Unfinished Lives

Unfinished Lives

Reviving the Memories of LGBTQ Hate Crimes Victims

STEPHEN V. SPRINKLE

RESOURCE *Publications* · Eugene, Oregon

For Sharon Groves,
my Diotima, who knows wisdom is found between, just like love.

Contents

Foreword

As DIRECTOR OF THE Religion and Faith Program of the Human Rights Campaign Foundation, I have unfortunately had many reasons to need a ready reference to the facts of representative hate crime murders over the years. In advocating for an end to such violence, I have needed to be able to review what happened, to whom, and under what circumstances. *Unfinished Lives* is the first book length work I am aware of that offers that information on diverse victims of hate murders across the spectrum of queer identities, from all walks of life and from all parts of the country.

But as important as the raw data is, I have needed more. I needed, as a healing exercise, to be able to moan in my spirit for the real people behind the headlines. I have needed a tombstone to stand before in order to bring the healing tears to my eyes in memorial lament. This book is a lovingly maintained cemetery for the LGBTQ communities and our allies to visit for a walk among our beloved dead.

And I have needed a resource that would help me digest the systemic causes of hate violence; to process how social justice advocates like me could intervene to tear out the ignorance and distrust and fear that are the roots from which hate violence springs. Stephen Sprinkle has given me—and everyone who cares deeply for LGBTQ people—that resource in *Unfinished Lives*.

I am proud to call Steve my friend. A road trip is a great way to get to know someone better. When the trip is centered around something as serious as a hate crime, the likelihood is high that travelers will learn a great deal about their fellow travelers and about themselves.

I took just such a trip with Dr. Stephen Sprinkle last summer and as the year begins to wane, the resonance of the lessons learned grows deeper every day. We flew into El Paso, Texas, rented a car and began the long drive south and east through the desert toward Brewster County. Our mission was a ministry of presence. We were headed to Brewster

County to remind elected officials there of their responsibilities to a young man who had recently been brutalized; first emotionally by his fundamentalist Christian family who made him homeless at seventeen because they perceived him to be gay; then physically by older, but still young, men from the vicinity; and finally by a school administrator who re-victimized the young man by denying him access to his high school, where he was in his senior year, because she said she didn't want to have (the gay) conversation in her school.

We went to Brewster County to remind that school administrator to whom public schools really belong. We also went to remind the local district attorney that the world was watching what was happening with the prosecution of the local roughs. We talked with officials of Sul Ross State University about the support the young victim of epidemic hate could expect from the university and about steps the school could take to help reduce the fear and lack of understanding that stems from and causes hate violence.

Each meeting with local officials was coordinated by an irreverent saint named Clarence Rousseau, an advocate for victims of domestic and other forms of violence in Alpine, Texas. Clarence is the sort of person who is motivated by gratitude for his own journey to accompany others in meaningful ways on theirs. Steve and Clarence had found each other in the ways activists do—each reaching out for help for the young victim until they found each other and teamed up.

What was remarkable about watching Clarence and Steve operate was the grace with which they confronted community leaders about their responsibilities toward the young man who had largely been failed by his family and community for much of his life. They assumed good-will toward the hate crime victim until someone, by their actions, proved themselves not to be a person of goodwill. They offered open hands and open hearts and lots of resources and several solutions to people seeking a way out of the cycle of hatred and fear—seeking a way where there appeared to be no way.

The end of this story is yet to be written, but it looks as if it will be a happy ending. Due to Clarence and Steve's diligent advocacy, the young man whose life almost ended in tragedy is safe and earning his high school diploma. The possibility of a college education awaits him and the community he left in an ambulance eagerly awaits his return home, ready to help him find a job and live in peace and mutual respect with his neighbors.

A book like *Unfinished Lives* cries out to be read—first because it chronicles the stories of the martyrs of the movement for LGBTQ justice, whose stories deserve to be heard again and again—but also in order to hold out hope that more stories might end like the one in Brewster County, Texas, and fewer like the ones chronicled here. In fact, this book demands to be read in order to glean from it the lessons that can help us prevent hate violence to begin with by working the deep roots of violence out of the rocky soil of denial and ignorance.

Stephen Sprinkle is uniquely qualified to write this book. An ethnographer in the tradition of Zora Neale Hurston, Steve makes real for us the challenges, joys, gifts and struggles of the people whose stories are told in *Unfinished Lives*. We hear their voices, we know their friends and family, we experience their work settings and the places they relaxed and played not just because Steve's a great storyteller, but because he has taken the time and emotional energy to literally walk a mile in their shoes.

Steve has done the heart breaking and time consuming work many of us have wished "someone" would do. He has painstakingly researched the facts of each case, then put the police blotters away and visited each site named in the police reports or newspaper accounts. He has sat, over coffee and beer and lots of food, with the loved ones left behind to grieve the loss of each hate murder victim. He has listened not just for the facts of the case, but for the nuances of the lives and loves of these folk who, in the eyes of those they left, are never "the victim," but are always Sakia, Billy Jack, _____, Matt . . .

In this book and on his website—www.unfinishedlivesblog.com— Steve has created a fit memorial for those who would almost certainly have been forgotten. Doing so would have been worthwhile in and of itself.

But this book does more. It speaks to the systemic denigration of LGBTQ people in the United States in the twentieth and early twenty-first centuries. This book offers insights into how misogyny and fear of loss of power feeds the beast that is hate violence in our beloved country. And it offers hope that the cycles of abuse and hatred and violence can be broken—one person, one family, one community at a time. A simple memorial would not have been enough. The blood and tears and anguished cries of the people whose stories are chronicled here demand more of us than that.

Stephen Sprinkle has offered us an icon through which to pray for solutions as we read about the systemic problem of anti-LGBTQ hate violence. I pray you will read this book with ears to hear what you are being called to do in response.

Harry Knox, Director
Religion and Faith Program
Human Rights Campaign Foundation
Washington, D.C.
October 28, 2010

Introduction

Why It Matters: Remembering Unfinished Lives

A READER WHO CONTEMPLATES investing time enough to read a tough book like this deserves to know why. What payoff awaits someone willing to face stories that trouble the soul, like these about LGBTQ hate crimes murder victims? A new sense of self is the chief reward. No one can encounter a threat to our existence, survive it, and expect to come out of that encounter unchanged. This is also true for communities. The fiery ordeal of attack and loss need not drive its targets into isolation and despair, despite the intentions of their adversaries. Assault upon a group of people may indeed have the opposite effect, calling forth a community where originally there was little or no commonality or social cohesion. For a community-still-in-formation like the LGBTQ community in America, remembrance of the dead and stories of the fallen can be particularly potent in shaping the soul of a people learning to value life and difference. A valuing of life and difference is the very tie that binds a distinctively queer commonwealth together.

TRANSFORMERS

People have been re-telling the stories of murdered human beings as far back as memory stretches, at least back as far as the *Epic of Gilgamesh* and the Genesis account of how Cain slew Abel. In the reading process, we vicariously face the ultimate human nightmare of a violent death, and escape it alive, cleansed by the *frisson* of horror, and then to return to our lives perhaps a bit more thankful for another day, or perhaps a bit wiser to the dangers that surround us. But to encounter homicide, even by reading about it, is more than that. It is a moment of unhingement, of dislocation, like a train car unhitched from its old locomotive, sidetracked until a new engine comes along. We are uncoupled from the old self we were, from our familiar, comfortably naïve ways of being in the world, and in these moments of disjointedness, we begin to imagine the unimaginable about ourselves. Stories of crime and murder seize our imaginations and work on us with an attraction hard to explain, causing us to recognize our own personal vulnerability, that such a chilling fate might just be *mine*, next time. We are drawn to stories of murder like moths to a flame, I suspect, because these narratives of death offer us the chance to reinvent ourselves, to rise out of the ashes of a death not our own, and to emerge from the experience personally renewed.

At first, it may seem counter-intuitive that stories about lesbian, gay, bisexual, transgender and queer murder victims could be as transformational for readers as the homicides of people not so specifically sexualized in twenty-first-century America. But when it all comes down to dust, outrage against murder is nearly as universal as birth and death. The cunning of the dehumanizers of history, exhibited in the horrors of the Middle Passage and Strange Fruit, the Witch Craze, the Inquisition, the Trail of Tears and the Nazi Holocaust (all of which for a time marshaled xenophobic hatred so effectively against blacks, women, heretics, native North Americans, and Jews), eventually failed. Xenophobes who banked on their ability to make their victims so sub-human that society would aid and abet their extermination or exile succeeded only for a season. The same is proving true in the case of queer folk in our own time. To dehumanize people for their sexual orientation is the first ominous step in denying them rights, employment, housing, health care, and protection from physical harm. A terrible and sustained decimation is stealing the lives and futures from thousands of LGBTQ women, men and youth in the name of skewed morality and bad religion. Yet, even though the numbers of bias-motivated crimes against LGBTQ people are increasing alarmingly today, and showing no signs of abating whatsoever, when someone is slashed to pieces or shot in two, the rawness of such a cold-blooded murder pushes many of us past our ideological hang-ups to a recognition that this gay victim was a fellow human being just like other people I know—*just like me.*

A metamorphosis takes place when the voices, lives, and sufferings of the oppressed are finally acknowledged to be fully human. The anti-Semitism of Elizabethan England notwithstanding, Shylock the alien-Jew shouts his protest in Shakespeare's *Merchant of Venice* and becomes Shylock the neighbor-who-happens-to-be-a-Jew before the eyes of the audience:

> Hath not a Jew eyes? Hath not a Jew hands, organs, dimensions,
> senses, affections, passions; fed with the same food, hurt with the
> same weapons, subject to the same diseases, healed by the same
> means, warmed and cooled by the same winter and summer as a
> Christian is? If you prick us do we not bleed? If you tickle us do
> we not laugh? If you poison us do we not die?

A similar transformation took place in the case of the archetypal gay hate crime victim of our time, Matthew Shepard. Police Commander Dave O'Malley, a twenty-seven-year veteran of the Laramie, Wyoming Police Department, experienced a life-altering moment when he investigated Shepard's hate crime murder in 1998. Though O'Malley spent the last eight years of his career as Chief of the Laramie Police Department Investigations Unit, he said that he had never witnessed a crime scene to rival the spot at the end of a lonely dirt road where two young Laramie men dragged Shepard to that infamous buck fence. Drag marks scarred the ground, and blood spattered over a fifty-foot radius where Matt tried to escape his killers as they whipped him with a stolen pistol until his skull cracked before tying him to the foot of the fence, leaving him to die of exposure in the cold wind. O'Malley, as hard-boiled a western lawman as there is, confessed to Bill Kurtis of *American Justice,* "I was a rotten son of a bitch when it came to dealing with gay issues. I had preconceived ideology that I grew up with, hearing it from my father and my friends... the jokes we used to tell and the things we used to say." In an interview on September 30, 2000 with Michael Janofsky of the *New York Times,* O'Malley explained how Matt Shepard's murder changed him. "My eyes got opened up," he said. "I didn't realize how a hate crime affects all gays, not just an individual. Matt's friends were scared to death. Some left town as a result of what happened. Some transferred to other schools. They knew if it could happen to him, it could happen to anybody. All kinds of people get killed every day," he went on, "but I'm not afraid to go down to the liquor store and buy a six-pack as some of these people were.... It's absurd that it took something this tragic to make it hit me." Now, O'Malley, Sheriff of Albany County, is an outspoken advocate for LGBTQ rights, all because of the personal transformation he underwent by encountering the gay son, brother, friend, and student—the real human being—who lay bludgeoned and bleeding to death, trussed to the base of a buck fence.

Anti-LGBTQ hate crimes murders are not tragic. They are outrageous, wicked, unjust, and terrible. But what *is* tragic is that when LGBTQ victims die at the hands of haters empowered to kill by the heterosexism, misogyny, and homophobia that persistently thrive in our society, only then, it seems, are some brought to see the equal humanity of queer folk who were denied equality in their lifetimes. They finally "get" what the poetry of Maya Angelou has been trying to tell us all along, that "we are more alike, my friends, than we are unalike."

SHOCK, HOPE, AND LGBTQ RELUCTANCE

Early in the research phase of this book, I wondered why no such anthology of LGBTQ hate crimes murder victims already existed in print. I now believe part of the reason lies in the literal sort of experience queer folk have while reading stories of anti-LGBTQ violence. Another reason is the tenuous state of a community that has not yet taken itself seriously enough to remember its dead. Neither reason seems to be sufficient to foreclose on this project, nor to excuse LGBTQ people from working their way through the hell of these stories to get to the other side, where these dead point the way to a more accountable and hopeful way of living in the adversity they must face for the foreseeable future in the United States.

Like captives emerging from the dark of Plato's Cave into the clarity of the midday sun, LGBTQ people cannot, without considerable pain, read about others like themselves so gruesomely slaughtered. There is an immediacy to these stories that communicates fear, and hooks self-loathing in the lives of queer folk that quite simply is absent for other readers. To avert one's eyes from such things is an understandable reflex. But while avoiding pain, if one can, is a rational response, avoiding reality is not. Too many bias-motivated deaths are occurring among LGBTQ people to permit denial and avoidance any longer. Admittedly, the statistics are daunting. The National Coalition of Anti-Violence Programs (NCAVP) report for 2008 shows a 28 percent increase of violent crimes against LGBT people over the previous year, with a 100 percent jump in murders over the same period. Commenting on these figures, Sharon Stapel, National Coordinator for the NCAVP, expects the totals to go higher along with the intensity of media coverage over same-sex marriage, hate crimes legislation, a transgender-inclusive Employment Non-Discrimination Act (ENDA), and the debates over repealing the Defense of Marriage Act (DOMA) and Don't Ask Don't Tell (DADT). "The more visibility there is the more likely we're going to see backlash, and that's exactly what we see here," Stapel says. Since the NCAVP reports anti-transgender hate crimes, in distinction from the annual FBI's hate crimes report that does not, Stapel is able to give us a more accurate picture of the landscape of peril in which LGBTQ Americans find themselves. Even so, organizations from only twenty-five of the fifty states report to the NCAVP, indicating that the actual number of bias-related hate crimes against LGBTQ people may be much higher. Additional factors arguing for higher numbers of these crimes than are reported by either the NCAVP or the FBI are the stigma and despair often associated with violent crimes against queer women and men. Local law enforcement agencies tend to skew their investigations away from anti-gay or transgender motives as a reflection of the bias rampant in their home locales. Victims often fear exposure and media scrutiny for themselves and their loved ones, and therefore do not report crimes against their persons. And since LGBTQ victims are often considered unreliable sources of information, and are routinely blamed somehow for their own misfortune, it is easy to see why so many simply endure the attacks in silence.

Not only has the number of these crimes risen sharply, but the brutality with which they are carried out, the sheer *overkill* characteristic of anti-LGBTQ hate crimes, has also intensified. The horror of these killings goes beyond the shock and bereavement of loved ones and friends. These are not usual homicides, as hateful as they may be: killings for money or drugs, domestic strife, or crimes of passion. In over half the anti-LGBTQ hate crimes murders recorded since 1995, the brutality visited on the victims involved some combination of shooting, stabbing, garroting, and bludgeoning, often including the desecration of the body after the victims had died. Killers of LGBTQ people usually express their utter disregard for the humanity of their victims by having to get in close, hand-to-hand, to do their bloody work. While there are some women and people of color who slay LGBTQ people, the general profile of those who carry out these murders is chillingly familiar: young heterosexual white males from the late teens to the mid-thirties. Violent attacks against LGBTQ people are perpetrated not just against a single individual. They are message-killings, assassinations meant to terrorize whole populations of queer people. As Richard Lacayo wrote twelve years ago in his famous article on the Shepard murder for *Time*

Magazine, "[Matt] was stretched along a Wyoming fence not just as a dying young man but as a signpost. 'When push comes to shove,' it says, 'this is what we have in mind for gays.'"

As alarming as these numbers are, in the thousands of annual incidents, and as hotly as the national debate rages over terms like "hate crimes," and "violent incidents," it all falls mute before the plaintive cry of a bereaved mother like Pauline Mitchell for her murdered Navajo Two-Spirit child, F.C. Jr. *"Please don't forget him!",* she says to everyone, but especially to LGBTQ people like her son. F.C. was her youngest, just sixteen, when unreasoning hatred tore him from her. She lamented that no one would ever know the beautiful transgender person he was becoming. Don't forget him amidst the controversy, and the politics, and the power struggles, she says. And don't turn away from him, either. For his story, as well as the stories of the other victims included in this volume, is strong medicine for queer women and men who wish only to see the world through lavender-colored glasses, yet so desperately need to break free of the deadliest of all the closets a heterosexist/homophobic culture has constructed for them—the closet of denial.

When you get beneath the layer of self-absorption with which many LGBTQ people have insulated themselves against prejudice, you find people who are highly sensitive to the wants and needs of others. Perhaps that is why there seems to be such a bond between LGBTQ people and straight women. They both identify with the underdog, and recognize something of themselves in the other. Like Suzanne Pharr says, they understand that homophobia is a weapon of sexism. They also exhibit a deep yearning for things of the spirit, and a desire to belong to something larger than their individual selves. The need for relatedness and spirituality is part of the furniture of the queer soul. Often the biological families of LGBTQ people have disappointed them, sometimes even to the point of rejection. Organized religion in the United States has been such a source of exclusion and pain for them that large numbers of LGBTQ people have left religious communities altogether, usually in their youth, about the time they began to be aware of their sexual orientation. Yet despite the problems gay folk have with traditional faith communities that still reject homosexuality, religious and spiritual patterns keep cropping up in LGBTQ life, especially at the tender spots where people either deepen and mature, or remain stunted. Call it metamorphosis, resurrection, or coming out, one thing all LGBTQ people have in common is a sense of what it means to die. The trauma described over and over in coming out stories is the fear of what lies beyond admitting that one is "gay" or "lesbian"—the sense that existence as one has known it will be over when the world finally knows *who and what I am*. In that way, the transition from the closet to what lies beyond it is a "death" of sorts. No amount of advice or coaching can take away the stress of the initial passage from one way of being in the world to another. Coming out stories also say that there is an unimaginable sense of freedom and newness of life on the other side, too, and that those who have passed from an old existence in the dubious security of the closet to a new, freer mode of life would never go back for anything in the world.

Like the 'never-ending story,' the LGBTQ passage from death to life goes on for many for an entire lifetime. And life as experienced by queer women and men on the other side of the closet is hardly fair, no matter the benefits honesty and openness deliver every day. It is dogged by inequality and the awful banality of bias. This is particularly true for queer folk of color, who must perform their masculinity and femininity under the awful effects of the history of racism, poverty, and deprivation of access in this nation, not only in American society at large, but also within the LGBTQ community itself. How to find support and solidarity in a world where the risks are real and the challenges are many is the place where so many LGBTQ people live in a country not yet willing to tolerate its queer children, much less claim them. Here is precisely where the lessons learned from LGBTQ people who have died because of their sexual orientation make the strongest medicine, person-to-person. As Minerva, the old low-country root doctor, says to John Kelso in the script of the film version of *Midnight in the Garden of Good and Evil,* "Boy! Take these words to heart. To understand the living…you got to commune with the dead."

Though LGBTQ people have good reason to fear what the world can do, as the stories in this volume testify, finding the courage to tell these stories makes the fact of that fear less and less important. Confronting the dangerous nature of these narratives of murder and loss carries with it a mission for each LGBTQ person, for all who have survived the worst the culture can do are survivors, and survivors have the duty and the dignity of becoming witnesses. Encountering stories of murdered LGBTQ people can indeed be a stark, literal experience for others who are just like the slain, causing discomfort and denial; but, dealing honestly with the apathy and hostility of an unfair world has called forth creativity and the will to flourish despite everything from generations of LGBTQ people before this one. In response to these stories, it will surely do so again. This is the transformational movement from beyond shock to hope. "Communing with the dead" in the sense of owning them as cherished fallen members of the queer family, and crying out for justice for their sake and for the sake of the living gives new power and depth to the lives of LGBTQ women and men.

QUEERLY BELOVED COMMUNITY

A significant reason the stories of LGBTQ murder victims remain largely unknown by the wider world is the reluctance of the queer community to take itself seriously enough to embrace the stories of those of their number who have been killed because of hatred. There is a direct relationship between the way LGBTQ folk are silenced and rendered virtually invisible in this country, and the way the underreported stories of their murdered comrades evaporate so quickly in American consciousness. If random people on the street are asked these days—perhaps even LGBTQ persons—if they know of anybody murdered for their sexual orientation, chances are they will say "no," not off the tops of their heads. And if anyone's name does happen to come to mind, it will almost invariably be Matthew Shepard, who is the public face of LGBTQ hate crime in America. In all probability, the average person will not be aware of anyone murdered in an anti-LGBTQ bias crime since Matt Shepard died over a decade ago. The slaughter of hundreds upon hundreds have gone unreported, or swiftly forgotten. Common decency and human dignity demand that this cultural amnesia be overcome. But how?

Admittedly, the hard work of becoming a community for LGBTQ people has not been going on for very long in historical terms. Many aspects of LGBTQ life are still in the "movement" stage, a reality reflected in every aspect of queer social organization. Barely a generation has passed since the Stonewall Uprising in the summer of 1969 in New York City. LGBTQ people are hardly used to being called "a community," much less living into what it means to be one. Even what to call this community as it comes into being is still up the air, a jittery jumble of the alphabet, perhaps because the prerogative for self-designation most groups take for granted has not been in queer hands for very long. I have become convinced of two assessments of queer community in the course of writing this book, both of them rooted in what I call "critical hope." First, until the disparate elements of lesbian, gay, bisexual, transgender, and gender-queer society regard themselves as a unified people more seriously than they do now, they will never develop into a true community on the American scene. I am not suggesting mawkishly aping heterosexist social entities either negatively or positively. LGBT and Queer thinkers have perceptively critiqued the patriarchy, coercion, ideological regimentation, parasitism and binary fragmentation of the straight world, and point instead to a sense of relatedness in queer life based on difference itself that has no need to "same" one another and the world. Still, though there are notable exceptions in the fields of advocacy, the arts, entertainment, and politics, in the main, LGBTQ social organization remains splintered, hedonistic, or just plain invisible in most of the United States. Our cultural cousins in Great Britain call the *gravitas* necessary to be taken seriously, "bottom." Risking the obvious pun, what they are talking about, and what I believe LGBTQ folk yet lack, is the groundedness of spirit to transcend accounts of irresponsibility and triviality too often associated with stereotypical LGBTQ practices, and become accountable to ourselves and others for the gift of life. As long as so many LGBTQ people remain content to abdicate their responsibility for the defense and development of their culture to a relative handful of activists, no matter how dedicated and talented these advocates are, queer life will continue to be a sideshow in the American panorama, and should expect to be nothing more. Just like the reportage done on LGBTQ hate crimes murders today in the mainstream media, they will be relegated for the foreseeable future to the back pages, buried somewhere beneath the fold. This book is a cry that such obscurity for both living and dead LGBTQ people is unacceptable. But I also sense that LGBTQ people want more, expect more, and *are* so very much more than that. To that end, LGBTQ people must move outside the cocoon, and dare to transform themselves and their people into a community as tough and resilient as the love they live to embody. LGBTQ folk have never been handed privilege or power willingly. They have had to pull together and fight for it. They must again prove themselves responsible to the best elements of their character, forged in the furnace of resistance and survival in the face of fickle civilizations that since the dawn of history, have benignly ignored them at best, and savagely persecuted them at worst.

Part of the responsibility and privilege of a community is to remember and tell the stories of the members of their group who have died unjustly. African Americans, for example, remember and witness to their dead: Emmitt Till, Medgar Evers, Martin Luther King Jr.; the four little girls blown up at Sixteenth Street Baptist Church, Addie Mae Collins, Carole Robertson, Cynthia Wesley, and Denise McNair; and thousands more like them. Jewish Americans join Jewry around the world in remembering six million gassed, shot, and immolated in the Nazi "Final Solution" of World War II. Buddhist Americans and their allies fold hundreds of thousands of colorful paper cranes each August to remember the people of Hiroshima and Nagasaki who died when the United States dropped the atomic bombs "Fat Man" and "Little Boy" on Japan.

How the living remember and honor their dead reveals the strength and character of a community to itself and the world. To date, LGBTQ people have not united in memory of their dead. Remembering and telling the stories of the unfinished lives of their assassinated sisters and brothers, however, is a promising start in that direction. Stories bring the memories of murdered people back from the dead. Telling the stories of slain LGBTQ people, stories that are largely unknown and swiftly forgotten, is a counter-cultural act of resistance and reconstruction in its own right. Stories give the voices of the murdered a chance to speak again, so the living may have another chance to understand them and the outrageous reasons for which they died. In learning how to "commune with the dead" by witnessing to the worth of their lives and the injustice of their deaths, a social transformation of the group takes place. The LGBTQ community deepens and strengthens as it learns about its assassinated sisters and brothers whose lives and deaths will remain unvindicated until their community suffers their fate no more. All across the country, in locations where LGBTQ people have died cruelly and alone, hundreds and thousands of witnesses have banded together around their memories in candlelight vigils, teach-ins, protests, and memorial marches that exhibit the ferocious, peaceful resolve of an aroused, committed population of LGBTQ people and their allies. Seats of government in Tallahassee, Denver, Sacramento, Lansing, Augusta, Albany, and the nation's capitol have experienced the power of a cohesive queer community determined to win protection for themselves and all Americans from hate crimes, and this newly awakened power has translated into a movement for equality in marriage, employment, and military service.

My second assessment of LGBTQ community is that the reluctance to heal and reconcile the two spiritual wings of the queer movement—LGBTQ people who eschew organized faith traditions, and LGBTQ people who belong to them—is an outmoded drain on the energy necessary to become an effective social and political witness to the larger culture. It is time LGBTQ people have the long overdue conversation about religion, spirituality, and faith. The memories of LGBTQ hate crimes murder victims are dear to both groups, and this common affection itself is a good reason to come together so that the fallen may be honored. The "angel" of a people is a way of personifying the genius or unique gift they have to give the world. The Greek way of referring to this winged image can prevent it from becoming too cherubic. They called it the *daemon* of the group. Anyone can see that a one-winged *daemon* cannot fly. It will only spin in place, which is uncomfortably close to the actual effect this internecine feud has had on LGBTQ political power. While post-mortems on the "No on Prop 8" campaign of 2008 in California are still being done, the attack of right wing religious groups like the Knights of Columbus and the LDS Church needed both secular and religious LGBTQ groups to blunt its impact, but queers of faith were not brought into the fray until the day had effectively been lost. If a single queer angel is too unitary an image to suit the competing groups, then let there be to be two angels with one wing apiece to express the incompleteness of both parties in this feud. Then let these two partners embrace each other tightly, so that finally, together, the gay *daemon* can use both its wings to fly.

Some friends have suggested what I am doing in this book is a sort of "religious honoring" of LGBTQ hate crimes victims. I admit it freely. The genius of the faith communities that have nurtured me, and with whom I have a lover's quarrel to this day, is their ability to remember and tell stories very well. Faith communities have a fiduciary responsibility to hand down the traditions that they have received from those who went on before them. The narratives they pass along are not just good advice or yarns. They are the building blocks of communities of character. I learned to honor the dead from the churches who reared me, and the counter-intuitive result has made me a social justice advocate for the living. Nothing could be less "other worldly" than that. Refusing to forget the fallen, remembering and honoring the dead, especially those who have died unjustly, makes justice an everyday concern.

Religion is a serious problem for LGBTQ people, and the problem will not go away anytime soon. But the cause of preventing LGBTQ hate crimes requires queer secular and spiritual people to unite in order to confront the religious question. No other form of contemporary bias against a social group is as theologically based as anti-LGBTQ discrimination. The last great demographic it is permissible to hate in American life is the sexual minority, and nine times out of ten, the justification given by those who kill LGBTQ people is rooted in religion as mediated by the rhetoric of theological hate: "God says kill fags." While I do not feel any need to conduct some sort of "rescue mission" on the Bible or benighted religious groups, I do believe the best way to fight fire is with fire—not hellfire and brimstone as the radical religious right employs against gay people, but the refining fire of truth and love, applied by religiously devoted LGBTQ Christians, Jews, Muslims, Buddhists, Hindus, Pagans and others who are coming out in larger numbers every year. Further, they are refusing to leave their faith communities, not matter the pressure applied to them to do so. Queer folk are finding out that they have allies by the millions in these faith groups who are just as incensed as LGBTQ people about "right wing nuts" who claim to speak for God on the matter of homosexuality and human rights. Struggles over separation of church and state, reproductive rights, and the ordination of homosexual people have been joined in every faith tradition in America, and though there are setbacks, there is also reason to hope that the tide will turn toward mercy, justice, and the Golden Rule. On the behalf of the whole sexual minority, LGBTQ people of faith and their allies are the very ones to join the battle for good faith against bad religion. Many are toeing the line for justice every day already.

There is a religious or spiritual aspect to every story in this volume. Some were stalked, tortured, and murdered by religious zealots, as was Ken Cummings Jr., the gay airline attendant from Houston, Texas. Others, like Satendar Singh, the gay Sikh immigrant who lived in Sacramento, California, were killed in the clash of cultures and religions over the question of what is moral and immoral. The grisly death of a lesbian carpenter, Talana Kreeger, fired the resolve of the LGBTQ community in Coastal North Carolina to establish a church of their own, so that they would never have to depend on straight Christians again for a place to bury their dead. There are stories of religious courage here, too, like the example set by the Jews and Unitarians of Bangor, Maine who spoke out against hatred when gender non-conforming Charlie Howard was thrown over the State Street Bridge and left to drown by a group of gay-bashing youths.

Dr. Martin Luther King Jr. conceived of a new social compact, rooted in the impulse of freedom he learned about in church at the feet of his father and mother. He called it the "Beloved Community," a vision he worked for until the day his life ended on a motel balcony in Memphis, Tennessee. Dr. King's dream of a community of love and reconciliation, where each person in every group would work in the best interests of all, remains an unfinished chapter in American history. It was an imperfect vision. LGBTQ people were left out of it originally, as the banishment of Bayard Rustin, the gay African American Quaker who was the genius behind the famed 1963 March on Washington, showed. But had Dr. King lived on, he would surely have joined his wife, Coretta Scott King, in asking Rustin's forgiveness, and worked for the liberation of LGBTQ people as she did all the days of her life.

Now is the time to renew the dream by making it more inclusive of sacred and secular, LGBTQ and straight; breaking down the binaries of inequality; and respecting the differences that make the dream stronger and more compelling to the American public, without the paralyzing criticism and backbiting that divide to no purpose. This dream renewed is a "Queerly Beloved Community." The role the unfinished lives of LGBTQ hate crimes murder victims can play among the "queerly beloved" is to serve as signs of the work that remains to be done by all queer folk until justice comes. Their truncated lives remain outcast and unfinished until their stories are fulfilled in a united LGBTQ community, ready to do whatever it takes to bring about change in this country. Their stories can be used to build bridges of communication and understanding with the straight majority, and to enable sharing between queer and straight people whose narratives and practices may be different, but whose reverence for life is held in common. For the LGBTQ community to capture the imagination of the nation, there need to be ambassadors who can get a hearing, and in a queer way. Those who have died because they were outcast, whose lives were cut short by brutality and hate, are those very ambassadors.

The American public deserves to confront the lives of their murdered LGBTQ children. Their amnesia, denial, and apathy helped create the climate that makes hate crimes like these possible in the greatest nation on earth. While the sense of personal identification the straight majority will achieve encountering stories like these may be more oblique, it is nonetheless profound. The survivable danger of these murder narratives gives them the chance to reorder their lives, as in the similar case of LGBTQ people. But the straight majority can go one step further than this: in reconstructing their lives and their understandings in the wake of these stories, they can reach beyond their comfort zone and claim the Other as their own people, just as deserving as heterosexuals are to live out their lives in a world without fear. When a face is put on American injustice, the "better angels" of the American spirit have a chance to act, and to put an end to it. Sharing these stories calls forth these better angels both from the teller and the listener, and opens the opportunity for America to embrace the hopes and dreams of *all* her children.

PERSONAL INVESTMENT

My investment in this book is personal. I experienced the false security of the closet for many years while I was a parish minister in Connecticut and North Carolina. After coming out as a seminary professor in Texas, I had a close call with hate crime myself.

For seventeen years, I served churches as an ordained minister. Though I was closeted and came out only to a few trusted friends, homophobia did not spare me. My home was defaced by anti-gay graffiti on two occasions; my car was vandalized; phone and television service were ripped off the back of my house; anonymous letters were mailed to church leaders about me; and my two pet dogs, my only companions in those days, were butchered and hung up in a tree in my parsonage backyard while I was visiting parishioners in the hospital. Today, I still have nightmares about that last act of terror. I dug in my heels, learned how to fight back against ignorant and dangerous haters, and refused to be driven away.

When I came to Texas to begin my divinity school career, I came out of the closet fully and never looked back. These sixteen years have been the most fulfilling of my life, but they have come with a cost. In the mid-1990s, Fort Worth was debating protection statutes for LGBTQ people, laws that were eventually passed, and that covered housing, public accommodation, and employment. In order to speak to the City Council, I had to give my name and address at the podium to establish that I was a citizen with a stake in the debate. Over four hundred people showed up to speak, and passionate arguments came from both sides of the issues. When I returned to my home, I listened to my voice mail, and heard a male voice threatening my life: "You are the faggotiest faggot I have ever seen! You make me want to puke! We know you walk to work every day! One day you just won't come back!" I had enough presence of mind to capture the number, preserve the voice mail, and call the police. They conducted an investigation, and identified the person who threatened me: a student at the university where I taught. I had no further trouble from him or anyone else, but I did quit walking to work, and learned to be more aware of my surroundings. The matter of hate crimes became real for me instantly. I count myself as one of the lucky ones, however. Unlike so many LGBTQ people, I have never been physically assaulted or severely battered. *I am still alive.*

After my brushes with hate crime, I began to pay attention to the few stories of LGBTQ assault and murder reported in the media. One particular incident from the past caught my attention, since it had occurred in Dallas. A young Vietnamese man, Thanh Nguyen, and his partner, Hugh Calloway, were shot in a downtown park in 1991 while picnicking after the bars had closed. Calloway survived, but Thanh died of his wounds. The Dallas paper carried a few stories, and the local LGBTQ paper carried a few more. But after the trial of his three assailants, the fact that a young gay Asian was shot and killed was simply forgotten. Calloway disappeared. By the time I investigated Thanh's story, it was as if the earth had opened up beneath him, and swallowed up his memory as if he had never existed. There is not enough information about his story even to write a partial chapter in this book. *How could someone die and be forgotten so swiftly?* I began to collect similar stories, and in short order I was overwhelmed with the number and brutality of them. So many! That is how this book was conceived.

WHAT IS HERE, AND WHAT ISN'T

Gathered here, and told in twelve chapters, are the stories of fourteen LGBTQ Americans murdered for their sexual orientation and gender presentation. I selected these particular individuals because each one represents the situations of other LGBTQ hate crimes victims, and the sum of them covers most of the major regions of the country. My aim and hope is that the reader would grasp how pervasive and national in scope this queer holocaust truly is. I also chose them because piecing these sto-

ries together like the parts of a puzzle from news reports, personal interviews, court documents, and my own travels to the murder sites caused
victim to live again for me. I never met any of these victims before they
died. Instead, I have caught reflections of them in the grief, laughter,
and outrage of their loved ones and friends as I listened to them—or,
failing that, from the printed reports of those who either knew them in
person, or who became committed to keep their memories alive after
they had died. Looking in the mirror of these reflections, I have caught
a glimpse of who each of them was, and I have tried to convey what I
have seen and felt as faithfully as possible to my readers. This book is not
journalism or academic research. Neither is it comprehensive enough to
be called biography. These are portraits of the women and men whose
memories have touched my own mind and heart. Nothing I have written
can convey sufficiently the vitality or the pain of a single life, much less
fourteen of them. Still, I cannot resist remembering, and cannot stop
myself from telling, what I have learned from each of these individuals.
These slain LGBTQ people have become my sisters and brothers—and
my teachers.

Though the victims are all members of the sexual minority, the
collective message they send us is universal: murder is an unparalleled
outrage against life, and no one should have to die solely for being who
they are. I have tried to find a common thread binding each of these
unique lives to all the others, and one similarity stands out in them all.
The one thing each of these victimized people share is an unfinished life:
love foreclosed, potential ripped away, relationships brutally terminated,
and future contributions stolen from us by outrageous, irrational hatred.
An empty feeling in the pit of my stomach attends each of these stories
for these very reasons. The loss each one represents is incalculable.

Though I have tried to include stories representing the national, sexual,
racial/ethnic, identity, and gender diversity of this awful holocaust, there
are notable gaps. First, the stories of women are fewer in this volume
than of men. Lesbian hate murders—for whatever reason—are harder to
find on record than the stories of gay men. This does not mean that lesbians are not being murdered in large numbers throughout America. I
believe they are, but the deaths of many lesbians, I suspect, are hidden in
the vast numbers of women who are outrageously raped and killed every

day. I did not find the story of a murdered bisexual person I thought I could tell well enough to include, and I regret that.

Second, each of these victims shares the fact of their otherwise unremarkable lives. They were the sorts of people who live in most every neighborhood in America. Had they not been targeted for such foul murder because of their actual—or suspected—sexual identification, they would have probably led decent, usual lives alongside the rest of their neighbors and friends. With the exception of Matthew Shepard, all the rest are relatively unknown either to the LGBTQ community or to the public at large. Though this book attempts to change their unknown status, I am convinced that the very normal nature of their lives makes the crimes that ripped the lives from them even more heinous. For that reason, I have resisted exalting them to celebrity, because I believe pedestalizing murder victims is not only a maudlin exercise, but it prevents us from having to deal with them as real people. Each one of these individuals could have been a son, daughter, neighbor, fellow student, or co-worker *of ours.*

I have not chosen to interview the convicted killers of these LGBTQ people. Arthur Dong, the Oscar-nominated gay filmmaker, has already done a remarkable job of that in his groundbreaking 1997 documentary, *Licensed to Kill.* Likewise, I have not chosen to contact the families of the killers, either, even though I respect their loss in these crimes. Like the families of the victims, they have lost someone dear to them because of unreasoning hatred, and for that I am sorry.

The real unsung heroes of these stories are the families of the victims, particularly the women who are related to them. Sisters and mothers of LGBTQ hate crimes victims never sought the spotlight, but when their beloved was murdered, many of them stepped up to the challenge, and became the most effective advocates for human rights in our nation. Kathy Joe Gaither and Vickie Saltsman, Billy Jack Gaither's sisters; Pauline Mitchell, F.C.'s mother; Elke Kennedy, Sean's mom; Pat and Lynn Mulder, Ryan Skipper's parents; Denise King, Simmie Williams's mother; and Judy Shepard immediately come to mind. Pat Mulder is working on a book from the perspective of the parents of these victims, the working title of which is *There is No Closure,* and I wish her the very best as she carries out her labor of love. Her work needs to be done.

I suspect that, like myself, readers of these stories will be left with many unanswered questions about the circumstances surrounding these

murder victims. What in the world compelled them to expose themselves to such harm? Why did Talana Kreeger get in the cab of a truck
with a virtual stranger in the dead of night? What lured Ryan Skipper to
drive down that eerie, dark dirt road with rough characters like "Smiley"
and "Bill Bill" (known methamphetamine addicts)? How could Matt
Shepard get into that pickup truck and sit between Henderson and
McKinney? Why didn't he just stay at the Fireside Bar and have another
Heineken? Frankly, I don't know. But I do know that only hindsight is
truly 20/20. And if I have come to believe that these victims were just
like most people I know, I also believe that none of them intended to put
themselves in lethal situations. While not one of these LGBTQ people
claimed to be angels or saints, they were not fools or demons, either.
Like most of us, they were works in progress, prone to make mistakes
sometimes, but possessed of great qualities, as well. My God, they were
human, and they longed for affection, intimacy, adventure, and meaning
in their lives. Just like straight people do every day in the exercise of their
normal humanity, they entered situations in which they might not have
felt completely safe, but they still felt safe enough. Let us be clear before
assigning blame hypocritically. None of these victims had a death wish.
And none of them were to blame for their deaths. Only their killers and
those who motivated them to kill are to blame.

LAST THINGS

I need to acknowledge the legion of people without whom this project
would have been impossible. Friends have supported this project at every turn with their time, their expertise, and their money to help defray
the cost of my travel and research. For each one, I am grateful—espe-
cially Harry Knox and Sharon Groves of the Human Rights Campaign
Religion and Faith Program; David Gary of Integrity Alabama; Todd W.
Simmons of Houston, my website administrator and copy editor; Charlie
Rose and Dan Peeler of Peeler/Rose Productions in Dallas, my illustra-
tors; Ryan Valentine of the Texas Freedom Network in Austin; Colonel
Paul Dodd, U.S. Army Chaplain (Retired) of the Servicemembers Legal
Defense Network; Sandy Brandon and Dean Nancy Ramsay of Brite
Divinity School; my teaching assistant, Matt Bridges, and my research
assistant, Egon Cohen; and my most faithful reader, Rob Rodriguez,
whose critiques have "kept it real."

The stories of many other LGBTQ hate crimes murder victims could have been chosen for this book. I am uncomfortably aware of the arbitrary nature of these selections, and ask that others pick up where I have left off. Errors in fact and misrepresentations written in this volume, though wholly unintentional, are solely my own.

Finally, no words of mine could offer closure to this essay better than these spoken by the most tireless advocate for erasing hatred from the narrative of this country, Judy Shepard, Matthew's mother. Here is a portion of her testimony before the Senate Judiciary Committee during one of many attempts to pass federal hate crimes protections for LGBTQ people in our country. For our sake and for the sake of our fallen LGBTQ sisters and brothers, we owe her our keen attention:

> *Matt is no longer with us today because the men who killed him learned to hate. Somehow and somewhere they received the message that the lives of gay people are not as worthy of respect, dignity and honor as the lives of other people. They were given the impression that society condoned or at least was indifferent to violence against gay and lesbian Americans. Today, we have it within our power to send a very different message than the one received by the people who killed my son. It is time to stop living in denial and to address a real problem that is destroying families like mine, James Byrd Jr.'s, Billy Jack Gaither's and many others across America.*

Stephen V. Sprinkle
Dallas, Texas
The Twelfth Anniversary of the Murder of Matthew Wayne Shepard
October 12, 2010

Matthew Wayne Shepard
December 1, 1976—October 12, 1998

LARAMIE, WYOMING

1

The Second Death of Matthew Shepard

*"Matthew Shepard, God bless you,
what else can we look forward to . . . ?"*

—Pride 2009, Jon Gilbert Leavitt

Another Mother's Day comes and goes, and another Father's Day, too. Matt Shepard's chair remains empty in the Shepard home in Casper, Wyoming—no card from him, or roses for his mom; no tie or set of slippers for his dad—for over twelve years. His parents, Judy and Dennis Shepard, and his younger brother, Logan, miss him every day.

Matt died at the hands of young men who targeted him because he was gay. The homicide case was cracked relatively quickly. Two locals were arrested, charged, booked, tried, and sentenced to life without parole for taking the life of the 21-year-old University of Wyoming student. That brutal chapter of the Matt Shepard story is officially closed. But some people are still getting away with murder.

Matt died a lingering death after Aaron James McKinney and Russell Arthur Henderson lured him away from the Fireside Lounge in Laramie, late on the night of October 7, 1998. In the men's room of the Fireside, McKinney and Henderson hatched a plot to entice the slim, blond man with the good shoes, who was drinking a Heineken, to ride away with them, offering him a fun night with two, hot young men. It was a lie calculated to fool Matt. They abducted him, beat him repeatedly with a .357 Magnum pistol until his skull cracked, robbed him, trussed him to a buck fence way out in the boonies high on a ridge, and left him to die of exposure. So cold it was! So agonizingly cold in his stocking feet with no shoes!

Virtually everything about Matt's murder took on symbolic status in the media frenzy and the political maelstrom that exploded around the hateful slaying of Judy and Dennis's boy. Wyoming still smarts at the memory of all the unwanted attention. Terrible things like hate crime murders are not supposed to occur in the "Equality State," and certainly not at the hands of young men from local families . . . but in fact they do. Laramie's pioneer days history, the railroad, Cowboy Pride at the University of Wyoming . . . all of it has been altered forever by the stinging memory of the slim, blond gay man who fell into a death coma under the cold October stars, strung up like a hybrid of Jesus and an abject scarecrow on a wooden fence.

Matt was morphed into an icon, both figuratively and literally. His delicate, almost asexual appearance in photographs arrested the attention of the public in a way no LGBTQ hate murder victim has before or since. The tousled straw blond of his hair, blue eyes wide with archetypal innocence, and the faint hint of braces beneath shyly parted lips made Matt erotically irresistible to some, and the perfect little brother of every white, middle-class, *Ozzie and Harriet* family in America. Hearts broke from coast-to-coast, and outrage burned at the savagery of his death. *The Laramie Project*, staged by the Techtonic Theater, seared the tragedy of Matt's murder and the horrible-to-contemplate possibility that anti-gay violence can break out anywhere in the United States into our cultural consciousness. Fr. William McNichols, a Roman Catholic priest, modeled Matt's bloody bust and torso into a stunning icon entitled, "The Passion of Matthew Shepard," dedicating it to the hundreds of gay and lesbian youth who commit suicide every year. Against the blue-black velvet of the Wyoming sky, the crimson image of Matt stands stooped before the cross ties of that notorious buck fence, cold stars and pale moon looking down.

In the culture wars that rage around sexual identity and orientation, Matt's murder is a time-splitter, marking all earlier time as BBF, "Before the Buck Fence," and all that has followed as ABF, "After the Buck Fence." Though thousands of LGBTQ people have suffered and died in the United States before his death and after, in order to find some small purchase of media attention, every story seeks some correlation to Matt's murder. Examples are sadly abundant: Charlie Howard of Bangor, Maine, thrown by three epithet-yelling juveniles off the State Street Bridge to drown in 1984 is "the Matthew Shepard before Matthew

Shepard"; Ryan Keith Skipper, stabbed nineteen times, throat slit, and dumped in a roadside ditch in Wahneta, Florida, has become "Florida's Matthew Shepard." All the myth making around Matt has turned out to be a Trojan Horse for the LGBTQ community. The less similar hate crime murder victims are to Matt, the less mainstream media seem to pay attention to their stories. If the slain person were female or transgender, black, brown or Asian, impaired, or not so young and attractive anymore, the story is buried in the back pages of the paper, if written about at all. Sadly, that tends to be as true for the LGBTQ press and blogosphere as for the mainstream media. Matt's myth carries all the usual pathologies of American prejudice in its Trojan belly, "-isms" and phobias that beset the sexual minority community as much as the public in general. Because of America's historical amnesia and fifteen-minute attention span, the average American who may remember something about "that boy killed in Laramie 'way back'" does not believe that anyone has died for being gay in the last decade.

Matt's parents have had to live with the effects of this myth making around their son. In the March 1999 issue of *Vanity Fair*, Judy Shepard reflected candidly with Melanie Thernstrom about her sometimes-depressed, and often too-naïve-for-his-own-good son: "It's a very frightening concept as a parent that your son now becomes a martyr, a public figure for the world. He's just our son." She was particularly concerned that some had likened Matt to Jesus Christ. "You must understand, it's like putting him on a pedestal that just won't work. I'm concerned that if people find out he wasn't a saint, they'll be disappointed or angry and hate him."

The real Matt Shepard died in a Fort Collins, Colorado hospital in the wee hours of October 12, 1998 with his parents by his side. Ironically, it was the day after America's observance of National Coming Out Day. His team of doctors and nurses, professional as they were, could not undo what hate had done to Matt. He never woke up from his coma. His heart gave out. The ventilator switched off, and Matt was gone. Our memory of him, however, cannot rest in peace. Not yet.

MURDERING MATT'S STORY

Revisionists are getting away with murder, working to change the subject of Matthew Shepard and alter the impact of his story for LGBTQ Americans. It is not just that they are trying to shift the conversation to something more palatable to the cheerful, "Good Morning, America" attitude so prevalent in this country; another sort of murder is afoot. The revisionists are working to change how Matt is remembered—to revise his story into the image and likeness of what queer folk are to them: so-called people of bad character, purported anti-saints whom Judy Shepard suggests face posthumous suspicion and revulsion. In science, if the epitome of a whole species is found to exist in a particular specimen, then that individual becomes the "holotype" for all that follow it. All other specimens are compared to the original that set the standard. Weaken the holotype, distort it, and you inevitably revise the meaning of everything else in its class.

The public outcry at Matt's cold-blooded killing meant the hate crime that cut his young life short became the holotype in the American psyche for all instances of oppression against people in the sexual minority. It also sent a chill into the bones of the religio-political Right Wing. Power to enact protection statutes for LGBTQ people coalesced around Matt's death so swiftly that the "Wingers" feared anti-LGBTQ hate crime legislation might actually become law. Their strategy was to kill the story, or failing that, change the narrative. Cut the power of moral outrage out from under Matt's murder, and they would blunt the mounting public sentiment for an end to anti-LGBTQ oppression, they reasoned.

Since Matt's story looms larger than any other account of anti-LGBTQ hate murder, attempts to discredit Matt and lessen the moral impact of his death are archetypal. The first attempt to kill the story and change the subject was made public during the trials of Henderson and McKinney. With the death penalty staring down at them, they swore they had never intended to kill Matt—just to rob him. Henderson and McKinney and their attorneys entered the primal homophobic defense ploy into the public record: Matt was actually *responsible* for his own murder. The killers' version of the story was that he hit on them in the pickup truck, making sexual advances. His abductors panicked, assaulted him without mercy, got on with their thefts (including Matt's wallet, credit card and shoes), drove him for miles, and tied him up in the remote Sherman Hills area east of Laramie where they left him to die in near-freezing temperatures—wouldn't anybody do the same in their situation?

As absurd as it sounds, the "gay panic" defense is a homophobic classic, and as the Matthew Shepard case shows, it can rise to dizzying heights of absurdity. In order for it to work, either in a court of law or in the court of public opinion, the gay panic defense must feed off of the irrational fear of homosexual latency, especially in males. The fabricators of the gay panic defense bet that male jurors are so terrified and insecure about their masculinity that making a charge of sexual aggression against a gay hate crime victim will infect the prosecution's account of the facts just enough to skew a verdict. It puts the victim on trial instead of the perpetrators. Sadly, the gay panic defense ploy works all too well.

"FRANKEN-MATT"

Regrettably, it does work, and here is how: Take the actual Matt Shepard, no paragon of male machismo (all 5'2" and 105 lbs. of him), raise doubts about his nature, turn him by imagination into a raging deviant bent on deflowering his two larger, stronger murderers, and to some degree average "reasonable" citizens lose their bearings in the thicket of anti-LGBTQ beliefs we all inherit in our country. Matt, the fragile-looking, average middle-class white boy, becomes "Were-Matt," or "Franken-Matt," an abominable sodomite who, in some measure, got what he deserved on that windy Wyoming ridge that full moon night. Like the Jews throughout Europe, some seventy years ago. Or like women who "get" themselves raped.

In fairness, the Albany County judge didn't buy it. He threw the "homosexual rage syndrome" defense out of his court. Apparently, the defendants in the Shepard case didn't really buy it either, since they abandoned that theory to turn against each other. Henderson, trying to portray himself as harmless as a choirboy, turned state's evidence against McKinney, whom he portrayed as a crazed, homo-hating meth addict, to avoid the death penalty. The gay panic defense went up in smoke, but Matt's story got changed ever so slightly, nevertheless. Some in the public started scratching their heads. The revisionist story killers were on their way.

Beth Loffreda, author of the finest book on the Matthew Shepard murder to date, *Losing Matt Shepard: Life and Politics in the Aftermath of Anti-Gay Murder*, notes that even a few of Laramie's gay men admitted wondering what Matt had been up to that night with rough trade like Henderson and McKinney. While we will never know the answer to that question, the fact that it lingers in the air around a gay murder victim is revealing. Loffreda's conclusion is that even a person like Matt, totally vindicated of inciting his own death by the City of Laramie Police Department and the Albany County Sheriff's Department, is still under the onus of sex and desire. Innocence and sexual appetite are uneasy bedfellows in this tragically repressed culture of ours. Was Matt a normal 21-year-old gay man with desires comparable to the passions usually assumed to possess normal straight men of the same age? Yes, naturally. Could that have figured into the mix of signals flying between Matt and his abductors that night at the Fireside? It would be surprising if longing, loneliness, and lust did not somehow inhabit the libido of any young university student like him. Name one for whom it doesn't. Mating impulses are acceptable among birds, bees, and straight people. But gays and lesbians suffer the taint of "the sin that dares not speak its name" for their urges. Even given the discovery that Matt was HIV-positive, a disease that refuses to discriminate against anyone of a sexual orientation, he cannot be held complicit in his own death. Matt was no better nor worse than anyone else looking for love, or at least pleasure, in the late twentieth century—no matter how uncomfortable that fact might make us feel.

As Loffreda sees it, Matt was a real person, not a hero or an altar boy. He was unique in the ways most young men normally are, and in that may be found the real, heinous nature of the crime that bludgeoned the life out of him. If culpability attaches to human sexual feelings, then by rights most all of us should have faced assassination on that cold ridge right alongside him. It is a cultural smear of the worst kind to attack any LGBTQ person's character because of the desires we all carry.

If Matt's murder is not about "the homosexual agenda," as the revisionists wanted to portray it, then their best strategy remained in distorting the precipitating factors leading to his death. The trials of his killers brought up a series of these scenarios: the killing occurred inadvertently—it was a robbery that got out of hand, or a drug deal that went bad. How plausible are these imaginative reconstructions of what happened at the buck fence that night? Robbery was an undeniable factor in targeting Matt. McKinney and Henderson saw a benefit in abducting him. They needed money, and Matt dressed pretty well, wore good leather shoes, and drank imported beer. Whether the dubious allegations that Matt either wanted to buy drugs from his killers, or that he had offered them drugs for sexual favors, in the popular mind, young men, theft, and drugs go together like ants and pie at a summer picnic. Framed in the right fashion, either scenario has a way of shifting anti-gay hatred out of the center of the buck fence story: "Matt wasn't killed because he was gay . . . it was because he was a naïve rich kid, a druggie on the make for sex and a high."

20/20 GONE BLIND

This second move to kill the story of Matt Shepard made its most audacious bid for legitimacy in an *ABC News 20/20* special in November 2004. Promoted as the "real story" of the killing based on "new information," the show advanced the theory that it was actually a crystal meth drug binge killing, and not an anti-gay murder at all. Its revisionist appeal lies in how credible drug-related crimes have become in our society, and in the seemingly inexhaustible power of denial in human psychic life. In this version of "Franken-Matt," he becomes a craven drug dealer or junkie who died plying his wares or whimpering for crank. Either revision of the story of Matt's last night in Laramie will do to blunt and confuse the account that he was truly targeted for being gay.

The so-called "new information" was not new at all—every seemingly substantial allegation in the *ABC 20/20* show had been floated to the public before, and had been knocked down. Henderson and McKinney's defense lawyers attempted to deflect first-degree murder charges with accounts of how the defendants only wanted to rob Matt, and things got out of hand. They also brought up the drug buy/drug swap for sex distraction to the court. Inspection of Letters to the Editor in the *Laramie Boomerang* shows that locals kept bringing up these theories for months after the trials were over. In September 1999, *Harpers Magazine* played up the methamphetamine connection. Five years later, the ABC story failed to present any new blockbuster revelations. All they actually had was old hat. What Elizabeth Vargas and her team at ABC managed to do, however, was to repackage Matt's murder on the television screen for the American viewing public—for voters. They presented a carefully edited, pseudo-documentary distorting Matt's story in order to draw a bead on the real target of their ire: anti-LGBTQ hate crimes, and any proposed legislation that would address them.

McKinney and Henderson were sentenced by the court to two consecutive life terms apiece, and are serving out their punishment in state prison. But the revisionists working so hard to change the subject, and kill the story of Matthew Shepard, are getting away with narrative murder, and paying little or no price for it.

1. Revisionists torture facts. They are not interested in facts for what they would otherwise faithfully reveal. They employ facts selectively, and strategically omit others in order to achieve a spin on an event that matches their ideological convictions.

2. Revisionists assassinate character. For them, the very idea that Matt was murdered because he was gay is repugnant. LGBTQ people are bad people to them, special pleaders who have an "agenda." LGBTQ lives are not worthy of the dignity and respect afforded to other people. In many cases, this revisionist point of view appeals to homophobic religious ideas that either tacitly condone violence against LGBTQ people, or openly sanction it. The full protection of the law is not for "queers," but for good, upstanding, moral citizens, whose way of life is threatened by the "homosexual agenda." Any right-thinking "homo" would never come out of the closet anyway, and those who do simply ask for the trouble they get.

3. People who get hurt or killed, as revisionists ratchet up rhetoric against LGBTQ claims of injustice, are no more than collateral damage to them. Revisionists take no responsibility for the violence their propaganda incites or permits. Anyone who says, "Sticks and stones may break your bones, but words will never hurt you," never lived in harm's way as LGBTQ people do every day in America.

The revisionist forces have a clear agenda: to keep LGBTQ women and men in their place, and to frustrate for them any attempt to secure equal protection under law. Even to admit there is such a thing as an anti-LGBTQ hate crime is to allow the proverbial camel to poke its nose successfully under the flap of the American tent. Let that happen, and pretty soon the whole camel will break in, humps and all! Knock down the premier American example of anti-LGBTQ hate crime, the Matthew Shepard story, and you have beaten the camel back, or at least significantly hobbled it. So, the ends justify the means: employ any argument that would damage the liberal, homosexual agenda, no matter how sufficiently these warmed-over arguments have been refuted in the past; deny any fact that does not support the status quo; and do what is necessary to swing public opinion against hate crimes laws. In other words, *get away with murder*—kill any support for social and political change arising from the Matt Shepard murder story, and do the same thing to any other sexual orientation, gender identity, or gender expression murder story that arises in the future.

From the outset, the whole point of the *ABC 20/20* show was to say only one thing about the murder of Matthew Shepard: "This was not a hate crime." Now that the twelfth anniversary of Matt's murder is upon us, the story killers will be at it again, working overtime.

Was Matt's murder *not* a hate crime? If robbery was the sole reason for the initial assault, why drive ten miles out of town with a fragile-looking person like Matt, who was easily enough robbed in the early stages of the abduction? Why bludgeon a person in the head eighteen times with a stolen revolver, someone who, by Henderson and McKinney's own testimony, was so scared that he offered to take them where they could steal far more than the $20 and the credit card he had on him that night? Matt's autopsy revealed the backs of his hands were bruised from trying to defend himself, and his crotch was traumatized where he had been repeatedly kicked. Was it just a meth crime, then, a robbery, or a drug deal that went bad because of too little money and too much crank?

The great flaw in the *ABC 20/20* theory, that something other than hate crime was afoot in the murder of Matthew Shepard, is the insupportable assumption that what had happened was "either/or." It had to be drugs *or* homophobia, theft *or* hate crime. Why? What in the investigations bears this out? Bias-related crimes are never clean, never neat. Slaughter is a nasty business, and those who carry it out often liberally mix other criminal activity with killing.

Judy and Dennis Shepard refuse to let their son's story be riddled with such confusion. They appeal to the confession tape Aaron McKinney made before he and Henderson established a line of defense attempting to muddy the waters. Repeatedly, McKinney made homophobic allusions and blamed his loathing of gays. In a letter he wrote to a friend from his prison cell, McKinney recounted why he had beaten Matt so severely: "Being a verry drunk homophobic [sic] I flipped out and began to pistol whip the fag with my gun, ready at hand."

For Judy Shepard, any attempt to fog the truth with the contention that her son's killing was not about his sexuality is bogus. Hatred of her son's homosexuality was at the root of everything: "There were a lot of things going on that night, and hate was one of them, and they murdered my son ultimately," she said on *20/20*. "Anything else we find out just doesn't . . . change that fact." Lest a mother's grief be thought to cloud the issue, the law enforcement professionals who spent months investigating Matt's murder remain clear about the motivation for Matt's killing. It was murder incited by hatred of homosexuals.

"ONE THOUSAND PER CENT TORTURE"

Laramie Police Commander Dave O'Malley, lean, tall, and mustachioed, forcefully disagrees with the belief that drugs motivated the attack on Matt. For O'Malley, a professional who left no stone unturned in his investigation, the murder was about one thing only: sexual orientation. "I really don't think [McKinney] was in a methamphetamine-induced rage when this happened. I don't buy it at all," he told reporters for *20/20*. "I feel comfortable in my own heart that they did what they did to Matt because they [had] hatred toward him for being gay."

O'Malley, now retired from the police force after twenty-seven years of service, was a registered Republican at the time of Matt's murder. He voted for Bush in 1992 and Dole in 1996. Now he advocates for hate crimes legislation to protect LGBTQ people. Matt's case changed the hard-bitten lawman, as he admitted to Bill Kurtis, host of A&E's *American Justice*: "I was a rotten son of a bitch when it came to dealing with gay issues," O'Malley said, emotion in his voice. "I had preconceived ideology that I grew up with, hearing it from my father and my friends . . . the jokes we used to tell and the things we used to say."

"My eyes got opened up," O'Malley said in a subsequent interview with *New York Times* reporter Michael Janofsky.

> I didn't realize how a hate crime affects all gays, not just an individual. Matt's friends were scared to death. Some left town as a result of what happened. Some transferred to other schools. They knew if it happened to [Matt], it could happen to anybody. All kinds of people get killed every day, but I'm not afraid to go down to the liquor store to buy a six-pack as some of these people were . . . It's absurd that it took something this tragic to make it hit me.

Commander O'Malley, who spent the last eight years of his career as chief of the investigations unit, said he had never seen a crime scene to rival Matt's murder site where the dirt road dead-ended at the buck fence. Footprints, drag marks, and tire tracks scarred the ground. Blood splattered over a fifty-foot radius, indicating Matt had desperately tried to escape his killers. McKinney admitted to investigators how Matt struggled for dear life to stay in the cab of the pickup truck. McKinney had to beat him with the stolen pistol to break his grip on the steering wheel of the pickup in order to drag Matt to the ground. Henderson's clothing was stained with Matt's blood, evidence that he had held their bloodied victim as McKinney rained blows on him with the butt of the gun. Matt's screams went unheard. The nearest house was hundreds of yards away. Matt's wounds were so brutally concentrated on his head and face that O'Malley concluded Matt's assailants warmed to their work. This was nothing less than an attack fueled by hate, up close and personal.

Detective Sergeant Rob DeBree, the lead investigator for Albany County, told Beth Loffreda in unmistakable terms that Matt's murder was unlike any drug-related crime he had ever seen. He and his team searched the pickup truck and the residences of both Henderson and McKinney, finding no evidence of methamphetamines. "From everything we were able to investigate," DeBree told Loffreda, "the last time they would have done meth would have been up to two to three weeks previous to that night."

DeBree is a big, bluff character, weathered tough on the prairie. Like O'Malley, DeBree was initially unsympathetic to hate crime claims made by LGBTQ people. Dave Cullen, a Denver writer who interviewed DeBree for Salon.com, described him as "a man who would be exceedingly out of place in the Castro or the East Village—the least likely sort of person to shill for the gay community." But like Commander O'Malley, in the course of the investigation, Detective Sergeant DeBree learned what being gay and lesbian is really like in small-town America. Most of all, what those two perpetrators did to Matt changed DeBree's mind.

"Nobody in this country ought to be having the fear [gays and lesbians] do," DeBree said to Bill Kurtis, "and if I can change my view, my supposed fears of what gays are and things to that effect—if I can change, anybody in this country can. Believe me."

"[McKinney and Henderson] knew damned well he was gay," DeBree told Cullen. "It started out as a robbery and burglary, and I sincerely believe the other activity was because he was gay . . . That was one thousand per cent torture, what occurred to that boy."

RESISTING THE SECOND DEATH

Matthew Shepard was pronounced dead in a Fort Collins hospital. In reality, though, he died on that lonely ridge tied tightly to the poles of a buck fence five days earlier. During the interim, after eighteen hours in the cold and wind before his discovery, and after two hospital staffs lost their battle to keep him alive, Matt's physical life ended. Because of who he was and who he has become in the American mind, some people are not satisfied with his physical death.

Whatever one believes about the afterlife, the struggle for a murdered gay man's memory goes on. People in Laramie wish to forget him, to lay Matt's memory to rest forever. It is a hard thing to hear from Rob DeBree, one of Laramie's own, that two local men, bone of their bone and flesh of their flesh, took Matt's life away because he was gay. Researchers who go to Laramie these days to get information about the Shepard murder, and ask for directions to the buck fence location, get told little or nothing. Sometimes they get threatened with arrest if they go looking for it. During my own search, two women from the Laramie Chamber of Commerce warned me, "You don't want to go there, mister; you really don't. We are not at liberty to tell you anything about that place, and if you go up there, you'll be arrested for trespassing." On the way from the Regional Airport, I asked the cheery Enterprise Rent-A-Car man about Matt's murder. He brushed off the question, saying, "Aw, man, everybody knows what happened that night was a drug buy gone bad. That boy wasn't killed 'cause he was gay." Conversations like these went on the whole week I was in Laramie. Like Dallas, Texas, where I live, proud towns have difficulty living with infamy.

Thankfully, no matter how one conceives of life and death, Matt is beyond harm now. There will always be those who feed on their fear and loathing for LGBTQ people. Fred Phelps and his lamentable followers are among them. I omit any theological title for Phelps—he doesn't deserve it. During Matt's funeral at St. Mark's Episcopal Church in Casper, where Matt was a member, Phelps and his hatemongers stood across the street in the park shouting slogans and brandishing signs like "Matt in Hell," and "Fags Die, God Laughs." Later, at the trials of Henderson and McKinney, he and his vulturine flock demonstrated outside the Albany County Courthouse. On Phelps's website, GodHatesFags.com, the centerpiece of his calumny is a digital image of Matt roasting in flames. If visitors to the site have the necessary computer "plug-in," they can hear screams of torment in the background. Matt is by no means the only target of Phelps's homophobia. Phelps has also drawn down on Diane Whipple and Billy Jack Gaither, to name only a couple of others.

Phelps and his ilk—for he is only one of too many like him in America—would have us believe that Matt, and Diane, and Billy Jack are among those suffering the miserable fate of the wicked dead in Hell. Anti-LGBTQ violence comes in many forms, and spiritual violence against Matt's memory is only another attempt to change the subject by making Matt seem responsible for his own death. It is hard to grant such blatant lunacy the same protections of the First Amendment, especially when the families, lovers and friends of queer folk suffer so much from hateful tirades. Spiritual violence does great harm to the living, and virtually every case of physical violence done to LGBTQ people has been justified theologically by their tormentors. But their version of the "second death," while despicable, cannot reach Matt and others like him anymore. For that, at least, we can be thankful.

The second death we must resist is the seemingly endless attempt to deny the truth of why Matthew Shepard died. Changing the subject to something else, anything else, murders something precious. While Matt himself is beyond harm, his memory is not. Amnesia, distortion, ignorance, political cynicism—even sincere desires to closet the lives of LGBTQ people and throw away the key—are at work to rob Matt's story of its moral impact on the conscience of the nation. We must not allow that to happen. The vigilant keepers of Matt's memory must not rest. The tellers of his story must not fall silent. His story once captured the imagination of a whole nation, and began to move people. The story, however, hasn't moved people far enough to make justice real for all the citizens of this country. Until it does, Matt's memory will uneasily remind us of how much work there is to be done.

Quite another Christ than the counterfeit version Phelps wielded as a weapon against LGBTQ people looks down from a stained glass window in the small ante chapel of Matt's church in Casper. The eyes of Christ are all-compassion. Like the unlocked door of the chapel, open twenty-four hours a day, Christ's hands are open to bless and heal any seeker. His words, "Come to me, all who labor and are heavy laden, and I will give you rest," are etched in the glass. This is the Christ who insures that no hater will ever have the last word. And, for those who draw comfort from this true Christ, there is strength to keep Matt's memory evergreen, along with the memories of all other LGBTQ people who died solely for being the people they were.

A DECADE AND MORE AFTER THE BUCK FENCE

Twelve years after the hate crime murder of Matt Shepard, what has *not* changed? Speaking recently to *USA Today*, Matt's mother, Judy, says the worst thing is that hate crimes killings continue unabated. "Hate is still out there," she said. "LGBTQ people are still being bashed and killed simply because they are different." During the interview, she referred particularly to the February 2008 shooting of Larry King, a 15-year-old middle school student in Oxnard, California, who was murdered by his 14-year-old classmate: "This terrible incident underscores the fact that we cannot let hate go unchecked in our schools and communities. Our young people need our direction and guidance to prevent this type of crime from happening."

The politicians and citizens of Wyoming have not yet seen fit to protect their LGBTQ neighbors and friends. And in Laramie, where Matt was murdered a decade ago, there are municipal ordinances against throwing rocks and spitting in public places, but no statute to criminalize bias crimes. The only thing the city council could muster in the wake of Matt's cruel demise was an ordinance directing the city manager to see that police were trained to identify such crimes, report them statistically, and include the figures in the minutes of city council meetings (Ordinance 1312 § 1, 2000).

Some things have changed, however. Matt's murder was a watershed in the human rights movement. The heinous nature of his death opened many eyes to the plight of LGBTQ people in America. In the months following Matt's murder, the Shepards received more than 110,000 messages from every state in the nation, and from every walk of life. The Matthew Shepard Foundation works each day to lessen the impact of hate in our society, a dream Matt shared with his parents before his death. Even Logan, his younger brother, has joined his parents in the effort to "Erase Hate" and promote understanding about queer youth. As Judy Shepard shared with the *Houston Chronicle*, campaigning for acceptance of LGBTQ people keeps her slain son alive. It prevents the Shepards from becoming victims, and moves them along in their grieving process. "[Doing this,] I get to keep Matthew with me," she said.

Most will say that the signal achievement attached to Matt's name is the passage of the Matthew Shepard and James Byrd Jr. Hate Crimes Prevention Act by both houses of the 110th Congress. After a decade of contentious debate and dogged advocacy, and after no fewer than fourteen separate congressional floor votes throughout the years, the dream of enacting Federal protections for LGBTQ people in the United States became a reality. When President Barack Obama signed the Byrd-Shepard Act into law on October 28, 2009 at the White House, he said:

> After more than a decade of opposition and delay, we've passed inclusive hate crimes legislation to help protect our citizens from violence based on what they look like, who they love, how they pray, or who they are. I promised Judy Shepard, when she saw me in the Oval Office, that this day would come, and I'm glad that she and her husband Dennis could join us for this event. I'm also honored to have the family of the late Senator Ted Kennedy, who fought so hard for this legislation.

The family of James Byrd Jr. of Jasper, Texas—brutally murdered and decapitated by bigots because of his race the same year Matt was killed in Laramie—joined the Shepards and the Kennedys at the signing ceremony: a show of solidarity in grief and hope by blacks and gay folk, facing the common ravages of hatred and terror with a determination never to let bigotry have the last word. Judy Shepard spoke to the nation on that red-letter day in the name of her slain son:

> We are incredibly grateful to Congress and the President for taking this step forward on behalf of hate crime victims and their families, especially given the continuing attacks on people simply for living their lives openly and honestly. But each of us can and must do much more to ensure true equality for all Americans.

Matt's name and image, used in the cause of hate crimes legislation throughout the world for better than a decade, has become the most recognizable LGBTQ identity in recent history—if not of all time.

But perhaps the greatest advance in the twelve years since Matt's hate crime murder is not the passage of the long awaited Shepard-Byrd Act at all, but rather something less dramatic. Far more significant is how Matt's death has changed the way homosexuality is approached and talked about in society. There has been definite progress here, of a kind. Judy notes that when she was growing up as a girl in Wyoming, "no one talked about it." The subject of homosexuality was taboo. Gays and lesbians were kept silent and invisible, even to their families and close neighbors. Since 1998, much of that has changed. Emboldened by the outrageous murder of their little brother, Matt, gay folk by hundreds of thousands all over America have come out of the closet, refusing to hide any more. These days, one would be hard pressed to find a segment of American life where issues surrounding LGBTQ life are not on the public agenda in some fashion, pro or con.

At the center of advocacy for LGBTQ freedom remains the enigmatic memory of the young, blond student trussed to that buck fence in Laramie. He has become the symbol, both here and abroad, for the hurts and hopes of lesbians, gay men, bisexual people, and transgender folk. For the millions who hear his story, curiosity or outrage at what happened to him usually begins a change in their hearts and attitudes about hate crimes. That alone is reason enough to tell and retell Matt's story, and the stories of so many other LGBTQ people who have died so brutally. But are we any closer to understanding the real person, or is that person locked away behind the closed door of a decade of myth-making and amnesia? For most Americans, other than his family and his closest friends, the only way we come to know Matt is through the veil of the savagery that cut his life short. He suffered the dying, but we suffer the effects of his death. There may be no way to recover Matt Shepard: the complicated young man who comes to life when his mother talks about his passionate opinions, his flashing temper, his generosity to a fault, his love of politics, his hopes of becoming a human rights advocate, and, we must add, his disturbing naïveté. The person he might have been is long gone. As Beth Loffreda says, what remains is the "whiplash" of his memory, haunting Laramie and haunting us, luring and stinging the conscience of our violent American society. Forgetfulness seems not to work. We can neither forget him, nor should we. In the act of telling and retelling how his life ended lies the hope that a grace of transformation may seize us, as it did Sergeant Rob DeBree and Commander Dave O'Malley. Justice may yet be done, and hatred may be changed gradually into acceptance: of LGBTQ people by others and by themselves, of those who strike out against persons they fear and do not understand, and ultimately, of the need to grant each other room to "live and let live."

Dennis Shepard, Matt's father, showed us, on the day he and Judy granted Aaron McKinney life instead of death, how this must be done. On behalf of the family, Dennis spoke unforgettable words to McKinney and Henderson, to the court, and to the world. His words of justice are juicy with grace:

[Mr. McKinney],

Matt became a symbol—some say a martyr, putting a boy-next-door face on hate crimes. That's fine with me. Matt would be thrilled if his death would help others. On the other hand, your agreement to life without parole has taken yourself out of the spotlight and out of the public eye. It means no drawn-out appeals process, [no] chance of walking away free due to a technicality, and no chance of lighter sentence due to a "merciful" jury. Best of all, you won't be a symbol. No years of publicity, no chance of communication, no nothing—just a miserable future and a more miserable end. It works for me.

My son was taught to look at all sides of an issue before making a decision or taking a stand. He learned this early when he helped campaign for various political candidates while in grade school and junior high. When he did take a stand, it was based on his best judgment. Such a stand cost him his life when he quietly let it be known that he was gay. He didn't advertise it, but he didn't back away from the issue either. For that I'll always be proud of him. He showed me that he was a lot more courageous than most people, including myself. Matt knew that there were dangers to being gay, but he accepted that and wanted to just get on with his life and his ambition of helping others.

Matt's beating, hospitalization, and funeral focused worldwide attention on hate. Good is coming out of evil. People have said, "Enough is enough." You screwed up, Mr. McKinney. You made the world realize that a person's lifestyle is not a reason for discrimination, intolerance, persecution, and violence. This is not the 1920s, '30s, and '40s of Nazi Germany. My son died because of your ignorance and intolerance. I can't bring him back. But I can do my best to see that this never, ever happens to another person or another family again. As I mentioned earlier, my son has become a symbol—a symbol against hate and people like you; a symbol for encouraging respect for individuality; for appreciating that someone is different; for tolerance. I miss my son, but I'm proud to be able to say that he is my son.

Mr. McKinney, one final comment before I sit, and this is the reason that I stand before you now. At no time since Matt was found at the fence and taken to the hospital have Judy and I made any statements about our beliefs concerning the death penalty. We felt that that would be an undue influence on any prospective juror. Judy has been quoted by some right-wing groups as being against the death penalty. It has been stated that Matt was against the death penalty. Both of these statements are wrong. We have held family discussions and talked about the death penalty. Matt believed that there were incidents and crimes that justified the death penalty. For example, he and I discussed the horrible death of James Byrd Jr. in Jasper, Texas. It was his opinion that the death penalty should be sought and that no expense should be spared to bring those responsible for this murder to justice. Little did we know that the same response would come about involving Matt. I, too, believe in the death penalty. I would like nothing better than to see you die, Mr. McKinney. However, this is the time to begin the healing process. To show mercy to someone who refused to show any mercy. To use this as the first step in my own closure about losing Matt. Mr. McKinney, I am not doing this because of your family. I am definitely not doing this because of the crass and unwarranted pressures put on by the religious community. If anything, that hardens my resolve to see you die.

Mr. McKinney, I'm going to grant you life, as hard as that is for me to do, because of Matthew. Every time you celebrate Christmas, a birthday, or the Fourth of July, remember that Matt isn't. Every time that you wake up in that prison cell, remember that you had the opportunity and the ability to stop your actions that night. Every time that you see your cellmate, remember that you had a choice, and now you are living that choice. You robbed me of something very precious, and I will never forgive you for that. Mr. McKinney, I give you life in the memory of one who no longer lives. May you have a long life, and may you thank Matthew every day for it.

THE SECOND LIFE OF MATTHEW SHEPARD

The true danger to memory is not forgetting. Rather, it is failing to remember. The dissimilarity between the two is as profound as the difference between sins of omission and sins of commission. Those who fail to remember are, as sages say, "doomed to relive their past." The revisionists of the religio-political Right Wing want us to believe the worst that could happen to Matthew Shepard's narrative is for it to be forgotten. Indeed, for Matthew Shepard to be forgotten, as have the vast majority of the 13,000 LGBTQ hate crimes victims in America bookending him before and after, would be a tragic loss. The real injustice revisionists still plot for Matthew is to render his story and memory unworthy to live and flourish. No matter the laws passed in Matt's name, they reason, if the leading symbol of the human rights movement can be discredited sufficiently, the discriminatory order of patriarchy and heterosexism can, and will, reassert itself. The queers will have to return to the closet. Many in this country are desperate to relive this version of the past, and will act violently to do so. As the National Coalition of Anti-Violence Programs statistics on anti-LGBTQ hate crimes for 2009 reveal, the second-highest total of murders in a decade took place the very year the Byrd-Shepard Act was passed—with by far the greatest number of violent attacks against the sexual minority taking place in October 2009, when the act was signed into law.

What is this phenomenon of violence? What does it portend? Could this be the inbreaking of backlash politics, the relentless, de facto repeal of a generation of work for the safety, liberty, and full equality of LGBTQ people in America, of which a fatal failure to remember Matt's hate crime story would be the leading edge, as the revisionist politicos desire? *No!*

Matt's story stands as a bulwark against the demons lurking in the American character, just as important to the rights and equality of all residents of this nation as the remembrance of the Holocaust is to the full humanity of the world. In monumental letters carved into eternal stone at the Dachau Concentration Camp are the words, *Never Again!*, in five languages. As Dr. Johannes Neuhäusler, Auxiliary Bishop of Munich and former Dachau inmate, said, "Dachau can and shall be a lesson! Therefore we dare not be silent about it, although the memory of it is sad and grievous." Remembering is a duty of the soul. As often as we rehearse Matt's story and the other "sad and grievous" stories of the LGBTQ women, men, and youths who died at the hands of unreasoning hatred, the intentions of the killers, the haters, and the indifferent bystanders are thwarted. Instead of succumbing to a second death, the murdered dreams of the lost are found, and acquire new life again.

Americans love stories of hope, renewal, struggle, and redemption. That is why the unvarnished story of Matthew Shepard will remain evergreen in the consciousness of the nation. The underdog will rise. The fallen shall not have died in vain. Love is more powerful than death. Fed on such manna, the "Better Angels of the American Spirit," as President Lincoln said in his Second Inaugural Address, gain strength to redress the injustices so many in this country like Matt have endured. In the *New York Times,* Mary Cable, the popular historian, said the best biographies "leave their readers with a sense of having all but entered into a second life and of having come to know another human being in some ways better than he knew himself." At the heart of the narrative of Matthew Shepard's outrageous murder is a complex young man, neither demon nor angel, flesh and blood, just like us. We connect with him. Our longing to change the conditions that took his life is the way we uphold his memory. His legacy belongs to the storytellers. His "second life" is living itself out in us.

For Greater Understanding

The Second Death of Matthew Shepard

BOOKS

Kaufman, Moises. *The Laramie Project*. New York: Vintage, 2001.

Loffreda, Beth. *Losing Matt Shepard: Life and Politics in the Aftermath of Anti-Gay Murder*. New York: Columbia University Press, 2000.

Shepard, Judy. *The Meaning of Matthew: My Son's Murder in Laramie, and a World Transformed*. New York: Plume, 2010.

Swigonski, Mary E., et al. *From Hate Crimes to Human Rights: A Tribute to Matthew Shepard*. Binghamton, NY: Harrington Park Press, 2001.

FILMS AND VIDEOGRAPHY

American Justice—Matthew Shepard: Death in the High Desert. The Arts and Entertainment Television Networks, 2008.

20/20 —The Matthew Shepard Case. ABC News, May 14, 2007.

ORGANIZATIONS AND WEBSITES

Gay & Lesbian Alliance Against Defamation (GLAAD): "10 Questions About ABC's 20/20 Show on Matthew Shepard," http://www.glaad.org/page.aspx?pid=582.

Matthew Shepard and James Byrd Jr. Hate Crimes Prevention Act, http://www.hrc.org /laws_and_elections/5660.htm.

Matthew Shepard Foundation, http://www.matthewshepard.org.

Unfinished Lives Project, http://unfinishedlivesblog.com.

Kenneth L. Cummings Jr.
September 11, 1960—June 4, 2007

HOUSTON AND PEARLAND, TEXAS

2

God Slain

Kenneth L. Cummings Jr.

*"This death is just one more smoking gun found at the scene of
another crime caused directly by fundamentalist Christian leaders
whose obsessive anti-homosexual campaign leads to tragic consequences they will not admit. Soulforce has been saying for years that
their rhetoric leads to suffering and death, and now—once again—we
have the sickening evidence to prove it."*

—REV. DR. MEL WHITE,
SOULFORCE FOUNDER, ON THE MURDER OF KEN CUMMINGS

TWO BIBLICAL TEXTS BOOKEND the senseless murder of 46-year-old
Southwest Airlines Flight Attendant Kenneth Cummings Jr. The
first, found in Malachi 4, is a fearsome prediction of wrath for "all the
arrogant and all evildoers" who will be burned up on the day of God's
judgment. God tells the prophet that he will send back Elijah to the earth
as a forerunner to inaugurate "the great and terrible day of the Lord." The
Righteous will leap for joy on that day "like calves from the stall." But
then the Righteous will trample down the wicked, who will be incinerated in the oven of God's anger, "for they will be ashes under the soles of
your feet" (Malachi 4:3). Ken's killer, Terry Mark Mangum, stalked Ken
with that very passage of scripture in mind—if you believe him. After
immersing himself in toxic anti-gay teaching for thousands of hours,
and calling himself by turns, "Elijah" and "Melchizedek," Mangum fatally attacked Cummings in his own home. "Sexual perversion is the
worst sin," he said. "I planned on sending him to hell."

The second biblical text, set in bronze atop Ken's grave, is from Jeremiah 20:11: "But the Lord is with me like a dread warrior; therefore my persecutors will stumble, and they will not prevail. They will be greatly shamed, for they will not succeed. Their eternal dishonor will never be forgotten." According to the text, the besieged prophet looks forward to the day when he will be vindicated by God, who will cast down his opponents, and rush to the aid of the needy who rely on him. Ken's family, as truly pious and charismatic Christians as their gay son had once been, chose this verse to cover his grave. It is an unusual choice for a tomb epitaph. According to a longtime friend from Ken's college days, Ken claimed this Jeremiah text as his own after watching a televangelist preach the scripture passage on the Trinity Broadcasting Network. Cast on the metal tablet, beneath his name and color portrait, these holy words shield Ken's remains from both the heat of the Texas sun and the animosity of the hateful.

People who kill LGBTQ folk almost universally seek to justify their murders by appealing to God's judgment and quoting scripture verses. They say that homosexuality is a sin, punishable by death according to divine authority, so their victims simply got what was coming to them. It all sounds mad. But to dismiss the self-appointed executioners of queer people as pathological is to miss the deadly rational simplicity of their logic. In Ken Cummings's case, it was as plain to Mangum as an inference from Aristotle is to a student:

> If all homosexuals are worthy of death, and Ken Cummings is a gay man, it follows, then, that Ken Cummings is deserving of death.

When religion is recruited by brute ideology to justify homicide, all that is missing is a willing perpetrator, someone who has the "guts" to do it. Take Matthew Williams, for example, one of two religiously motivated brothers who slaughtered gay life-partners Gary Matson and Winfield Mowder in their California home in July 1999. Williams made no bones about his reason for slaying these so-called abominators. "It's a part of the faith," he argued. "So many people claim to be Christians and complain about all these things their religion says are a sin, but they're not willing to do anything about it. They don't have the guts." Terry Mangum could not have said it better. Hence, the diabolical syllogism once again:

> If true followers of God do what God requires, and God requires
> that homosexuals die violently, then a true believer must act on
> God's requirement and kill homosexuals.

But just because it is "logical" doesn't mean that it isn't monstrous. Ken Cummings was not a syllogism's middle term or minor premise. He was a real, flesh-and-blood person who did not deserve to be incinerated by a deadly ideology masquerading as biblical truth. Neither does it mean that an apprehended and convicted killer—acting as judge, jury and executioner—is solely responsible for the act of hate crime murder. Terry Mark Mangum did indeed wield the knife that cut short the life of a man who was a beloved son, brother, uncle, co-worker and friend . . . but Mangum was a cat's-paw for others who were just as culpable of this hate murder as he. There were many people besides Mangum responsible for the death of Ken Cummings Jr. Very many, indeed.

THE SPIRIT AND THE FLESH

As the tumultuous 1960s began, Kenneth L. Cummings Jr., was born in Galveston, Texas on September 11 to "Big Kenny" Sr. and Martha Cummings. He was their first child and only son, to be followed in time by a sister, Lori. "Little Kenny," a moniker he would carry until the day he died, grew up in the Gulf Coast oil boomtown of Texas City where his father worked for the Marathon Oil Company. The post-war petroleum industry was a Mecca for thousands of men like Ken Sr., who worked hard, lived frugally, and tried to give their children two basic gifts: the cherished values they had inherited from their own parents, and the chance for a better life. Ken's mother was a stay-at-home mom, a homemaker who gave the little family stability, while dad labored at the huge Texas City oil refinery that ran full-throttle, twenty-four hours a day.

Like most Texans of that era, the lifestyle of the Cummings clan was a blend of Southern culture, Western enterprise, and Lone Star independence. They valued family, patriotism, and church—in their case a robust form of Pentecostalism as practiced in the Assemblies of God. In Texas City and throughout the state, hard-working, blue-collar folk populated the pews of the Baptist Churches, the non-instrumental Churches of Christ, and the Pentecostal fellowships, providing the backbone atop which the upper classes of Texas life were built. "Little Kenny" grew up comfortably with the customary "roughneck" rivalries: between the Texas City High "Stingarees" and their football adversaries, between Democrats and Republicans, between Rebels and Yankees, and between the denominational groups that vied for members in the neighborhoods that comprised his hometown. He grew up learning to chuckle at the objections out-of-towners made to the noxious odor brewing up from refinery exhausts and the miasma of the ship channel, and to rebut their delicacy with the canned retort, "Smells like money, doesn't it?"

While the rest of the country churned with the social upheaval of the 1960s and 1970s, "Little Kenny's" youth was relatively calm and All-American in Texas City. The secular verities emblazoned on his high school seal *Trust, Believe, Accomplish* reflected the optimism common to towns with big shoulders: a positive outlook that a high school diploma could still open doors to success for a youth who was willing to work hard and play by the rules.

By the time he graduated from Texas City High School, Ken Jr. had grown into a fine looking young man. He was 5'10" tall, slender, with a head of rich, brown hair and an olive complexion that could really hold a tan. He cut a sharp figure in his stylish clothes. Among his talents were a good singing voice and a sweet touch on the piano. He dated girls off and on, and was a perennial favorite of his classmates for his great sense of humor. As so many said at his funeral, he could always make you laugh.

Ken's jovial personality had a magnetic effect. He had lots of friends, and established an early pattern of welcome and inclusion that lasted throughout his life. Rick Maloch, another "Stingaree" alumnus, recalled how Ken invited the "new kid" to join him at his table of friends in the school cafeteria. "That's Ken in a nutshell," he said, "always willing to share his most cherished gift, his friends."

He was keenly attuned to others, respectful of his parents, and aware of the attitudes and feelings of his friends. One might say he was considerate to a fault, sending greeting cards and messages to family and friends for even the most obscure holidays on the calendar. As Sharon Jones recalled, Ken remembered her on every holiday and birthday, never forgetting to call or send flowers, "even on St. Patrick's Day." Testimonies abound to demonstrate how that was typical of the way Ken attended to his friends. Clearly, he was a skilled "bridge-person," building connections between people he liked, linking person-to-person. But while he kindly attended to the needs of so many, much was stirring within him that could not be expressed, needs and feelings of his own that he must have often denied and tried to pray away. He was different from others, and that difference would cost him dearly as he grew to understand what his sexuality truly was.

The Assemblies of God church where Ken came to faith as a boy, understood life in stark Manichean terms—a battle between light and darkness, truth and error, spirit and flesh. Sin abounds everywhere in the carnal world. Customarily, he would have attended church two or three times a week, and very rarely outside his own denomination. From the pulpit, he would have listened to what a leading Assemblies of God progressive has called "a drumbeat of scriptural negativity" concerning human sexuality. The nuclear family exemplified God's created order for human relationships, and, throughout Ken's impressionable early years, everything taught in church would take for granted that everyone in the congregation was straight. The AG church preached against masturbation. He would have regularly heard a strong emphasis on virginity, sexual purity, and abstinence in his AG youth group meetings. Sexual activity was ordained by God to take place legitimately only in the bonds of marriage between one man and one woman, "the heterosexual fulfillment of both man and woman," as the Assemblies' 1979 position paper on homosexuality states. Further, the church taught, "In total contrast, the lifestyle and practice of homosexual couples establish a social unit that thwarts [the propagation of the human race] and the creative purposes of God for humanity." Homosexuals were condemned as "depraved" and as "abominations," dehumanizing stereotypes driven home by blatantly negative sermons on Leviticus, Sodom and Gomorrah, and the first chapter of Romans. A practicing homosexual, according to all these teachings, could never inherit the kingdom of God.

Strict adherence to biblical teaching, interpreted as the "plain sense" of scripture, holding fast to "sound doctrine," including the experience-based manifestations of the Holy Spirit; and ascribing to an uncompromising moral code of behavior all served AG church members as bulwarks against the temptations the world afforded. Temptations of the flesh, though, were among the deadliest in the Devil's arsenal. In this context, we can better understand the urgency of the Assemblies of God's teachings about homosexuality, which it considered to be the epitome of fleshly corruption. While Ken was still a teen, his denomination fired this broadside against the supposed "sin" of homosexual conduct:

Today homosexuals have become aggressive in pushing their agenda. The church has been forced to answer ... Lowering God's holy standards to mankind's sinful preferences is an abomination in God's sight. As members of the Body of Christ, we must not ignore God's clear admonitions . . . and we must never let the declining moral climate of our nation pressure us into condoning what God condemns (excepted from the 1979 position paper of the Assemblies of God on Homosexuality).

Ken heard these teachings constantly throughout his formative years, and, like his peers, took them to heart. Sectarian Christians always see themselves as chosen by God to live exemplary lives, but the Assemblies of God see themselves as a distinctively holy people, "a people apart," and inculcated that responsibility in their members. Though all independent evangelical Christians share a literalist way of interpreting the Bible and a common conservative social agenda, Southern Baptist and Church of Christ congregations harbor a thinly-veiled contempt for Pentecostals, calling them "bird people" and "holy rollers" for their emphasis upon receiving the Holy Spirit, prophesying, healing, and "speaking in unknown tongues," or what is known as *glossolalia*. Elders in the Assemblies churches regularly preach that their members should "stay in the fold," refrain from dating outside the denomination, and, for God's sake, never marry anyone who is not baptized in the Holy Spirit. One Texas AG minister recalled that when he dated a Baptist girl, "It was a big deal," and he was clearly frowned upon for doing so. Belonging to the group was constantly communicated as a matter of life and death for the soul. Pressed to the margins even of evangelical Christian life, many preachers and members of the Assemblies of God saw their personal trials as the unfolding of biblical prophecy, evidences of the "Last Days" when they as God's righteous remnant, would be sorely tested by the Devil. If the pious proved faithful to God's Word and remained securely within the fold, then they would be vindicated as the true "Bride of Christ," while God's foes would be cast into the lake of fire for all eternity.

As a sensitive young person, finely attuned to the lives and attitudes of family and church, "Little Kenny" was put in a truly difficult position. He increasingly found members of his own gender attractive. If he revealed his feelings for other men, he risked a social death among his peers, and another one perhaps worse than the community shunning that accompanied it. He stood to lose his family, and to face reproach and condemnation from his church. Worst of all, Ken felt the fear of losing his whole frame of reference for who he was supposed to be, the future of wife, children, and a family of his own (the hope instilled in every young Texan of his era). The loss of his entire future story was too terrible to contemplate, and so Ken took the crown of thorns of a conflicted life, and placed it on his own head. As so many LGBTQ people before and after him, Ken believed that in time he could change. He did, but not at all in the ways he expected he would.

WAXAHACHIE AND "BABYLON-ON-THE-BAYOU"

While many of his school buddies married right out of high school and went off to work at construction sites or take jobs at the local refineries, Ken had other ideas. He set his sights on Houston, the sprawling first city of Texas. In order to succeed there, however, he knew he would need a college degree. That goal led him in 1979 to Waxahachie, Texas, the home of Southwestern Assemblies of God College (SAGC), a four-year undergraduate institution founded by the church. He enrolled in the Junior College section of the school, and set about earning a Business degree.

Even if a student came to SAGC for a so-called "secular" degree, like Business, the environment and the training one received there was intended as a safe haven, a "bubble," to keep Pentecostal young people from the taint of the world. That is a major reason why Ken and his peers chose to attend Southwestern rather than the University of Texas at Austin, Texas A&M, or any of the other larger, better known, more "worldly" universities in the state: as AG members, they could not have imagined themselves anywhere else. Everyone enrolled in SAGC, regardless of study plan or major, was required to attend chapel on campus five times a week, Monday through Friday. Every night, Resident Assistants led devotions in the dormitories. Students were required to attend church every Sunday morning, Sunday evening, and on every Wednesday night. If what an Assemblies youth was looking for was a "holy" place to get a degree and find a spouse, SAGC was the right college.

Ken Jr.'s roommate in Davis Hall was Andy Harris, a Louisianan who came to Southwestern to study for the ministry. Ken and Andy bonded in "The Harvesters," a gospel choir of twenty to twenty-five students who traveled throughout Texas and Louisiana representing the school. They became fast friends, with Ken serving as a groomsman in Andy's wedding to Sheryl Lyn Thompson in 1981. Theirs was a friendship that lasted the rest of Ken's life. They got to know each other's families, staying in touch intermittently through the years. Andy said they might not hear from each other for months, but when they finally made contact again, they "just picked up right where we left off." The shock and anguish of Ken's brutal murder has been hard on Andy. "I miss Ken," he sighs. "No one deserves to die the way he did."

In those days, Andy never suspected that Ken was gay. Ken gave no indications of it, and he actually dated girls. Now an Assemblies of God pastor in Bossier City, Louisiana, Andy says, "He was straight as an arrow." There were other gay men at SAGC during Ken's college days, and he probably knew who most of them were. In the estimation of a friend of LGBTQ people at SAGC during that era, most of them did not cope with the oppressive atmosphere very well. After a semester or two, most closeted kids found it too tough, and they just left. A few attempted suicide. Some others like Ken stuck it out. They dated to pass as straight, or even, perhaps, to find the "right woman" to "cure" their struggle with homosexuality.

Like the rest of Ken's friends, Andy expected Ken to take a big corporate job after graduation. Instead, Ken was among the first group of men to be hired as flight attendants by Southwest Airlines in 1983, a career that had been a female preserve up until that point. When Ken asked Andy about whether he should take the job, something he obviously wanted to do, Andy quipped, "That'll be alright until you can get a real job!"

Ken was brilliant at his new career with Southwest Air, and served with distinction for twenty-four years. He spread his wings, and literally flew. If you really want to know someone, the next best thing to living with that person is to work with him. Ken's work ethic would have done a Calvinist proud. From the start he was highly conscientious, professional, and hospitable. He was a "day flyer," preferring to work the morning run so that he could have the nights for himself, for his friends, and for his family. Co-workers remarked on how punctual he always was about signing up on time for the morning flight schedule so that he would not be bumped to nighttime. This habit was so characteristic of Ken that when he missed signing in for the upcoming round of morning flight assignments in that fateful June of 2007, his friends suspected something amiss almost immediately.

The same magnetism that Ken exhibited in high school and college also drew people to him at work. Co-worker David Kirtley, probably the closest friend Ken had for the last twenty years of his life, met him after missing a flight. Ken helped David take the flub in stride, and before he knew it, Ken had him laughing about it. One might say that Ken had a knack for befriending lost sheep. Sherilyn Gerhardt, another of his colleagues, noted that no matter how many times she got something wrong when she was flying with Ken, he always had a forgiving spirit. In the crew lounge, his outrageous hijinks attracted friends like bees to honey. On lay-overs, other flight attendants would seek him out, and anyone who got an invitation to vacation with Ken's crowd in New Orleans, or New York, or Honolulu knew a special time was in store for them. His buddy Paul Jones said that his best memory of Ken was cruising down the street with the top down on a convertible, "listening to Kool & the Gang, singing out together, 'Celebrate Good Times, Come On!' . . . If Ken was going to be there, there wasn't a dull moment, for sure!" Hal Scott, who met Ken at Lake Travis in Austin, was also impressed with how he enjoyed life, never seeming to have a bad day, and, like a *yentl*, constantly introduced friends to each other. "If it wasn't for him," Hal said, "I wouldn't have met many of the people right now at the core of my life. God bless Ken for all of the little things that he did for people."

Though Ken's family was always paramount for him, his career broke him free from the orbit of relatives and church, and afforded him the chance to reinvent himself. His sublimated gayness emerged among other young, good-looking men who took to the skies above Texas. Like the population at large, some of these men in their smart uniforms were gay and some were not. The jokes about gay flight attendants, "trolley-dollies" and "air queens" were grounded in at least this much fact: aspiring young gay men could make a good living in the travel industry, one of the few relatively hassle-free career paths open to them. During those early years at Southwest Air, Ken was based in Dallas and Austin. While he was in Austin in the mid-1980s, he met the first long-term love of his life, Guy Cleveland. They moved in together, and shared their lives for two years. Guy still credits Ken with helping him through one of the hardest times of his life, the death of his father.

Either out of respect or shame, or a combination of both, Ken kept the two parts of his world separate. During all their time together, Guy never got to meet "Big Kenny," Martha, or Lori. Ken never took Guy to see them. Ken's old friend Andy Harris blames his career for changing Ken. Though Ken and Andy stayed in touch, there was a tacit agreement not to talk about Ken's love life. They were two men living out different dreams, Andy as an ordained minister among the Assemblies of God, and Ken as a flight crew professional. Andy never agreed with what Ken was doing with his life. "What he chose was not part of God's plan for him," he said with sincere regret in his voice. "It is so sad." While a written life-story like this one is not the place to debate whether sexual orientation is a choice, the strains of coming out in a conservative culture like the Assemblies of God in small-town Texas are too familiar. Ken's college roommate and he had become like the elephant and the whale: both God's creatures, but dwelling in two different realities. As happens with so many other LGBTQ people, a chasm deepened between his emerging life as an adult gay person and his continuing life as a son, brother, and school chum. Ken spent the rest of his years negotiating the passage back-and-forth over that divide.

One of the early casualties of his new life was participation in church. What happened depended on which side of the question you were on. He either chose to wander like the prodigal son in the "strange land of unlikeness" (as ancient St. Augustine had called it), or the inhospitality, or maybe even the hostility of his old spiritual home evicted him. Ken's sister, Lori Franks, testified at his killer's sentencing hearing that Ken would still attend church with his parents and her family from time to time, singing solos and duets, playing the piano. He loved children, she said, and when she and her husband Chris had kids, he enjoyed helping out with children's church. Andy Harris knew the other side of the story, though. Ken had no church to call his own when he died. The church where his funeral was held, Christian Temple, a large Assemblies church in south Houston, was picked to accommodate the massive crowd, not because Ken had any particular association with it. In the latter years, Ken was pretty much reduced to watching TV preachers on the Trinity Broadcasting Network.

Ken confided to his close friend, David Kirtley, that though his parents always loved and accepted him, his sexual orientation was a significant source of friction and discomfort, especially for his dad. "Big Kenny" agonized about his son, worrying about whether he was staying safe from disease, and was pretty much of the mindset that "Little Kenny" could just say "no" and walk away from his "lifestyle." In a climactic conversation that must have been difficult for both of them, Ken pleaded with his father to understand what it would feel like. What if he were told that he could not look at, or date, or love a woman ever again, never being allowed to hold hands with her or share life with her? According to David, Ken felt he began to get through to his father just a bit that day. "Big Kenny" confessed to his son that he still couldn't really understand, but now he had a new way to think about what his beloved son faced.

In the latter years of his life, Ken made it to Houston, Southwest Air's headquarters city. And when his family moved to Pearland, a small 'burb swiftly being enveloped by Houston's urban sprawl, Ken Jr. decided to live there, too. He bought a fine brick home with a big bay window in the 1100 block of Sussex Trail, where he hosted his folks every Christmas. He threw parties there for his friends and neighbors, and when he dated, he liked to share his home with his dates, too. His Pearland retreat was close enough to get to the airports easily and to the Montrose area of Houston, the center of LGBTQ life on the Texas Gulf Coast. Montrose itself was also just far enough away from Pearland to offer a separate world for Ken.

Houston, Texas, is a Manichean's wet dream. Not only is it the largest city in Texas, but it also has the twelfth largest population of LGBTQ people in the United States. Gay life in the '80s centered on the Montrose neighborhood, a Bohemian enclave of queer folk, hippies, artists, and a home to the hottest gay bars and nightclubs on the Texas Gulf Coast. The allure of the culture and sexual permissiveness of Houston for the young was decried by social and religious conservatives who saw its gleaming towers and steamy fleshpots as a cross between Sodom and Babylon. No matter how much "woe" was pronounced on the city by the preachers, however, country boys and girls flocked there from the hinterlands for adventure, romance, and freedom.

THE TERROR THAT PROWLS THE DARKNESS

Ken chose not to live in the Montrose area itself, but he was a regular there when he was off duty. The bars and clubs were a great place to dance, decompress, meet friends, have some drinks, and enjoy the "eye candy." Though the bar scene had cooled down from its crest in the 1970s, '80s, and '90s (thanks to the advent of the internet), it was still a magnet for gay men, young and old, in the summer of 2007. South Beach, the glittery new nightclub, was packing them in with "hot twinks on the box," beefy bartenders, a driving dance beat, and strong, cheap drinks. Ken's taste drew him to more intimate neighborhood bars like EJ's on Ralph Street, and reliable standbys like JR's on the Pacific Street strip.

One might say that, at 46 years of age, Ken had the best of both worlds. When he wanted it, he could travel from his house in Pearland for half an hour and immerse himself in a thriving gay scene he never dreamed possible as a boy in Texas City. Afterward, whenever he liked, he could return to suburbia, to his quiet street and his nicely appointed home, and be near his family. Ken had done well at Southwest Air. He not only had a fine brick veneer home of which he was proud, but he also had a good portfolio of investments. He was generous with what he had. When Grandmother Nebout needed living room furniture, Ken bought it for her. After his brother-in-law Chris was injured in a work-related accident, Ken helped him pay the cost of attending college. Most of all, he adored his four-year-old niece Kelli and his 18-month-old nephew Joshua. His sister Lori revealed to the press soon after his murder that Ken had made a long-term commitment to finance their education, having established college funds in each of their names.

June 2007 found Ken in a down mood, according to Andy Harris. They had spoken by phone, and Ken confided in his old college buddy that his current "roommate" had moved out, and left him depressed. Seizing the moment, Andy broke his rule of silence about Ken's sexual identity, and urged him to repent of his sin and find his way back to church. The last thing Ken ever said to him was that Andy was probably right, and that he would think about it. Ken didn't need someone to room with him to help pay the bills. What he had hoped for was a relationship that would last, and it hadn't worked out. Now, on top of his depressive funk, in the name of care, Ken's old minister friend had confronted him about his life. Whatever his open ended answer to Andy actually meant, it offers us a window into Ken's psyche during his last weeks. He was in a period of transition and self-doubt, and he needed some time to sort through things.

He turned to his local friends and decided to hit the Montrose area on Monday, June 4. The first long weekend of June was clear and hot in Houston. A strong jet stream was pushing Tropical Storm Barry, brewing in the Gulf of Mexico, toward Florida. That was doubly good. It would miss the Texas coast entirely, which meant good flying throughout the week. In order to give himself something to look forward to, Ken had planned to go see his sister's family on June 5, and then to visit friends in Fort Lauderdale during a June 6 lay-over.

He and his friend, Craig Farrell, went out to lunch at Café Adobe on Westheimer Road, spent part of the afternoon shopping, and then dropped by EJ's, a friendly neighborhood gay bar with a steady Houston clientele. Just beyond the main bar there was an area with a pair of pool tables. Some men were engaged in a game of 8-ball. One of them, a flirt, caught Ken's eye. The man was about 5'8", slender with brown hair, and wearing a pair of blue jeans, a white shirt, and a ball cap. Ken sent him a drink, and they struck up a conversation. The three men played pool together. The young man told Ken and Craig that his name was "Dylan." Craig testified later that, since he was flirting so shamelessly with Ken, he naturally assumed "Dylan" was gay. He and Ken exchanged cell phone numbers. After they parted company, while Craig and Ken were still out on the town together, "Dylan" called Ken's number, and they talked. Everything seemed normal. The two friends had dinner together, hit a few more bars, and then Craig said goodnight and went home. Ken called him later from JR's, normally a bustling gay venue in the heart of Montrose. The place was dead and he was bored, Ken told him. Craig suggested that he should just call it a night. Ken agreed that he would. But in fact, he did not. He called "Dylan" and arranged a hookup.

"Dylan" was the assumed name for Terry Mark Mangum, a 26-year-old ex-con who had just gotten out of prison that May after serving a sentence for robbery. Mangum did not go to EJ's to play Monday after-noon pool. He was executing a plan he had been devising for weeks, to stalk and kill a gay man "in the name of God." Like bait on a hook, he pretended to be gay, and trolled the bars in Montrose to lure his prey. Tragically, Ken took the bait.

A surveillance video from the Montrose area supermarket that gay men called "Mary Kroger" showed Mangum and Ken together buying beer and wine later that evening. After the short trip down to Pearland, Ken unlocked the deadbolt to his comfortable suburban home, and trustingly let his killer in.

We do not know what passed between Ken and Mangum sexually that night, or if anything occurred at all. Piecing together Mangum's confession, his court testimony, the forensic evidence, and the available details from the murder investigators, however, we get a gruesome picture of how this latter-day "Elijah" carried out the "code of retribution" he claimed to have received from God against gay men. "Bottom line is I stabbed him in the head with a six-inch blade," Mangum matter-of-factly admitted in a jailhouse confession. Though he felt no remorse for killing a gay man—even going so far as to refer to Ken as "it," rather than a human being—he was concerned that people might think him odd. "It's not that I'm a bad dude," he confided to *The Facts* reporter John Tompkins from the Brazoria County Jail. "I love God."

Mangum's laconic attitude belied what really happened—a five-hour (or maybe more) torture spree before the *coup de grace*. The coroner reported two deep gashes to Ken's head in addition to the stab that broke the knife blade off in his fractured skull. Trauma to the right part of his chest cavity had filled it with blood. Ken's Adam's apple had been slashed three times, and he had been strangled. Family members said to friends that Ken's eyes had been put out. Mangum apparently had gotten tired and hungry during his grim work. He paused in mid-execution, fixed himself a bowl of oatmeal in Ken's kitchen, and then dispatched him. Sometime during the day of June 5, after cleaning the house of gore as best he could, Mangum bundled the corpse into the trunk of his 1992 Toyota, and headed out into the country to finish his mission by immolating the body as a burnt offering to God.

Not reporting to work was so uncharacteristic of Ken that his flight attendant friend, David Kirtley, Ken's sister Lori, and trusted neighbors suspected trouble within a day. David had a key, and went inside the house on Sussex Trail looking for any sign of Ken. His home alarm system was disarmed: an ominous sign. The den and the kitchen area were eerily calm, with a glass of red wine sitting on the windowsill as if its drinker had only left it here the moment before. But the small area rug David had given Ken was gone, an afghan was out of place, and, upon close inspection, something like tiny spatters of blood showed on the wall. David and a neighbor called the police. The subsequent investigation, which used a chemical agent called "Bluestar Forensic," revealed a large area of blood smeared liberally on the bar, the floor, on a computer chair, and around the base of an entertainment center. Invisible to the naked eye without Bluestar, the reagent interacted with the copious amounts of blood and the cleaning agent used to erase the evidence, and produced a vivid, luminous blue glow. Somebody had been grievously injured or killed in that room, and Ken was nowhere to be found. His white 2003 Saturn L300 was still in his garage, but with new damage to the passenger side and front bumper.

UNGODLY NEWS

As the investigation went into full swing, an intensive search began for Ken in Pearland and Houston. Dozens of volunteers began combing through the rural areas near his home. Ken's family and his friends at Southwest Air enlisted the aid of Texas EquuSearch, a mounted search and recovery team made nationally famous by its involvement in the 2005 disappearance of Natalie Holloway in Aruba. "Big Kenny" still held out hope that his boy would be found alive. "What's going through my head is not something that's good," he told a reporter for KPRC television. "A lot of things could have happened and we're trying to hold out hope."

The search moved two hundred miles west into the vicinity of south San Antonio, when a trace of Ken's credit cards uncovered three local purchases in the very early hours of June 6: cigarettes, a butane lighter, and a flashlight all bought from a store in Schulenburg at 3:16 am; another cigarette lighter, lighter fluid, charcoal briquettes, and a drink at a San Antonio convenience store at 5:06 am; and then about an hour and a half later, more drinks and some hydrogen peroxide at the same store. The morning clerk remembered the man who came in to her shop for the second time. He had muddy hands, and a couple of gashes on two of his fingers he said he got from using a borrowed shovel. He used the peroxide on his cuts after washing off in the restroom.

On June 11, a week after Ken disappeared, Terry Mark Mangum was arrested and charged by Pearland Police with the murder of Kenneth L. Cummings Jr. He refused to disclose where Ken was. The EquuSearch effort near San Antonio grew to over six hundred volunteers, many of them Southwest Air employees, and focused on the fifty-acre ranch in Poteet belonging to Robert Mangum, the suspect's grandfather. Investigators discovered that Mangum, released from prison on May 18, had attended his grandfather's ninetieth birthday there on June 2. The searchers concentrated on the area of a dry stock tank not too far from the road, a likely place to bury a body where someone driving a regular car without 4-wheel drive could get to. David Kirtley was examining a shallow incline near the back of the stock tank when he kicked over what appeared to be a charcoal briquette partially buried in the pale dirt. Almost at once he saw a charred bone poking out of the ground that later was identified as his friend's kneecap. David believed Ken had reached out to him once again, this time wanting to be found.

On June 16 Ken's remains were carefully unearthed from the crime scene. Mangum had prepared a shallow pit and covered the body lying face up with charcoal and lighter fluid. A human body is notoriously difficult to burn up. The whole lower cross section of his torso had resisted the flames. All his facial features had burned away from the head, leaving his jaw and teeth enough for a positive dental ID. Though Mangum's stated intention was to offer God a "flesh offering" of a sodomite, the unspoken consensus was that the grisly scene resembled a bar-b-cue pit.

Father's Day came on the day after the authorities exhumed Ken's charred remains from their shallow grave. "Big Kenny" Cummings told *Houston Chronicle* reporters that it would be the saddest Father's Day he could imagine. "I'm not holding up real well, but I feel a little bit better than I would if they hadn't found him," he said. But the Cummings family was not the only one devastated by the horror discovered at the Mangum ranch. "Mark," as Mangum's family and friends called him, had bitterly wounded his own family, too. Old Mr. Mangum, the 90-year-old patriarch of the clan, whose grandson had done this unimaginable thing, broke down in tears at the news, vowing that there would be no more parties at his house, only his own funeral. According to friends of the family, Grandmother Mangum couldn't sleep after hearing what had happened. Kent Mangum, Mangum's father, and a law enforcement officer himself, contended that his son was mentally ill. As a friend of the Mangum family said, "They must face each day knowing that their son and grandson was a part of this horrible act."

Mangum had been involved with a woman, and had sired a son by her. Probably the harshest consequence of this tragedy is the scar it leaves on his child. A woman named Ashley, claiming to know the family well, wrote a comment to a blog called "Last Row," attempting to get a message directly to Mangum:

> Why, Mark? Don't try to conjure up some bogus religious mumbo jumbo. Your son will now grow up without his dad. What will he feel when he learns of your actions? Have you loved your neighbor as God commanded you to? Your son needs a role model. Your son needed a dad to be there for him. You can never

be those things for him now. What would God say to you about that? I know there is goodness in you. I have seen it. But now there is this horrible dark side as well.

Ken's funeral was a big event for the city of Houston. Media swarmed everywhere. Over six hundred mourners attended the service, held on June 23 at the Christian Temple Church, an Assemblies of God congregation. A former AG pastor from the Cummings family's Texas City congregation officiated. Many of the employees of Southwest Airlines sat together, dressed in their uniforms in tribute to their friend.

Mangum liked to gab. While sitting in jail on Friday, July 13, to the chagrin of his defense counsel, he gave reporter John Tompkins of the Brazoria County newspaper, *The Facts*, a full admission of guilt for Ken Cummings's murder. Mangum gave the whole world the rationale for what he had done, too. He went out of his way to explain that he was definitely not a homosexual. Far from it. God had commissioned him to hunt down and kill gays, "just like it says in Leviticus," he said. After "thousands and thousands and thousands of hours" of Bible study, he told Tompkins, he decided that the victim he was to offer God had to be a man because men "carry the harvest of the sinner." Sexual perverts deserve to die, period, and he saw himself as the instrument of God, just as the prophet Elijah and the high priest Melchizedek had been. While Mangum deliberately went to the Montrose area hunting a gay man to kill, he said he had nothing in particular against Cummings. "He was just the one I bumped into." With chilling sincerity, Mangum concluded the interview, "I believe with all my heart that I was doing the right thing."

Tompkins, unable to resist the scoop, went to press with the whole story the next day. That earned him a date in court testifying at Mangum's capital murder trial, and the judge overseeing the case slapped a gag order on everyone. Nothing more was to be said by either side until the trial.

While psychiatric specialists were called in to determine Mangum's fitness to stand trial, the courtroom of public opinion was roiling with full-throated theological combat. An outfit calling itself "The Army of God" out of Chesapeake, Virginia, leapt to the barricades on its website defending Mangum's actions and calling for Christians to support him:

[Mangum] came to the biblical truth that homosexual sodomite sex perverts deserved the death penalty for their sins against God. Terry had the courage to obeyed [sic] our LORD God and took

out one of these sodomites who are defiling our land . . . Terry
deserves our support . . . Now I know why God wrote Leviticus
20:13.

Rev. Don Spitz agreed. On a Houston blog site called "By the
Bayou," he wrote, "The Bible is clear that homosexuals are sexual perverts. Whatever you think, you will not be able to change God's Word
and will one day have to pay the price for not believing what God has
written." Spitz went on to quote the twentieth chapter of Leviticus 20 and
the first chapter of Romans.

John, the Houston blogmeister who founded "By the Bayou," took a
more balanced approach to the religious argument over the Cummings
murder in his home metro area:

> Now, it doesn't take religion to make someone a killer. And plenty
> of non-religious people do things as awful as what Mangum did.
> But there's something incredibly creepy about the way that "God
> told me to do it" can make someone feel so justified about bru-
> tally murdering another human being. There's not even the usual
> excuse: *the gay guy hit one me and I freaked out,* or anything like
> that. Just *God said this was bad, so I had to carefully make a plan
> to snuff out another human life.* And now he feels good about it.
>
> Of course, the various preachers who tell their flocks that
> gay people are the worst and most dangerous thing ever will no
> doubt say they never meant anything like this to happen. And
> they probably didn't, any more than the somebody who gets a
> friend drunk and then watches him get behind the wheel of a
> car *meant* for him to get into a car crash that leaves himself and
> others dead.
>
> But don't expect any consideration of what responsibility
> might be there. I expect they'll tell us it was God's will.

Another respondent to Rev. Spitz was not so moderate. "Uncle
Mike" shot back:

> Even the devil can quote scripture, Don. I assume from your
> love of the Old Testament, that you abhor shellfish, never touch a
> menstruating woman, stone to death disobedient children, never
> shop on Sundays, and never wear 50/50 blends.

Theology and insanity were at the heart of the defense of Terry Mark
Mangum. On August 7, 2008, Mangum's attorneys entered an insanity
plea on his behalf, claiming that he was delusional, schizophrenic, and

mentally ill. As the trial progressed at the Brazoria County Courthouse, the defense tried to counter the damning evidence and Mangum's jail-house confession by insisting his religious justification for the murder was an obsession and evidence of his mental illness.

The Facts Senior Reporter John Tompkins took the stand for the prosecution, detailing Mangum's confession to him in July 2007. He testified to the court, "It's hard to recall exactly what he said. More or less, he believed he was justified through God in killing a homosexual man." Mangum had told Tompkins homosexuality was an abomination. "I asked him if killing [Cummings] was like stomping on a bug," Tompkins testified. "He looked at me kind of confused and I rephrased, 'Like swatting a mosquito?' He said, 'Yes.'"

With that, the prosecution rested its case.

The defense put mental health experts on the stand twice during the trial, trying to establish that Mangum had no real, deeply held religious convictions, and that he suffered from a combination of schizophrenia and antisocial personality disorder. Kristi Compton, a forensic psychologist from Dallas, called her multiple interviews with Mangum "hours of prophecy," rambling discourses on prophetic interpretations of scripture that she did not understand and found difficult to follow. Michael Fuller, a psychiatrist with the University of Texas Medical Branch, testified that Mangum's "bizarre religious beliefs" were mixed with other delusional beliefs to the extent that it was hard to know how religion alone motivated him. Instead of concurring with Compton's assessment that Mangum was schizophrenic, Fuller diagnosed him with "severe anti-social disorder."

Mangum's father, Kent Mangum, took the stand to testify that his son had claimed at times to be beset by Satan, and at other times to be the Holy Spirit and Jesus. Letters Mark wrote to the elder Mangum from prison in 2003 had convinced him that his son was mentally ill.

In the end, the jury didn't buy the insanity plea. The six man, six woman jury returned a guilty verdict in less than an hour and a half. On Wednesday, August 13, 2008, Terry Mark Mangum was sentenced to life in prison for the murder of a gay man who was no more consequential to him than a mosquito. Though eligible for parole in thirty years, the jury believed Mangum had committed the murder because Ken Cummings was gay, and attached a hate-crime enhancement to the verdict that would come up for consideration at the time of his parole hearing.

Reporting for *The Facts*, John Lowman recounted the testimonies of Ken's longtime friend, David Kirtley, and his sister, Lori Franks, during the sentencing phase of the trial. David looked into Mangum's eyes as he accused him of twisting the message of the "God in the Bible," using that as the justification for "taking a most kind person from his family." Kirtley continued,

> You brutally attacked Ken from behind, the act of a true coward. The impact of your actions are [sic] impossible to convey to you because you are evil. To the rest of your family, I offer condolences. They did not make you do this. No one on earth or heaven made you do this. Go and spend the rest of your days in jail where you will be able to inflict no pain and suffering on anybody else.

In turn, Lori recounted the qualities that made her brother such a special person: his thoughtfulness, humor, and his loving generosity. Most of all, she testified, Ken made holidays special for her family. "He never missed an anniversary or a holiday," she said. "For the last ten years, he hosted the entire Cummings family at his house for Christmas dinner. He sent my mother a poinsettia every Christmas."

No one in the courtroom could miss the pain in her voice as she concluded, "Last Christmas, his friend, David, sent it."

A SCORPION INSTEAD OF AN EGG

Ken Cummings's brutal murder will teach nothing to anyone as long as his memory remains a battleground between religious rivals: Right versus Left, fundamentalists versus moderates, anti-gay Christians versus pro-gay Christians. Ken's story gets lost when one group labels itself "true prophets" and their opponents accuse them as "false prophets."

The theological issues his death raises, however, are more interesting and potentially fruitful. This hate murder, done in the name of God, evokes some necessarily ugly questions about the nature of a religion that can accommodate such lethal social teachings against any segment of the human family. Ken grew up in the church. His parents taught him to honor its teachings. He was a baptized believer, both in water and in Spirit. The pastors and teachers who shepherded Ken tried to involve him with the best of their faith. From every indication, especially in the early years of his life, Ken Jr. tried with his whole heart to uphold a tradition that, in the end, betrayed him by demanding he deny who he truly was in order to belong to it. He was not sanctified by his church's heterosexism and homophobia—he was marginalized and alienated by it. Ironically, the same sort of Christianity that could not tolerate Ken's homosexuality most certainly did accommodate the deadly intolerance that tore his life away from him.

Who bears the blame for Ken Cummings Jr.'s murder? Mangum, of course. But there is a whole phalanx of unindicted religious leaders who fed the hate machine that stole away the joy of Ken's religion long before Mangum took up the calling to kill. Pope Benedict XVI, Pope John Paul II, Billy Graham, W.A. Criswell, Fred Phelps, Rick Warren, Jerry Falwell, Pat Robertson, Phyllis Schlafley, James Dobson, Oral Roberts, Bishop Eddie Long, Anita Bryant, Franklin Graham, Francis Shaeffer, John Hagee, Rod Parsley, Jimmy Swaggart—all the mouthpieces of intolerance should share the indictment for this, or any, hate crime murder, if not the sentence for it. But theologically and spiritually, the burden of guilt must be shared even more broadly than that. The whole of Christianity must share in the blame, especially the theologians. Ken Cummings's slaying was not simply a hate crime murder case. It was a failure of Christian theology.

In the eleventh chapter of Luke's gospel, Jesus of Nazareth says that no self-respecting parent would give something poisonous to a hungry child:

> Is there anyone among you who, if your child asks for a fish, will give a snake instead of a fish? Or if the child asks for an egg, will give a scorpion?

What about a faith community? When people come seeking food for the soul, would a bowl of something homicidal be in order? If, as Bishop Gene Robinson says, 95 percent of the perpetrators of anti-LGBTQ hate crimes justify their violence by quoting a Bible verse, or a church teaching, then all churches have some intense soul-searching and atoning to do until the violence and intolerance stops. Completely.

Jesus goes on to say:

> If you then, who are evil, know how to give good gifts to your children, how much more will the heavenly Father give the Holy Spirit to those who ask him!

Sometimes in a blinding insight of almost unbearable pain, we finally understand who it *really* is who died for our sins. Like now.

For Greater Understanding

God Slain: Kenneth Cummings Jr.

BOOKS

Boyarin, Daniel. "Against Rabbinic Sexuality: Textual Reasoning and the Jewish Theology of Sex. In *Queer Theology: Rethinking the Western Body*. Edited by Gerard Loughlin. Malden, MA: Blackwell Publishing, 2007.

Cobb, Michael. *God Hates Fags: The Rhetorics of Religious Violence*. New York: New York University Press, 2006.

Gomes, Peter J. *The Good Book: Reading the Bible with Mind and Heart*. New York: Bard/ Avon, 1996.

Helminiak, Daniel A. *What the Bible Really Says about Homosexuality*. New Mexico: Alamo Square Press, 2000.

White, Mel. *Religion Gone Bad: The Hidden Dangers of the Christian Right*. New York: Tarcher/Penguin, 2006.

FILMS AND VIDEOGRAPHY

For the Bible Tells Me So. First Run Features, 2007.

ORGANIZATIONS AND WEBSITES

Faith in America, http://www.faithinamerica.org.

Human Rights Campaign Foundation Religion and Faith Program, http://www.hrc.org /issues/religion.asp.

SoulForce, http://www.soulforce.org.

Unfinished Lives Project, http://unfinishedlivesblog.com.

Talana Quay Kreeger
September 25, 1957—February 22, 1990

WILMINGTON, NORTH CAROLINA

3

Time Favored Her At Last

Talana Quay Kreeger

"In an expanding universe, time is on the side of the outcast. Those who once inhabited the suburbs of human contempt find that without changing their address they eventually live in the metropolis."

—QUENTIN CRISP, *THE NAKED CIVIL SERVANT*

IN THE DAYS FOLLOWING the murder of Talana Quay Kreeger by manual disembowelment, law enforcement officials warned leaders of the Wilmington, North Carolina LGBTQ community that it would not be in the interest of their "people" to be too visible. Fearing reprisals, Talana's heartbroken friends planned a quiet funeral for her at a Baptist church in nearby Ogden, believing that her sexual orientation would not be known outside of town. Forbidden by authorities to post signs directing mourners to the church, organizers tied bunches of white balloons along the route up Market Street, the main drag leading out of town. It was a signal that only people in the funeral caravan would know.

At the last minute, the service was called off in Ogden. Someone had gotten to the pastor, and explained that Talana was a lesbian. It was no skin off the pastor's nose to cancel the funeral, really. He had only agreed to accommodate the service as an expression of Christian charity. Talana was not a member of his congregation, and besides fearing repercussions from holding a lesbian's funeral in his sanctuary, he didn't condone "that lifestyle" anyway. Wilmington Police halted the procession of cars already en route, and ordered them to turn around. How the police department knew so quickly that the funeral had been scrubbed over in

Ogden is one of the lingering mysteries surrounding that awful day. In the scramble to find someplace, *any* place for the funeral, and with the presence of more than two hundred grief-stricken, frustrated mourners, someone contacted the Reverend Burton Whiteside, a sympathetic Episcopal priest in downtown Wilmington who opened the Church of the Good Shepherd for the memorial service.

Talana Kreeger, 32, was well known and well regarded in the closely-knit lesbian and gay community. She was a journeyman carpenter of considerable skill, and she had volunteered her time to remodel the Park View Bar and Grill, a haven for Coastal Carolina lesbians since the 1980s. Her murder by long-haul trucker Ronald Thomas terrorized and enraged the entire LGBTQ population of New Hanover County. Talana's gruesome death caused Southeastern North Carolina queer folk to find their own voices. They vowed never again to rely on straight people to furnish them a church for the funeral of one of their own.

Like the lure of the ocean for a poor swimmer, the lurid account of the manner in which she died threatens to drown the untold dimension of Talana's story: her humanity. Friends who knew her noted the same phenomenon in 1990, as the media reported on both her murder and the man who killed her. Ronald Thomas was humanized in the press as his defense lawyer skillfully shaped public opinion in the days running up to the trial for one of the most sensational murders in North Carolina's history. Talana, on the other hand, was fixed in the public mind as little more than "a body in a field." Her life and death were surrounded with sexual innuendo, but never one clear word was printed in the papers about who she was personally and spiritually—a lesbian. A "sexual act" had taken place in Thomas's truck late that dark February night, the press said. The body of the victim was "white as bone." There was dried blood at the kill site in the woods behind a pool hall, and drag marks, and the riveting details of her disembowelment "by hand," but no hint of the real flesh-and-blood woman who had begged her killer, "Leave me alone and let me die."

All this dehumanization abetted the reduction of the life and death of this friend to many, and the lover of some, to a cold corpse clutching longleaf pine straw in a coastal woodland. It was an expression of the closet that hedged in so many Southeastern North Carolina queer folk from the 1990s until this present day. Behind the veil of official concern that details of Talana's "lifestyle" would prejudice any New Hanover

County jury against her and adversely influence the case, lurked a deep-seated loathing of queers who lived and worked in their city. Paranoia also skulked around Wilmington about what the LGBTQ community might do if they rose up in anger in response to such an outrageous death of one of their own. And Talana somehow got lost in all the sensationalism, the fear, and the calculation.

For twenty years, the story of Talana's disembowelment, and the stifled velvet fury it created in the soul of Wilmington's sexual minority, has simmered and stewed. A courageous straight social worker and local documentary filmmaker, Thomas A. "Tab" Ballis, eventually took matters into his own hands, and with the help of other filmmakers, sought to resurrect Talana's story and exorcize the demons that still hold the LGBTQ community in psychic bondage. "The Park View Project" brought together queer civic and faith leaders, law enforcement and legislators, the arts community, helping professionals, and Talana's lovers and friends in order to "out" her story to the world. Time seems finally to have turned 'round right for "Talana with the wild blonde hair."

TALANA'S PORCH

Talana could swing a hammer with the best of them. Everybody who worked beside her at Laney Builders knew it. With her shoulders loose, a grip firm around the neck rod and handle of a 500 gram striker, and her wild blonde hair swept back under her carpenter's cap, she was a lesbian John Henry: a steel-driving woman, 5'2" tall, and 140 lbs. She won her respect the hard way. Like the old Black Gospel song says, she had "come 'round the rough side of the mountain."

Born in Missouri to parents of modest means, Talana grew up in Jacksonville, North Carolina, hard by Camp Lejuene, the largest U.S. Marine Corps base on the East Coast. Her dad was a truck driver who died early, and her mother, a full-blooded Cherokee, remarried a cruel man who was rumored to have raped Talana underneath his sickly wife's nose. Talana learned to endure almost anything for the sake of her mother. Talana even dropped out of school to tend to her mother during her lingering battle with cancer. As soon as her mother died, Talana's stepfather drove her out of the house to fend for herself in any way she could.

She had no marketable skills and no high school diploma. What she did have, though, was rare beauty in the years before life wore her down. A photo reveals her bright green eyes, slender figure, high cheek-bones, silken complexion, and the flowing blonde hair that became her signature among the forty thousand young, lonely, and horny Marines on the base. Her smile revealed cute little dimples. Like so many other impoverished, good-looking young women, she got by working in massage parlors in Jacksonville.

Talana rebuffed offers of marriage. She was neither a whore nor a trophy wife. Instead, she was attracted to other women, usually older than she. One of them, a successful journalist named Debbie Dunn, scooped Talana up. Because of her job, Debbie moved around a lot, to Raleigh, and then to Stokes County in the North Carolina Piedmont. Debbie had a son name Ian, and Talana helped her raise him. With her lover's support, Talana earned her GED. Eventually they moved back down the coast to Wilmington. There they joined the intimate, friendly lesbian community made up of natives and transplants who banded together in the Port City.

One of North Carolina's oldest cities, Wilmington survived the Civil War largely intact, and prospered in the late nineteenth and twentieth centuries as a major sea port and shipbuilding center on the Cape Fear River. By 1990, the city of 61,000 residents had become a tourist magnet and a filmmaking Mecca. Wilmington's seafaring attitudes and its arts orientation made it more conducive to diversity than any other Coastal Carolina city or town. Though not huge by any means, it boasted the largest population in Eastern North Carolina, a place where youth exploring their sexuality could blend in, find friends, and not draw unwanted attention to themselves. Lesbians and gay men from all over the rural counties along the coast, who looked to have any sort of social life and business opportunity, uprooted to settle there. Wilmington was one of the earliest cities in the state to have a gay bar, and, in time, to develop a lesbian bar named the Park View.

Talana grew into a powerful, confident woman in Wilmington. Folks said she reminded them of Elly May Clampett from popular 1960s television show, "The Beverly Hillbillies." Those who knew her best called her "caring" and "fearless." She laughed a lot, had a fun personality, and was good at a party. She loved Bluegrass music, and she could drain a six-pack as quickly as anyone. As one of her friends said, "Talana was up for anything." She was proud that she could beat men arm wrestling. Unfortunately, her teeth were always a problem, and in her late twenties she had to get dentures, a partial upper plate. She was self-conscious about her dentures, and would reflexively put her hand over her mouth to cover her smile. She always loved the outdoors, and since she displayed an aptitude for woodworking, her lesbian friends introduced Talana to carpenters so she could apprentice. Coastal Carolina was booming in the 1980s, and there was a lot of work available building houses.

By the time she was in her thirties, Talana had risen through the ranks as a carpenter to earn both good money and the respect of women and men in the regional construction trade. Lynette Miller, a lesbian girlfriend of hers who worked construction, too, had plans for Talana. Lynette wanted to own a construction company, and to make it a success, she wanted Talana to work it with her. Now a general contractor in Wilmington, Lynette said that one of the first things she thought after facing the initial shock of Talana's murder was, "This can't have happened! Not to Talana! Who the hell am I going to run my construction company with now?"

After the relationship with Debbie Dunn ended, Talana eventually moved outside of Wilmington to the Pender County community of Hampstead, a settlement deep in the country. There she bought a two and a half acre spread with a pond where she could fish and indulge the real love of her life, her pets. Talana loved animals. By the time of her death, she had amassed a menagerie on her farm that included three dogs, five cats, and a number of chickens and goats. She even named one of her dogs for her favorite skill saw, "Makita." Friends used to joke with her that she was a bumpkin, living like Eva Gabor on the television show, "Green Acres." Talana retorted that she was a lot more like Eddie Albert, thank you. She said she wanted to live out in the open where she could build a bonfire just for the hell of it and drink beer anytime she wanted to. Wanda Whitley, a lesbian friend who owned the Park View Bar and Grill, reminisced to local reporters about how compassionate Talana was, gently capturing spiders she came across on the job to set them free rather than kill them.

Like some lesbians, Talana had a fascination with motor vehicles. Motorcycles, trucks, and cars of all types interested her. Perhaps it was her love of the open road, the freedom to hop on her motorbike, toss care to the wind, and cruise through the salty breeze beside the Atlantic with her unkempt blonde hair streaming. Some of her friends couldn't handle the daily thirty miles back-and-forth between Wilmington and

Hampstead where her farm was. But the miles measured how far she had come in her tough life. From clawing out a way to survive after the early death of her mother and the bum's rush she endured from the stepfather who had molested her, Talana had become a vital member of the lesbian and gay community in Wilmington, and a skilled contributor to society to boot. Everyone knew and liked her at David's Lounge and Mickey Ratz, the local gay bars, and, of course, at the Park View.

As far as we know, she kept in touch with only one cousin, Billie Pelzer, who had married and moved to South Carolina. They routinely telephoned each other, and shared recipes. The summer before Talana died, they met for a short vacation at Topsail Beach. Then, in September 1989, Talana and Billie had weathered Hurricane Hugo together. According to her cousin, Talana was a woman who enjoyed her life fully, loving nature, the beach, the sunrise, and, most of all, people.

She never forgot others, even though her generosity of spirit cost her. As often as not, she would help folks out for a discount price, or for free, especially if she knew and liked them. Besides working construction for Laney's as her main employment, she picked up odd carpentry jobs on the side. On the night of her murder, Talana was working after hours to remodel the back bar at the Park View for her friend, Wanda Whitley. If Wanda threw in a couple of beers, and shot a game or two of pool with her, then so much the better.

While conducting my own research, I discovered that people in Wilmington still remember the quality of her work, how it manifested the strength of her spirit. It's just a short walk from Michael Moore's fashionable antique store on Castle Street to Priscilla Asbury's house with the big porch. Talana left footprints on the souls of them both. Michael credits her death as the reason for his coming out as a gay man. "I was terrified by what that man did to Talana," Moore said, "and angry, too. If someone could do that to her, then they could kill me, also." Instead of paralyzing Michael, the thought of dying as Talana had, galvanized his resolve. "I said to myself, if that might happen to me anyway, I would want it to happen when I'm out and proud." Then he said, "You should visit Priscilla down the street in the big lavender house, the one with the porch on the front that Talana built for her. I'll call down there for you."

Priscilla was waiting at the house she had shared for twenty-one years with her late partner, Martha Nesmith. She showed me pictures of Talana no one else knew about, pictures of a young, green-eyed woman in blue jeans sitting on the knee of her lover, Debbie, and drinking a beer with friends upstairs at Priscilla's and Martha's. Years later, Priscilla said, she asked Talana to build her a porch, the very one we were sitting on during that cool evening. It was large, well constructed, and structurally solid, even after eighteen years. "This was one of the last things she ever built. Talana built things to last," Priscilla said. "You know, Talana was the last person I expected to die like this," she went on. "The strongest one among us died." Then Priscilla paused for a moment before continuing, "I guess she never knew this old porch would last longer than she would."

CONSPIRACY OF SILENCE

Talana was murdered about the same time documentarian Tab Ballis moved to Wilmington. The story shocked him. Drawn into the plight of New Hanover County's lesbian and gay community by Talana's story, Ballis uncovered what amounted to a "conspiracy of silence" surrounding the pain and suffering of thousands of queer folk "Down East." He still argues that Talana's heinous murder is of a piece with a constant, withering attack on the LGBTQ community throughout the 1980s. The "Leland Five," a gang named for a town in Brunswick County five miles west of Wilmington, went on trial in 1984 for enticing gay men from downtown Wilmington into secluded rural areas where they beat and robbed them. In 1988, the naked corpse of Randy Lee Hockabout was found butchered near Greenfield Lake about two miles south of Wilmington, a murder widely believed to be an anti-gay hate crime.

Ronnie Butts, a friend of Talana's throughout this period, explained how rough life was for lesbians and gays in Wilmington. Bullying and physical violence were rampant against anyone perceived to be different. As a high school student, Ronnie had been harassed for being gay and sodomized with a stick by a gang of boys. Like many others, he feared for his safety every day in school. He couldn't wait to get out of Wilmington, so he moved to California and lived there for years. Butts returned home for family reasons and met Talana, who was already an established fixture in the gay community. "Everybody liked her," he said. "I can't tell you in words what being gay in this town was like," he said, with a tear brimming in his eye. "It was just hard, is all."

Frank Harr, a leader of the Wilmington LGBTQ community for many years, spoke candidly of those awful years. "It had got to the point that we were losing a gay man [to violence] about every year or so," he said in his gentle, Southern drawl. "That was the price we thought we had to pay for living in paradise." Harr's account of the losses the LGBTQ community endured just to exist in hostile territory conjures up a parallel in literature: Richard Adams's story of the "Warren of Snares" in his 1972 novel, *Watership Down*. Fleeing their home warren, a band of male rabbits finds refuge and abundance in the burrows of a melancholy rabbit named Cowslip. Cowslip's Warren was almost too good to be true. Situated in a plentiful garden where rabbits could eat their fill, and where the farmer who owned it routinely shot their predators, the nomad rabbits settled into a false sense of security. Then the awful truth crashed in on them when one of their number was snared by the "shining wire" of the farmer's traps that he set to catch rabbits for meat. Cowslip, when confronted by his angry guests, was philosophical about the loss of an occasional rabbit, an appeasement to stave off peril, as if the deaths were all simply a matter of "risk management."

Though Harr never acquiesced to the violence as Adams's character does in the novel, what the two narratives *do* share besides the terrifying sacrifice exacted from the group for living in a comfortable place, is the monstrous *banality* of such an evil system. Like collateral damage in war, the decimation of gay men was acceptable to a majority of Wilmington's citizens. These were the kind of people who would never bloody their own hands, but neither would they actively suppress homophobic attacks because they secretly agreed with the sentiments behind them. As long as "those people" persisted in their unmentionable "lifestyle," the city fathers reasoned, they had to expect that one of them would get killed every once in a while.

As in the case of racism in North Carolina, civility, "knowing one's place" in the system, trumped civil rights every time. What made lesbians and gay men "good ones" or "bad ones" was whether they remained silent and invisible to so-called decent society. It was all right to like "one of them" individually, to get one's hair done by one, even perhaps to commit an indiscretion with one, now and again; but there was a tacit agreement that everybody involved would surely have the good taste not to mention it publicly. This was the damnable closet with a Southern-fried aroma, and it horribly disfigured Carolina gay folk for generations. This was Talana's world, the one she lived in . . . and died in.

Gay bars in Wilmington bore the same deformity as LGBTQ individuals did. Establishments such as David's, and later Mickey Ratz, were purposely hard to find. Though they both operated downtown, and fronted on busy streets, their presence was virtually unknown to passers-by. They had no discernable entrances or exits on major thoroughfares. A person wanting to visit a gay bar to socialize and relax in relative safety had to know which darkened alley to go down, and then what unmarked door to open. In the '80s and '90s, there were virtually no gay-friendly places to congregate on the coast other than Wilmington's few bars. Though city officials knew where the gay bars were located, they mostly turned a blind eye. While lesbians were certainly welcome at David's and Mickey Ratz, they needed a place of their own. The Park View served that purpose.

Unlike the bars catering to gay men, the Park View was situated in the open on a main traffic artery, beside the Y-shaped intersection of Front Street, Third Street, and U.S. Highway 421, also known as Carolina Beach Road. Greenfield Lake and the park that lent its name to the bar were directly across the highway, famous in the area for stands of flowering magnolia, dogwood, long-leaf pine, and live oak, many hung with Spanish moss. There was no hiding the Park View. "In a way, it was ahead of its time," said Tab Ballis, who believes that the story of the Park View is integral to Talana's story. Throughout the 1980s, it attracted thirsty workers from the nearby State Port. Lonely out-of-town truckers like Talana's future murderer, Ronald Thomas, knew about the bar, too. But the Park View's lesbian clientele made it truly distinctive in Southeastern North Carolina. Same gender loving women from surrounding rural counties, like Brunswick, Columbus, Bladen, Pender, and Duplin, drove the distance to enjoy the easy ambience of the little bar where they could drink, smoke, shoot pool, and unwind without having to look over their shoulders. Or, at least they thought they could.

KILLER TEDDY BEAR

Talana was a regular at the Park View. She was close to Wanda Whitley, the Park View's owner, and Heidi Crossley, Wanda's lover. Rumors persist that Talana and Wanda were secretly interested in each other. In any case, when Wanda expressed interest in remodeling the back area of the bar, Talana signed on to help out after her day job. The Park View was a simple rectangular building with a spacious window at right angles to the stool-lined main bar that looked out onto Carolina Beach Road and Greenfield Park. Another bar and a couple of pool tables were in the back area, and a door opened onto a patio with outdoor tables and chairs.

Wednesday, February 21 was a mild day on the coast. The high climbed into the low 60s, but when the sun went down, the temperature started to plunge. It was going to be an unseasonably cold night. Priscilla saw Talana that morning, and tooted her car horn at her. "She was wearing a striped Izod shirt and blue jeans," she remembered. "She looked good, like she had lost some weight." After work, Talana headed to the Park View to measure the back bar for its remodeling. About 11 p.m., a tall, heavy-set long-haul trucker came into the bar and ordered his first beer. He told the bartender his name was Ron, and that he had a trailer-load of oranges he had to drop off at Hoggard High School the next morning. The students were going to sell the citrus for a fund-raiser. He saw a blonde in the back talking with another woman. The blonde reminded him of one of his ex-wives, so he took his next beer to the back bar to chat her up. Talana, Wanda, and Heidi were playing pool. The big trucker seemed friendly enough, and so the four played a few games together as he downed one brew after another. What the women did not know was that Ron had already been to another bar, Dot's Tavern, and had actually started drinking an hour earlier. New to Wilmington, he had asked about other local watering holes, and if there was any action in town. A guy told him about the Park View just down the road, saying, "You oughta go down there and check out them dykes!" Witnesses said Ron was getting loud before he left Dot's, bragging about how he was "gonna go down to that Park View and get me a lesbian!"

Ronald Sheldon Thomas, 32, was easy-going around his friends, so much so that one of them described him as a "teddy bear." This "teddy," however, had a rabid streak and an alcohol problem. He was a formidable man, mustachioed, dark-haired and broad-faced, measuring 6'3", and weighing in at 265 lbs. Thomas grew up in northern Alabama, the son of a fundamentalist preacher. His parents had split up when he was a child, and he had been left to grow up under the harsh discipline of his father. In adulthood, he had moved to Lewisburg, Tennessee and developed a troublesome drinking habit. He tried marriage multiple times, but it never seemed to work out. By 1990, he had gone through three divorces.

At the Park View, the lesbians had expressed interest in Ron's big white eighteen-wheeler, so he offered them his keys, and Wanda and

Talana went out to inspect the rig. Other than the junk that cluttered the front passenger seat and floorboard, they were impressed by what they saw. The cab had a sleeper compartment, fully equipped with a TV and a VCR. They brought the keys back to him, and played another round or two of pool with the big Tennessean. He had proved good for business. By closing time, Thomas had sucked down ten beers in less than an hour and a half.

The conversation turned to food around the pool table as the last customers drifted out the door into the increasingly cold night air. Thomas wanted to know where to get something to eat. *He was starving,* he exclaimed. The women told him there was a Hardee's burger joint that stayed open late on Carolina Beach Road, about a mile and a half away. Since they were hungry, too, the four agreed to meet at Hardee's fifteen minutes later for some breakfast together. Wanda and Heidi had to shut down the Park View, so Thomas offered to drive Talana. She seemed glad about that, since she had never ridden in an eighteen-wheeler before.

People have wondered why she got into that truck with a man she barely knew. Priscilla Asbury said, "That was just Talana. She was a free trusting spirit. She trusted everybody, too much. And Debbie [Talana's former partner] wasn't there anymore to make her stop and think that it might not be a good idea." So, Talana climbed over the junk in the front seat, got into the sleeper compartment, and Thomas cranked up the big rig, heading out into the darkness.

Just as agreed, Wanda and Heidi closed down the bar, stopped momentarily at Heidi's house, and got to Hardee's about a quarter hour later, sometime between 1:45 and 2 a.m. There was no big white semi in the lot. Thomas and Talana never showed up. Sensing trouble, Wanda sounded the alarm, calling friends around town to find out if anybody had seen Talana. No one had. Before long, most of the core group of the queer community in Wilmington had been alerted that Talana was missing with a truck driver twice her size. Wanda and Heidi set out frantically, searching for their friend. For three hours they looked everywhere they knew. It was fruitless.

Ronald Thomas "had a thing" for lesbians. A psychiatrist could have a field day with his attraction-revulsion response to women who loved women. The tip that there was a "dyke bar" down the street launched him in the direction of the Park View. After his arrest, he told investigators that he "could tell that the three women [Talana, Wanda, and Heidi] were lesbians by the way they were acting." Feelings of sexual inadequacy, titillation, homophobic rage and an oceanic misogyny bubbled just beneath his teddy-bearish façade, like magma on the boil. When Thomas got Talana alone in his tractor-trailer cab, all of it erupted.

Talana did not survive to tell her side of what happened in that truck, of course. All we have is Ron Thomas's account of the way the attack unfolded. But we do know that she was trapped in the small, confining space of a sleeper compartment, 3' x 6' x 5', by an intoxicated, testosterone-crazed man who outweighed her by more than 120 lbs. Thomas's guilt-ridden confession, coupled with forensic evidence, establishes the probable sequence of events that snuffed out Talana's life so cruelly. Though she had no chance against her much heavier attacker, the evidence suggests that Talana did not go to her death willingly or easily. As her cousin Billie Pelzer put it, "She fought for her life and she lost it."

Thomas confronted Talana with her lesbianism almost as soon as they had pulled away from the Park View lot. He wanted to know why she and the other women were queer. Talana would have characteristically thrown the question back on Thomas. She was unapologetic about her sexuality, and needed no approval from him. The argument heated up. Thomas said he needed to "take a leak," and pulled off the road behind a warehouse and a pool hall, beside a dense patch of woods. He stepped out of the cab, relieved himself, and climbed back in. Talana was still in the sleeper. Thomas pressed her again about why she was a lesbian, asking whether she had ever been "satisfied" by a man before. He reached up to grab her breast. She defended herself with all her considerable strength, slapping him backhanded. He hit back with such force that it knocked teeth out of her partial upper denture, teeth that were later recovered in the truck's cab by crime scene investigators. She fell back into the sleeper. He moved toward her again, and Talana landed at least one good fist to his chin. According to police records, at about 2 a.m., a woman was filling up her car at the Gas World service station on Shipyard Boulevard. The woman heard a loud scream out of the darkness, and then a faint one.

Thomas said at that point he "lost it," and attacked to subdue her once and for all. He punched her multiple times in the head, until she started bleeding from her mouth, her temple, and the back of her head. Thomas then threw all his weight on her, kissing her mouth, and mauling her breasts with his teeth. The medical examiner testified that a chunk of flesh was missing from her right breast and her right nipple had nearly been bitten off. In fear for her life, Talana bought time by stripping for him, saying, "You're going to rape me. I've been raped before." Thomas invaded her vagina with his fingers, preparing to rape her. Then, thinking better of it, he said, "My little [penis] ain't gonna do anything for you," and he reached for a jar of "Go Jo," a creamy hand cleaner mechanics use to remove stubborn grease and oil when soap and water alone won't work. Slathering it on himself, Thomas jammed his whole lubricated hand up past his wrist inside her twice. He heard her grunt, and thought she was "getting into it." Then he realized that there was something sticky all over his hands and arms. Blood was everywhere, on Talana, on him, and on the sleeper bed.

HORRORCORE

There is no language adequate to describe the vicious way Ronald Thomas killed Talana Kreeger. It is the very definition of a hate crime. "Savage," "grisly," "heinous," "brutish"—the words pale before the act. The nearest we can get for those two unspeakable hours in which an innocent lesbian was gutted by hand and left to die might be a nightmare soundtrack, what rappers call "horrorcore," "tha' wicked shit"—a subgenre of gangsta rap devised by lovers of hardcore sadism and horror movies, wrapped in hip hop and rock music. If we take offense or blanch at the mere retelling of the event, what must have the experience itself been like for Talana?

State pathologist, Dr. Charles L. Garrett, performed the autopsy. He confirmed that to cause the damage done to Talana's pelvic area and viscera, Thomas must have thrust his hand up into her vagina and rectum multiple times. He pierced her peritoneal wall between her vagina and rectum, seized her right kidney, and unseated it from the kidney bed. Approximately twenty inches of her small intestine had been dragged out of her body. Renal, intestinal, and colonic blood vessels had all been ripped in two.

The pathologist went on to testify that she would have endured all of this while still conscious. As a matter of fact, he said, she would have remained conscious for ten to twenty minutes after the attack, "during which time she would have experienced considerable pain."

Time must have stood still for Talana. She mumbled that she had to urinate. Thomas went around to the passenger side of the truck and opened the door. Talana fell naked out of the cab and hit the concrete face first. Thomas reached down, grabbing her by the arms, and started dragging her into the dense underbrush and woods. In all, he dragged her 128 feet, dumping her nude body into leaves, nettles and pine needles. The last thing he remembered Talana saying was, "Leave me alone and let me die." Investigators found that she had survived long enough to crawl on her belly, first for four feet, then for two more before she succumbed on the forest floor from what the pathologist described in chilling clinical jargon, "massive exsanguination" . . . she slowly bled to death in the winter cold. Records show temperatures dropped to 33 degrees that night. Thomas turned away and left her to die . . . simple and hideous.

In his courtroom summation to the jury, District Attorney Jerry Spivey asked the jurors to try and imagine what Talana must have thought as she lay fully conscious on her stomach in the woods as Thomas left. "She hears him go back in that big truck, crank it up, lights come on, and sees it pull off . . . There it goes," he said to the jurors. "That's her last hope forever."

Thomas had every intention of hiding any evidence of the killing. After abandoning Talana in the woods, he drove to a nearby convenience store and asked for directions to Hoggard High School. He drove there and parked at the school so that he could make his drop later in the morning, doing his best to clean up the gore and hide Talana's clothes before going to sleep. It was about 4:30 a.m. when the "teddy bear" fell asleep in the very same compartment where he had taken Talana's life.

At 8 a.m., he reported to school officials who told him he could unload his freight at the school dock in an hour. While he was waiting, the phone rang at the school, and Wanda Whitley asked if there was a man named Ron with a white truck making a delivery that morning. The school official called Thomas to the phone, and Wanda confronted him about Talana. Ron denied knowing anything about a woman by that name, or that he had ever been to a bar called the Park View. Thomas dropped off his load of oranges, and headed out of town going north toward his next stop in New Jersey. Undeterred, Wanda got the name of the trucking company and called to inform them of her certainty that Ron had been somehow involved in Talana Kreeger's disappearance.

MORAL FIG LEAF

To get out of Wilmington, Thomas had to drive past the turnout where he had dumped Talana in the woods. Beset by guilt and fear, he got only as far as Dunn, North Carolina, less than two hours away, when he pulled off of Interstate 95 at the Robin Hood Truck Stop. Reverting to his youth in a parsonage, he called a minister listed in the Yellow Pages, Reverend Ken Spivey, pastor of Bethesda Friends Meeting. We can only guess what combination of remorse and calculation went on in Thomas's mind. But Thomas surely knew he had "been made" by Wanda Whitley, and that it was therefore only a matter of time before a manhunt tracked him down for the murder.

"I need some help, preacher. I've done something terrible," he told the Quaker minister on the phone. Rev. Spivey replied, "I don't care what you've done. The Lord can forgive you." "Not for this He can't," Thomas retorted. He said he had beaten up a girl really badly, and left her in a wooded area in Wilmington. He didn't know whether she was dead or alive.

The minister offered to meet Thomas at the truck stop, but he let him know he was going to bring a deputy sheriff with him. Thomas agreed, and Rev. Spivey and Harnett County Deputy Lymon McLean met him at his truck. In tears he confessed his crime to the two men, and they escorted him into the truck stop restaurant for a cup of coffee. His biggest concern at the time, Rev. Spivey remembered, was how this news would affect Thomas's father, the fundamentalist preacher.

Deputy McLean put a call in to the Wilmington Police Department, speaking to Detective Pat Pridgen, who asked to speak directly to Thomas. Thomas described the spot where he left "the girl" whose name he said he couldn't remember. Only after retrieving Talana's clothes and purse from the truck could she be identified by her driver's license. Detective Pridgen said that Thomas wanted to know if they found the girl and to get her some help if she was still alive. Following Thomas's directions to the turnout near Carolina Beach Road and Shipyard Boulevard, Pridgen and another detective found Talana lying prone in the woods, pale as alabaster. She was dead. Her naked buttocks were bloody. There had been a shower of rain that had washed enough gore from her body to show a length of her entrails hanging across her leg. When they turned her body over, Pridgen recalled that her hands were clutched in fists around pine straw and other forest debris.

Lesbians showed up at the kill site as rescue workers tagged, bagged, and rolled Talana's body out on a gurney to a waiting ambulance for transport to the medical examiner. In a *Star News* photograph published the day after her body was discovered, the initial response of the LGBTQ community to Talana's murder has been captured forever. Three of Talana's friends stood together in a tight triangle as they reeled from what they had just heard and seen—one of their own had been eviscerated alive. The horror on the face of a woman with her hands clasping either side of her head is as easy to read as the twisted features of a mask in a Greek tragedy. Police forbade them to identify her body at the scene. Heidi Crossley followed the ambulance to the morgue and identified the friend with whom she had laughed and shot pool just the night before.

Ronnie Butts remembers that everybody was in shock from the news. They all met, women and men, at the Park View the first night after Talana's body was discovered. The group nervously traded rumors. Someone said that "possums were eating her insides" when the detectives discovered her. "We all just leaned on each other that night and cried," Ronnie said.

Thomas was taken into custody and charged with first-degree murder and first-degree sex offense. Emotions in the tightly woven queer community went wild, ranging from disbelief to nearly insufferable anger. Some were fearful of imminent attacks on themselves or on the LGBTQ community. Others were in an eye-for-an-eye mood. When the authorities stepped in to get gay leaders to calm things down "for their own good," ill feelings intensified. News of who the suspected killer was spread like wildfire from person to person. Talana's best friends, Wanda, Heidi, Priscilla, Martha, Lynette, and the regulars at the Park View were particularly inconsolable.

The debacle over Talana's memorial service simply heaped coals on the fire. The pent up fury of years of anti-LGBTQ oppression focused on the humiliation of a whole community forced to beg hat-in-hand for a church that would permit the funeral of one of their own. That anger made Wilmington city fathers nervous. No one could predict what the lesbians might do. They were flinty, redoubtable women in a situation dry as a tinderbox. One errant spark might just set them off. Gay men had also been pushed too far this time.

Veterans of those days remember how the lesbian sisterhood rallied to overcome their fears, and by sheer force of presence, kept pressure on the court to do right by Talana. Ronnie Butts said that even though some people withdrew into their closets, "the girls went to the court-house every day." It was a brave thing to do in Eastern North Carolina in 1990. Being seen at the justice center day after day amounted de facto to coming out to the whole world. Priscilla Asbury said, "All those women stood in the gap for [Talana]. That made a real difference. Those girls stood up to let everyone know that justice had to be done."

Mustering great effort, the LGBTQ community remained self-con-trolled. As Thomas went on trial in the spring of 1993, rumors surfaced that the D.A. was going to plea bargain the case, and let Talana's killer off easy. Court officials enforced extraordinary security measures, limiting the number of queer folk who could attend the trial, threatening harsh punishment for any outbreak of emotion or demonstration in the court-room. Two mitigating factors argued for a lighter sentence than death for Thomas, the defense argued. First, the defendant hadn't been in trouble before, and, second, Thomas had turned himself in. He displayed re-morse. The prosecution countered that the deliberate, heinous nature of the murder, and the callous manner in which Thomas abandoned his victim without so much as an anonymous call to get Talana help mandated the supreme penalty. In the courtroom of LGBTQ opinion, however, a sentence had already been delivered. Frank Harr understood as well as anyone how his community felt about city officials who had patronized gay folk for so long, and looked the other way whenever a gay man was bashed or killed. This atrocity, however, was different. This time the victim was one of their women, and queer Southern honor de-manded satisfaction. "For the first time," Frank said, "we felt that the life of one of ours was just as good as one of theirs. One of ours was dead, and one of theirs needed to die, too—a life for a life, you might say."

At the climax of the trial, Thomas, clean-shaven and wearing a new three-piece suit, broke down weeping before the jury. Encouraged by his attorney, who leaned over to him and said, "Just say what's in your heart," Thomas began:

> The night this happened, it wasn't me. I wouldn't want to hurt nobody. I asked God why it happened, and He ain't told me. But He gave me peace of heart. I have got to answer to Him. But I know in my heart I didn't mean to do what I did. And I just ask y'all to give me a chance.

Following a recess, District Attorney Spivey made his closing state-ment for the prosecution. "There's no way you could have convinced

Talana Kreeger that Ronald Thomas was just a good, cuddly teddy bear," he said. The D.A. graphically recounted the ghoulish details of the murder and abandonment of the innocent victim Thomas had disemboweled with his own hands. The only remorse Thomas had, the D.A. said, was for himself, not for Talana. Thomas knew Wanda Whitley had fingered him, and that it was just a matter of time before he was caught. So he tried to limit the damage while he could, to avoid the death penalty.

The jury of seven men and five women deliberated for just an hour and a half before rendering their verdict—guilty on both counts of murder and sex offense. They recommended two life sentences instead of the gas chamber. Thomas stood calmly as the judge read out the sentence. He would serve two back-to-back life sentences. Legal experts explained later that Thomas would be eligible for parole after forty years.

According to the *Wilmington Morning Star*, fifteen of Talana's friends bolted out of the courtroom after the sentencing. They were deeply disappointed that the judge had not sentenced Thomas to death. Lisa Ward, one of Talana's friends, complained bitterly to a reporter, "Nobody helped her when she was pleading for her life! Nobody gave her a second chance!" Wanda Whitley was even more pointed in her feelings. "I'm not pleased and I'm not satisfied, and I'll never be able to rest or let Talana rest until he's gone!" she shouted on the courthouse steps. Neither Thomas's minister-father nor his stepbrother, who was also a minister, made any comment to the press.

The jurors defended their verdict. A member of the jury told reporters that they had no difficulty in recommending life instead of death. They were not convinced that the crime rose to the ultimate penalty. While it is tricky to second-guess the legal process, the sentence seemed to satisfy the majority of Wilmingtonians. The majority sentiment seemed to say, maybe now things could get back to normal. Equilibrium could set in again. Everybody could find their customary place, and just settle back in. But that would not be the end of it, not by a long shot.

The sentence certainly did not quell the passion of the New Hanover County queer community. True enough, as Gandhi had said, an eye for an eye makes the whole world blind. But the decision of the court was hardly Solomonic. The same jury member reported that the penalty had not been arrived at with particular difficulty. Instead, the verdict and the sentence were little more than a "moral fig leaf" covering the injustice routinely visited on gays and lesbians throughout Eastern North Carolina.

Nothing much genuinely changed. There was no hate crime statute on the books in the whole of the Old North State. Tarheels continued to like their queers silent and invisible . . . and dependent on the goodwill of the decent Christian citizenry. All the Thomas trial did in Wilmington was to drive the anguish and frustration of LGBTQ people underground. Like Ronnie Butts said, people who had begun to feel safe downtown retreated into the closet out of fear. Looking over one's shoulder became a reflex once again on the Carolina Coast. But this time, though Talana's story would still roam the Park View and other gay haunts like a hungry ghost for two decades, her people were not going to accept crumbs from the masters' table any more. Queer folks found their own voice because of Talana, and upon her story, they built a church.

FORGOTTEN SAINT

Frank Harr and his partner of thirty-two years, Ken Cox, knew Talana well, and loved her. They, and a core group of other lesbian and gay friends, resolved they would never be put in the same desperate situation they had to face on Talana's funeral day. Two years after her murder, Frank, Ken, and a few dozen others founded a church affiliated with the Universal Fellowship of Metropolitan Community Churches (MCC). They named it "St. Jude's" after the Patron Saint of Desperate Causes. On first impression, St. Jude's looks and sounds pretty much like any other Protestant church: hymn-singing, Sunday School classes, Bible study, and the staple of all church life, pot-luck dinners. But St. Jude's ministers openly to LGBTQ individuals and families as well as to straight ones in the full light of day. Same-sex life partners hold hands during services unselfconsciously. Visitors don't have to search to find the colors of the rainbow flag in the handsome building on North Twenty-Sixth Street; they are proudly on display for all to see.

Tradition teaches that St. Jude (Thaddeus), one of Christ's apostles, was wrongly confused with Judas Iscariot, the man who betrayed Jesus. In the early days of Christianity, this confusion caused many to avoid venerating St. Jude or establishing churches in his honor. Historic churches of St. Peter and St. Paul are everywhere, as well as churches dedicated to the memory of hundreds of other saints and holy martyrs who died defending the faith. But churches named for the Saint of Desperate Causes are hard to find. He is often called "the Forgotten Saint" because of this misunderstanding, to the point that only those in the most precarious situations remember and pray to him.

Talana Quay Kreeger was no martyr. She didn't die to establish a church. The story of her murder is so brutal that there are many who find it too disturbing to remember. Still, without the events of her life and death, there would be no St. Jude's in the Port City. In that sense, it is Talana's church, and she is its "forgotten" saint. The founders of St. Jude's vowed that they would have a church open to everybody because of the desperation they had felt when Talana's funeral was nearly derailed by anti-lesbian bias. The way Frank put it, "Never again would we have to hunt for a place to bury you or to bless our unions. Never again would we have to depend on anybody else." Though her name is not found on the church cornerstone, there are signs that she is still remembered. The church members have always insisted on large double doors anywhere their congregation has met, so that a casket can be easily rolled into the sanctuary.

Talana and St. Jude's live in a symbiotic union of sorts. Just as there would be no St. Jude's without "Talana with the wild, blonde hair," her story rests in memoriam with a community that refuses to forget her. "The Park View Project," now filming a documentary about her, is also closely related to the church. Workshops on grief, dedicated to her memory, are held at St. Jude's. A prayer garden in her honor is currently planned for the church grounds. The congregation is the launching pad for social justice and anti-hate crimes efforts along the Carolina Coast so that what happened to Talana will never happen again.

Shortly before he died in 2008, Frank mused on the meaning of what happened to his friend, Talana. "She was one of our girls," he said in an interview for *Park View,* the name of the film Tab Ballis is shooting. The straight community viewed her killing as no more than a "happenstance." "We still live in a society where Talana's life has no real value," Frank said, his soft voice building in power. "We expected payment due for her life. Straights couldn't comprehend that we considered our lives of equal value to theirs. They expected us to value Talana's life less than that man's who killed her."

Talana used to come to Frank in a dream, he said, urging him, "Scream about it, Frank! Tell them about it! Don't let them forget me!" After a long pause, he composed himself and began the interview again: "We deal with tragedies around here in a more quiet way. We've moved on, we buried our dead and moved on. That would have been what Talana really wanted . . . You gotta keep the greater picture in mind." And then he delivered her epitaph as eloquently as any preacher: "There may not be any grand monuments to her, but she has not been forgotten. She is loved and valued by our people."

Though her memory, like her body, was left for dead, time kept turning and turning, like the hands of a great clock. The sweeps of the hands of time extended their reach, little by little, making the circumference larger and more inclusive each year. She died a horrible death as an outcast, it is true. But Talana's memory refuses to die. She is no longer just "a body in a field." Unique among lesbians and gays cut down by violence and hate, her story has given birth to a church, one that, to hundreds of people, has become a crossroads of hope. Someday—soon perhaps—after Tab Ballis's film is finished and released, the great arc of time will sweep her memory from the periphery and into the center of North Carolina's struggle for human rights . . . and the world will truly see how much she is loved and valued by her people.

For Greater Understanding

Time Favored Her At Last: Talana Quay Kreeger

BOOKS

Comstock, Gary David. *Violence Against Lesbians and Gay Men*. New York: Columbia University Press, 1995.

Suzanne Pharr. *Homophobia: A Weapon of Sexism*. Inverness, CA: Chardon Press, 1997.

FILMS AND VIDEOGRAPHY

Park View. The Park View Project (in development).

ORGANIZATIONS AND WEBSITES

Kathy's Lesbian Life Blog, http://lesbianlife.about.com/b/2007/03/30/gaylesbian-hate -crimes.htm.

National Gay and Lesbian Task Force, http://www.thetaskforce.org/issues/hate_crimes _main_page.

Park View Project, http://www.parkviewproject.com.

St. Jude's Metropolitan Community Church, Wilmington, NC, http://www.stjudesmcc .org.

Unfinished Lives Project, http://unfinishedlivesblog.com.

Billy Jack Gaither
January 21, 1960—February 19, 1999

SYLACAUGA, ALABAMA

4

Southern Gothic

Billy Jack Gaither

"When the Fox hears the Rabbit scream,
he comes a-runnin', but not to help."

—THOMAS HARRIS, *THE SILENCE OF THE LAMBS*

BILLY JACK GAITHER DID not intend to go out Friday night, especially when he had to work the next day. He was a computer distribution specialist for the Russell Athletic Corporation in nearby Alexander City, and he was conscientious about doing his best. According to his older sister, Kathy Joe, he was in his room, settled in for a quiet evening of his favorite television shows, comfortably surrounded by his beloved *Gone With The Wind* collection. The phone rang, and Billy Jack answered it. The next thing Billy Jack's father Marion knew, Billy was getting ready to head out.

"Where're you going this time of night, Son?"

"I'll be back in a little bit, Dad," Billy Jack told him. He stepped out of the white clapboard house on Pelham Avenue, where he lived as primary caretaker for his disabled father and his ailing mother, and backed his car down the short driveway into the cold darkness of a February night. That was the last time any of his family saw him alive.

Sylacauga, Alabama like so much of the rural Deep South remains a difficult place to be gay. The fact that LGBTQ people are as numerous there as anywhere else is one of the most closely guarded Southern secrets. Citizens would rather not talk about it, sort of like the existence of the crazy uncle who hides up in the attic, or of Boo Radley (of *To Kill a*

Mockingbird fame). As long as "they" keep out of sight and quiet like they are supposed to, God-fearing folks can basically deny their existence. In Sylacauga, it is generally agreed that "they" should just move away to Birmingham or Atlanta if they are going to insist on being "that way." Some do make a break for the big cities, but many like Billy Jack stay behind for a whole variety of reasons. On the surface, rural Southern LGBTQ folks live supposedly normal lives, passing as straight: going to work, tending to family, and singing in the church choir, just like Billy Jack did at Shelvin Rock Baptist Church in nearby Fayetteville. Beneath the veneer, however, are lives complicated by fear, often wracked by guilt, and haunted by loneliness. Exposure of one's genuine sexual orientation can inflict social death, dishonor, and perhaps even physical harm.

Before the savage murder of Billy Jack Gaither, Sylacauga had three claims to fame: the whitest marble quarried in the world, the acting and singing career of its favorite son, Jim Nabors, and a falling star that hit a local woman in the early 1950s. Like a sleepy lint head who worked in its now-largely-defunct textile mills, the whole town of 13,000 reclines on a bed of marble thirty-two miles long by a mile wide; thus, its alias, "Marble City." The United States Supreme Court Building and Detroit's General Motors Building are constructed of its cream white stone. Jim Nabors, the local boy made good, got away from Talladega County to pursue his dream of an acting career in Hollywood, becoming a TV star on the 1960s hit series, *The Andy Griffith Show*, and then as Private Gomer Pyle in another popular show, *Gomer Pyle, USMC*. Locals also boast of the two dozen albums showcasing the singing talent of Nabors, their native son.

But it was the Hodges Meteorite that really lifted Sylacauga out of the ordinary. The only meteorite ever to have struck a person, an eight-and-a-half pound space rock, hit Ann Hodges as she napped on her living room sofa in the early afternoon of November 30, 1954. It slammed through the roof, smashed a Philco radio, and bounced off her hip. News of the invasion from outer space electrified Alabama for a short while and made an over-night celebrity of Mrs. Hodges. *Life Magazine* printed a photo of the big bruise made by the fallen star fragment, and Mrs. Hodges appeared on the TV quiz show, *I've Got A Secret*.

Given the national storm of controversy surrounding the anti-gay hate crime murder of Wyoming's Matthew Shepard barely four months earlier, the gruesome torture and immolation of closeted Billy Jack overshadowed every other notoriety Sylacauga claimed. Though homophobia and Southern shame are woven into the fabric of education, religion, and family values in rural Sylacauga, the news that the charred remains of a quiet, pious, well-liked Sylacaugan were discovered still smoldering on a pyre of kerosene-soaked tire carcasses hit the community like a bolt out of the blue.

"BRIGHT AND SHINING STAR"

Southerners, by reputation, love and respect their parents, regardless of whether children actually conform to the cultural stereotype or not. Family is *the* overshadowing reality in rural Southern life. It is the nexus of everything else Southerners hold dear: economics, religion, politics, heritage, and sexuality. "Daddy and Mama" stand at the pinnacle of the family unit, and families, tiered by custom and social rules, are the mortar that binds the fabric of Dixie together. From the time Southern babies can crawl, Black or White, the Fifth Commandment, "Honor thy father and mother" (plucked from the King James Version of the Bible, of course), is virtually graven on their foreheads. No greater accolade can be given to any son than to say that he took care of his parents.

Billy Jack had earned his laurels. He was a model son to his parents, Marion and Lois. Though he was born fourth in a family of two sisters and five brothers, he was the designated caretaker, the unmarried child so familiar in the rural South upon whom the chief responsibility for aging parents falls. The rest of the Gaither siblings could freely pursue their lives and loves because Billy "liked" to stay home and see to Daddy and Mama. Some of the others would occasionally pitch in when he would break away to Atlanta or to Panama City, Florida, for an annual beach trip with his aunts, but there was no question who bore the main burden. The duty had devolved on him, and he embraced it with rare commitment. It was not a matter of fairness; rather, Billy Jack's life was a study in unfairness, particularly since he was gay and closeted even to his parents. His younger brother William said that "he didn't bring that stuff home out of respect for Mom and Dad." As in so many Deep South households, Billy's homosexuality was kept in deep background. As William said of the Gaithers, "they knew about Billy, but at the same time, they didn't."

Billy Jack was a tree of life for his folks. There was no question that they needed him. His father had suffered thirteen surgeries, and Billy

Jack was always there to support him. He shopped for groceries, ran to the pharmacy, took his mother and father to doctors' appointments and to church, cleaned house, and kept the yard mowed and trimmed—all while holding down a full-time job. In return, his parents gave him free rein to decorate the house. He painted and wallpapered, and in the main living spaces hung a picture of the Last Supper and a copy of the Ten Commandments. The dead giveaway to anyone questioning his orientation was the set of pink chiffon curtains he hung on the windows in his room. His room was his sanctuary, the one place he could create an alternate world for himself. He chose to turn it into an echo of Tara, the storied plantation home of Scarlett O'Hara. Movie memorabilia graced the walls: images of Scarlett, Rhett Butler, and gallant Ashley. *Gone With The Wind*, with its antebellum glamour of a bygone South, and the bittersweet melancholy of the Lost Cause, offered him reverie and release from an otherwise schizoid existence.

Kathy Joe, Billy's older sister, estranged from her father and stepmother most of her adult life due to her open lesbianism, especially appreciated how he sacrificed his independence to take care of Marion and Lois. "Mom and Dad were in bad shape, and Billy really stepped up," she remembered. "He gave up his life for them. Sometimes he would talk about moving away somewhere he could lead his own life, but then he would say to me, 'I just can't leave Mom and Daddy,' and then he would just stay." Billy Jack was on an elastic string, tugging away toward the affectional life he so desired with men from Birmingham or Mobile, but then pulled back by duty and love for his family. William, voicing his own regret about how barren Billy Jack's life became at home, speculated that had Billy been able to have relationships with good men from out of town, he would not have gotten involved with narrow minded, dangerous locals like his murderers. "They were the ones who were here," William said.

There was a persistent light in Billy. He sparkled with good humor and laughter, no matter what else he faced in his private life. He was tall like the rest of his brothers, 6'2", with a dark complexion, carefully coiffed dark hair that ranged from Versace-short to Billy-Ray-Cyrus-long, and he possessed a ready smile. For glamour shots, he hid his glasses, which he had needed since his boyhood teammates noticed that he couldn't see well enough to hit a fastball. He took care of himself, and was meticulous about his clothes. His little smirk was unforgettable, and when he laughed, it came from a deep place within him, bending him double.

Billy Jack was not typically "pretty," but despite a mild battle with his weight in his thirties, women still thought him attractive. Men did, too. He had tried to date women some, flirting with a notion that the right woman could change him, but as his sister Kathy Joe recollected, "it just wasn't Billy." His heart was drawn to men.

Coming of age for any gay boy in the South is tricky, fraught with heat and smoke, and not much light. Approaching puberty, Billy experimented sexually like all boys do, awkwardly discovering who he was becoming, learning by trial and error the taboos of Southern homosexuality, and understanding how to get around them. He could be disarmingly naïve about his identity. His siblings remember how funny it was one hot summer day when boys in a passing car wolf-whistled at him for wearing short shorts in the yard. Confused, a little scared, and perhaps not a little flattered, he protested, "Why are all those guys whistling at me?" Kathy shot back, "You know very well why!" He did, of course, though there were certainly many times he prayed it wasn't so. He joined the church, got saved, tried to be a good Christian boy, and read his Bible nightly for years until his death.

As scripture says, though, you can't keep your light under a bushel for long. Kathy Joe was naturally more sensitive to matters of sexuality than other members of the family, but even she couldn't see what was coming. Birmingham was her stomping ground, her fertile field to sow her wild oats, and she had a reputation as a "cutter" up there, a tough, motorcycle lesbian. In the late 1980s, she went to The Lighthouse, a now-defunct gay bar, and the manager accosted her with a shout, "Your sister was up here this weekend!"

"My sister, Vickie?"

"Naw, BJ!"

"My brother, Billy?"

Thus the owner of The Lighthouse Bar unintentionally outed Billy Jack. "Yep, he got up on the table and danced . . . He's a good dancer!"

Kathy Joe sped home and confronted Billy Jack, "You can't go up there and be doing that, BJ! I've got a reputation to uphold!"

"He started laughing at me," she said, and then he shared his sexual identity with her. "Well, you knew!" he said. For the rest of their lives, they were powerfully bonded to each other: gay brother to lesbian sister.

Then Kathy Joe's chuckle falls silent, and the tears well up again no matter the passage of the years. The jagged ache in her heart just won't go away. "Agree or disagree [about his sexual orientation], you don't have to hurt nobody! He was a beautiful son, brother, and uncle. He didn't get to be thirty-nine but one month! We lost a bright, shining star," she sighs, "He could have had a wonderful life!"

SHOCK KILLING

Around midnight, Marion and Lois got so worried about Billy Jack's failure to return home, they called his Aunt Pat, and then his mother went out looking for him. Billy just wouldn't stay gone like that, especially on a work night. They didn't have long to wait. The authorities let the Gaithers know that a car matching the make and model of Billy's had been found burning in extreme northern Coosa County, but Billy was missing from the vehicle. Later in the day on Saturday, a young hunter moving near an old bridge across Peckerwood Creek in Talladega County caught sight of a blackened, charred hand held aloft over human remains, still smoking in the oily ashes of burnt tires. Then the smell hit him. What he stumbled on was so horrific, so bizarre, his mind struggled to cope with it. He told people later that, at first, he thought he was looking at a mummy that had been set afire.

Before becoming a trash dump, littered with shattered glass, tin cans and all the other things people were too lazy to take to the landfill, this boat access near the old bridge had been used for generations by Baptists and Pentecostals as a baptismal site. As a local man said of the horrific scene, "Hell burnt slap through up there that night!" The dump's remote location in dense woodland, a full half-mile down a dirt road, and at least that far to the nearest house, made the Peckerwood Creek site wickedly perfect. There was a concrete slab suitable for the pyre, and room enough for a car to pull in and turn around. This place had been well cruised beforehand, selected carefully. Early discovery was not likely. Had the hunter not stumbled on the kill site by happenstance, the hate crime scene might have gone undiscovered for days.

What remained after the fire was positively identified as Billy Jack. Gold jewelry he had been wearing when he left the Gaither home, a bracelet, a neck chain, and a ring he loved were discovered in the ruins of his body.

Coosa County Officer Michael Taylor told a reporter for *The Daily Home* that the body appeared to be mutilated and bludgeoned, facts later confirmed by the coroner. A three-year veteran of the force, Officer

Taylor admitted that he found the scene offensive, "too gruesome and heinous. This is the gruesomest [murder] I've seen, one of the most vicious and heinous in this region's history."

By six o'clock on Saturday evening, the whole Gaither family had been notified and was gathering in grief, anger, and disbelief. Detectives from Coosa and Talladega Counties intensified their investigation, but quietly, asking the family to make no statements to the press. The tight-knit, but necessarily discrete gay community in town was also asked to keep their misgivings under wraps for the time being, so that the investigation could explore the anti-gay angle of the murder unimpeded. The Alabama Bureau of Investigation was called in. Billy Jack's remains were shipped to forensic pathologists in Birmingham as the news spread rapidly throughout Sylacauga and Central Alabama. *The Daily Home,* local paper for Sylacauga, Talladega, and Pell City, carried its first story on page one, Tuesday, February 23. Then local reporting fell silent as an intense manhunt progressed.

"CHARLSEY" AND THE SKINHEAD

Charles Monroe "Charlesy" Butler Jr. was johnnie-house drunk, stinking of moonshine, when he stumbled home in the wee hours of Saturday morning. Boyish-looking at twenty-one years old, the 5'3", 120 lb. resident of Fayetteville looked enough like Opie to have been cast for *Mayberry RFD,* according to one of the prosecutors on the Gaither case. His father wanted to know where he had been to get so "stewed." *In Vino Veritas.* He confessed to the elder Butler, "Daddy, we kicked a queer's ass." Distraught, Charlsey tried to sleep, but had nightmares. He tried to eat, but couldn't keep his gorge down. Because neither Butler could keep a secret, both of Billy Jack's killers were under arrest within a week. Daddy Butler told a family friend, who tipped off the police and then convinced Charlsey to turn himself in.

Steven Eric Mullins, 25, also of Fayetteville, was under arrest on unrelated charges by late the same afternoon that Charlsey was singing to investigators like a caged bird. If Butler was a wuss, then Mullins was a thug. Mullins's little accomplice feared him, saying to *Frontline's* Forrest Sawyer, " You've seen him for yourself. Steve's a big ol' boy."

Mullins, an ex-con, 6'1" and 200 lbs., sported a Neo-Nazi "SS" tattoo on his right hand and shaved his head like a skinhead. More accurately, he was a skinhead wannabe. Mullins strutted around local bars like a bully, wearing "White Power" tee-shirts and spewing racist epithets. He wanted—nay—he *needed* to have people think he was a big man, and little Charlsey was the perfect accessory for his tough guy conceit. While sitting in a Coosa County jail cell, Mullins told Sheriff's deputies that he had a statement to make because he had all-of-a-sudden gotten religion. "God told me to confess," he said.

Given his wolfish malice toward gays and lesbians, more likely Mullins didn't want Butler to get all the credit for luring Billy Jack to his death a week earlier. While Charlsey seemed tormented by what he had done, Mullins never showed any sign of remorse. He confessed that he and Butler had planned to murder Billy Jack for two weeks. His motive? Gaither was gay, and Mullins had "gotten tired of his being queer."

Ironically, Billy Jack had befriended both of his soon-to-be executioners for a number of weeks. With no car, and no prospect of getting one, Butler and Mullins mooched rides off of the big, good-natured country boy. He took them to the grocery store and other places from time-to-time in the champagne colored Honda of which he was so proud. If Mullins and Butler had ever wanted money from him, they would have come up empty, because Billy had learned the hard way not to loan money. But rides were another matter. According to his older sister Vickie, "Billy was bad about picking up people on the side of the road." When she tried to warn him about being too trusting, Billy gave her that impish little grin of his, saying, "Naw, I'll be alright."

Everybody who frequented the bars in Sylacauga likely knew each other. There just weren't that many places to go. Mullins and Butler probably met Billy at the Tavern, where Billy loved to enjoy cheap Bud Light beer and dance with Marian Hammonds, the owner. The Tavern, self-described as "The Hottest Bar in Town," is a nondescript gray building just off the Birmingham highway. In severely devout Talladega County, the Tavern was an oasis for backsliders who needed an escape from Mama, Daddy, and Wednesday night prayer meeting. On the bar's 'fridge, an old bumper sticker proclaimed, "Everybody needs to believe in something. I believe I'll have another beer!"

Tavern regulars knew Mullins was a bad seed, a red-thumb racist in a historically racist town. Some of Billy's friends also knew that Mullins was a violent homophobe who hurled the word "fag" like a brickbat at any man he thought was sissy enough for him to dominate. Noticing Billy Jack's association with Mullins, a friend who had had a previous run-in with the thug told Billy to watch his back. But if he had any inkling of danger around Mullins—the way Mullins could "sweet-talk" Billy into doing things for him—then Billy's belief in himself as a former Marine overcame it. Behind Billy's back, Mullins and Butler were ridiculing their benefactor, advising others without transportation to get Billy Jack to give them a ride: "We know who to call. This queer, Billy Jack'll carry you to the store if you give him money for gas or do other things for him."

In the end, loneliness for intimacy made Billy vulnerable to Mullins, a man whose raw physicality reminded some Sylacaugans of the World Wrestling Federation's professional wrestler, "Stone Cold" Steve Austin. Billy's trusting nature and his need for male companionship turned out to be a two-edged sword. A female co-worker and confidant, Bobbie Jo Story, remembered that Billy had broken up with a married man just a few weeks before his murder, and the loss had hurt a great deal. Twice-a-month trips to Birmingham's Tool Box, a popular gay bar Billy used to frequent, no longer satisfied him, and he had become concerned about driving home more than forty miles after drinking. Diabolically, Mullins and Butler plotted to offer Billy sex in order to lure him out of his home that February night. In court, Mullins testified that Billy had propositioned him on an earlier occasion, prompting him to take action to kill him two weeks later. Admitting his inability to do it by himself, Mullins said he enlisted Charlsey Butler because he could control him with fear, and besides, Butler "didn't like queers either." Mullins testified that he called Billy Jack and promised him sex. All we have is the word of a self-serving, homophobic murderer about the content of the call that night. Some believe it to be a plausible scenario, and some don't. But we do know that emotionally, Billy was vulnerable. Even members of the Gaither family acknowledge that there might have been a brief, furtive sexual relationship between Mullins and Billy that Mullins would have had to initiate, an affair Mullins refuses to confess to this day. The deepest, deadliest form of homophobia is the internalized sort, marinated in the toxic stew of religious hate speech and social shame. Mullins was plague-ridden with it.

The Associated Press reports the court testimony this way:

"Are you telling these ladies and gentlemen that one of the reasons you set Billy Jack Gaither up was because he was gay?" [Charlsey Butler's] defense attorney Billy Hill asked.

"Yes, sir," Mullins replied.

"And you hate gays?"

"Yes, sir."

SAVAGERY IN THE PITCH BLACK DARK

Mullins and Butler stuck to their proposition story, but those who really knew Billy Jack say that his discretion and non-aggressive demeanor make such a scenario unlikely. His sisters and brothers agree that Billy never denied his gayness in his adult life, but he didn't volunteer the fact either. His older brother Rickie remembers that other kids in school made merciless fun of him, enough so that Billy Jack learned how to carry himself if he was going to survive in Deep South Alabama. "Oh, yeah," Rickie said to Forrest Sawyer for *Frontline*, "They'd call him names, a fag, a queer. It was hard for Billy to deal with because Sylacauga's a little town. Everybody knows everybody. So if you breathe the wrong way, they knew about it." When Sawyer asked if people knew Billy was gay in later life, Rickie replied, "Billy didn't deny anything about himself. He had gotten to the point where he felt good, and everybody who knew Billy, knew Billy was gay, and accepted him that way. Billy could be Billy everywhere he went. He wouldn't hide anything. He wouldn't come up to you and say, 'I'm gay.' But if you asked him, he would tell you, yes."

Doug Burke, Billy's hairstylist and good friend, told *The Advocate* that though Billy was searching so hard for a real relationship with a man, he would never have approached Mullins and Butler for sex. It was not his style. "Someone would have had to make the advance at him because I can't ever see Billy Jack taking the lead," Burke said. "I didn't see that in his makeup. He was too shy. He was not an aggressive person at all." Billy's co-worker, Mike, who would not give his full name to *The Advocate*, agreed with Burke, "He would let people know in a minute that he was gay and not ashamed of it. But he never made a pass at any of the guys he worked with." Marian Hammonds, owner of the Tavern and one of Billy's dance partners, had observed Billy's bar behavior for years. She told Richard Jones of the *Philadelphia Inquirer*, "He was very discreet. We're a straight bar, and he acted straight when he was in there. Sometimes he'd tease us about who he was seeing or whatever, but he never named any names." Hammonds also doubted that Billy Jack ever came on to Mullins and Butler.

On his thirty-ninth birthday, Billy came to Kathy Joe disturbed. He told her he was afraid that a couple of people wanted to hurt him. He had given them rides home when they were too drunk to get home by themselves. Now, they wouldn't leave him alone, he said. Since the two men hung out at the Tavern, Billy said he hadn't felt comfortable about going up there lately. Though he wouldn't tell her who they were, he did say that they wanted to "do a threesome with him," but he didn't do that sort of thing. His refusal had angered them.

"Then don't have anything to do with them," Kathy told him, "Don't be going around them!"

"Well, okay," Billy replied.

Then the conversation turned at once playful and somber.

Kathy teased him. "When I die," she said, "you're gonna take me and walk my casket."

"No, I won't," Billy teased back. "You ain't heavy. You ain't my brother." Then he said, "It would be perfect if we could just trade bodies."

"You know that won't work, Billy!" Kathy shot back. "You know I don't even like men!"

Gales of laughter replaced his disturbing concern, and they both went back to the birthday party. But when she knew Billy had been murdered, Kathy remembered the prescient conversation, and told her father about it. Marion Gaither took the account with a grain of salt. Yet when a version of the threesome story emerged later in court testimony, Marion put his head in his hands and grieved, "My God, Kathy told the truth about that one!"

Mullins testified that he had awakened the morning of Billy Jack's murder determined to kill him. "I was going to do whatever I had to do…To me it didn't seem like it was any different than waking up and saying, 'I'm going to the grocery store this afternoon,'" he told *ABC News 20/20*. Telephone records show Steven Mullins called his little sidekick Charlesy Butler just after 8 a.m. and then again just before 4 p.m. to finalize arrangements. The Gaither siblings have always maintained that there were supposed to be at least two other men involved in the plot to murder their brother, two who could have warned Billy Jack had they chosen to. One, a cousin of Mullins, was picked up by deputies for questioning, but never charged. Another man, according to Billy's folks, got a case of cold feet. Rather than cross Mullins, he turned himself in to authorities in Alexander City for failure to pay child support in order to give him a perfect alibi. Assuming these two alleged bystanders knew of a murder plot against Billy Jack, the stain of his blood is undoubtedly on their hands, as well.

Billy Jack went to his death giving rides to men who, if they were anything to him, should have been his friends. He first picked Mullins up at his trailer, and then dropped into the Tavern, cryptically saying to his friend Marian, "Now, don't worry about who I've got out there in the car." Marian has always wondered if Billy was trying to tell her something that night. Perhaps he already knew by then he was in trouble. If he was asking for help, it was a strange way to do it, and it went completely over her head. Billy left the Tavern with Mullins to get Butler at a pool joint called "The 11th Frame," where Charlsey was playing in a tournament. They rode out to a boat ramp at an old reservoir. As Billy got out of the car, Mullins struck out at him with a small-bladed pocketknife. He slashed at Billy's throat, delivering a deep gash, but not a killing cut. Mullins did not intend to end Billy Jack Gaither's life quickly. He had torture on his mind.

Billy fell to the ground on his hands and knees, pleading for his life. "He asked me to let him go . . . and told me he wouldn't say anything. I told him it was too late because he was a faggot," Mullins told *20/20*. He stabbed the little blade into the side of Billy's rib cage twice, as Butler popped the trunk open, and then ordered Billy who was both dazed and wounded, to get into the trunk of his own car.

Mullins drove to his trailer to collect two old tires, a gallon of kerosene, kitchen matches, and an ax handle. Butler remembered how quiet Billy was in the trunk of the car when Mullins dumped the tires on top of him, blood covering half his face, and Butler assumed Billy was either unconscious or dead already. They rode for miles, and then turned down Peckerwood Creek Road, following the dirt track in the inky dark until they stopped to unload at the old baptismal ground by the sluggish stream. Charlsey and Mullins set the kerosene and the ax handle beside the car, took the tire carcasses out of the trunk, and reached for Billy's bloody body. Billy Jack sprang up, taking Mullins completely by surprise, hitting him so hard that Mullins tumbled down the steep creek bank into the dark water. Charlsey hightailed it into the woods, as Billy dashed for his life into the driver's seat of his car, desperately searching for the keys. Mullins clawed his way up the bank, howling that Billy wasn't going anywhere because he had the car keys. In a last ditch attempt to save his own life, Billy locked his hands onto the steering wheel as Mullins dragged him by his legs out onto the ground. The ferocity of the death struggle was so great that the steering wheel was bent almost back to the steering column before Mullins broke Billy Jack's grip.

Crazed by embarrassment and rage, Mullins grabbed the ax handle and started beating him, grunting and yelling as he cracked open Billy's skull with frenzied blows. According to the autopsy report, death came by "severe blunt force trauma" to the head. Charlsey finally returned from his hiding place as Mullins continued to beat Billy's lifeless body with the ax handle. Tearing off his own shirt, Mullins ordered his jittery accomplice to take it and wipe Billy's blood out of the car, while Mullins never missed a stroke with the ax handle. Charlsey remembered the sound of the wooden handle striking Billy's then lifeless body as a dull "thump—thump—thump." Butler then soaked the tires with the kerosene and set the pyre ablaze as Mullins continued to swing the ax handle. "I beat him until I couldn't do it anymore, until, you know, all the adrenaline was gone. The fire got going and the tires started burning real well and I drug him into the flame and uh, we stood there for a few minutes and then we left," Mullins told reporters.

The killers had to get rid of the car. After driving Billy's car back to Mullins's trailer, they took showers, changed clothes, and then asked to borrow a friend's car on the pretext of going bar hopping. After buying a gallon of gas with the money they had stolen from Billy Jack, Mullins and Butler drove both vehicles out to an old landfill in the next county where Charlsey soaked Billy's Honda with the gas, and torched it. Then, as if nothing particularly troubling had just happened, Mullins and Butler partied the rest of the night away with the remainder of Billy's money at the Southern Station, another bar near Sylacauga.

WHITHER, ALABAMA?

Remorseless after initially pleading not guilty, Steven Mullins coldly admitted later that he killed Billy Jack because he was queer. He testified against Charlsey, who had already pleaded not guilty by reason of mental defect. Apparently, a mentor's loyalty goes only so far when the electric chair is a concern. Both Mullins and Butler attempted versions of the gay panic defense in order to soften the sentencing. In court testimony, Mullins's secret sexual peccadilloes with several other men came to light, vindicating Rickie Gaither's belief that Mullins's macho posturing hid a fear of exposure that he projected onto Billy Jack with fatal effect. According to *Frontline's* Forrest Sawyer, who reported on Mullins, "He has no doubt that he is heterosexual, despite his reported sexual experiences with other men."

Though the rest of the family was in an eye-for-an-eye mood, Billy Jack's father said only God should have the right to take a life. Marion did not believe that Billy would have wanted the death penalty, and Billy's father struggled with the exposure the anti-gay aspect of the trial would bring upon him and his family. All he and Lois knew is that they missed their son with a sort of pain they had not thought possible. "Whatever he did," Lois said to David Firestone of the *New York Times*, "he never brought it home. And whether he was [gay] or not, it don't make me love him any less. He was my young'un."

The court sentenced both Mullins and Butler to life in prison without parole.

Was justice done in "Sweet Home Alabama"? African American poet, Duriel Harris, sets the question up succinctly by asking whether the killers "own" Billy Jack's story. After all, his killers are still alive, and Billy is dead. What is the meaning of another average gay man's murder in the Deep South?

Trash. With the kind of cruel irony only bigotry could contrive, Billy Jack's murderers took the life of a truly good human being, and burned him like trash on a garbage dump. They chose a trash-strewn landfill as the site for disposal of his car, as well. And some, in blunt Southern parlance, could accuse Billy's killers as the real trash for what they had done to Billy. "Trashy is as trashy does," one might say. But it is just not that simple.

To treat Billy Jack Gaither's anti-gay murder as an isolated incident carried out by aberrant, misfit men is precisely what the White South had become expert at doing to Blacks during the great struggle for civil rights—localize the blame, subtly re-victimize the victim, and quarantine the moral impact of hate crime brutality so that none of the sources of bigotry need to change. Civility displaces civil rights. In a world divided between "good ones and bad ones," that is, those who know their place and those who don't, there is never a way to be different and good at the same time. The situation of LGBTQ people differs from the Black experience in one crucial way, however: Blacks, who are emerging as a power in the New South, and their former White oppressors essentially agree about the necessity of keeping LGBTQ people "in their place."

Though it would be a terrible mistake, Mullins and Butler may be easily dismissed as "Sorry White Trash," dissociated from the religious, social, and political institutions that nurture hatred toward LGBTQ people to this present day. Billy Jack, who necessarily kept his sexual orientation hidden, may be just as easily dismissed as an example of "the gay lifestyle": a weak sort of person who did not deserve to die as he did, but who supposedly "chose" to live as a homosexual and therefore "chose" the circumstances that led to his death—similar to an alcoholic, a drug addict, or a kleptomaniac.

Neither of these assertions is true. To let such misconceptions go unchallenged would miss the *real* meaning of Billy Jack's murder—that the savagery perpetrated against a lonely, middle-aged gay man was the lethal result of casual, everyday hatred and soul-crushing rhetoric bred into the bone of small town America. There are aspects of Billy's case that are peculiarly Southern, but oppression of LGBTQ people is not exclusively a Southern phenomenon. Sylacauga—like Laramie, Wyoming, or Cortez, Colorado, or Bangor, Maine, or Pearland, Texas—was an incubator of fear and loathing for LGBTQ people, solely because of who they are. District Attorney Fred Thompson put succinctly in his opening remarks to the jury at Charlsey Butler's capital murder trial: "[The murder] was hatred—hatred of someone perceived to be different. Billy Jack Gaither was a homosexual and that is the only reason they killed him."

"This is not the type of place where this happens," said George Carlton, President of the Sylacauga City Council. "Just because you don't like someone, you don't beat them to death." Though denials like this one may be spoken with a Southern accent, hatred and the permission to despise people who are different is handed down from generation to generation almost everywhere. Mullins and Butler learned to dehumanize others, and Billy learned to internalize self-loathing in Dixieland. Yet had they been born and reared in another part of the country, they could have learned the same lessons. Most people don't foist their loathing in direct ways onto others, but far too many readily tell ugly, demeaning jokes on the sly, gossip at the beauty parlor, or refuse to hire a person because she is perceived to be too masculine, or because he is thought to be too effeminate. These seemingly minor infractions participate in the same violence that took an innocent life on the banks of Peckerwood Creek. The difference is one of degree, not of kind. Anyone who hears a child ridiculed as a "dyke," or a "fag," in school, and who still subscribes to the dangerous little bromide, "Sticks and stones may break my bones, but words can never hurt me," has too narrow a definition of hate crime. Unsafe schools and unsafe houses of worship inexorably lead to unsafe neighborhoods. Hate speech leads to hate actions. Billy's life and death teach us that lesson, and offer us a mirror in which we may see ourselves as we are, not as we pretend to be. It wasn't Alabama stars that fell on Billy Jack that chilly February night a decade ago; it was the hatred of local men who learned from their own community that it was all right, even righteous, to make a gay person suffer and die.

At least one of his killers can quote scripture these days to justify what he did to Billy Jack. Mullins's version of God aided and abetted his character disorder during the killing itself. Since incarceration, he has become something of a Bible student, but with a bigoted twist. For ABC's *20/20*, he shared his conviction that homosexuality is evil, and that while Billy Jack is now in eternal hellfire, when Mullins himself dies, he will go to heaven. "God forgives for everything. If you ask, you shall receive. And I asked for forgiveness, and that's what I got. I repented," he asserted. "[Billy Jack's] in hell because he's a homosexual and it tells you in the New Testament that that's wrong." Disturbingly, even some members of Billy Jack's family seem to agree with Mullins's basic theological point, albeit with a different outcome for Billy. Billy's younger brother William also believes that unrepentant homosexuality will send a person to hell. "I'm glad that Billy suffered some before he died," he admits, "so that he didn't die right away, but had time to pray and ask Jesus to forgive him. He had to be praying in the trunk of that car. I believe I'll see him in heaven, I really do."

Mel White of Soulforce contends negative religious attitudes toward LGBTQ people had dire consequences for every major participant in Billy Jack's story. White speaks from the authority of his own experience as a gay Southern Baptist himself:

> Billy's suffering began long before they beat him with an ax handle and tossed his body on a pile of blazing tires. If you are a lesbian, a gay man, a bisexual or a transgendered person, you know well how Billy suffered during those endless decades living in his lonely little closet in Sylacauga. If you are a parent, a family member, or a friend, you, too, will understand the suffering.
>
> Billy grew up listening to the anti-homosexual rhetoric from Baptist pulpits, reading it in Baptist magazines and mailers, hearing it on Baptist radio and television programs from Baptist evangelists like Jerry Falwell.

Did the rhetoric confuse Billy Gaither? Is that why he lived for at least a quarter of a century in his lonely closet and eventually died there? Did Billy wonder if his homosexuality was a sickness and sin? Did he live in fear of failing his parents and his God by "giving in"? When he "gave in" did he suffer guilt and more confusion? (Were the boys who killed him also victims of the rhetoric?).

Though the murder of Billy Jack Gaither was the direct responsibility of the two young men who carried out the deed (and indirectly the responsibility of any others who knew of the plot and yet refrained from warning Billy about it), culpability for Billy's suffering belongs to the society that still believes LGBTQ lives are not as valuable as everyone else's. To deny corporate culpability for creating and maintaining a climate of spiritual, social, and familial violence against men and women like Billy Jack is ultimately to concede to the killers the story and memory of every murdered LGBTQ citizen.

To tell Billy's story, and to act for change because of it, is to frustrate the intentions of the killers. Many rallied to Billy Jack's memory in the days and weeks after news of his murder spread. Demonstrations and vigils for him took place in dozens of locales throughout Alabama and the nation, one of them drawing as many as three hundred people. Progressive clergy and LGBTQ allies in the religious community spoke out against anti-gay hate crimes. Episcopalians made pilgrimage to Peckerwood Creek to exorcise and bless the site that had been desecrated by Billy Jack's slaughter and immolation. Media converged on Sylacauga for a time, causing local reporter Jason Landers to write, "As if the days of segregation had returned, Alabama was again on people's minds because of hate." *Dateline, American Justice, ABC's 20/20,* and *PBS's Frontline* telecast exposés on the Gaither killing, and editorials decrying the plight of LGBTQ Americans ran in papers from the *New York Times* and the *Philadelphia Inquirer* to the *St. Louis Post-Dispatch* and the *San Francisco Chronicle.*

Some who were horrified and enraged by Billy Jack's murder went the proverbial second mile, and acted to change the climate of fear LGBTQ people endure every day. President Bill Clinton vowed to work for federal hate crimes legislation in response to the killings of James Byrd Jr. in Texas, Matt Shepard in Wyoming, and Billy Jack Gaither in Alabama. Hate crimes were not recognized in the state of Alabama at the time of Billy Jack's death, and still aren't. But thanks to Billy Jack's story, the tide mounted high enough for legislation to pass the Alabama House, and came near to passage in the Senate. Sponsors have not given up. One day they hope to enact "Billy Jack's Law" into the state criminal code.

The Southern Poverty Law Center in Montgomery understood that Billy Jack's story must not be forgotten as the long march to freedom continues for minorities in Alabama and throughout the South. At the national Civil Rights Memorial Center, a large, compelling tablet bearing Billy's likeness and the account of his murder hangs beside those of martyrs in the struggle for African American civil rights. Thousands of visitors read it with horror and wonderment every year, especially the young, who are learning that LGBTQ people are worthy of protection and respect—thanks to Billy Jack.

Though most of the ardor that mounted in the aftermath of Billy's murder has cooled as Alabamians have gone on with their lives, a small group of committed LGBTQ people and their allies refuse to let Billy Jack's story belong to the killers, or to vanish into amnesia. Dr. Beverly Hawk, Director of the Crossroads Community Center at the University of Alabama at Tuscaloosa, remains determined to see "something of lasting beauty come out of something so ugly." She and her allies have established an annual vigil on the anniversary of Billy Jack's murder, and created the Billy Jack Gaither Humanitarian Award, given to a champion of human rights each year. In Birmingham a gathering of LGBTQ activists, with parents of gay and lesbian children and other pillars of the city, fund research into Billy Jack's story and the stories of other LGBTQ hate crimes murder victims throughout the country. David Gary, a key figure in this group, stays in touch with the Gaither family. He says the whole way Alabamians think about hate crimes changed because of Billy Jack. Through a network of contacts Gary has built as a founder of Alabama Integrity, a group of pro-gay rights Episcopalians and others have monitored subsequent hate crimes, such as the hate murders of Roderick George in Montgomery, and Scotty Joe Weaver in Bay Minette. If Billy Jack's memory continues to be remembered and not forgotten with the passage of the years, leaders of conscience like Hawk and Gary will have made all the difference. They and their networks of friends are the keepers of the flame.

Kathy Joe Gaither remains the fiercest keeper of Billy Jack's memory. Confined to an oxygen tank and an electric scooter chair by the lung disease she believes will take her life, she tells Billy's story to whomever will listen. Proudly, she shows visitors the Resolution of Respect posthumously awarded her brother by the Los Angeles City Council, and the personal letter of condolence her family received from President Bill Clinton. Her tiny apartment in Wadley, Alabama, which she shares with Pablo, her ancient Chihuahua, is full of papers, photographs of a young Billy Jack with "that little smirk" on his lips, and of Billy's beloved *Gone With the Wind* collection. Her husky voice, made raspy and weak by lung disease and too many cigarettes, rehearses funny anecdotes about her brother, outlines of events of his murder, and proffers theories about why Billy's killers took someone so precious away from her. She is full of love for anyone who will help keep Billy Jack's memory alive, like Beverly and David, but full of contempt for the men who killed him.

Her dying wish—besides passage of hate crimes legislation in Alabama to protect LGBTQ people—is to confront Steven Mullins and Charlsey Butler. "I want to see them, face to face, eye to eye. I want them to tell me the truth, and I think I can get it out of them," she says with controlled fury, "'cause I don't think the truth came out in the trial. I want them to tell me why they did it." Then, the old, familiar pain of loss returns to her eyes, and her voice trails off as she remembers, "Daddy said, 'Before you get to heaven, you're going to have to forgive Mullins and Butler, so you can see Billy.' That one's hard . . ."

"You know," Kathy Joe says, Pablo sitting in her lap, before her visitors leave, "Billy's still with us, no matter what. You get him into you, and you cannot get him out."

So long as Billy's story is still alive, as the poet Duriel Harris says, *"he ain't dead."* Every time his story brings people of goodwill together, the culture of violence and the intentions of the killers are thwarted. Just as the fox does not have the last word on the hare, murderers cannot extinguish the memories of those they kill. Change does not come overnight in "Sweet Home Alabama." But as long as the memory of Billy Jack Gaither rises again in hopes of a better world, it will come, slow but sure.

Naw. He ain't dead.

For Greater Understanding

Southern Gothic: Billy Jack Gaither

BOOKS

Gold, Mitchell, and Mindy Drucker. *Crisis: 40 Stories Revealing the Personal, Social, and Religious Pain and Trauma of Growing Up Gay in America.* Austin, TX: Greenleaf Book Group, 2008.

Levin, Jack, and Jack McDevitt. *Hate Crimes Revisited: America's War on Those Who are Different.* Boulder, CO: Westview Press, 2002.

FILMS AND VIDEOGRAPHY

Frontline – Assault on Gay America: The Life and Death of Billy Jack Gaither. Public Broadcasting System, 2000.

ORGANIZATIONS AND WEBSITES

Crossroads Community Center at the University of Alabama, http://crossroads.ua.edu.
Equality Alabama, http://www.equalityalabama.org.
National Civil Rights Memorial, http://www.splcenter.org/civil-rights-memorial.
Southern Poverty Law Center, http://www.splcenter.org.
Unfinished Lives Project, http://unfinishedlivesblog.com.

Fred C. Martinez Jr.
March 15, 1985—June 16, 2001

Cortez, Colorado

5

Changing One

Fred C. Martinez Jr.

Earth's body has become my body
by means of this I shall live on.

Earth's mind has become my mind
by means of this I shall live on.

Earth's voice has become my voice
by means of this I shall live on.

—Navajo Blessingway Chant

"F.C." IS WHAT HIS friends called him. His people, the Navajo of the high, dry, Four Corners region (the intersection of Utah, Colorado, New Mexico, and Arizona's borders), knew him as *nadleeh,* a Two-Spirit person who at 16 years old was becoming comfortable living both as a male and a female. From time immemorial, the Navajo have accepted and honored members of the *Dineh* who harmonized male and female characteristics within themselves. F.C. was more complete than any simple gender category white people are comfortable with. As *nadleeh,* a reconciling sexual entity, he could have become a shaman, an artist, or perhaps even a theologian for the *Dineh.* He was becoming more beautiful, walking the Navajo way of beauty. Murder by blunt force trauma and a slash to the abdomen on the night of June 16, 2001 tore that possibility away from him, and away from those he loved and cared for in Cortez, Colorado. The *nadleeh* transformation the Navajo have known so well for centuries, and which is woven into the fabric of myth and reality that is their heritage both on and off the reservation, was violently unraveled by a hate-filled young man with a rock and a blade in a dark canyon called "The Pits." No one has lamented the loss more perceptively than F.C.'s own mother, Pauline Mitchell: "Because he was different his life was taken from him, and we will never know the person Fred would have become."

Depending on how you look at it, Cortez, Colorado, whose population is about 8,000, is either a crossroads of cultures, or a battleground. As the largest town in the Four Corners, where Colorado touches the great Navajo reservation in New Mexico, Utah, and Arizona, Cortez is home to a First Nations minority population of around twenty percent. The region is home to Utes of the Southern and Ute Mountain Clans, Navajos off the "Rez," and other descendents of the prehistoric Basketweaver Indians and their successors, the ancient Pueblo civilization who inhabited the Great Sage Plain for thousands of years. Tourists flock here to experience the rumors of warriors and sages that whisper through the towers and kivas of Mesa Verde National Park and Hovenweep National Monument. Atop the Escalante Pueblo ruins in nearby Dolores, Colorado, a person standing in one spot can turn in a full 360 degree circle and behold the great sacred hoop of the Navajo cosmos in a single breathtaking panorama. Standing on that high hilltop in the wind, and amidst the broken stones the Ancient Ones left behind, a person gets the strange sense that F.C. and his ancestors have been here forever, and will continue to be here forever. According to the Navajo emergence myth, First Man and First Woman escaped into this land from the three worlds below this one. Some clans teach that when the Third World was destroyed by flood, the ancestors climbed up a hollow reed to find safety here in the land they call "The Glittering World."

Today, though, Cortez is not glittering at all for anyone born Navajo and poor. For F.C., who was himself a crossroad of cultures, genders, and phobias this was especially true. He tried to fit in. *Bellagona* (Navajo for "honkie") social expectations were tough to handle even for a 6'1" boy. F.C. never found passing for straight a natural thing to do.

TWO SPIRITS IN ONE

F.C. shared most things with his peers in small town Colorado. He loved *Hot Wheels* cars, and apparently collected them. He played the clarinet. Rap and hip hop music provided the soundtrack for his life. Puff Daddy and R. Kelly were among his favorite artists. F.C. idolized Tupac Shakur and mourned his assassination. When "Homies," the tiny plastic toy barrio kids, became the rage for other youth his age, he played with them, too, and probably identified with the outsider feeling these teeny toys conjured in the psyches of middle school students. Like his peers, he dreamed of a career, perhaps making it as a computer specialist or a fashion designer in a big city somewhere. Anywhere but Cortez.

Like any other teen, F.C. was a bundle of contradictory facts and feelings. He was big for his age, and strong. Yet he preferred the company of girls, and towered over them, head and shoulders. He loved to put up his hair attractively, and found makeup alluring and expressive of the true person he was becoming. He owned purses and carried them in public. He let his fingernails grow, and manicured them himself. In a snapshot taken by a friend, he appears unaffectedly feminine, eyebrows plucked and penciled in archly, a coquettish "Mona Lisa" smile on his lips. His girlfriends loved him and reinforced his budding transformation. To them he was "Fredericka." At the same time, he was also *Dineh,* one of *The People*, something beyond the comprehension of most of his school friends. F.C. was proud of his Navajo heritage, and yet as a poor Indian kid from the trailer parks, he must have felt the paradox of being a Navajo in a complex, sometimes hostile world. Like his entire tribe, he was an alien in his own country. Among *The People*, F.C. found the quiet, spiritual support he needed as he learned how to navigate the contradictions of his young, changing life. F.C. found personal significance in the Native American Church, so he joined and was an active member, though he never talked about it much, even to his best girlfriends.

Above all, F.C. was a real, flesh-and-blood kid, neither an angel nor a demon. Sometimes he drank too much. He carried Zig Zag rolling papers and condoms in his pockets. He loved life—loved to laugh and to make other people laugh with him. He loved to joke around and basked in the attention he drew to himself. His teachers and friends said he could brighten up a room just by walking into it.

At home, he was the baby of the family, the last of six brothers, and some of them kidded him about being spoiled. F.C. loved and respected his dad, Fred C. Sr., but it was clear that his best friend was his mother, Pauline. F.C. missed her badly while she was away in Durango making a living for her family as a domestic housekeeper. When he was just six, she was compelled to take the out-of-town job to help the family make ends meet. Although F.C. lived with his brothers in her mobile home just across the street from the high school, the periods of separation when she had to be away at work had been hard on Pauline and her youngest son.

Though the whole family loved and accepted him, no one loved him like his mom. Speaking out to the press after his murder, Pauline said,

> My son is beautiful. He was *nadleeh*, Two-Spirit, and he could comfortably walk the path of both male and female. He never saw another person as a stranger, but as a fellow human being and was always ready to give a hug or compliment to anyone who he believed to be hurting. The most important thing I can say is that I loved Fred. I loved my son exactly for who he was, for his courage in being honest and gentle and friendly. What I wanted for my son was for him to be accepted and loved, just like I accepted and loved him. Fred was always proud to be Navajo. Fred did not struggle with who he was, but he was hurt because of the people who had problems with my son expressing himself honestly.

More than anyone else, his mother knew that he sometimes just needed to be alone. Like any youth his age, and much less one dealing with the complexities of a life like his, F.C. needed elbow room. Sometimes, she said, he would set out on foot to stay at friends' places for a couple of days at a time, just to get away.

PANTHER COUNTRY

School was a pressure cooker of conflict for the young Navajo. F.C. had a tough freshman year at Montezuma-Cortez High School. Officials sent him home because the makeup he wore and his feminine accessories "distracted" other students. Students taunted and harassed him, calling him "faggot" and *"joto"* ("bum-boy") both behind his back and to his face. MCHS sophomore Jessica Wilson confirmed as much: "People talked behind his back, but I'm sure he knew." As another former schoolmate of his, Tyson Garland, said, "Everybody knew he was gay." What that meant in practical terms was that no matter how well grounded and self-aware he was, trouble was a fact of his life as a high school student. MCHS was not a safe place.

When verbally assaulted, he was neither defensive nor apologetic about his identity. He had never kept his homosexuality a secret, as the *Cortez Journal* pointed out after his murder, when the paper was criticized for printing that he was gay. If F.C. was not ashamed of it, the editorial staff wrote, why should anyone else be? Gender identity and expression, however, are just not that simple. To cope, F.C. cultivated a public self and a private self. Counselors and casual friends found him to be at ease about who he was and outwardly unruffled by the intolerance he faced. High School Counselor LouAnn Burkett, said, "He was really happy with himself—he didn't seem to have any guilt or any complex about [his homosexuality]. He enjoyed himself and the way he was and kids accepted him." Under the surface though, F.C. suffered from the constant corrosion of taunts and thinly veiled hostility. He didn't trouble his mother with his problems. Around her he played the joker, though she intuited that school was tougher than he let on. Only after his death, Pauline learned from F.C.'s girlfriends and from their mothers about the full degree of violence he faced in school. Priscilla Scott, who saw F.C. frequently when he visited her daughter Marlene, admired and loved him, but was also worried about him. It hurt her to witness how kids would accost him, saying, "Here goes that faggot!" His personal resilience to the harassment amazed her, but she suspected the razzing pained him deeply: "He used to say, 'I don't care what people think about me.' He could be so degraded and just have a smile on his face and blow it off. There was a lot of love in that kid."

Warning signs began to crop up. F.C. started skipping school. To his close friend, Robin Flores, who was also sixteen, he confided that he wished he were a girl and not a boy. At one point he took an overdose of pills and wound up in intensive care. When his friends asked him why he did it, he told them he didn't know. The Four Corners Gay and Lesbian Alliance for Diversity arranged counseling services for him. One of their leaders, openly gay Cortez resident John Peters-Campbell, told reporters after F.C.'s murder, "From what I understand, there was a significant shift in his outlook after that."

Flores said that in the months following his suicide attempt, F.C. seemed happy. He told Flores he wanted to be nicknamed "Beyoncé" for the lead singer in the female R&B group, Destiny's Child. "He would stand in front of the mirror for hours, checking his makeup and his hair. He was so much fun, the best girlfriend in the world." Reprieved from death by overdose, he had turned a significant corner in his personal development. F.C. was gradually becoming reconciled with his identity as *nadleeh* in a *bellagona* world.

Like all transgender people in an ignorant society, F.C. had to negotiate his self-disclosure to others according to the capacity of the persons he encountered. Transgender life is complicated, and F.C.'s own accounts of who he was becoming reflected that fact. To most people, like his classmates at Montezuma-Cortez High, he was gay. To those he trusted to be able to handle it, he was transgender. To the Navajo people, his family among them, he was Two Spirit, *nadleeh,* an identification that harmonized gay, queer, and trans realities. This is not to say that he had split personalities or that he was confused. Rather, it is a testimony to the clarity he had achieved about his sexual identity since the transformation began when he was thirteen. Cathy Renna, Media Director for the Gay and Lesbian Alliance Against Defamation (GLAAD), saw it this way: "Fred was totally comfortable with who he was—he was Fred. I don't think Fred needed a label for himself that was any one word or any one category . . . We all go through our own growth in identity and who we are . . . Fred was a very complex young man who was transforming into his own identity." In the process, F.C. had learned his audiences, and understood how to navigate his complex life in the midst of them.

In February of 2001, he broke with Montezuma-Cortez High and started attending the Adult Education Center in town. Evening adult education classes offered him the outlet he needed. Evening classes were a haven of sorts for him, a way to learn in a more mature, tolerant atmosphere. As Barbara Burroughs, one of his school teachers, said to the *Cortez Journal,* "He was being harassed, and you don't want to go to school every day if your are going to be harassed. He came to the Adult Ed center because it was a learning environment where he felt safer." Ann Miller, another of his teachers at the Center, saw him begin to flourish in the security he found there. She admired him. "He knew others did not care for the way he looked, but he did not hold it against them," Miller said to the *Cortez Journal.* "He was very forgiving, and he really liked people, even if they were less than polite. He had a lot of pain in his life, but he never felt sorry for himself." Instead, she noted, "When people felt down in the classroom here, he wanted to help them; he could put people at ease. He had an incredible spirit that was very pure and very admired." Summarizing her experience of F.C., Miller said, "He had a woman's mind, soul and heart in a man's body. If he had been a woman, he would have been the most popular girl in town."

The Adult Education Center opened a window to his future. He was working toward his GED with an eye toward college and a good career. F.C. was intelligent and perceptive about his options in Cortez. He knew he could never attain full Two Spirit status in such a cooped-up environment. After his death, an artist who knew him well drew his totem spirit on a memorial to him. The totem was an eagle, and beneath F.C.'s photo, the artist drew two crossed eagle feathers united by a rose in full bloom: beauty, freedom, and strength, together in harmony. A free bird knows to get clear of snares so that it can stretch its wings out and fly. F.C. was never to know the full freedom he needed for his change to become complete. The violence that stalks those who are different set its snare on a summer's night after the rodeo.

MONSTER THAT SUCKS IN PEOPLE

The Ute Mountain Rodeo and Carnival is the biggest event of the summer for Cortez and the surrounding country. Adding to the excitement of bronco busting, calf roping, and bull riding at the annual rodeo, a carnival also comes to town and sets up rides and a midway on the Montezuma County Fairgrounds. Festivities kick off with the Annual Rodeo Parade that rolls down Main Street, replete with floats, marching bands, fire engines with lights flashing and sirens wailing, military veterans in pickup trucks waving American flags, and the Montezuma County Sheriff and his Posse mounted on tall horses. Youth are everywhere, showing their "Panther Pride," and sporting school colors. People come from all over the Four Corners to cheer the parade, watch the spills and thrills at the rodeo, spin and whirl on a ride or two at the carnival, and party until the wee hours each night.

F.C. said good-bye to his family the first night of the Rodeo on June 16. He was headed to the carnival. He wore a gray sweatshirt, tan pants, and black work boots that concealed red nail polish he had recently applied to his toenails. Under his sweatshirt, he was wearing a small, unobtrusive bra. His mother later remembered that F.C. was sporting his best blue bandana when he walked out the door. It would be the last time she saw him alive.

When hatred, violence, or cruelty—the "ugliness" of discord—breaks out anywhere, the Navajo believe this disturbance can be traced back to the selfishness of a man and the ravages of a monster. When First Man was escaping the flood that destroyed Third World, the world before this one, he could not bear to leave his bundle of selfishness behind. So, First Man sent a diving bird back into the water to recover his destructive greed and to return it to the Glittering World. At the same time, a terrible, man-eating giant followed First Man from the underworld, the "Monster That Sucks In People," *Ye'iitsoh*. *Ye'iitsoh*, resembling the "Four Horsemen of the Apocalypse" all wrapped into one, oversaw this bundle of "ugly conditions" and inflicted them on the *Dineh* at every opportunity. It took the combined strength of the original Navajo holy family, Father Sun, Changing Woman, and her twin sons (Monster Slayer and One Born for Water), to defeat *Ye'iitsoh* and restore harmony to the Glittering World.

The vestiges of that mythical warfare ricochet within every crime and brutality human beings inflict on each other. That is what makes death-dealing selfishness so destructive and monstrous in its effect. Beyond the ravages suffered by individuals in any violent event, the simultaneous and greater atrocity rips apart the harmony that holds this whole world together. Every instance of violence threatens to plunge this world back into the chaos and destruction that originally drove humanity upward from the Three Underworlds before this world.

When F.C. set out for the Ute Mountain Rodeo and Carnival on that June summer night, he was unaware that he was about to become a victim in the great cosmic struggle between good and evil. He was just looking to have a good time. Then, he got sucked in by the Monster.

GANGBANGER

Shaun Murphy, an 18-year-old hard case, left his pregnant woman and toddler at home in Farmington, New Mexico, to hook up with his buddy, Clinton Sanchez, for the trip back to his old stomping grounds in Cortez. They had methamphetamine to sell, and wanted to cash in at the Ute Mountain Carnival, but they got a late start. By the time they arrived at the fairgrounds, the carnival was winding down for the night, so they went over to a jam-packed house party instead. There they saw a tall Navajo boy wearing a sweatshirt, tan pants, and a distinctive blue bandana. He had his hair done up in a ponytail. Murphy was apparently acquainted with him, and they struck up a conversation.

Though F.C. was taller and heavier than Murphy, who stood at 5'8" and weighed about 140 pounds, the Anglo was a danger to be reckoned with. Murphy worked the oilfields, and had a reputation as a tough customer with an anger problem. His gang sign was "13." A "banger" in the East Side Locos Trece, a gang that had been involved in hate-generated violence against Navajos before, Murphy was trouble waiting to happen. Genevieve Jackson, herself a Navajo, said that Farmington, New Mexico teenagers consider the torture and murder of Navajos a "rite of passage," and the documented instances of such attacks stretched back there thirty years. As Tiger Carillo, who heads the Gay, Lesbian, Straight Education Network in nearby Gallup, New Mexico, notes, adding anti-gay bias to the attacks makes the encounter with gangbangers all the more dangerous.

Murphy's violence was rooted deep in his childhood. Originally from Cortez, he was expelled from the sixth grade for what Cortez Middle School Principal Byron Wiehe called, "violent behaviors." He didn't last long at Montezuma-Cortez High School or Southwest Open, the alternative secondary school, either. Principal Wiehe recognized Murphy's name immediately when the police went public with his identity. "We knew the name just because he had problems and he was young when we expelled him," he said to *Cortez Journal* reporters. "Just for that short time, it got to the point that he was considered by state law as a habitually disruptive student."

Murphy was taught to hate his absent father by his mother, Angel Murphy Tacoronte, who was an addict herself, and, ironically, a self-identified lesbian who dated Native American women. Young Murphy had a long criminal record. He had been repeatedly charged with assault. He beat his own stepbrother into unconsciousness, and, as a child, had been charged for assaulting a police officer, ramming a man's head into a wall, and breaking a beer bottle over a drunken man's head. After serving time in a secure youth facility, he fell into small-time drug dealing and gang life. In 2000 he moved to Farmington with his common law wife and child. Since he was a parolee in New Mexico, the trip back up to the Ute Mountain Rodeo in Colorado, across state lines, was a violation that could have sent him back to jail.

The summer moon rose pale, a waning crescent in the dark sky when F.C. set out on foot from the party at the Sleeping Ute Apartments where he had seen Shaun Murphy. By most standards, nowhere is too long a walk in Cortez. A walk with a killer, however, turned out to be the longest walk of Fred C. Martinez Jr.'s life.

According to testimony at F.C.'s murder trial, Shaun and his "Cuz," Clinton Sanchez, left the house party between two and three o'clock in the morning. They landed at another friend's apartment located at Seventh and Madison Streets, and got hungry. On the way to a nearby Handy Mart to get pizza, Murphy and Sanchez saw F.C. standing in front of the high school on Seventh Street, just across from Elmwood Trailer Park where he lived. Sanchez told police they offered F.C. a ride, and he got in the back seat. While Sanchez went into the Handy Mart, Murphy, who was the driver, stayed behind in the car with F.C. They talked, and during that conversation, Murphy sized up his victim.

On the way back, F.C. asked to be let out at the corner of Seventh and Madison. After he got out of the car and had walked out of earshot, Sanchez asked Murphy, "Do you think he thought we were gay?" Police believe that Murphy already knew something about F.C.'s sexuality, and that what he knew contributed to the attack that night. Murphy and Sanchez drove back to their friend's place. Shortly after, Murphy told his friend that he was going out "to get a joint," and left alone. When Murphy returned about twenty minutes later, Sanchez testified to the court, his buddy was covered in blood. Murphy had gotten into a fight at "The Pits" (a narrow box canyon bisecting the southern part of town), he said, and then bragged that he had "bug-smashed a *joto*" (Spanish slang for "faggot"). Murphy took a shower at the apartment, changed his clothes, put his bloody things in a bag, and asked a friend to drive Sanchez and himself an hour's trip down to Farmington, New Mexico. On the way, Murphy threw his bloody socks out of the window, one of which was later recovered by investigators.

ABANDONED TO DIE

What exactly happened in The Pits, that long gash in the earth, between Shaun Murphy and Fred C. Martinez Jr. is ultimately unknowable to us. Murphy knows, but has given three different and inconsistent accounts, all of them self-serving. Perhaps F.C. and Murphy agreed to meet later to smoke marijuana out of sight in the canyon, as Murphy claimed to authorities, which was just a short walk from the trailer park. Perhaps not. Pauline Mitchell will always believe that her son would never have gone down into that foreboding place in the dark of night without being forced. "How could someone so small take on my son?" she asked later, saying that there had to have been more than one person involved in the attack. "There's no way Fred ran into the dark canyon . . . they dragged him there."

We can say one thing conclusively about the attack that took place that night: the transformation F.C. was experiencing as *nadleeh* was savagely arrested in that dark, lonely place. He was murdered in cold blood. Changing One would change no more. *Ye'iitsoh*, the Monster that Sucks

In People, had struck out at human beings again, this time with unusual cruelty and callousness.

F.C.'s skull was cracked open with a big rock that was found later at the crime scene, covered in his blood. His wrists were injured, and he suffered a lateral slash across his abdomen. Clutching his stomach from the pain, he fell on stony ground in a brush-choked area of the canyon between two boulders. His blood seeped out on the ground, *so much blood!* Investigators found bloody streaks up the steep nearby wall of the canyon, where F.C. apparently tried to escape his attacker. Murphy got one thing right about that night: it was indeed a "bug-smashing."

After pocketing about $40 off of him, Murphy left F.C. mortally wounded to die alone. Coldly, he just walked away. He didn't return, even to check on his handiwork. He didn't send anyone else, or even place an anonymous call to try and get F.C. help. This *joto* was finished.

For five days, F.C.'s corpse lay there on his back in his cruel cradle of stone and scrub, dead eyes scanning the sky, dead arms clutching his wounded stomach. Ironically, his head was facing east, the direction the door a Navajo female hogan (home) faces so that a family can greet Father Sun each morning. The autopsy suggests that he died from the combination of a severe blow to the head by a blunt object, massive blood loss mainly from his stomach wound, and exposure to the elements. It was a hard death, slow and agonizing. The sun beat down at ninety degrees and more for those five days. The carrion creatures did their grim work. To compound the tragedy, F.C. had died less than a quarter-mile from his home.

On the fifth day, June 21, two boys from the nearby Happy Valley Trailer Park went down into The Pits to play. There they stumbled on the remains of a man, not far from the sewage disposal ponds belonging to the Town of Cortez Sanitation District's complex. The little boys sounded the alarm . . . five days too late. By the time law enforcement officials and emergency medical personnel got to the crime scene, there was little left of F.C. that remained identifiable. It took dental records to settle who this had been. When his mother was finally called to the funeral home to identify the body, she said that what was left was "unrecognizable as the beautiful boy I had seen a week before. I had to identify that body by the hair band F.C.'d been wearing."

INVISIBLE WOMAN

When F.C. did not come home from the carnival or contact his mother, Pauline reported him missing to the police. The authorities ignored her pleas to find her son. "I was worried sick when he never returned," she said, "but I never thought it could be this bad. I don't know how long he lay there suffering. I don't know what his last thoughts were."

Pauline Mitchell is a proud woman with three strikes against her culturally and racially. She is a single mother, poor, and Navajo in a *bellagona* town. English is not her first language. Her mother tongue is Navajo. White aggressiveness did not come naturally to her. She is a soft-spoken housekeeper. Navajos are not rude or pushy. They do not interrupt when another is speaking. Her appeals for help would have been answered more quickly if she had been dealing with Navajo police, but she was not, and the neglect she suffered should never have occurred to anyone.

Mothers of other queer youth reached out to Pauline and helped her find her voice. They showed her how to rattle cages, network to find allies, and work the system. Most importantly, these mothers could empathize with Pauline, because they had endured the same sort of ordeal she and her family were going through. With their encouragement, she went to the press to gain a hearing:

> I am angry that the police have not taken the time to explain what is happening and help me deal with this. I don't want to read new things in the newspaper. I reported that Fred was missing on June 18. Two days later I called the police again, and on June 23 I read about a body being found near our home. I phoned the police again, but they told me the body had not been identified. Since June 25, when the police told me at work that Fred had been murdered, I wondered if it was because of who he was and how he expressed himself.

Sadly, the authorities in the police and sheriff's departments and District Attorney Joe Olt still kept her in the dark. They did not even tell her the results of the autopsy, as the District Attorney had promised. She and her family had to read the gruesome details for themselves in the newspaper.

The strain took its toll on Pauline and F.C.'s brothers. Before the year was out, Pauline had suffered two heart attacks. At a community forum held in Cortez by LGBTQ organizations and covered by the *Cortez Journal*, F.C.'s brother, Jervis Mitchell, spoke through his tears about what happened to his little brother: "I felt a lot of anger that I couldn't be there [when F.C. was attacked]. Every night I stayed up until four or five in the morning thinking about him. Finally, one morning I went to sleep," he said. In a dream, his little brother came back to him. "I grabbed him in a hug, and I asked him, 'We have been worried about you. Where have you been?' He looked at me and said, 'I'm alright, I'm okay.' I still miss him, and I will always think of him."

BELLAGONA JUSTICE

Murder is big news. The Four Corners media got hold of the story, and spread the word down to Farmington. When Shaun Murphy heard the news of F.C.'s death on television, he blurted out to his "Cuz," Clinton Sanchez, "Killed that fool, huh?" He showed no remorse. A tipster "dropped the dime" on Murphy, and police staked out his apartment. They watched as Sanchez threw a plastic bag into a dumpster. The bag was filled with clothes, belts and shoes speckled with dried blood. Forensics matched the bloodstains to F.C.'s blood type.

Murphy was arrested on a Colorado murder warrant on July 3, the same day F.C.'s obituary came out in the *Cortez Journal*. At first he was charged with second-degree murder. Later, upon establishing that Murphy had robbed his victim as well, the D.A. changed the charge to first-degree murder, a charge that carried the death penalty or life in prison. Finally, the waffling D.A. offered Murphy a plea bargain that reduced the offense back to his original deal. Murphy pled guilty to murder in the second degree, a crime that carried a sentencing range of only eight to forty-eight years in prison. Seeking to justify his actions, D.A. Olt told Montezuma County Commissioners that a full-blown jury trial would have cost $60,000, and bankrupted the county. It just made good financial sense to do things this way, he explained.

Controversy threatened to swirl out of control around F.C.'s memory in the aftermath of Murphy's arrest. Reporters from Durango, Farmington, Denver, and the Navajo Reservation converged on the community, digging for stories. Because of the similarities between F.C.'s murder and the hate-killing of Matthew Shepard in Laramie, Wyoming back in 1998, national attention was drawn to Cortez.

Initially resistant to the idea that F.C. had been the victim of a hate crime, investigators uncovered more and more evidence that anti-homosexual bias had motivated Murphy's assault. By mid-July, law enforcement officers openly broached the possibility that F.C. died because he was gay and/or transgender. Pauline was already certain that her son had died because of his sexual identity and gender expression. To the media on July 18, she declared, "Violence was a common part of his life, and as I learn more, I know that this was a crime based on anger and hate." News of Murphy's boast, that he had "bug-smashed" a faggot, and his callous response to the report of F.C.'s death clinched it. Cortez residents had to admit that a hate crime festered in their own backyard.

YANKING AWAY UGLY THINGS

The Navajo believe wicked things strongly attach themselves to someone suffering from dis-ease. These recalcitrant things do not release a sick person willingly. *Dineh* ceremonials prescribe several rites that are intended to remove "ugly things" from a person. The "Unraveling Ceremony" is one of them. A shaman, called a Singer or a *Hatalii*, binds bundles of feathers and powerful herbs together with strips of the yucca plant, and presses them against the patient's ailing body. With a swift motion, the *Hatalii* yanks the bundle away, removing the "ugly things" now entangled in its contents.

In February 2002 Shaun Murphy agreed to plead guilty to second-degree murder to avoid the death penalty. Later he reversed his decision, and said he wanted to reject the deal. During his months in prison, Murphy exhibited the same violence he had been known for as a youth in Cortez, and then in gang life in Farmington. He plastered his gang sign, "13," on his cell mirror. He fought with other inmates, and at one point attempted to escape from jail.

By May 2002, Murphy reversed himself yet again, and took the deal the D.A. originally offered him. In a letter to District Judge Sharon Hansen quoted in the *Cortez Journal*, he stated that he feared losing his case and receiving a life sentence. "I have two kids that i would really like to be a father to and if i get a life sentence then I cant do that," he wrote in a nearly illiterate scrawl. But then he equivocated in the same letter, scrawling again, "i would have a chance to get a lesser charge if i would take this all the way . . . Ma'am i didn't intentionally or even knowingly allegedly kill this guy I'm being tried for." Sentencing was set for June 3, 2002, just shy of a year since F.C.'s murder.

At 9 a.m. on Monday, June 3, the all-day sentencing hearing commenced in the Montezuma County Courthouse. Murphy sat at the defense table wearing black boots and a too-large grey shirt left untucked over a pair of black pants. His ankles were chained with manacles, but his hands were unrestrained. Murphy had a nearly-complete buzz-cut, except for a little ponytail he fiddled with from time to time. Murphy's mother and grandmother took turns pleading with the judge, asking for mercy for their boy. In a moment of high drama, his grandmother, Angie Murphy, grabbed her chest and collapsed after testifying on her grandson's behalf. The judge cleared the courtroom so that Mrs. Murphy could be carried to an ambulance. Shaun sat unmoved by his grandmother's crisis.

The greatest suspense of the day, however, surrounded F.C.'s mother as she rose to read her statement to the court. Steady and resolved, Pauline Mitchell outlined the life of her youngest child, his sweetness and honesty. She talked about the obstacles F.C. faced as a poor, but proud Navajo *nadleeh* in a school that never accepted him as she and his brothers had—just for the beautiful person he was. Then she expressed the devastating toll his death had taken on herself and her family, and the horror of the way he died in that lonely, dark canyon. Members of both families were crying as she spoke about her grief and loss.

At the climax of her statement, she addressed Shaun Murphy directly:

> Mr. Murphy, you took my son away from me in the most vicious way I can imagine. You smashed his head with a rock. You were covered with his blood. When you left him that night a year ago in The Pits, not even a mile away from here, you knew you beat him with a rock and you felt it break his skull. You knew how much he was bleeding because you were covered with his blood. You deliberately left him there to die—or already dead. And my son lay there for a week and all you said about it was that you had "bug-smashed a fag."
>
> I think you should be put to death for that. But I know that will not happen. It doesn't even seen to me like you care about what you've done. It looks like you have only cared about yourself since you were arrested. You say you want to be a father to your child, but what kind of father can take a mother's youngest child away from her with no apology whatsoever? It looks to me like you are a dangerous, violent person. The idea that I might see you on the street before too long, free to live your life, is an insult to me and to the memory of my son, Fred. I believe you should be in jail for as much of your life as the law will allow. Because of

you Fred can never become the person he might have been and the world is less for that. Whatever life you have left to you, in jail or not, and whatever freedom you might have after is more than you deserve. You stole my son's life. You broke my family. And you broke my heart.

Throughout Pauline's statement, Murphy remained stone-faced. In his appeal to the court, he pleaded to be understood as a person who was overcome by anger, "a human being who has made a terrible mistake." He must have been hoping that the judge would sentence him on the lighter side of the eight to forty-eight years in prison a conviction of second-degree murder carries with it in Colorado. He apologized to Pauline, asking her to forgive him for taking her son's life because, "My state of being was of intoxicated confusion."

Judge Sharon Hansen agreed that the circumstances of the crime were deplorable. She said, "It's a very tragic situation when we have two young people whose lives have either been ended or altered." And then, with breathtaking swiftness, the judge yanked the tangled bundle of "ugly things" away.

Judge Hansen declared, "Your crime is horrific. I believe you are sincere in that you didn't want this to happen — however, you knew you had injured someone and didn't even make a call. It might have made the difference between life and death." She sentenced Shaun Murphy to forty years in prison for the murder of Fred C. Martinez Jr., plus $300 in court costs and time already served. The gavel came down . . . hard!

Murphy's mother, Angel Murphy Tacaronte, gasped in disbelief, "Did she say forty years? Oh, my God!" As they led him away to begin his sentence, his mother cried out to him, "I love you, son! I love you!"

As sheriff's deputies led him out of the courtroom, and Shaun finally shed tears . . . for himself.

Speaking to a reporter from the *Durango Herald*, Pauline Mitchell dismissed Murphy's apology as insincere. "It was just something that he felt like saying to make him look good," she said. "I don't have any feelings for him. He didn't have any feelings for my son." Questioned by the *Cortez Journal*, John Peters-Campbell said he would have preferred the maximum sentence of forty-eight years. "But this was very close. My main concern was that Pauline would run into [Murphy] on the street five to ten years from now, and that's not going to happen."

GIFTS OF THE CHANGING ONE

If you go to Cortez these days, there is no hint around town that Fred "F.C." Martinez Jr., a Two Spirit lad, ever lived or died there. His memory is a source of discomfort to a community that just wanted to move on after Shaun Murphy was dispatched to prison. Tourists still throng to Cortez that bills itself the "Gateway to Mesa Verde." The calendar is packed with events, seminars, and history tours focused on the ancient Puebloan civilization that built Cliff Palace, Spruce Tree House, and Sun Temple seven hundred years ago.

The stone Panther etched in deep relief outside Montezuma-Cortez High School snarls at passers-by as it did F.C.'s freshman year. Elmwood Trailer Park, its trailers in various stages of disrepair, seems not to have changed either. The Pits still cuts through the south side of town like a scar, and kids still sneak down by night to screw and party, away from the prying eyes of their elders. Poverty and privilege, Navajo and Anglo and Latino, still sit cheek-by-jowl in Cortez, and the queer and the straight still glance over their shoulders at each other, not saying much about how they feel. In June, the Ute Mountain Roundup Rodeo and Carnival comes back to town, filling the dry, cool night air with excitement and the whinnies of stamping horses . . . Just as it did in June of 2001.

No one has started an LGBTQ youth center or Two Spirit program in the Montezuma Valley. Though Coloradans finally saw fit to pass anti-hate crime legislation, they have also passed a state referendum banning same-sex marriage. Even the Navajo Nation, forgetting the immense contributions of Two Spirit people, have clambered on the *bellagona* anti-gay bandwagon, and banned same-sex marriage on the "Rez." But some still refuse to forget F.C. More accurately, they cannot forget the glittering fact of him, in this place of the ancestors, where the *Dineh* find the path of beauty.

"DON'T HATE ME BECAUSE I'M BEAUTIFUL"

The only shrine to F.C. is by the grave where he is buried in the Cortez Cemetery: Block 13, Plot 14. If you are looking for a monument, you won't find one. His grave remains obscure, except to those who know how to find it by heart. Like a metaphor for F.C.'s memory, the small metal marker that bears his name is partially hidden by grass and fading plastic flowers of red and blue. The marker reads, "Fred C. Martinez Jr.

1985—2001. Ertel Funeral Home." The large, expensive portrait head-stone of a beautiful young woman, buried next to F.C. in 2003, obscures his resting place even more. Visitors' eyes are drawn past his resting place to her likeness, fully the woman F.C. had always wanted to be-come, someday. How truly ironic.

Someone attends the grave of F.C., often it seems. Around the nameplate, underneath the trellis of red and blue flowers, someone has arranged *Hot Wheels* cars, and the whimsical little toy Homies, laid low by the wind. Attached to the back of the flowers is a big, blue plastic clothespin, securing four items. One is a weathered, black-banded LED wristwatch, perhaps one that belonged to F.C. himself. The other three items are key rings, the kind with witty, little sayings done in silver and blue. *"Princess,"* is inscribed on one, *"I Have An Attitude, and I Know How to Use It,"* is on another, and the third tugs at the heart: *"Don't Hate Me Because I'm Beautiful."* Most prominent in the modest shrine is a small ceramic of a sad-eyed little boy wrapping his arms around a Mother Goose shoe. On the side of the shoe, in raised, powder blue let-ters, the caption reads, "Baby Boy." A handful of cats-eye marbles fills he shoe, just the sort of things a boy might want to play with if he got bored or lonely. This makeshift memorial is a work of love and remembrance. This is the work of a mother.

According to the "Say Yes Quickly Arts and Media Company," who have filmed a documentary about F.C., his mother Pauline is the one who has left these gifts for him at the grave. On the website announcing the film project, the webmaster writes, "Fred's mother Pauline Mitchell visits the grave with such regularity that two depressions can be seen where she kneels to talk to him in Navajo and English . . . Fred's family has not been able to afford a headstone, but his brothers have designed a modest monument they hoped could someday honor his memory and bring dignity to his final resting place." The filmmakers intend to fund the long-overdue monument at the same time they make their film.

There is strong medicine in the F.C. Martinez Jr. story. It is the med-icine that heals as often as it is told. This is medicine anyone can make who responds to Pauline Mitchell's request, "Please don't forget him."

At the conclusion of the Navajo Night Sing, the *Hatalii* raises the chant called, "The House Made of Dawn." The ailing one, now freed of violence, sickness, and terror, inhales the Dawn's breath to the sound of singing:

Happily I recover.
Happily my interior becomes cool.
Happily my eyes regain their power.
Happily my head becomes cool.
Happily my limbs regain their power.
Happily I hear again.
Happily I walk.

By the restoration of the one who was dis-eased by the ugly things of life, all *The People*—women, men, and *nadleeh* alike—live together in renewed harmony:

Happily the old men will regard you.
Happily the old women will regard you.
Happily the young men will regard you.
Happily the young women will regard you.
Happily the children will regard you.
Happily the chiefs will regard you.
Happily, as they scatter in different directions, they will regard you.
Happily, as they approach their homes, they will regard you.

In the Changing One, all are reconciled. The opposites are united, as two halves of a whole. The stranger becomes the friend. The victim and the offender live in forgiveness. This is the strong medicine the Changing One brings, when "us" and "them" are no more, and everyone is transformed by the beauty that heals:

In beauty I walk.
With beauty before me, I walk.
With beauty behind me, I walk.
With beauty below me, I walk.
With beauty above me, I walk.
With beauty all around me, I walk.
It is finished in beauty,
It is finished in beauty,
It is finished in beauty,
It is finished in beauty![1]

"*Hozhoni, F.C., hozhoni!*": Peace be with you, F.C. Your feet have found the path of beauty.
"*Ya'at eeh!*"

---

1. Bierhorst translation, University of Arizona Press, 1984

For Greater Understanding

Changing One: Fred C. Martinez Jr.

BOOKS

Bierhorst, John. *Four Masterworks of American Indian Literature: Quetzalcoatl, the Ritual of Condolence, Cuceb, the Night Chant.* Tucson, AZ: University of Arizona Press, 1984 (from which the translation of the "House Made of Dawn" is gratefully acknowledged).

Gilley, Brian Joseph. *Becoming Two-Spirit: Gay Identity and Social Acceptance in Indian Country.* Lincoln, NE: University of Nebraska Press, 2006.

Newcomb, Franc J. *Hosteen Klah: Navajo Medicine Man and Sand Painter.* Norman, OK: University of Oklahoma Press, 1964.

Roscoe, Will. *Changing Ones: Third and Fourth Genders in Native North America.* New York: St. Martin's Press, 1998.

Tanis, Justin. "Trans Issues: Defining Transgender." In *Transgendered: Theology, Ministry, and Communities of Faith,* 13-23. Cleveland: The Pilgrim Press, 2003.

FILMS AND VIDEOGRAPHY

Call Me Malcolm. Filmworks, Inc., 2005.

Thorn Grass. Light Circle Films, 2002.

Two Spirits: The Fred Martinez Film Project. Riding the Tiger Productions LLC, 2010.

ORGANIZATIONS AND WEBSITES

Four Corners Gay and Lesbian Alliance for Diversity, http://www.4cglad.org.

Native Out, http://www.nativeout.com.

Unfinished Lives Project, http://unfinishedlivesblog.com.

Scotty Joe Weaver
May 26, 1986—July 18, 2004

BAY MINETTE, ALABAMA

6

Perfect Hatred

Scotty Joe Weaver

"They hated Scotty with a perfect hatred."

—J. DAVID WHETSTONE, ESQ.,
BALDWIN COUNTY (AL) DISTRICT ATTORNEY

SCOTTY JOE WEAVER'S LIFE and death, like a babushka nesting doll, are more than initially meets the eye. Inside the *babushka* (Russian for "grandmother") several figurines nest, each one within the next. The characters within the doll alternate genders as they diminish in size: female to male, male to female. Finally one gets to the enigmatic last figure, the baby, who is indivisible and cannot be opened further. To recover who Scotty Joe was in life, to get to his indivisible, convoluted soul, we have to get past his babushka, "Ol' Granny Death." The first thing the outside world ever knew of Scotty was the manner of his murder. It is unlikely that we would ever have noticed him otherwise, just another young gender non-conforming person forlornly scratching out an existence in rampantly anti-gay South Alabama. Like the portly babushka who holds a rooster in her arms and all the other figurines inside herself, Scotty's tortured death overshadows his life and contains his manifold mystery. Granny Death holds his multiple identities deep within her viscera: Scotty the little boy, Dolly the drag queen, Martha's dear son, gay brother Lum Jr.'s flamboyant little bro, Alabama's forgotten child. The investigation of one aspect of his life leads to another, and another, and another. At the core lies the soul of a person caught between youth and adulthood, scarred by disappointments and struggles most young men his age never have to face.

Scotty, who was murdered at the hands of three houseguests who should have been his friends, seems outwardly to have been a simple person. Like other 18-year-olds from Baldwin County, just thirty miles northeast of Mobile, his life was circumscribed by the rural culture of South Alabama. Though Mobile's skyscrapers were visible from across the Bay, Scotty's family could just as well have been socially and culturally on the far side of the moon rather than just across the bridge and through the Bay Tunnel. Mobile's population of 200,000 bears the heritage of the plantation South, haunted by memories of the War Between the States, festooned with banks of azaleas and draperies of Spanish moss hanging from the live oak trees. Scotty's hometown, Bay Minette, population 7,800, inherited the lot of the sharecropper South, old mules and hard memories. For generations, Mobile has been the Big House; Baldwin County has been the outbuildings where "the help" lives.

Scotty Joe was born into a family of hard-working, blue-collar folks, the baby of four brothers. He dropped out of high school. Those who knew him predicted that had he not died such an untimely death, Scotty would have lived a normal lifespan in Bay Minette in relative anonymity. He had gotten a job he liked well enough, working as a "traveling associate" (a short order cook) for Waffle House. He also waited tables, ran a cash register, and cleaned up wherever he was assigned in the general area. Like half the residents in Bay Minette, he lived in a mobile home. He was proud that he could finally afford his own place, and liked to show off the aluminum-sided trailer he rented in the Dobbins Trailer Park.

MAKE-A-WISH BOY

As District Attorney David Whetstone put it, Scotty was a "good boy with limited horizons." His dearest wish when he was a little boy reveals the set of blinders he wore, and the small world he inhabited. Scotty was a "Make-A-Wish Child." When he was ten, he contracted an ear infection, and a knot rose on the side of his neck that grew as big as an egg. The diagnosis was Hodgkin's disease, a form of glandular cancer often fatal in children. His mother Martha, reflected with a reporter for the *Mobile Register* on his childhood ordeal, and she wept as she recalled how hard it was to watch him suffer. "I came close to losing him then," she said, biting her upper lip. "I was afraid they were going to come in and say the treatments were not doing any good." During the harsh, two-year regimen of chemotherapy, someone nominated Scotty to the Georgia-Alabama Chapter of the Make-A-Wish Foundation for a final dream-come-true. His situation was dire enough that the foundation board granted it.

Many Make-A-Wish children from Alabama set their sights on Disney World, or want to see New York City, or go to Hollywood, or wish to meet an astronaut. Not Scotty Joe. His fondest wish, the experience most vividly mirrored in his mind, was to go the thirty miles west across the bridge and attend a Mobile Bay Bears minor league baseball game. The constricted diameter of his world would remain the same throughout his life.

While most children struggling against a deadly disease have their hands full with the day-to-day business of survival, Scotty was different. Rather than hungering for reassurance from his parents, he reached out to comfort *them*. Throughout his illness, he was curiously strong. Leigh Ann Kircharr, a niece of Scotty's uncle by marriage, recalled for the *Mobile Register*, "He was really tough. He was strong. He always said, 'This cancer's not going to beat me. I'm going to beat it.'"

Scotty beat his disease by grit and hope. Though the chemotherapy ravaged him, he somehow managed to keep most of his ample brown hair. The battle with Hodgkin's did not embitter him. The sensitive and affectionate side of his personality actually improved in the wake of his ordeal. He became more affectionate, more attentive to the needs of others. Kircharr remembered, "He made sure he told people he loved them if he did."

By the time he turned fourteen, Scotty faced another crisis in his young life. His father, Lum Sr., died unexpectedly at the age of forty-two, leaving his mother, Martha Varner Weaver, to rear him as best she could. D.A. David Whetstone said of her, "She was uneducated, with limited resources, poverty stricken . . . her children were so important to her." With four boys, she had her hands full. Two of them, Lum Jr., the eldest, and Scotty Joe, were both gay. Martha knew about her two gay sons. She always said, "If you love your child, it doesn't matter." But she worried, especially about Scotty.

GAUNTLET RUNNER

Bay Minette, Alabama is not the sort of place to grow up gay and be comfortable about it. The county seat of rural Baldwin County, Bay Minette is a hard-working, God-fearing community of blue-collar folks. People mostly make their living off the land, though, as the locals say, "right many" of them work in the big International Paper container plant where they make corrugated boxes and egg crates. To say growing up as a gay adolescent in the Bay Minette public schools is a "challenge," is too timid a word. Public school was hell for Scotty.

To friends and relatives who did not know about Scotty's evolving queer identity, his trouble adjusting to school must have looked like a combination of usual teenage angst and distress over his father's death. His cousin, Tonya Miller, mirrored that too-simplistic understanding of Scotty's struggle throughout his mid-teen years. "He was just real depressed and would act out," she told the *Mobile Register*, "but I think that's normal teenage stuff." Scotty began to rebel against his mother, refusing to listen to her, spiraling into discouragement. The missing piece of the puzzle, even to those closest to him, was that his sense of ostracism from other boys his age was increasing week-by-week. He was discovering gay thoughts and feelings he could share with no one in the family, with the possible exception of his older brother, Lum. Unlike Lum, however, eight years his senior, and who had cultivated the ability to pass as straight, Scotty either couldn't pass or didn't want to. Lum tried to talk with him, to warn him about what could happen to him if he didn't watch out. In the end, however, Lum had to accept that "[Scotty] was just being himself." He was developing a reputation for being "that way" in school, and kids were beginning to sling epithets at him because he presented more femininely than other boys and even a few of the girls. His voice was effeminate, high pitched, a sure trigger for catcalls and bullying. School had become an exercise in running the gauntlet, a place of dread where the lessons he learned were that he was not welcome or even safe. For four months following his daddy's death, Scotty sank deeper into depression, and got in trouble in school. After he took off in a funk one day with her car, Martha decided to send him over to Dothan, two hundred miles to the east, to try going to middle school there.

He came back to Bay Minette and enrolled in high school for the 2001–2002 school year. After only three months back home, he was identified as an "emotionally troubled youth," and was enrolled in the county mental health department's "ACE initiative," self-described as "a therapeutic program for high school students whose emotional and behavioral problems hinder their normal functioning in school and at home." There he met the person who would be his best friend for the duration of his life, Justin Toth. They were the same age. Like Justin, Scotty loved music: rap, hip-hop, and pop. They appreciated the same sorts of movies, too. But what truly bonded Scotty and Justin was the fact that both of them were gay in hostile territory.

Both boys struggled with depression. Little wonder. According to Michael Faenza, former president of the National Mental Health Association, 78 percent of teens who are suspected of being gay are harassed in school because of it. "When bullied, gay youth and those thought to be gay face an increased risk for depression, anxiety disorders, school failure and suicide," Faenza writes for the Trevor Project Hotline, a service designed to help LGBTQ youth in danger of killing themselves (www.TrevorProject.org). Justin and Scotty had all the risk factors. Scotty skipped town on more than one occasion, offering his friend no other explanation than that he was "staying with somebody in Mobile." When pressed about why, or with whom he was staying, Scotty didn't want to talk about it. When they both turned sixteen, Justin said, they made a suicide pact. Justin claims that he never took their oath seriously—they didn't even set a date to carry it out. But Scotty embraced it with deadly seriousness. He acted on it. Four or five months after he had sealed the pact with Justin, Scotty Joe slashed his wrists. Justin says he never knew what set his friend off, but as a result, Scotty was sent away to a state mental health facility for several months.

The next two years in school proved unendurable. Though he returned to Baldwin County High School in September 2002, he dropped out after a few weeks. Martha didn't know what to do anymore. The courts ordered him to return to the ACE program. Scotty tried one more time at BCHS, starting the 2003–2004 school year there. What was going on behind the scenes was the public schools' open secret: *Queers attend at their own risk.* Classmates tormented Scotty for his homosexuality daily. Students constantly called him "weird," "queer," and "faggot." Justin remembered, "He was ridiculed pretty hard for [being gay], because it was Bay Minette. Bay Minette is pretty old fashioned about that." Destannie Edmonson, a student who knew Scotty, told *WKRG-TV*, "Everybody talked about him real bad, and they acted like they hated him." Another of his classmates, Jessica Jones, revealed her astonishing naïveté to the

Mobile Register about what was swirling around Scotty Joe. "It was pretty much kids being kids," she said. "I didn't think they took it to the point where it was harassment. I never thought it got to the point where he wouldn't finish school."

The crisis came later that year when a gang of boys shouting slurs at Scotty cornered him in the school toilet, threatening "to beat his ass." No one in authority at school ever protected him. BCHS Principal Eddie Mitchell refused to allow that Scotty was at risk in his high school. The way he presented Scotty Joe to the press after his murder subtly insinuated that Scotty was an ongoing problem, bouncing in and out of school, facing court-mandated ACE attendance, all of which was true from a certain point of view. Mitchell claimed that he had no recollection of Scotty ever complaining to school officials about any form of bullying. "Certainly, if we know of it, and it's reported to us, we address it and come to some sort of a solution," he told investigative reporter for the *Mobile Register,* Brendan Kirby.

Principal Mitchell was well aware of Scotty's troubled school career. He could not have avoided noticing how Scotty spoke and presented himself. The conditions were ripe for anti-gay harassment in the corridors of BCHS. School staff had to have been deaf, dumb, and blind not to know it. Scotty's previous difficulties and personality should have been red flags to any teacher or administrator. But Scotty had not squealed on the bullies in the toilet, and for good reason. To snitch on them would probably have made their violent retaliation even more certain. If the teachers and administrators were in touch with negative community feelings about homosexuality at all, we are left to wonder at the degree of official denial—or perhaps possible collusion with student bias—Scotty had to face simply to remain in school. In effect, they had washed their hands of him. No one from the school system seems to have investigated why he finally dropped out. For Scotty Joe, the risk he faced had become too great. Justin said, "He felt that if the school couldn't provide a safe environment, he wasn't going to go there."

BACKWOODS BARBIE DOLL

Things began to click for Scotty Joe once he dropped out of high school. He flirted with getting his GED, and told friends he would like to be an architect or a health care professional some day. But school was finished for him for good, and he needed a job. He applied to be a grill operator at the local Waffle House, and started work right away: minimum wage, $5.15 an hour. The "WaHo" subculture appealed to him. The diner started him off on second shift, when business was lightest, to learn the routine alongside a senior cook. A grill operator is the key to making profit in the Waffle House system. A good grill operator with a blue star certification can sling $200 worth of hash an hour by himself, or $250 with an assistant line cook at his side. *Hire 'im cheap, train 'im good, push 'im hard*, and a WaHo grill master can earn the store enough in an hour to pay for his salary all week.

Scotty Joe's co-workers liked him. He was easy to talk to, good with the wait staff, quick with a spatula, and nice to the customers, even the drunks during the wee hours of the graveyard shift. Though he was obviously gay, that was seldom a problem, because, as one of his neighbors said, "He wasn't cartwheel gay," at least. Management promoted him to "traveling associate," which meant he was assigned as needed to any of the area WaHo locations. It also meant that he could work double shifts, bringing home from $400 to $500 in a good week.

Scotty Joe was rockin' and rollin'. He had money to save for the first time, and usually had enough money on him to help people out, if they asked him. His family and friends began to feel that he had turned a corner in his life. He was happier, better able to cope, and as his friend Justin said, "less my-way-or-the-highway." When he approached his mother to ask for financial help with the deposit to rent and fix up a two-bedroom trailer he could call his own, she was receptive. In a relatively short time, Scotty had gone from being a besieged student who couldn't seem to catch a break to a self-sufficient, confident corporate employee. Nothing seemed to make him prouder than to visit his mom on payday to repay her, and help *her* out for a change.

Scotty's newfound freedom caused his feminine persona to blossom, too. From his boyhood, he had been attracted to cosmetics and cross-dressing. Lum Jr. had also dabbled in female impersonation, and Scotty used to borrow makeup from him, experimenting with wigs, dresses and high heels. Leigh Ann Kircharr recalled the first time she passed Scotty dressed like a woman on the street. Scotty was wearing makeup, a tight shirt, and girl jeans, complimented by a set of high heels. Leigh Ann told reporter Brendan Kirby that she did a double take, but realizing it was Scotty, she just "wrote it off" as part of his nature. As his circumstances changed, he was becoming more comfortable with his sexual identity. Though he started appearing in public more often as a woman, he knew he couldn't do so everywhere. He dressed as expected for work, and around his mother and brothers. Leigh Ann like others in the family didn't think less of him for the feminine way he presented himself. As she saw it, he was just being consistent with who he was. "He was still Scotty," she said. "His personality didn't change."

It must have been exhilarating for Scotty to flout convention, spread his wings, and try out aspects of his sexual identity that he had dared not express publically before. Like a butterfly emerging from its chrysalis, Scotty Joe was testing the limits of his own psyche and of his conservative hometown. Boundaries between male and female had always been blurry for him. Now, he was actively transgressing those boundaries with a frequency and a boldness that began to concern his inner circle of support.

His cross-dressing morphed into a full-blown drag persona. The weekly "Drag-o-rama" contests at the Emerald City, a gay dance club in nearby Pensacola, Florida, gave him an outlet to "get fixed up" and strut his stuff. Open to all forms of drag, "Em City" lived up to its name for many South Alabama and Panhandle Florida queer folk. "Dorothys" from all the surrounding small towns followed the storied yellow brick road in search of good times, adventure, glamour, and fame. Unlike Mobile, where admission to gay bars was by membership only, and restricted to 21-year-olds and above, Pensacola was less uptight about the age of drag contestants. Gay teenagers could get into Em City legally and compete with veteran drag queens and other budding princesses like themselves for cash prizes and gigs on the drag circuit.

Scotty Joe idolized Dolly Parton, and chose her to be his drag avatar. Dolly, a gay rights advocate, claims affinity with the men who impersonate her. She once said to her gay fans, "It's a good thing I'm a real woman, because if I wasn't I'd have to be a big ol' drag queen!" Seeing men who come to her shows looking more like her than she herself does delights her. "I think its cute and fun and a great compliment," she says. "Lots and lots of drag queens come to my shows. I change the words to 'Jolene' for them," and then she belts out, "'Drag queen, drag queen, drag que-e-een, I'm begging of you please don't take my man!'" With her Pigeon Forge twang and a toss of her bottle blonde locks, she laughs, "They get a big kick out of that."

Scotty modeled his stage character on Dolly's floozy sassiness. He must have identified with her refusal to submit to a moral straightjacket.

Dolly had broken free of the puritanical taboos of the hills and hollers where she was born. Offered only two choices by her native Pentecostal, holy-roller church culture, either to be a married woman and have a bunch of kids or remain single and have a bunch of kids, she chose to shave her legs and wear makeup like a local prostitute she admired. "I felt this woman was absolutely beautiful," she said. "She wore short skirts, high-heeled shoes, hair piled on top of her head and lipstick and nail polish." Though everybody called her "trash," Dolly defied them all, and chose this fallen woman to be her ideal. "I thought, 'That's what I want to be when I grow up,'" she said, looking back on her youth.

Dolly's rags-to-riches story inspires devotees all over the globe, and impersonating her on stage gave Scotty a chance to hitch his hopes to her pink Cadillac, if only for the little while he was on the Emerald City catwalk. With a regular paycheck, he could afford some stylish, flashy dresses, great heels, and a knock out blonde wig. Photos of him in full Dolly drag show that, for an amateur, he had her down pat. Lum attended Scotty's rehearsals, and suggested how to make his routine better. "He loved to be onstage, and he loved to make people laugh," he said. Like a thousand other men across the drag spectrum, Scotty perfected lip-synching Dolly's classic hits, most popular among them, "I Will Always Love You." He was good enough to place second at Em City, winning a cash prize and a performance slot on another fabulous night at the Drag-o-rama.

SWIMMING WITH 'GATORS

Martha Weaver worried about Scotty Joe performing his drag routine in public. She confided to Baldwin County District Attorney David Whetstone that she had warned him to be careful. "She worried someone could really hurt him," Whetstone said. Though the D.A. never met Scotty in life, he became a student of him in his death. Now retired to the South Baldwin town of Gulf Shores, Whetstone received his post when Governor George Wallace appointed him in 1984, and kept his position until 2006. "Scotty was a good boy," Whetstone says, "very friendly, easy to talk to. He was very trusting. But his sexual attraction to men made him a target. I think his lifestyle made his life not as valuable in some people's minds." Justin Toth, Scotty's best friend, agrees. Like some other gay men, Scotty seems to have been infatuated with straights as possible sex partners. "Scotty had a little problem with coming on to straight men, and he'd get in trouble," he told the *Mobile Register*.

To Whetstone, the problem wasn't so much that Scotty Joe was gay, or even that he was attracted to straight men from time to time. The problem was Scotty's obvious gender presentation. "In Bay Minette," Whetstone said, "it would have been very hard to have sex with Scotty. He was too female in aspect, he drew attention to himself and any prospective partner." He went on, "Scotty's way of being gay would give offense while the manner of some other homosexuals would not." North Baldwin County was slow to change its attitudes about sexual orientation. Whetstone pointed out to *Mobile Register* reporter Samira Jafari, "In Alabama, we have very little violent crime against race. We've gone past that in our state. We're not there yet in lifestyle changes," he continued. "We haven't arrived yet to more acceptance."

Unaware of his impending peril, Scotty Joe was running out of time. From the date he rented his green-trimmed trailer on approximately the first of July in 2004, he would have less than three weeks to live. For one thing, "WaHo" (Waffle House) wasn't "WeHo" (famously gay West Hollywood). Some bad seed knew where he worked the graveyard shift, and they were bent on harassing him. Scotty's mom told the local NBC-TV affiliate about some young men who barged into the Waffle House in early July during third shift, calling him a "faggot." It happened more than once in those few weeks. In a response on a blog, an anonymous Bay Minette resident recalled that about a week before Scotty's murder, she and her husband went out on the town, and stopped by the Waffle House late before going back home. "Scotty just happened to be working that night," she wrote *Frank's Wild Lunch*, a popular blog. "Some guys were giving him a hard time and he was trying to be so nice. For some reason, he kind of stuck in my head. When I saw on the news what happened, I was so sad, like I had lost a friend as well."

The taunts troubled Scotty Joe, maybe even scared him. Like his elder brother, he knew about "smear the queer" rituals locals carried out when the sun went down. Lum recounted how nighttime was the most dangerous for LGBTQ people. Since everybody in a small town knows everybody else, gay residences were easily targeted by hoodlums speeding by in their muffler-less pickup trucks. Screeching the Rebel Yell and shouting obscenities, they would hurl beer bottles against the sides of trailers at any time of night. Some of Lum's friends found "faggot" spray painted on the sides of their cars. It was not unusual for gay youth to be beaten, if they were caught out alone. Scotty also knew about the super-pious folks locals called "Bible-humpers," who regularly breathed fire and brimstone against gays and lesbians, invoking the wrath of God to destroy them. District Attorney Whetstone doesn't mince words about the responsibility of the religious community in Scotty Joe's death. "As long as people preach hatred," he says, "things like these are going to happen."

Looking back, the stage had been set for murder in twenty-first-century Alabama years before a knife ever grazed Scotty Joe's throat. For example, the furor over Billy Jack Gaither's murder in Sylacauga with an ax handle back in 1999 had already died down after his killers were locked up for life without parole. Billy Jack's murderers had written the need for anti-LGBTQ hate crimes legislation in innocent blood, but supporters in Montgomery couldn't find the votes to pass it.

The same sort of unholy alliance between religion, vigilante justice, and the courts that had fueled KKK lynchings of Blacks in the twentieth century formed again to lash out at LGBTQ people and their allies. Barely three years after Billy Jack's murder, Chief Justice of the Alabama Supreme Court, Judge Roy Moore, issued one of the most homophobic judicial opinions in the history of the United States. Moore, who gained national notoriety by planting a Ten Commandments monument the size of a fifty-five-gallon garbage barrel in front of the state judicial building, attached a fourteen-page "special concurrence" to a decision which denied a lesbian mother custody of her three teenage children. In it, Alabama's top judge went on record, pontificating that homosexuality was "abhorrent, immoral, detestable, a crime against nature." Same-sex practice, he declared, is "an act so heinous that it defies one's ability to describe it," an "inherent evil" which "should never be tolerated." Moore then inveighed against those who persisted in gay sex, threatening that the state might need to exercise the biblical "power of the sword" against such abominators.

Journalist Bob Moser remembered that long-time LGBTQ rights advocate Ken Baker predicted what would happen to LGBTQ Alabamians as a consequence of Judge Moore's screed. Barely two years later, Scotty Joe was tortured to death. "All [Judge Moore] didn't do was hand out the rope," Baker said.

TEAM ROPING

Nicole Kelsay had a baby boy, but no husband and no job. Her boy-friend, Chris Gaines, didn't have a job either, and they needed a place to stay. It was high summer, and hot in Bay Minette. Generous to a fault, Scotty Joe invited them to stay with him in his newly rented trailer. We do not know the terms of their agreement. Were his houseguests to help with the rent, or to buy groceries? Early friction between them suggests that they initially agreed to such a deal, and that they skunked their host. What we do know, however, is that nothing in Scotty's life could have turned out worse.

Nicole Bryars Kelsay, 18, had known Scotty Joe since the first grade. Scotty also knew 20-year-old Christopher Ryan Gaines from grade school. Maybe Scotty's special feelings for Nicole and her infant son moved him to offer the trio a place to stay. Nicole is a willowy girl with long, mousey brown hair that dangles to her waistline. She has sleepy brown eyes, and a vanishing chin. A ninth grade drop out, she told investigators, "I don't understand school." She thought she was in love with a man once (before she took up with Chris Gaines), married him, got pregnant by him, and then couldn't stand him any longer. At least she thought her husband was the father of her child. She couldn't be sure. Soon after getting married in January 2004, her newly minted husband turned himself in to jail on a robbery charge. The breakup was ugly. Though she had temporary custody of her baby boy, her ex contested her in court for the child. She was not the sort of girl to be alone for long, and she struck up a hot new romance between herself and Chris Gaines.

Scotty's mother, Martha, said to the press after his murder that Scotty was "confused" about his sexuality. Scotty's affection for Kelsay seemed to support her claim. Martha said that besides "loving her to death"—to the point that Scotty Joe would have done "anything for her"—he had actually proposed marriage to her. Martha, however inadvertently, was also the person who outed Scotty Joe's gay sexual orientation and his participation in drag contests to the press. Martha's sense of betrayal toward Kelsay grew strong enough to make this shy woman confront Kelsay during her sentencing hearing, demanding why she had done such a terrible thing to her son. Perhaps Scotty's mother counted on a marriage between the two of them more than he himself did. Was he as "confused" about his sexual identity as his mother wanted to believe? Whatever Scotty would have said about his sexual attraction for Nicole, we cannot know. Yet he was not the first or the last predominantly gay man to seek out a relationship with a woman. Whether he was attracted to her sexually or not, Kelsay was unavoidably aware of Scotty Joe's sexual interest in men, and she and Gaines claimed to have gone with Scotty to gay clubs in Pensacola and Mobile.

In those summer days of 2004, Scotty felt his possibilities open up wide. School was little more than a bad memory for him by then. The Waffle House gave him a sense of purpose and a paycheck that had put rent, food, cosmetics, stylish clothes, and generosity within his reach for the first time in his life. What was to stop him from believing he could also have a family, a wife and a baby that he could care for as his own? He could work more double shifts. He could quiet some of the rampant objections to his effeminate manner with a woman he cared about, and besides, didn't she already know everything about how he was?

Chris Gaines didn't like Scotty's encroachment on his girlfriend. He objected to a "queer" like Scotty having anything beyond friendship with a woman, much less *his* woman. Gaines, a slight man with dirty blond hair and icy blue eyes, sported a ring in his left ear lobe. Among the thirteen or fourteen tattoos inked on his body are a Nazi swastika and another that reads, "Little Psycho." Thanks to the work of David Ferrara of the *Press-Register*, we know a good deal about his background, none of it good. Gaines flunked out of high school. He had a vicious disposition, and was quite capable of hurting somebody. After a donnybrook with his stepfather in 2002, Gaines faced a charge of third-degree domestic violence. The judge dropped the charge when Gaines enlisted in the Alabama National Guard, the 711th Signal Battalion. He lasted for five months, until December 2003 when he was discharged for reasons the Guard kept quiet. Had he remained in the service just one more month, he would have shipped out with his unit to Iraq.

The law caught up with Gaines in March 2004. Arrested for six counts of writing bad checks, he pleaded guilty. The judge sentenced him to a ninety-day suspended sentence for each count, and he received twenty-four months of probation. Two charges were still pending at the time he moved into Scotty's trailer with Kelsay. Though Scotty Joe paid for the roof over his head and his other living expenses, Gaines chafed at the arrangement in the trailer, and tried to assert his dominance. He, not Scotty, was supposed to be the man of the house. What kind of "man" was Scotty, anyway? Gaines's ill feelings toward Scotty lurked in the background, dating back to high school. Destannie Edmonson, a schoolmate of both Chris and Scotty Joe, said that Gaines acted like he hated Scotty, something she knew for a fact, since she had heard the way he talked about his homosexuality "all the time" behind his back.

There was an uneasy truce between Scotty Joe and Gaines for the sake of Kelsay and her child until Robert Holly Loften Porter showed up. Kelsay started letting him sleep on the couch while Scotty was work-ing late nights. Scotty had made no agreement for a fourth free rider (including Nicole's baby), but Gaines started acting like an "alpha dog," asserting that he ought to have the say about who could come into the house. Tensions built between the three men, with Scotty reminding them whose trailer home it was.

Porter, 18, a friend of Gaines's from their days together in juvenile detention, is dark haired, mustachioed, and feral in appearance. Like Gaines and Kelsay, he was broke and had no job. He was born in Bayou La Batre, a fishing village in extreme southern Mobile County. By the age of two, his family had moved to Bay Minette. He just couldn't get along with other kids, landing into trouble often as a youth. He spent two years at a disciplinary boot camp in Montgomery as a teenager, but eventually dropped out of school anyway. Brendan Kirby, reporting for the *Mobile Register*, uncovered that Porter had plenty of legal trouble. He had a violent streak, and went wild when he got mad. Earlier that July, he and an older woman harassed and attempted to beat up another Bay Minette woman who filed a complaint of criminal mischief against them for trying to break down her door in the middle of the night. "He just had a wild look in his eye," the victim said to Kirby. "It really freaked me out."

In Scotty's absence, the bitching and backbiting rose to a fever pitch. Gaines complained about Scotty Joe's expectations and his gall, believing he of all people could be affectionate toward Kelsay. Scotty told neigh-bors in the trailer park that Kelsay and Gaines had stolen food and tips from his Waffle House job, and had refused to pay rent. He tried to evict them, but they wouldn't leave. Porter was an instigator. He was vocal about hating all homosexuals, and "that fag" in particular, and declared that he wanted to kill Scotty. Within three days of Porter's arrival at the trailer, a lethal plot started to form against Scotty. Gaines told Kelsay and Porter that things were coming to a head and somebody was going to have to move out. When it came to making somebody move out, Porter said he knew how to do it, "Tony Soprano style." On July 16, only two days before the fatal attack, Porter nearly assaulted Scotty in the parking lot of a convenience store, and Gaines had to restrain him.

In the early hours of Sunday, July 18, Scotty dropped by his mother's place after working the graveyard shift at the Bay Minette Waffle House. He repaid the loan she gave him to help him rent the trailer, and then went back home to get some rest before his early shift the next day. He fell asleep on the couch. Kelsay, Gaines and Porter slipped into the trailer, and ambushed him in his sleep. The boys garroted him with a rope they had bought at Wal-Mart. Their plan was to tie Scotty up, drown him, tie his body to a rock, and sink him in Mobile Bay for the crabs to take care of the body. It didn't work out that way. In fact, what unfolded as the struggle ensued, and as Scotty pleaded with them for his life, stretches the limits of horror.

In retirement, former Baldwin County District Attorney Whetstone has a freedom to speak out in a way he could not as an elected official. He headed the investigation team that apprehended Scotty's killers. He built the case against Kelsay, Gaines, and Porter. At his order, Scotty's charred remains were shipped to a top forensic pathology team to reconstruct the details of the attack. The only reason Whetstone says that he regrets retiring is that he personally wanted to prosecute the Weaver case. "A lot more happened to him than came out in court or in the media," he said. "It was a heinous, atrocious, and cruel crime. If everything had gotten out," which he says would have happened under his authority, "it would have shocked the country."

Whetstone recounts, "This was a calculating, cold-blooded, savage murder—it wasn't a spur-of-the-moment murder. They did a poor job of choking him down—it was harder to do than they thought it was going to be—and then they tortured him for hours." Porter held his feet as Gaines throttled Scotty with the nylon rope. According to court testimony, Scotty begged for his life, "Please, Chris, stop! Please, Chris, stop!" Kelsay idly by, witnessing the whole horror show, hearing his screams and pleas. She could have warned him not to go into the trailer that night. Instead, she was part of the plot from the beginning, helping to lure Scotty unsuspectingly to his doom. To Whetstone, though she was less hands-on than Porter and Gaines, Kelsay held her benefactor in no less contempt than the men. To them Scotty was no more than a "meal ticket." "His life didn't count to any of them," Whetstone said.

"They believed him to be sub-human, and in their minds justified what they were doing, thinking, 'This guy needed killing.' But first he needed to suffer, to feel pain."

The old D.A. acknowledges that robbery figured into their motives for murdering Scotty Joe. Saturday was a payday. Porter lifted less than $80 out of his pockets during the slaughter. Gaines drove around with Scotty's bankcard, cell phone, and ID in his glove compartment days after the murder. Whetstone believes they expected to get between $200 and $500 that night. But he is rock solid in his professional assessment that this heinous murder was triggered by anti-gay prejudice. "At least 60 percent of the motive [for this homicide] was his lifestyle. I am sure of that," he said, reiterating for emphasis, "I am *convinced* they targeted him because of his lifestyle."

Forensic evidence describes how Scotty Joe was strangled, beaten, and then tortured with "edged weapons"—probably wielded by more than one assailant. Gaines and Porter inflicted multiple jab and stab wounds before Scotty Joe's death, and then they mutilated the body after he died. During the early days of the investigation, Whetstone noted the "overkill" Scotty's murderers indulged in, characteristic of anti-LGBTQ hate crimes, only hinting to the press about "curious" wounds imposed on the corpse. Now unrestrained by pending trials, the retired D.A. candidly revealed the bestial lengths to which anti-gay hate killers will go. "Before [Scotty Joe] died, they carved the letter "H" for "homosexual" in his cheek. They also mutilated his genitals," he said. "And, the pathologist reported that his anus was carved out with a knife of some kind." Courtroom testimony of Dr. Kathleen Enstice of the Alabama Department of Forensic Sciences established that Scotty suffered two stab wounds to his face, at least nine to his chest, and multiple other cuts to several parts of his body.

WILEY OL' HE-COON

To Whetstone, the attack on Scotty Joe's anus is the signature of pure hatred for who he was. "What they did to him was awful," he said, "an act of unmitigated hate. Their hatred caused Scotty to suffer more than other people because they just wanted him to." The press had dubbed D.A. Whetstone a "he-coon" in honor of the way he survived and thrived in Baldwin County, prosecuting such high profile cases as the murder and immolation of an alleged child molester, bringing the killer of over three thousand greyhound racing dogs to justice, and investigating the arson of two North Baldwin Black churches in Alabama's first anti-religious hate crimes trial. A "he-coon," in southern-speak, is the smartest raccoon in the pack, the one wise enough to elude all his predators and survive. Bringing his lifetime of expertise and savvy to bear on the evidence carved into Scotty Joe's body, Whetstone surmised that one or both of his young male attackers penetrated Scotty sexually while they were killing him. Though he admitted that the evidence was inconclusive, and that the anus could have been sliced out of the boy either while he lay dying or very soon after, he has no doubt that rape was involved. "Although we could not find enough evidence one way or another, I believe those boys had anal sex with him," he said. "They stabbed him and jabbed him with knives, and in an act of total disrespect for him, they desecrated his body." With anger under careful control, D.A. Whetstone growled, "They cut out his *anus!* They assaulted his sexual organ as a rapist would assault a woman's *uterus!* It is not uncommon to see attacks on genitals. Either they were striking out against the part [of his body] they hated, or they were trying to make sure that no evidence would remain of what they had done." After a long pause, he continued, "Those boys would rather go to the electric chair than to admit they had sex with him."

Then they delivered the *coup de grace*: they partially decapitated him, rolled him in a blanket, dragged him from the floor into bed, and finally left Scotty Joe undisturbed for the first time since the unspeakable horrors began hours before.

Kelsay, Gaines and Porter had originally intended to throw his body into the bay, but he had died too slowly, and his body was too heavy for them to carry out to the water. So they bought gasoline, since they reasoned that it was cheaper and easier to burn him than to sink him, and on the way returned the rope they hadn't thrown in the bay to the Wal-Mart in Loxley. They exchanged it for a refund of seventy-seven cents. Then, they bought themselves Slurpees which they enjoyed before going to Kelsay's mother's house to play dominos and cards. Only afterward they went back to collect the body.

Porter and Gaines went back to the trailer after their Slurpees. Retrieving Scotty's ravaged body and then dumping it in the trunk of Gaines's car, they drove eight miles out to a deserted place in the woods. Lying him on the ground face-up, they urinated on him as a last act of desecration, soaked his remains with the gasoline, and torched him. There his body lay, burned beyond recognition, decomposing for four days.

Kelsay, Gaines, and Porter coolly went about their daily lives as usual after the murder. Gaines later claimed that he and Kelsay had sex in Scotty Joe's bed a couple of days after they killed him. When Scotty didn't report for his shift on Sunday, and didn't call his mother, an ominous feeling crept into Martha's heart. It wasn't like him not to let her know where he was. Two days after Scotty disappeared, Kelsay and Gaines dropped by to see her, feigning worry, and asked if she had heard from Scotty. Something about their demeanor triggered her fears, and on Thursday, July 22, she filed a missing person's report with the Sheriff's Department.

On that same day, a man driving an all-terrain vehicle off of a dirt road eight miles from town, nearly drove through the charred remains of what had been a human being. Dental records were the only means of establishing that the body was Scotty Joe's.

ODE TO SCOTTY JOE

As news spread throughout the Bay area and around the state that Scotty Joe had possibly been murdered so gruesomely because of his sexual orientation, alarm spread in the LGBTQ community. Though Mobile has a large gay and lesbian population, it is by no means comfortable being "out." Long-time leaders like Tony Thompson, an executive of the historic Battle House Hotel, and Suzanne Cleveland, organizer of Mobile's PFLAG (Parents and Friends of Lesbians and Gays), reached out to other activists throughout Alabama to converge on Bay Minette and bring national attention to Scotty Joe's murder. Encouraged by the vigor with which District Attorney Whetstone was pursuing this case, Thompson, a founder of Bay Area Inclusion, Mobile's LGBTQ service center, hastily organized a vigil in Mobile's Washington Park. Few who knew Scotty Joe were there, but over a hundred people gathered to hear speakers from Mobile, Montgomery, Tuscaloosa, and Birmingham call for justice for a boy crushed in the jaws of homophobia.

Eight days after the discovery of Scotty Joe's charred remains, a standing-room-only crowd of 250 mourners converged on tiny Cross Roads Church of God for his funeral. A dark blue casket sprinkled with images of small white turtledoves occupied the front of the little chancel and held what was left of his body. A blanket of gorgeous red roses, Scotty's favorite flower, covered the lid. Someone brought a photo of him, young and full of life, smiling as he sat in a red kayak. The whole family attended: Martha, supported by Lum, and Scotty's other brothers, Cecil Lavon Weaver and David Weaver. Many in the congregation that morning were LGBTQ people, who came to support the family, grieve, and honor Scotty Joe.

Precious little comfort came from the pulpit for anyone that day, however. Reverend Helen Stewart seized the opportunity to confront so many queer folk with the error of their ways. "She made a lot of people mad, saying basically that Scotty Joe was in hell," Lum recalled. "She told us pretty much that we were all going to hell if we didn't change our ways." When the anti-gay tirade got so bad, several people just walked out. Martha and her family had turned to the only spiritual home she knew, and it betrayed them when they needed its love and support the most.

D.A. Whetstone and the Sheriff's Department pursued their investigation with a passion and professionalism that surprised the citizens of Baldwin County, and caught Scotty's killers off guard, too. Swiftly, Kelsay, Gaines, and Porter were in custody. They were shocked that anyone would care about a "queer" like Scotty. According to Whetstone, the murderers assumed that they would be able to get away with murder because of who and what Scotty Joe was. Even Martha Weaver "was not expecting the strength of our response to her son's murder," Whetstone recalled. The D.A. and his team knew the case would serve as a referendum on a small town like Bay Minette—and its most deeply held beliefs about LGBTQ people. "An insistence that justice will be done drove us," he said.

Attitudes about the impending trials were split, Whetstone remembers. Some in the religious community contended that these young people were the instruments of God's wrath on gay people, that what they did "was not a problem, but a solution." Even people who sincerely regretted what had happened to Scotty Joe came to the D.A. and asked, "Do you really think you can get twelve people to convict these three of capital murder, considering what he was?"

Whetstone understands why his successor, Judy Newcomb, chose to plead the three killers out rather than go for the death penalty. It would have been a hard conviction to get from a South Alabama jury. So, after Whetstone's retirement, he sits back and muses about whether justice was done for Scotty Joe. The grisly details of the torture and desecration of the body never came out in open court, so the press couldn't communicate a sense of outrage to the state and the wider world. Whetstone regrets that, since Alabama is still considered a bastion of anti-gay prejudice, and the truth about the Weaver case had the potential to help the state leap over its bias against LGBTQ people. He says, "This was a great issue for the State of Alabama. You cannot do this to any human being, no matter his orientation, no matter who he is. The truth can change hearts and minds."

The new D.A. got convictions in all three cases in 2007. Gaines pleaded guilty to avoid the death penalty, and received life without parole. He turned on both Kelsay and Porter. Porter got two life sentences to be served consecutively, but because he was perceived not to have hatched the plot against Scotty Joe, he was given enough leniency to qualify for parole in sixteen years. Kelsay was the last to be convicted. She agreed to a twenty-year sentence, but because the severity of her crime was believed to be less than Gaines's or Porter's, she may be out on the street within six years.

Few still remember Scotty Joe. For Martha and Lum Jr., Scotty's murder is a lingering nightmare. Martha was devastated by the loss of her baby boy. Lum says that she cries most all the time. She doesn't know who to trust anymore, and cannot understand how Kelsay and Gaines could have done something so malicious to Scotty. As she sobbed to David Whetstone, "If they had only really known him, they wouldn't have done this to my baby!"

Lum tried to represent the family and his brother's memory for a while, making himself available to the press. He and Martha made a brief appearance in the 2006 documentary film, *Small Town Gay Bar*, telling Scotty's story. "There's no doubt in my mind that homophobia killed my little brother. No doubt in my mind at all," he told a reporter for *365 Gay*.

It is virtually impossible for a family to hold onto supporters in the midst of an ordeal like this. They cannot be expected to. Friends and supporters must resolve to hold on to the bereaved family, instead. Very little of that has happened in the Weaver case. For a short time, people in Mobile like Suzanne Cleveland reached out to Martha and Lum. She invited them to a performance of *The Laramie Project*, the play about the 1998 Matthew Shepard murder in Wyoming. Cleveland says that Martha said very little during the performance, just wept softly most of the time. As Rev. Helene Loper, a lesbian pastor from Tuscaloosa, says, the cultural differences between Mobile and Baldwin County are so great that they are nearly insurmountable. LGBTQ people have support systems, service centers, a social scene, and quietly friendly churches in Mobile. In Bay Minette, even the funerals of slain gay boys become platforms for anti-gay rhetoric, and anyone suspected of being gay is "asking for it." Unlike the Billy Jack Gaither story, kept alive by a small group of dedicated activists and academics who regularly keep in touch with members of Billy's family, Scotty Joe's story wanders on the outskirts of memory like an orphan these days.

Tony Thompson is still angry about what happened to Scotty Joe. When asked about the message of Scotty's life and death, he refuses to temper his words:

> Some folks got the message. They're still out there, hidden. To them, the message of Scotty Joe's murder is that he could be *you*: split from stem to stern with his dead ass set on fire. They crawled back into the closet, and are still there. Hopefully, they will figure things out before they kill themselves, that they *can* have happy, healthy lives being who they are. That's what I wish the message of Scotty Joe could be, that young gays don't have to face what he did . . . that they *can* be healthy, happy, and productive.

"Scotty's death brought media attention to the importance of people sticking up for family and friends who are gay," Thompson continues. "If you have a child who is coming out, love them! Keep them close! Do not drive them away!"

David Whetstone, the old "he-coon," has a more sanguine view of the meaning of Scotty Joe's story. Scotty's case could have been just another "court-cost killing," but it wasn't. The term refers to cases deemed unlikely to get a conviction, so they are quietly plea-bargained away. The intense media scrutiny surrounding Scotty's murder prevented that outcome, Whetstone says. He regrets deeply the suffering in Scotty's life, saying, "What the community did to that boy was terrible. I might not like it if my child told me he was gay, but I wouldn't love him any less." He also mourns the effective loss of the lives of three other young people, victims in their own way of the prejudice that caused them to target Scotty for a "horrendous, painful, violent death."

Nonetheless, Whetstone is sure that Scotty did not die in vain. "He caused quite a stir in Baldwin County, bringing something in his death that couldn't be brought in any other way." Instead of remaining reflexively biased against LGBTQ people, this horrible atrocity forced the citizens of Bay Minette to take a second look at their core beliefs. "I saw a change," Whetstone says. "It may be temporary, but people started reflecting on the humanity of people who are different, like Scotty. Folks came up to me on the street and said, 'Everybody needs to have somebody in their corner, don't they?'"

Ol' Granny Death, Scotty's backwoods babushka, enfolds his memory in her ample arms. It is horrible to go through the tragedy in her bosom to get to the identities and roles he had only 18 years to fulfill. But in another way, there is no way to understand his life without being forced to examine our own fears, and core beliefs, and biases. Granny Death is a stern teacher, but an honest one. If we wish to reach out and touch the wounds of Scotty Joe, we must start by touching our own first.

Scotty was laid to rest in Bryars-McGill Cemetery, down a dirt path to the most remote section of the graveyard. To get there, you have to go "down yonder" to Perdido, taking a two-lane country road that winds miles and miles from anywhere. His grave backs up to a field of rusty, derelict farm implements bordered by a broken-down barbwire fence. The designs on Scotty Joe's headstone continues the theme in his casket, of little turtledoves with olive branches in their beaks, crosses, and praying hands. Inscribed in the stone near where his head rests are the words, "We love you and miss you."

Listen carefully. The stillness speaks in Southern graveyards. In between the hissing of the summer sun on the cemetery lawn and the thrumming music of the cicadas in the trees, you might just catch the faintest hint of someone a little bit country singing softly to Scotty Joe, "I . . . I will always, *always* love you . . . "

For Greater Understanding

Perfect Hatred: Scotty Joe Weaver

FILMS AND VIDEOGRAPHY

Small Town Gay Bar – Magnolia Home Entertainment, 2007.

ORGANIZATIONS AND WEBSITES

Dolly Online - http://www.dollyon-line.com/archives/ts/lkl_030703.shtml.

Equality Alabama - http://www.equalityalabama.org.

Find a Grave: Scotty Joe Weaver, http://www.findagrave.com/cgi-bin/fg.cgi?page=gr&
   GRid=9272618.

Memorial Hall: Scotty Joe Weaver, http://andrejkoymasky.com/mem/weav/weav1.html.

PFLAG (Parents and Friends of Lesbians and Gays), Mobile, Alabama Chapter, http:
   //www.angelfire.com/ab3/pflagmobile/.

Towleroad.com, "Dolly Parton: I'm Not Gay . . . And God Should Judge, Not Other
People," http://www.towleroad.com/2009/02/dolly-parton-im-not-gayand-god-should
   -judge-not-other-people.html.

The Trevor Project, http://TrevorProject.org.

Unfinished Lives Project, http://unfinishedlivesblog.com.

Ryan Keith Skipper
April 28, 1981—March 14, 2007

WAHNETA, FLORIDA

7

Keeper of Hearts

Ryan Keith Skipper

"You can love more than one person at a time,
and I don't give a damn what the self-help books say."

—RITA MAE BROWN, *FULL CRY*

O N A FOGGY WEDNESDAY, March 14, 2007, the eve of the *Ides of March*, two young Polk County men killed Ryan Keith Skipper in cold blood. William David Brown Jr., the 20-year-old nephew of Skipper's landlord, and Brown's friend, Joseph Eli Bearden, aged 21, chose knives for their act of assassination. Cassius and Brutus, the first-century (CE) Roman conspirators, also drew their knives and cut down Julius Caesar in the Senate House. But Brown and Bearden are hardly noble Romans, though their purpose was just as bloody-minded. They were hard luck "gators" up to no good, Central Florida white boys with little insight into themselves and even less ambition beyond drinking, violence, theft, and getting high in their trailer park homes. Both were known methamphetamine addicts and small time crooks. Bearden had served time for grand theft auto, and had pled "no contest" to charges of battery when he was a teen. Brown had been arrested just six days prior to the Skipper murder for "cyber stalking," and had four previous arrests in Polk County. Their intended mark was a gentle, fun-loving 25-year-old native of the Auburndale area, who lived with two girlfriends he loved like sisters in a little red rental house at 211 Richburg Road. To the red neck conspirators, Ryan Skipper was an uppity queer who flaunted his new car and his big shopping mall job, and he needed what they were about to give him: several inches of sharp steel.

A PRINCE OF OUR DISCONTENT

Folk wisdom says that the last thing a murdered person sees at the moment of death is imprinted on the tissues of the eye. Were that image retrievable and reproducible, then the dead could speak beyond the grave: we could see the killer. The residue of murder leaves indelible images of the victim, too, seared into the emotional memories of those who loved him. When someone so beloved and so loving is cut down savagely as Ryan Skipper was, the whole event of him is seared into the tissues of the souls he touched when he was alive. Murder doesn't make a person better or worse than he was in life. It can, however, make him unforgettable.

Ryan had many hearts in his keeping. Dozens called him "my best friend." They each loved him specially, differently, and he loved them back the same way. That was Ryan's gift, to focus his concern and care so fully on each of his lovers and friends that they seemed not to mind all the others. Instead, they seek each other out to this very day, so as not to forget, and to celebrate who and what he was. The lakeside home of his mother Pat and stepfather Lynn draws them like a magnet, and reflections of Ryan flicker back and forth in the stories they tell, in their laughter, in the memories they share, and in the way each of them seems to tend a wound that just cannot quite heal.

Ryan's portrait is a mosaic made of mirrors, showing other things besides glimpses of the boy and the man, and his strengths and weaknesses. It reveals something of the people who knew him, something else again of the troubled county in Florida where they continue to live after his murder, and something even more sinister than that. Looking into the life and death of this young man exposes something about a culture so disordered that it frequently cannibalizes its own young, especially when they are homosexual.

Ryan was a beautiful boy, the second son of Pat and Durl Skipper, born under the sign of Taurus the Bull. He had dishwater blond hair, and sparkling soft brown eyes. In a crowd of other children, he stood out as the skinny kid with the great big smile—an ear-to-ear grin that would open hearts to him all his life. He was outgoing and friendly, a happy boy. Ryan also had something sweetly naïve about him, almost gullible. His older brother, Damien, routinely talked him into escapades that would dupe Ryan into getting caught while Damien went scot-free. Damien and Ryan had two distinctly different personalities. While Damien, three-and-a-half years his senior, was more assertive and dominant, Ryan always sought to please everyone and to make peace. Still, Ryan voiced his own feelings and opinions, and had a stubborn streak, but he shied away from conflict, preferring instead to mend relationships whenever he could. Ryan adored his brother. It was mutual. Damien remembers how Ryan would never part from him without saying that he loved him.

The family had an inside joke on Ryan. He would take the most absurd explanations for gospel truth, and then stubbornly argue against any suggestion to the contrary, building up an alternate reality for himself that his mother Pat labeled, "Ryan's World." His stepfather, Lynn Mulder, put it this way: "If his friends believed that the green dye in Mountain Dew would make you impotent, well, it was true . . . if he thought he was right, there was no changing his mind." To anybody who would listen, Ryan would readily assert that the human head weighed twelve pounds—no more, no less—and that a set of human intestines would stretch around the circumference of the world. It was all true "in Ryan's World," and his family and friends had great fun with his dogged, good-natured sense of fantasy. "Ryan always had a good sense of humor and he could give it as well as take it," Lynn remembered.

That same gentle tenacity set Ryan's friendships apart. He was sweetly other-directed toward strays. At Thanksgiving and Christmas, when Pat would cook enough food to provision an army, Ryan would bring more guests home than anybody. He loved his friends like he loved his family. He fretted over the wellbeing of his housemates, Kelly Evans and Joyce Fraley, refusing to go to bed at night until he knew they were safe and sound. Ryan pledged himself utterly to his oldest and dearest friend from school days, Stephanie Schiff, becoming "god-fairy" to her baby girl, Kayden; He bridged the age gap with his more mature lover, Karl von Hahmann, to become Karl's "Mini-Me." Ryan loved whom he loved, and whoever disapproved could simply go to hell. That's just the way it was "in Ryan's World."

Boyhood for Ryan was anything but idyllic. Early on, his mother Pat, a Registered Nurse, sensed that he was hyperactive. A physician confirmed Pat's suspicions. Her marriage to Durl Skipper "hit the rocks" about the same time as Ryan's diagnosis, and she developed a special sense of responsibility for her son that grew into a powerful bond between them. Pat met Lynn Mulder, an operating room nurse, at Winter

Haven Hospital where they both worked. They married, and Lynn assumed the role of Damien and Ryan's true dad, the one they never had before. Ryan struggled with his hyperactivity, and keenly felt disappointment with his biological father. It was during this period of serious discontent that Ryan started acting out in school, and after a series of frustrating incidents, Pat and Lynn decided to remove him from the public schools. They enrolled Ryan in Winter Haven's Grace Lutheran School, a pre-kindergarten through eighth grade parochial outfit run by the Missouri Synod Lutheran Church. Grace Lutheran offered Ryan the discipline and personal attention he needed, and there he remained until he graduated and went to high school in the public education system.

HEART OF FLESH

About age 13, Ryan began realizing that he was far more attracted to boys than to girls. Central Florida is hardly sympathetic territory, either politically or religiously, for a young gay person to explore his sexual orientation. The battle raging in that region of the Sunshine State between censorship and First Amendment rights to free speech, and between conservative and progressive community values, makes being gay or lesbian in Polk County especially problematic.

Polk County, part of the "fly-over country" between Tampa and Orlando, is mainly rural, with orange groves, phosphate-mining pits, and a military bombing range. Shifting political winds in this strategic region of Central Florida have made it a cultural "Tornado Alley," where traditional Cracker conservatism and more progressive values routinely clash with stormy results. Though safely conservative in religious matters, Polk County's vote is part of the hotly contested I-4 corridor that girdles Florida from west to east, and has shown signs in recent elections of breaking nearly 50/50 for the Democrats. In the 2008 General Election, though John McCain edged Barack Obama in Polk County by seven percentage points, Hillsborough County (Tampa) to the west, and Osceola County (Kissimmee) and Orange County (Orlando) to the east went decisively Democratic-Blue, clinching Florida's electoral votes for Obama. Polk has become Purple like a bruise, with the right wing ramping up its rhetoric in order to hold onto power against changing cultural tides.

Staunchly conservative Polk County Sheriff Grady Judd, a major figure in Ryan Skipper's murder case, promotes himself as a Christian lawman guarding the population against obscenity, pornography, and degeneracy. He is firmly entrenched with the local media, especially the county newspapers, feeding them "propaganda," according to First Amendment Attorney Lawrence G. Walters of Altamonte Springs, Florida. Since Judd, who is used to running for re-election unopposed, represents a widespread community opinion that homosexuality is abominable and obscene, LGBTQ people who live in his county necessarily tread lightly. "Polk County is an anomaly in Florida, it really is," says Walters. "I don't know how to put this politely. It really hasn't evolved." As Karl von Hahmann said, "You would not drive down the street and see rainbow flags in Polk County. You would not be able to hold your boyfriend's hand or your girlfriend's hand here as readily as you could in a larger city." For gay people, the Auburndale, Lakeland, and Winter Haven area is no *Magic Kingdom*, no matter how nearby Disney World may be. This is storm country.

For five years, until he was 18, Ryan fumbled his way toward sexual maturity through trial and error, discovering smoking and alcohol along the way. At some point he also tried marijuana, and liked it. Smoking pot became a sort of self-medication for his hyperactivity; it calmed him down. Though his friends say that he quit abusing marijuana after his second arrest for possession just after graduating from high school, it was always easy enough to get in Polk County. In anyone else, taking a drink or occasionally smoking pot would be winked at as juvenile peccadilloes, but in a young *gay* man, such behavior would permit a brutal double standard to clamp down on him like the jaws of an Everglades alligator.

He came out to his folks at 18. Their acceptance of him was immediate and total. All his best friends, and many of his classmates already knew. His mom told him to keep his gayness under wraps in Polk County. "I said," she recalled, "'Ryan, Honey, it's not that I'm ashamed of who you are, but people around here will hurt you for that.'" She said he was worried about being gay-bashed, too. He had reason to be. A pattern of name-calling and physical threats began during his adolescence and continued into early adulthood, though he rarely mentioned it to anyone. As early as age 15, Ryan had a brush with violence for being perceived as gay. His mom got a distraught call from him because a group of boys roughed him up at a local strip mall, calling him a "faggot," and stealing his cap. He was scared and bewildered, she remembered. The loss of the cap was particularly bitter for Ryan because it had been a present from his brother Damien.

He also told his mother that he was worried about himself spiritual-ly. Little wonder. First Missionary Baptist Church in Auburndale, where Ryan attended as a boy with his family, is a heterosexist/homophobic congregation like so many southern Protestant churches. During Ryan's youth, graduates of Jerry Falwell's hard-right Liberty Baptist University had pastored the church. FMBC instilled less of the love of God in Ryan than fear of going to hell. The church's beliefs statement includes this ominous warning:

> We believe ALL MEN ARE BY NATURE AND CHOICE SINFUL
> AND LOST . . . that the spirits of the unsaved at death descend
> immediately into Hades where they are kept under punishment
> until the final day of judgment, at which time their bodies shall
> be raised from the grave and they shall be judged and cast into
> Hell, the place of final and everlasting punishment [emphasis in
> the original].

Grace Lutheran, where Ryan served as an altar boy, proved no better. As part of the right wing Missouri Synod, Grace Church might have talked love and forgiveness for LGBTQ people better than First Missionary Baptist, but there was very little graciousness to be found for gay people at Grace. Homosexuality was taught to be "intrinsically sinful . . . a person who persists in homosexual behavior stands under the condemnation of God's Word," according to a church pamphlet on the subject, easily attainable by a boy like Ryan. The only hope the Missouri Synod held out to a gay kid was the "therapy" offered by "The Keys Ministry," a Minnesota-based group dedicated to freeing people from "homosexuality and lesbianism."

Spiritually, Ryan's matter-of-fact naïveté worked against him. He admitted to his mother that for years, because the church taught that gay people like him were condemned and going to hell, he simply assumed it was true. Aghast, Pat assured him that God loved him just the way he was, no matter what the churches said. She remembers how amazed he was at the news that he was not bound for hell after all:

"Does God make any mistakes?" she asked him.

"No," Ryan admitted.

"Then, Honey, God didn't make a mistake when he made you, ei-ther. How could God condemn someone he made right the first time?"

In that sweet, naïve way of his, Ryan's face lit up with astonishment, "Mama, I never thought about it like that!"

In reality, the spiritual damage took years to heal, but as Stephanie Schiff said in an interview for the *Lakeland Ledger*, "I know his philosophy was that, 'God's not going to discriminate against me because of my sexuality.' He made peace with his faith and homosexuality in his own way."

Ryan's rocky re-entry into the public school system verified that Winter Haven High was a tough place for anybody "different." One student from those days who still wishes to remain anonymous said he and Ryan had similar experiences: "There was not one morning he set foot on that campus without feeling a deep sense of dread because he knew what was coming that day." Yet Winter Haven High was also where Ryan met his soul-friend, Stephanie Schiff. He had grown into a strikingly handsome young man, 6 feet tall, 165 pounds, flashing that infectious smile that made "Steph" love him. He took her under his wing like a real older brother, teaching her how to drive a stick shift, listening endlessly to her, and engaging in "girl-talk" in the best tradition of gay boys. He kept his sexual orientation a secret even from her, however, fearing that she would reject him if she found out. Stephanie already knew. When Ryan finally broke down and admitted that he was gay, she affirmed even more love for him because he had been honest with her at last.

The acceptance of the high school drama club became crucial to him. The drama club gave Ryan a place to belong, a rare oasis of calm in an otherwise hostile environment. He excelled among the troupe, rising to become the club's president. The students who gravitated toward theater banded together by necessity. One student said, "Freaks and geeks got to stick together." Ironically, the Polk County School System administration refused to allow the drama club to put on a production of Moïses Kaufmann's play about the murder of Matthew Shepard, *The Laramie Project*, declaring that it was "inappropriate for school-age children." This is the same school system that turned a blind eye toward the verbal and physical harassment of LGBTQ students, the same one that produced the likes of Ryan's murderers. School was the kind of battlefield where students like Ryan routinely faced hell. WHHS students were not called the "Blue Devils" for nothing.

Ryan was bullied in high school for being gay almost from the first day he attended. Though many students tolerated him, and most didn't really care one way or the other, the "red necks," as Stephanie called them, went after him verbally and physically. "People would call him a 'girlie man, gay boy, fag, queer' push him in the halls and throw rotten oranges, sticks, coke bottles and rocks at his car most every day," she said. Ryan would just endure the abuse. Depressed and angry, he expressed his frustration to Stephanie who often caught a ride with him and witnessed these attacks, "I don't bother anybody! Why don't they just leave me alone?" Unable to sit idly by and watch the red necks bombard him again, she made him stop the car as she jumped out, cursing back at his antagonists, pelting them with the same oranges and rocks they had thrown at her friend. She was not about to see him hurt, and her fury on his behalf was a wonder to behold. Her love and respect helped him learn to love himself, and over time, he began to defend himself and not let the harassment tear him down any longer. "He'd smile at them because they were ignorant," she said to *Ledger* reporters. "I don't think it bothered him that he was gay. Ryan was happy with who he was."

Early Ryan's last year and a half at Winter Haven High, Pat and Lynn built a comfortable lakefront home in Auburndale, and sold the little house where the boys had grown up in Winter Haven. Damien had moved away to college. When his parents moved, they asked Ryan to go with them, but he refused, opting instead to get his own place and finish high school with his friends. He was eighteen, a junior, and wanted to try and make it on his own. After graduation in 2000, he drifted back and forth between jobs. Though he was always employed, he never seemed able to find what he was meant to do.

THE PLEASURE OF HIS COMPANY

During Ryan's period of indecision, his folks and some of his friends suggested that he should probably move to a large city like Orlando, where it might be safer for a gay man, and where he could live more openly. In hindsight, there were enough omens of violence to make leaving Polk County behind seem like the right thing to do. Ryan had lost at least one job because of his sexual orientation. That was not the reason given for his dismissal, of course. Only a matter of days after he filed a grievance against a co-worker for calling him a "fucking faggot" on the job, the shop manager canned Ryan on the technicality of tardiness. The offending employee was never disciplined. At Stephanie's apartment where Ryan was rooming, a man barged in totally uninvited, spewing malice. He grabbed Ryan by the collar and slapped him around for being a "queer." Though Ryan reported the assault, filled out a report, and had witnesses to back him up, the Polk County Sheriff's Department never followed through. At another time, his friend and future housemate, Joyce Fraley, remembered how Ryan frantically banged on her door in the dead of night. The moment she opened the door she could tell from the look on his face and how hard he was breathing that he had just been jumped. There were other minor incidents, the numbing repetition of slurs and insults LGBTQ people face regularly, the small slights and the humiliations that one learns to endure in order to get by. Right up to the very night he was murdered, there were intimations of danger. Ryan racked up these warning signs to "the way things are when you are gay." The banality of homophobia is that queer folk come to think of such hurtful things merely as ordinary.

Ryan entertained the idea of moving away more than once. Fort Lauderdale and Miami's South Beach glitter like Shangri-La on South Florida's rainbow coast, offering lesbians and gays large, diverse communities, employment and nightlife. Ryan's friend Dotty Petersen had lived down there before she moved to Polk County. More than once he quizzed her about what it would be like to uproot and start his life over. The great thing to him about making such a move was that he would no longer have to stifle his feelings and emotions. He also shared with Dotty his deepest fear—to be hurt or killed in a hate crime. Though gay migration looks like a rational thing to do in hindsight, to fault Ryan or any other LGBTQ person for not becoming a refugee is wrong-headed if not downright heterosexist. Polk County's prejudices are replicated thousands of times throughout the United States. What says that any new place would be safe from the long, crooked arm of anti-gay violence? Instead of putting the onus on LGBTQ people to go into exile, why is it not the responsibility of government at every level to see that *all* its citizens are reasonably safe?

For three generations, Ryan's family had lived in Polk County. He grew up there. It was the only home he ever knew. Any flirtation with living somewhere else withered before that fact. His mom and stepdad anchored his heart in Auburndale. His best friends in the world, the ones who had loved him in bad times and good, lived in Winter Haven, Lakeland, and Auburndale. He was not about to move from the area. Instead he found a sweet little cottage, red as a Winesap apple, in rural Wahneta off of Rifle Range Road, just south of Winter Haven. Wahneta, population 4,700, is an unincorporated working class community that people are more likely to move away from, than into. It had a rough reputation, more than its share of derelict, rusting cars and churches, high fences and bad dogs, but unarguably it was affordable for young people with modest incomes. The 900-square-foot, one-bathroom cottage rented for $350 a month with utilities added. Ryan, Kelly Evans, and Joyce Fraley set up home together, split expenses, and loved every minute of it.

Beginning in late 2005, and throughout 2006, his life took an obvious turn for the better. Everyone could see it. He had enrolled in Traviss Technical Center in Lakeland, majoring in Computer Science and Repair. He loved computers, and was well on his way to a real career. Ryan's employment situation had greatly improved, as well. He secured a job he really enjoyed, as manager at the Sunglass Hut kiosk in Macy's Department Store in Winter Haven. He was saving his money, planning for the future. His stepdad, Lynn, said, "He was finding his way in life and had become comfortable with himself. He had found pursuits he could be excellent at. It was so rewarding to see Ryan thrive. It was one of those things that makes a parent proud." When Damien came home for the 2006 holidays, he found his kid brother happier and more self-assured than he had ever seen him. They went out for oysters and beer at a local joint. Damien remembers a wonderful night. Before they parted company, Damien told Ryan how much he loved him, hugged and kissed him. He would never see his brother alive again.

Despite being in the 'hood, life was good for Ryan, Kelly, and Joyce at 211 Richburg Road. All three of them knew each other well. Back in 1999, when Ryan was still a teenager, they met and became close friends while working together at K-Mart. The house was like a twenty-first-century film set for the Three Stooges. Ryan was "Queen" of the house. Everyone remembers the hilarity of the night he twanged on the guitar, singing "Over the Rainbow" so off-key it made dogs howl. Though Kelly was the de facto "mom," she also had the wildest streak. She and Ryan invented their own private nonsense language, a jibberish of purrs and yelps and grunts that reduced Joyce to tears, while she laughed at them acting so crazy. Kelly's boyfriends would come over to the house and wonder what the hell was going on with her and this gay boy, yammering away at each other like geese on acid. To Kelly, he was "the best room-mate and friend I have ever had." Joyce felt like Ryan was her brother. "He may not have been my blood, but he was my brother," she said with a bittersweet edge to her voice. "We just clicked." She and Ryan loved to pick back and forth. She kidded him that he would still be chasing young boys when he was shuffling along with a walker, and he fired back that she would still be waiting to find a girlfriend when she was 90. Ryan wanted to learn to dance, and Kelly tried mightily to teach him. "I didn't have much luck," she admitted. Repeatedly, she and Ryan attempted to get Joyce on her feet to boogie with them, but she would have none of it, remaining a dedicated wallflower. Both women still laugh about how Ryan was so deathly afraid of spiders, to the point of shrieking and running out of the house whenever he saw one, leaving the disposal of the beastie to them. It didn't matter if he was just out of the shower and naked—one glimpse of a hairy, eight-legged terror, and he was stampeding out the door, his towel flapping in the wind. Bottom line, they were a family in Red Neck Town, and they loved each other fiercely.

Kelly and Joyce were his girls, and along with Stephanie, they were the sisters he had never had. He capered like a clown for them, faithfully standing watch over them like a big sheep dog. His sense of responsibility for Kelly and Joyce was so great that he struck a bargain with Angie Justice (another dear girlfriend of his who battled cancer). Ryan promised to watch over her children if anything happened to her. In return, he asked Angie to promise that if anything happened to him, she would look after his two housemates. Joyce still cannot get over the gaping hole left in her life by Ryan's murder. She shakes her head, dabbing at her eyes, and says, "How am I going to get through the rest of my life without talking to that boy?"

The last six months of his life, Ryan established a relationship with Karl von Hahmann. They met in October of 2006 at Macy's in Winter Haven where they both worked. The friendship was truly blossoming between them by early March 2007. Ryan told Karl that he had never owned a diamond, and really wanted one. Since Ryan's birthday was coming up in April, Karl went out and bought him a surprise diamond ring. He picked it up on the afternoon of March 13, the day before the love of his life was murdered. Now he wears Ryan's ring on his right index finger so that he will never forget.

Karl was taller than Ryan, at 6' 3", and Ryan's senior by 12 years. His success in business and sales, his dark good looks, and his way with clothes attracted Ryan. Karl was completely taken by this passionate, funny, younger man. Ryan was Ricky-Martin-good-looking, joyous, vital, and had the most genuine heart Karl had ever known, "the kind of person I wanted in my life," as Karl put it. They were constantly in touch. Karl and Ryan had taken trips together to Orlando and Tampa.

Whenever he got done at work, Karl would go over and just hang out with Ryan until he finished at the Sunglass Hut. Then they would usually share a meal, either at a local restaurant or at Karl's Orchid Springs home in Winter Haven.

The one thing Karl was determined to work on with Ryan was the way he dressed. Ratty jeans and raggedy tee shirts were just not "getting it"! Though he dressed well enough for work, most of what he had in his closet was run-of-the-mill khakis and long sleeve shirts—too boring! Karl felt a man as handsome as Ryan needed to take more care and pride in what he wore, and he made it his mission to show Ryan how to do it. Before long, Ryan started dressing like Karl, who affectionately nicknamed him, "my Mini-Me." To see the photos of his young protégé striking a pose with cigarette in hand beside a limo, decked out in a black Italian-cut three-button suit, maroon shirt, and sporting a primo silk tie, one has to concede that Karl had outdone himself with Ryan. Ryan had become, in the words of another of his friends, "impeccable."

Most of all, the two of them just had fun together. Karl loved traveling, going to movies, art galleries, and the theater; and Ryan's antics, remarkable spirit, and brilliant smile had brought *joie de vivre* to Karl in an unprecedented way. Karl calls Ryan his angel, who watches over him still. Though Ryan's murder brought devastation to everyone who knew and loved him, Karl's grief is particularly sharp. "He was the best friend I ever had," he says. "Ryan was outgoing and had no prejudices. He was a very trusting person, which was one of his downfalls. He was really too trusting . . ." Karl's voice trails off as he fingers the ring he never got to give Ryan. "You lose people, you know, like in a car accident, which is bad," he says, "but it's nothing like this."

At the time of his death, Ryan had not yet introduced Karl to his parents. They heard about him, of course. They also saw Karl's effect on him: how happy he was, and what a fine, new sense of fashion he had developed. Ryan wasn't necessarily keeping the relationship "on the down low," but at the same time he had not fully opened up this part of his life to the other vital centers of intimacy and support he relied on. There were decisions about life and love, about friendship and romance that he had not yet made by the time the Ides of March caught up with him. Though Karl knew Joyce and Kelly, he would have to wait to meet the Mulders on his own . . . after Ryan was gone.

NAILS AND THORNS

Nothing epitomized Ryan's developing self-confidence more than the purchase of his brand new car, a "bad-ass" little powder blue 2007 Chevy Aveo. He had become a regular at all the junkyards in the area, trying to keep his previous rides on the road. No more "hoopdies" and "rust buckets" for him. God, he was proud of that car, and he showed it off all over town. His new purchase was a major achievement, a sign that he was turning the corner financially as well as psychologically. Ryan had barely scraped by for a long time. The jobs he had, at K-Mart, as a telemarketer, and the Dockside Bar & Grill, for example, paid poorly and had no benefits to speak of. Since landing the job at the Sunglass Hut, however, he had been making better money, and his hard work and thrift were paying off. Karl loaned him enough money to pay the car down within his reach, and he was making the monthly payments with no difficulty. His friends remember how he parked that sweet little Chevy in the lot next to Macy's, and jumped out with a big grin, inviting them all to get in and breathe in that new car smell.

One evening during the first week of March, after dinner at Karl's home, Ryan and Karl were making reservations together for a Spring Break trip. They were going to South Beach, where Ryan had not been in a long time. Ryan's cell phone interrupted them. It was Kelly, and she was upset. She said there had been gunfire at the house, and somebody had shot the windows out of Joyce's mother's car. Ryan said, "I gotta go make sure my girls are alright!" and headed immediately for his car. Karl had been worrying about where Ryan lived, and had even asked him to move in with him. But Ryan was comfortable in his little red house with his girls, and chose not to acknowledge the potential dangers of living in rural Wahneta. Barely a week before these gunshots, Kelly's tires had been slashed. Karl said, "I begged him not to leave that night to go back to the house because he didn't know what he was driving into. But he insisted that he had to go back and see for himself that those girls were okay." Ryan's stubborn sense of loyalty had kicked in, and no one could dissuade him. That was his character.

When he was younger, a fire started in the elevator shaft of Winter Haven Hospital where both Pat and Lynn worked. Pat remembers that there was smoke billowing out of the building, and fire trucks were everywhere. Though his parents were in no actual peril, Ryan had no way of knowing it. So he stormed past the firefighters, regardless of the smoke and the potential danger to himself, and raced around the corridors until he found his folks and saw for himself that they were safe. Ryan demonstrated the same character when his housemates were in potential danger. Regardless of personal safety, Ryan believed he had to get to them as quickly as he could. As Karl said, "He loved those girls. He would have done anything for them."

Joyce filed a Sheriff's report about the vandalism. It got nowhere. Wahneta was notorious for being a drug and high crime area, regardless of all the proud signs Sheriff Judd prominently displayed around the tiny business district proclaiming it a "COP Community (Community Oriented Policing)." Days passed after the drive-by shooting, and things at 211 Richburg Road settled back to normal for Ryan and his girls. Grinding poverty was all around them, but since Wahneta was full of good, hardworking White and Hispanic people, it was easy to overlook the punks and the meth heads. The gunshots? Hearing an occasional "pop-pop-pop!" outside might be troubling, but it didn't happen that often. Most every Saturday and Sunday morning, Ryan and the girls would wake up to a curbside littered with beer and liquor bottles carelessly dumped there by weekend delinquents. Cleanup was one of the consequences of cheap rent in Red Neck Town. Kelly remembers how they seldom locked their door in the evening, since Ryan, Joyce, and she got home at about the same time of night after work. The first one in would just leave the door unlatched for the others. Nobody thought anything of it, like nobody thought twice about the annoying visits of Bill-Bill "Dirty Foot" Brown.

William David Brown Jr., called "Bill-Bill" by his friends, didn't own a car or have easy access to one. He had earned the nickname "Dirty Foot" from Ryan's girlfriends who watched him peddling a bike up and down the gravel roads barefooted, rain or shine. Thin as a rail, with a buzz cut and a scraggly dusting of whiskers on his chin and upper lip, 20-year-old Brown often appeared in Wahneta's dingy little grocery store, bare dirty feet and all. Hispanics in the area called him "the skinny White dude." He was a neighbor of sorts, living in a woebegone trailer jungle a couple of streets over from Ryan and the girls. He was also their landlord's nephew. "Dirty Foot" made it his business to check up on what was going on over at the little red house.

Ryan certainly knew who Bill-Bill Brown was. He had come to the house several times, at first looking for his cousin, Richard, a former tenant there, and then to talk to Ryan. Joyce remembers him riding up on his bike twice in one day. At another time, Bill-Bill knocked on the door and asked for Ryan who was in the shower. Joyce told Ryan there was "some guy" outside wanting him. In due course, Ryan spoke with him, and Bill-Bill pedaled away. Sometimes Bill-Bill would ask Ryan for a ride since he didn't have a car. There was nothing to arouse Kelly and Joyce's suspicion about Brown's periodic contacts, and Ryan never seemed concerned. Whether the friends knew about "Dirty Foot's" extensive criminal activity in Polk County, especially his penchant for stalking, is unknown. Instead of being ominous, his visits seemed irritating and ill-timed. He was one of a hundred losers in the Wahneta area. No one suspected how lethal he would prove to be.

Brown's friend from nearby Eloise, Florida, Joseph Eli Bearden (aged 21, and whose alias was "Smiley") had recently gotten out of jail for auto theft. In late December 2006, Bearden set up a MySpace profile in order to troll for contacts. He was 5'3", 130 lbs., and had brown hair and eyes. The photo he posted is set none-too-subtly with a bed in the background. His prison haircut had grown out, and his gaze at the camera, meant to exude availability, was oddly sphinx-like. His self-description bears repeating in full:

> I'm Joseph, I live in Auburndale, FL. I'm a songwriter for a band called Nails & Thorns, which is going to be the one of the hottest, Christian Metal bands ever. Some of my interests include cars, hunting, snakes, fishing, going to church, X-BOX, and of course hot girls (in no particular order)!!! Goals are to finish chooling, [sic] and find myself a stable career that I love to work for.

His favorite books are listed as the Bible, anything written by Stephen King or Tom Clancy, and reference books which he found "fascinating." His musical preference was for Christian Metal, and his top motion picture choice was Mel Gibson's film, "The Passion of Christ, or anything with a good moral message to it." In an attempt at humor, he wrote that those most important to him were his pet snake, named "Charlie," and his parents, parenthetically speaking "in no particular order." Who he'd most like to meet are God, "and any hot Christian woman out there (notice I said HOT and W-O-M-A-N. NOT GIRL!!!)." His use of keyboard capitalization is telling. He wanted no doubt to linger in anyone's mind about his macho credentials. Smiley Bearden saw himself as a testosterone-charged Christian, a real man.

Behind the songwriter-choir boy façade was a little man, rawhide tough and ready to strike like the snakes he kept as pets. His police record showed Bearden was no stranger to violence. In February 2007 he had attached himself to the brothers Robert "Rock" Aguero and Daniel "Disco" Aguero, notorious drug dealers in nearby Haines City. Their sister, Maria, remembers that Smiley was a "banger," who "slammed" crystal meth intravenously. He and Dirty Foot Brown made a dangerous pair, and Ryan Skipper, the local gay guy with the new Chevy had become their person of interest. They colluded with Brown's cousin, 20-year-old Ray Alan Brown, called "Ray-Ray," who also lived in the Wahneta area. Though he was initially charged for Ryan's murder and quickly released for lack of evidence, Ray-Ray Brown was fully aware of the plot. The Polk County Sheriff's Complaint Affidavit quotes witnesses attesting that "Bill and Ray said that the victim was a 'faggot' and they should rob him."

"JUST GETTING RID OF ONE MORE FAGGOT"

Ryan's stalkers sharpened their knives, and set their plan in motion. They got high to pass the time until their quarry made it home from work.

Tuesday, March 13 had been out of the ordinary for Ryan. Normally, he worked the evening shift at the Sunglass Hut in Macy's at the Old Winter Haven Mall. Instead, he subbed at the Lakeland location until closing time, locked up, and then met Karl for dinner at Mimi's Café. On the way home to Wahneta, he was to drop the kiosk key off at the home of a young woman who would open the store the next day. Ryan hadn't smoked pot in weeks, but occasionally he needed a joint to help him relax, and this was going to be one of those nights. Karl gave him $40 to buy the marijuana, because Ryan was low on cash. No big deal. Karl picked up the meal tab with a credit card at ten minutes to eleven. Since tomorrow was going to be an early school day, Ryan collected his leftovers, and, almost as an afterthought, told Karl that he was the happiest he had ever been in his life. He got into his powder blue Chevy, and pulled out onto the highway with Karl following in his own car. They had agreed Karl would call him before bed to make sure Ryan had dropped the key off as planned. They drove side-by-side for several miles along the dark highway. Karl remembered waving to him as Ryan turned off to head south.

Just as agreed, Karl called Ryan's cell phone after giving him time to get home. It was 11:10 p.m. Ryan answered, but the contact was strange. They spoke no longer than ten or fifteen seconds, just long enough for Ryan to say that he had dropped off the key. Ryan seemed in a hurry, and there was something odd in his voice. Karl simply assumed that Ryan was distracted by one of his roommates, and thought nothing more about it. Early the next morning, Polk County Sheriff's Detectives pounded on Karl's door.

Joyce was not home yet. Her boss asked her at the last minute to work late, and she didn't make it back to the little red house until 3 a.m. with a case of the tea Ryan liked. He wasn't home, which was unusual to her, but she assumed that Ryan had stayed over at Karl's place for the night, and so she went to bed. On the other hand, Kelly had heard Ryan come in. Since she was the first one home, she had left the door unlocked for him and Joyce. She heard him open the refrigerator door, and then close it. Everyone knew that Ryan was "OCD" about his leftovers, because in Ryan's world, you had to get them into the 'fridge as quickly as possible to avoid food poisoning. Kelly thought she heard somebody else, too, but thought no more about it. No cause for alarm. She just rolled over and went to sleep. The pounding fists of police officers woke both girls up the next morning, too, and the nightmare of what had happened in the cruel dark folded its arms around them.

Bill-Bill, Smiley, and probably Ray-Ray, too, were thieves intent on robbing Ryan for drug money. Chronic meth use had addled their minds, obliterating emotions that would normally inhibit harm against another human being, and triggering instead the violent rages common to meth addicts. But Ryan was gay, a vulnerability that brought on an entirely different dimension of spite and wrath to their plan to rob him. To them Ryan was subhuman, scum, a "fag" who didn't deserve the new car and the fancy clothes he wore. He wasn't normal like they were—he was a pervert, and the fact that he had more than they infuriated them. To them Ryan was soft, weak, an easy target because he was gay. Like Smiley Bearden later admitted to Rock Aguero, as he was trying to sell him Ryan's stolen car, they had no remorse for "fucking him up." Rock testified at Bearden's trial what Smiley had said: "We were doing the world a favor, just getting rid of one more faggot."

The most likely reconstruction of the events of that night is that one or more of Ryan's assassins waited in the shadows until he got home. To begin with, they probably asked for a ride to the store, something Ryan was naïvely apt to do. Some have conjectured that Bill-Bill and Smiley may have told Ryan that they had a good local source for weed, and he could score some, too, if he would only take them to their supplier. Others suggest that Ryan's killers threatened to harm his housemates unless he went with them quietly. For whatever combination of reasons, neighborliness, self-interest, heroism, foolhardiness, or fear, Ryan rode out into the night with the men who would kill him. Bill-Bill's uncle, J.T. Brown, had a house trailer, where his son Ray-Ray lived, one that ran on a gas generator. Ryan took Smiley, Bill-Bill, and Ray-Ray to the store to get gas for the generator between 11:10 p.m. and midnight. Ray-Ray testified to the court that as he poured the gas into the sputtering genera-tor at his daddy's trailer, he saw Bearden and Brown get into Ryan's car with Ryan and drive away. Ten or fifteen minutes later, Ray-Ray said, the little Chevy pulled up into the yard again, but this time only Bill-Bill and Smiley were in it, and they were covered in blood.

Unless one believes that Ryan went quietly to his death, force surely came into play on that final ride. At what moment Ryan realized he was in serious trouble, we cannot know precisely, but almost surely cold ter-ror seized him as he turned down Morgan Road, a dirt track barely two-and-a-half miles from his little red house. The moon was in the third quarter that evening, and it was just rising over the southern horizon at midnight, hiding half of its face in the dark. Ryan never got to see it.

The fatal attack was sudden and savage. According to the Associate Polk County Medical Examiner Vera Volnikh, Ryan fought a losing bat-tle for his life. She counted nineteen stab and slash wounds on his body during the autopsy. He had five defensive wounds on his hands, wrists and arms. The rest were cuts and stabs of varying depths, suggesting that Ryan's flesh and bone had blunted more than one blade. "It could have been two different knives," she testified in court. The killing stroke was delivered from behind, across Ryan's throat, a 3.5-inch-deep slit from left to right that severed his jugular. He bled out in a very few minutes after that, dying in his seat belt. Ryan's autopsy also revealed that his eye socket was caved in from blunt force trauma, probably a stomping or kicking injury. This was no ordinary robbery. Ryan's killers had come armed for wet work. The attack bore all the hallmarks of a hate crime killing: a combination of stabbing, slashing, and bludgeoning, brutally delivered in a pattern of rage.

Charlotte Upchurch, a neighbor on her way to the store, found Ryan's body lying in the road about 1:30 a.m. on March 14. It looked to her like somebody had "turned on a sprinkler full of blood." Ryan lay lifeless, face down in the dirt and gravel. "There was a man's body lying in the road," she testified. "I called out to him and there was no answer and no movement."

THE CUNNING OF POLITICS

Brown and Bearden drove the blood-soaked car to nearby Haines City, where Smiley had been living with the Agueros. When Maria came home in the early morning hours, she found Smiley and the "skinny White dude" cleaning the car. She could tell that both of them were wasted, and the Bill-Bill was trembling as if he were chilled to the bone. They tried to fence the $15,000 car to the Agueros for $1,800 and a few ounces of meth. Rock refused to buy a stolen car with no title. As Ryan's killers took a joy ride around town, bragging about how they had "fucked up a faggot" and taken his car, they repeatedly failed to get something for it, and for a broken laptop computer Ryan was trying to fix for someone. The car was too hot to sell. It had turned into a millstone around their necks. As day neared, their fear of discovery rose. They drove out to a boat ramp on Lake Pansy with gas to burn up the car and eradicate the evidence. Someone has suggested that Bearden and Brown must be among the "greatest dumbasses" of all time—when they set the car afire and ran from the scene, they shut the door with all the windows rolled up, smothering the flames.

In an interview for *Accessory to Murder*, a documentary film on Ryan's death, his mother Pat related what happened when she went to the door of her home, awakened early in the morning:

> It was one of those parent things. You open the door and see detectives standing there with their badges, and I knew before they ever said anything that it was Ryan and someone had hurt him . . . and I never let myself think that it would be something more than hurting him because he was gay. It never, ever, ever crossed my mind! I never considered having to worry about somebody murdering my child!

Dazed, the Mulders fielded phone calls and personal visits all day. Pat stayed in her pajamas and robe until late. No one believed that something so horrific could happen to Ryan. Stephanie was questioned like all the others. The detectives told her that her best friend was dead, that fingerprints confirmed it was Ryan. But she couldn't let herself accept it. She sat at home until midnight, watching the road, hoping it was all just a bad dream. "I kept thinking that any minute I would see his little car boppin' down the road to see me like always," she said.

For Pat, the monstrosity done to Ryan did not hit home until the funeral directors suggested she pick out a high-collared shirt for him to wear in the casket.

Once the car was found, the Sheriff's Department swiftly identified three possible killers, Smiley Bearden, Bill-Bill Brown, and his cousin, Ray-Ray. Interest settled on Smiley and Bill-Bill, and they were arrested within seventy-two hours, charged with first-degree murder and felony robbery. In a deft display of blaming the victim, Sheriff Grady Judd pandered to his right wing political base, spinning the story to put Ryan's character on trial as well as his alleged killers. Soon after a solicitous visit to Ryan's parents at the funeral home, where Sheriff Judd accepted their thanks for such swift police work and pledged to them that Bearden and Brown would "never breathe a single hour of free air again," the Sheriff held a press conference unusual for its candor. Judd portrayed Ryan as a homosexual with a record of marijuana arrests, someone who "picked up the wrong people" while "cruising for sex." There was no doubt, the Sheriff told the local press, that this murder was a hate crime, perpetrated on Ryan Skipper "because he was gay." Further, Judd averred that Ryan and the suspects were "smoking marijuana," and were involved in a criminal check-washing scheme, using a laptop that belonged to Ryan, in an effort to procure drugs.

The Sheriff's allegations against Ryan were subsequently refuted one-by-one:

1. Ryan did not own a laptop, and the one found in the car was inoperable.

2. Ryan's possession arrests were minor when he was under age, with no bearing on his murder whatsoever.

3. The autopsy revealed no trace of marijuana in his bloodstream, so he could not have smoked pot that night with his assailants, as the Sheriff claimed.

4. The check-forgery allegation was spun out of thin air, forcing the Polk County Sheriff's Office to issue this statement one day shy

of a month after Ryan's murder: "There is no indication that Ryan Skipper was involved in any illegal activity . . ."

5. Finally, Ryan had never been in the habit of cruising for sexual partners. There was no need. He was a popular, handsome man, interested in relationships, not tawdry one-night-stands.

The damage to Ryan's reputation, however, was already done. As Brian Winfield of Equality Florida said to the *St. Petersburg Times*, "They've characterized Ryan as a pervert, a drug addict and a felon. In the eyes of the media, [the story] didn't carry the human interest that it should have." Whether or not Sheriff Judd intended to blunt the effect of Ryan's story in order to avoid the attention of the nation to Polk County's systemic homophobia, that is what happened anyway. The only source for the Sheriff's allegations must have come from the accused murderers themselves. Judd became their megaphone, spreading false rumors of "gay criminality" to a population already inclined to believe that somehow Ryan had deserved what he got.

News outlets, starting with the local press, regurgitated the unsubstantiated smears against Ryan's character, and then the metro Florida media repeated the same slander and libel. In a sad parody of "monkey-see, monkey-do," even progressive news organizations and the LGBTQ blogosphere picked up the negative spin without bothering to investigate the facts for themselves. Intentional or not, the anti-LGBTQ political calculus is cold and inexorable. Consequently, the moral impact of Ryan's hate crime murder remains obscured. Negative stereotypes of gay men and poor white men were reinforced in the popular mind, so the victimization of both classes of people continues unchallenged by the truth. The story of "Florida's Matthew Shepard" never had a chance to be told, and lives of potential LGBTQ victims who might have been otherwise saved, such as 17-year-old Simmie Williams Jr. in Fort Lauderdale less than a year later, have also been lost. The status quo rolls on relatively undisturbed in Central Florida. Grady Judd remains the White Knight of Polk County. He has never apologized to Ryan's family and friends. In 2008, he was re-elected Sheriff with 96 percent of the vote.

BRAVE WINGS

Two of Ryan's murderers have come to justice. The third suspect never stood trial. Joseph "Smiley" Bearden was found guilty of second-degree murder in February 2009, and sentenced to life in prison. William D. "Bill-Bill" Brown Jr. stood trial for his life in December of the same year. Bill-Bill was sentenced to life without parole for first-degree murder, and an added life sentence for armed robbery with a deadly weapon. Ray Alan "Ray-Ray" Brown is still a free man. The prosecution never formally charged Brown or Bearden with an anti-gay hate crime, opting instead for a capital murder case and the death penalty. Ryan's parents urged that the death penalty be waived so that the trials could proceed.

The Mulders and Ryan's elder brother, Damian, have gone on to become the most persuasive advocates for LGBTQ equality in Florida, and among the most respected social justice advocates in the nation. As vigils sprang up throughout the state and beyond, calling attention to the heinous murder of their innocent gay son, Lynn and Pat tirelessly traveled and spoke out for hate crimes legislation, safe schools, and LGBTQ rights. Both have become leaders in PFLAG (Parents and Friends of Lesbians and Gays). Damien became deeply involved in the campaign to elect LGBTQ-friendly Barack Obama as President, and made a video appearance on Obama's behalf that went viral on the internet. One of the proudest achievements of Ryan's family is the passage of an anti-bullying law for Florida's public schools in Ryan's memory, so hate violence can be addressed and arrested where it often starts.

Others have rallied to Ryan's memory. Scott Hall, a native of Central Florida, learned of Ryan's murder and established the Gay American Heroes Foundation which strives to chronicle hate crimes against LGBTQ people, and plans to build a national memorial to Ryan and the hundreds of other queer folk who have died because of their sexual orientation and their gender identity. Vicki Nantz and Mary Meek, lesbian partners from Orlando, wrote, produced, directed, and filmed a remarkable independent documentary, called *Accessory to Murder: Our Culture's Complicity in the Death of Ryan Skipper*. Ryan's dearest friends and family, as well as academics, clergy, activists, and law enforcement officers offer a penetrating analysis of the cultural roots of homophobia and hate crimes.

In Auburndale, Ryan's grave is marked by a strikingly handsome headstone of black granite. Carved under a rainbow are a cross and the words of 1 Corinthians 13, "So these things continue forever: faith, hope, and love, and the greatest of these is love." Ryan's gravesite is immaculately tended. As the many gifts left there testify, it is frequently visited. Among these little remembrance gifts is a faded plastic fairy with a broken wing.

Wings motifs keep coming up in relation to Ryan's memory, a theme embraced by his loved ones. Karl cherishes Ryan as his angel, and believes he is still watching over him. Stephanie has tattooed her ankle with Ryan's name, crowned with a halo, and mounting up on wings as if to fly, so that in her flesh she remembers him every day. The same sort of commitment is true for Kelly, and Joyce, and Dotty, and dozens more who recall the boy with the amazing smile and the good heart: the one who protected their hearts as if they were his own. Fittingly, now, their hearts keep memory alive.

On the mantle of the Mulder home, where Ryan's cat "Baby" patrols daily, still looking for her master, Pat and Lynn have put a framed photo of a snow-white egret in the Everglades. The egret stands in the blue water, surrounded by the submerged green-black menace of a school of large alligators, any of which could make a meal of her with one snap of its terrifying jaws. Yet the egret stands among them, beating her wings forward in an act of feathered defiance, steady as an Amazon warrior facing battle. An inscription in ink on the photo reads: "Brave Wings." Lesbian friends gave the photograph as a gift to the Mulders, a tribute to their son. Lynn shows it off proudly, gratefully. "That's Ryan to us," he says, "brave wings and all." And then, after a pause, "He was courageous like that, living here as just who he was, wasn't he?"

For Greater Understanding

Keeper of Hearts: Ryan Keith Skipper

BOOKS

Herek, Gregory M., and Kevin T. Berrill. *Hate Crimes: Confronting Violence Against Lesbians and Gay Men.* Newbury Park, CA: Sage Publications, 1992.

FILMS AND VIDEOGRAPHY

Accessory to Murder: Our Culture's Complicity in the Death of Ryan Keith Skipper. Ryan Skipper Documentary Project, 2007.

ORGANIZATIONS AND WEBSITES

Beyond Homophobia, http://www.beyondhomophobia.com/blog.
Equality Florida, http://eqfl.blogspot.com.
Gay American Heroes Foundation, http://www.gayamericanheroes.info.
Ryan Skipper Documentary Project, http://www.ryanskipperdocumentary.com.
Unfinished Lives Project, http://unfinishedlivesblog.com.

Sakia LaTona Gunn
May 26, 1987—May 11, 2003

NEWARK, NEW JERSEY

8

Justice Deferred, Justice Denied

Sakia LaTona Gunn

*"I remember how being young and black and gay and lonely felt.
A lot of it was fine, feeling I had the truth and the light and the key,
but a lot of it was purely hell."*

—AUDRE LORDE

SAKIA GUNN HAD A tiger swimming in her blood. She was brave. God knows, she needed to be. She was born black and poor, deep in the "'hood," into a broad-shouldered, blue collar city plagued by urban blight and cultural ills. She lived her 15 short years, and died in Newark at the point of a switchblade knife because she was "SGL," Same Gender Loving, and dared to be proud about it. No glib accounts of racism, skin privilege, sexism, or even homophobia can finally explain or expunge the grief and loss of her unjust end—not if we truly want to catch a true glimpse of this strong, gender non-conforming girl who lived life on her own terms. Sakia LaTona Gunn was far too formidable and complex for that.

If Sakia is remembered at all, Sakia remains a tantalizing enigma, a riddle wrapped in the mystery of her personal awareness about her sexual and social identity. She was a precocious child. As early as 11 years old, she announced to her mother, "Ma, I don't like boys. I like girls." Her mother LaTona Gunn took the news in stride, but knew through hard experience that the people of Newark would hardly congratulate her eldest daughter for such candor about whom she loved and why.

LaTona counseled her child never to be afraid of who she was. Sakia took her Ma's words to heart and grew up unapologetically. Her older cousin Anthony Hall told reporters after her death that Sakia was clear about who she was, and happy. "No man or woman can judge her," he said, "only God can judge her."

She was a good kid, the first of three girls and a baby boy that LaTona and Grandmother Thelma Gunn reared in Newark's far western Vailsburg section. "The Peacemaker," is how her mother described Sakia's role in the family. She could give up without giving in. Grandmother Thelma, Sakia's legal guardian, experienced this gift of hers early on. A devout Jehovah's Witness, she naturally wanted her eldest granddaughter to go to church. But Grandmother wasn't about to have Sakia accompany her to Kingdom Hall wearing the saggy-baggy jeans and an oversized boy's shirt she preferred to wear. No, ma'am! To please her grandmother, Sakia agreed to wear a pink dress and sweater picked out for her, if and only if Grandma would drive the car close enough to the church entrance so the fewest number of people would see her dressed up like a girl. The compromise worked. Sakia proved she could go along in order to get along, and her grandmother loved her so much that she laid aside her scruples about her granddaughter's soul. Beyond any doubt, Sakia knew who and what she was, and Grandmother Thelma understood there was no sense trying to change her.

According to her friends and kinfolk, Sakia was a charismatic, dynamic girl. By the time she reached her mid-teens, Sakia had matured into a promising young sophomore athlete, 5'3" tall and 130 lbs. She had musical talent, and wanted to join the West Side High School Rough Rider Marching Band as a drummer. But basketball was far and away Sakia's greatest interest. "B-ball" was her game, and she loved it. She tried out and earned a guard slot on the women's varsity squad. Her grades slumped, and Sakia had been suspended from the team, but lately her grades were steadily improving. She expected to be reinstated soon. Her fondest dream in the whole world according to her Ma was to play ball in the pros one day, for the Women's National Basketball Association.

LIKE A RAINBOW IN THE NIGHT

LaTona Gunn didn't want to see her beautiful Sakia traumatized by the perils poor urban women of color, straight and lesbian alike, face every day of their lives. Misogyny is shocking, brutal, and cruel. Let it become internalized, though, and sexist fear turns not only into a mental jail-house of the soul, but a physical one, as well. Women who absorb the brute whim of an unfriendly erection, a fragile male ego, and a switch-blade knife seldom sleep undisturbed in their beds, even when they are safely alone.

Denied skin privilege, robbed of gender esteem, and burdened with poverty, black lesbian youth in the 'hood are geared for same-gender love in a world of male hypocrisy. This obdurate reality is an important key for understanding how brave Sakia truly was. The endowment of slavery makes black men vigorous defenders of their women against whites, but too often this patriarchy works as a screen behind which the criminal abuse of black women goes on and on. Same Gender Loving African American women, however, face intensified discrimination within their own historically discriminated-against communities. SGL female subculture necessarily formed as an outsider community inside their own black culture. Their families of origin often disown them. The Black Church preaches against them. The selective shield of black male protection is reserved for conventional women, not "queers." Abusers find SGL sisters easier prey than others. Lesbians and bisexuals of color are all-too-often left to rear the children irresponsible men sire and abandon—men who depend on these very women—yet who openly disdain them for being same-sex-loving. The white gay and lesbian com-munity offers them no refuge, either. Racism, the ugly open secret of LGBTQ community, is commonly more blatant among white gay people than even their heterosexual counterparts. This is the lonely hell lesbians of color know so intimately, from Audre Lorde to Alicia Banks. As the refrain of the Negro spiritual goes, "Run to the Rock to hide your face; Rock cries out, 'No hiding place!'"

Sakia, however, owned an identity that tied her to a subculture of a subculture: she and her best friends where self-identified "AG-lesbians," "Aggressives." Not only are they geared emotionally and sexually for their same gender, but these young women of color express a complex interplay of masculine and feminine within themselves making them non-conformist even among other SGL women. Neither drag kings nor female-to-male transgender people, Aggressives have taken up the hip-hop life in earnest: the dress, the affect, the total defiant ambience that once made hip-hop a risky proposition before commercialism tamed it for the consumer market. They are "gangstas" of love, "sheroes" of the 'hood. Aggressives have declared their independence from mainstream lesbian subculture constructed on the butch-femme binary, opting instead for individual stud identities as black dykes who love femmes, but who may just as likely fall in love with other studs like themselves. Even among their SGL sisters, then, Aggressives are often targets of a lingering internalized heterosexism that brands them as disturbing gender outlaws—"too gay."

By her mid-teens, Sakia had grown into a SGL woman routinely mistaken for a male. She shunned frills and little pink dresses for the ubiquitous hip-hop uniform: low-slung jeans, a head rag, and a white tee shirt. Her best friend and cousin, Valencia Bailey, burst out in spasms of laughter when someone asked her who that *boy* was up in her room. She delighted to reveal that the so-called *'boy'* was "'Kia! You know, 'T'!" as Sakia's intimate friends preferred to called her.

Besides Valencia, with whom she shared most everything, Sakia found others who dressed and presented masculinely like she did. The group gave her an important sense of teenage belonging, even to a girl as strong as 'Kia. At West Side High, she had found a girlfriend, a quiet femme named Jai. She also found comfort and strength in a sympathetic high school teacher, her basketball coach, Shani Baraka. Though Newark is the largest city in New Jersey and the second most diverse in the whole state, it offered precious little refuge for any of its LGBTQ kids, much less Aggressives like Sakia's crew. The poor, crime-stricken neighborhoods on either side of Newark Penn Station the girls knew so well were like a palette of competing hues—brown and black, smudging into each other: Salvadorans, Hondurans, Puerto Ricans, Brazilians, West Indians and Blacks, living cheek-by-jowl. Street preachers harangued the foot traffic around the bustling bus stops in the daylight, and hookers "ministered" to the night people when the sun went down. Carloads of drunk, high, cat-calling men cruising for sex, plied the wet streets under the glare of the dripping overhead lamps into the early morning hours. Cops huddled together for safety, ignoring the homeless people and the junkies who mostly just wanted to be left alone. Newark seemed not to know there had ever been a Stonewall Rebellion for gay and lesbian rights in 1969 just over the river in Manhattan. There were no rainbow flags floating in the long Jersey night. A veteran political activist described Newark as "one great big closet." The city had no organized LGBTQ groups, no gay pride parade, no gay community center—not even a single bar dedicated to lesbian or gay clientele. So Sakia and her friends, like so many other Jersey queer kids of color before them, looked east to the bright, shimmering lights of the Big Apple.

As often as they could, the girls would get permission from their parents to take the PATH train from Newark Penn Station to New York City, just across the Hudson River. The fare was less than two bucks, and in twenty-five or thirty minutes they could be on Christopher Street in Greenwich Village, the pulsing heart of Manhattan's historic gay and lesbian district—a place where young Aggressives could breathe free. Sakia's mother said that when her daughter talked about traveling over to "the Vill," her eyes sparkled; it was like she was going on a "mini-vacation." Valencia Bailey, who often made the trip with 'Kia, told CNN's Maria Hinojosa:

> When you go to the Village, it's like a different environment. It seems like the gay community [is] as one, we don't play no nonsense. There's no beef there . . . You can just go and you can just relax, but you ain't got to worry about like nobody fighting.

As if teleported into another world, the girls landed in a "gayborhood" of narrow streets jammed with boutiques, cafés, sex shops and legendary bars—the iconic Stonewall Inn, and the Monster on Sheridan Square, the ever-popular Ramrod Bar for the leather crowd, the Cubby Hole and Chi Chiz that catered to lesbians, and Peter Rabbit's with its black queer clientele. Though Sakia, Valencia, and their friends were underage and the clubs were off-limits, it was just a short walk from the heart of "the Vill" to the Chelsea Piers, recently refurbished, jutting out into the Hudson River. Every gay tribe seemed to have a hangout there. The Piers had become especially popular with LGBTQ teens of color by the Spring of 2003. There they could smoke, dance, meet new people, drink the alcohol they had sneaked, talk and laugh as loud and hard as they liked, and make out under the lamps that burned up and down the Piers after dark. Usually after 2 a.m., they would make their way back past the 9/11 ruins of the Twin Towers to the PATH train. They rode it to Newark Penn Station, debarked, and caught a cab home if they had the money, or walked to the bus if they didn't. If they chose to walk to the bus and save a little money, the trek was four city blocks up the Broad Street corridor to the bus stop at Market and Broad Streets. Even though it was late in the night when they reached the bus stop, street lamps lighted the area well, and there was a big blue and white Newark Police booth situated on the corner where officers were supposed to be stationed all of the time.

DREAM-KILLER

The evening of Saturday, May 10, 2003 had turned fair, and the breeze was gentle. It was Mother's Day eve. Sakia, Valencia, Kamiya, Chantell and their friends, none of them over 17 years of age, hopped the PATH train to the Chelsea Piers. Like usual, Sakia's significant other, Jai, stayed home. Jai thought it was safer to stay in Newark than exposing herself to people she didn't know. Reflecting on that night a year after her lover's murder, Jai told Daisey Hernandez of *Fierce NYC*, "I don't go out. I go to school. I come home. Me and Sakia were total opposites. She was the type to go out and hang out." The girls were ready for a good time as their train headed toward "the Vill." They were decked out, pumped up, and full of bravado. Kia had on her favorite baggy jeans, her best white do-rag, and her white "wife beater," a classic tee shirt with no sleeves. A half-hour later, they were on their way down Christopher Street to the Piers. The night was vibrant and randy. The Village was a hive of throbbing activity, and the girls let loose. Valencia remembers that their favorite jam, Lumidee's brand new hit, "Never Leave You / Uh Oh!" was blasting out of passing cars, and the girls gyrated and danced to the pounding beat. That tune was going to be their theme song for the whole coming summer. The Piers vibrated with youthful joy and pent-up passions until the girls realized the hour was getting 'way late. They had to make it back for Mother's Day, the day of all days the black community sets to honor the women who sustained them.

By the time they got back to Newark Penn Station, it was after 3 a.m. One girl in their crew hailed a cab, and the rest were about to get in when Sakia said she wanted to walk up to the bus stop instead. She was the leader, and the others followed her up the corridor. It was about 3:30 when they arrived at the bus stop. The big police booth across the street, supposed to be manned 24/7 (a campaign promise made by Mayor Sharpe James), was empty that night. As they waited for the #1 New Jersey Transit bus, a white station wagon cruised slowly past the girls, and a big man leaned out of the passenger window suggesting lewdly that he could make them feel real good. "Yo, shorty, come over here!" he shouted. Richard McCullough, their harasser, was 5'9" and 265 lbs. of sexual frustration that night. He was 29 years old and the biological father of two children, yet obviously not mature enough to know better than to cruise for teenage girls. "You girls looking for some fun?" he leered. Sakia spoke up matter-of-factly for them all, saying "No, we're okay—we're not like that; we're gay." A storm broke in McCullough's head at their refusal—who did these little dykes think they were to rebuff him? Since the murder, pundits have debated whether McCullough went over the edge because Sakia announced she and the girls were lesbian, or whether he already suspected they were "dykes." Did he make sexual advances out of a perverse desire to evoke a response from them? None of these questions matter—the responsibility for what happened next was all his. Whatever ignited him, McCullough was well and truly poisoned by the same toxic mix of hypocrisy, misogyny, and homo-hatred that still infects so many other insecure, macho men in the 'hood. Now in a rage, he yelled out the window at the girls, calling them sluts, whores, fags, and dykes. His driver, Allen Pierce, yanked the station wagon to the curb and slammed the stick to park. He and McCullough boiled out on the street to assault the girls. Pierce picked up a bottle from the street, but put it down and backed out of the fight when Sakia and Valencia defiantly balled up their fists at him.

The attack proceeded with staccato fury. McCullough grabbed young Kamiya and put her in a headlock. Sakia shouted at him to let her go, moving swiftly to her friend's defense. Kamiya's mouth started foaming as she struggled to breathe. As she doubled over in pain and suffocation, the big man abruptly threw her down. He angrily ordered Sakia to come to him. She refused to move, saying, no, he wasn't her father. As Valencia recalled it, McCullough grabbed at Sakia, drew his switchblade, and they scuffled. Roaring more homophobic slurs, he took her by the throat, and as 'Kia swung her fist at him, she broke free of his hold. McCullough clumsily grabbed her again, this time pointing his 'blade at the base of 'Kia's throat. As she squared up to swing at him again, he stabbed the knife through her wife beater, deep into her chest. Valencia related her memory of that moment to black gay journalist Keith Boykin for his anniversary article about Sakia's murder: "She runs behind me and starts taking off her shirt. Her wife beater went from white to red. I ran toward her and she went into a state of shock. 'Kia, 'Kia! Come on! Get up! You have to get up!" Valencia screamed.

When Sakia fell to the pavement bleeding, the two men fled back to their station wagon and sped away. Valencia still had enough presence of mind to get the license number. She frantically flagged down a passing motorist, named Patrick Musa, and begged him to rush them to nearby University Hospital. Time ran out for the young tigress. Sakia hemorrhaged in her friend's arms, her chest gushing blood like a fountain, as they raced the short half-mile down the street to the hospital's emergency entrance. The doctors and nurses on duty fought to save her life, exercising all their skill, but without success. In the E.R., 'Kia's eyes rolled up into her head until all Valencia could see was the white, she testified at McCullough's trial. Then her friend went limp, her head lolling heavy and still in Valencia's hands.

NOTHIN' BUT A 'SMALL MURDER'

Mother's Day morning in the Vailsburg neighborhood swiftly shattered into a fractured jar of broken dreams. LaTona Gunn got the emergency call to come to University Hospital. The caller said her daughter, Sakia, had been stabbed. She and her mom, Grandmother Thelma, got down to the E.R. as quickly as they could, but LaTona never let the possibility enter her mind that her child could be dead. Quoted in Keith Boykin's anniversary interview about Sakia's murder, LaTona recalled that she was preparing to say, "Told you so," to her daughter for not carrying Mace with her as both LaTona and Grandmother Thelma had repeatedly advised. Then, intending to tease her a bit, LaTona meant to comfort Sakia about her first real "battle scar." After the head nurse confirmed LaTona was indeed Sakia's mother, and informed her face-to-face that her daughter was dead, even then the horrible news just wouldn't sink in. LaTona told Boykin she assumed the nurse had made some sort of awful mistake—surely someone else's daughter must have died. Not Sakia. But as Grandmother Thelma heard the same terrible news, she knew instantly it was true. Sagging in her waiting room chair, she clutched at her chest and fell to the hospital floor, stricken by a heart attack. In one of the cruel coincidences of such hate crimes, Sakia's grandmother was treated for cardiac arrest in the same E.R. where her beloved granddaughter had been pronounced dead just hours before. Only when LaTona was brought into the room where her slaughtered child lay covered with a sheet—only then—did the horror strike home. Sakia *was* dead, and LaTona's world was changed forever.

Stacy Nickerson was one of the first adults outside the Gunn family to reach the hospital early that morning. Stacy was the mother of

Sakia's ex girlfriend, Toni Nickerson, a 15-year-old lesbian who had only recently broken up with Sakia. During the three months of the girls' courtship, Stacy got to know Sakia well, regarding her as another daughter. After begging the Roman Catholic Chaplain to get her past security, Stacy entered the trauma room and held Sakia's body. She described the scene to reporter Mick Meenan of the *Gay City News*:

> [Sakia] was laying there with a plastic tube coming from out her mouth. Her body was covered by a white sheet. It appears that they had unhooked everything because they couldn't save her. But there was blood everywhere. She had on her white do-rag she always wears and it was filled with blood. Both her hands were full of blood.

News of Sakia's murder spread like a shockwave throughout the black lesbian community. E-mails flew, cell phones erupted, and the informal rainbow network of Newark's black queer youth rallied to the memory of their AG sister. The intensity of grief and anger unleashed by her death caught the mayor and city officials totally by surprise. Droves of black teens converged on the corner of Market and Broad Streets where Sakia had been fatally stabbed. Within a couple of days, mourners built two makeshift shrines at the murder site to honor her. One was a wooden wall constructed between a couple of upright girders, where scores of lesbian youth signed their names, wrote messages, and pinned up pictures, flowers, stuffed toys, and other mementos. The other was row-upon-row of foot-high votive candles surrounding Sakia's plainly visible rusty bloodstains on the sidewalk. Balloons, rainbow ribbons, and rainbow flags seemed to have sprouted up out of the concrete. Mourners wrote sentiments like "R.I.P. Sakia—A.K.A. 'T'" and "We Love You, T" on the pavement in bold letters with multicolored chalk and crayons.

The Gunn family was deluged by phone calls and requests for interviews, to the point that LaTona left home and sought refuge with trusted friends where she could grieve undisturbed. Sakia's favorite teacher, Shani Baraka, checked-in daily with the family to help them through their bereavement. Grandmother Thelma, still in the hospital, was moved to a cardiac care unit three floors above the trauma center where Sakia had died. There she struggled to recover from the double assault on her heart: a mild heart attack from which the doctors felt she would fully recover in time, and a broken heart she knew would *never* heal.

Stung by criticism about the deserted police booth at Market and Broad, the Newark Police scrambled to find leads. By Monday, police issued descriptions of two men to the public: both black, dressed in white tee shirts and blue jeans, in their mid-to-late twenties. The white station wagon was found abandoned thee miles away in East Orange early Tuesday morning. Police identified Richard McCullough as their chief suspect in the murder and released his picture to the media. Late Thursday afternoon, just as hundreds of angry black mourners converged on City Hall to protest Sakia's murder, McCullough, in the company of his attorney, turned himself in to the authorities. Police charged him with felony murder and a raft of other crimes that, in total, could have locked him away for 118 years. Then the dealmakers got involved, street rage was contained to a relatively small segment of the population, and the media downplayed the killing of a teenage girl McCullough chronically referred to as "the little dude"—the black lesbian kid who dressed up like a hip-hop boy.

Professor Kim Pearson, a Communications scholar from the College of New Jersey, who blogged about the Gunn murder from the earliest days of the story, noted how the passion surrounding Sakia's story never quite translated into "spreadable news." For a time, the 'hood was aflame with both anger and sorrow. On May 15 hundreds of LGBTQ youth of color attended a vigil in Kia's memory held on the steps of City Hall, and then marched to the bus stop where she died. On May 16, the day after the massive City Hall rally, a crowd estimated at 2,500 gathered for Sakia's funeral. City dignitaries, aspiring politicians, and Mayor Sharpe James himself attended along with Sakia's family. A crowd of grieving black lesbian, gay, and transgender teens congregated in the hundreds. Jim Fouratt of the *Gay City News* counted only *eight* whites attending the funeral, none of them from any of the major media outlets in the metro area. As if her story were smothered in insulation, the energy surrounding 'Kia's murder remained bottled up in Newark. Black activist and scholar Darnell Moore, living in South Jersey at the time, recalls that the word about Sakia did not even reach Camden, eighty-six miles away. Though vigils and memorial gatherings sprang up in a few cities as far away as Boston, Duluth, Minnesota and San Francisco thanks to news carried by a small number of bloggers, Sakia's name had a disturbingly short shelf life for LGBTQ human rights activists. As Professor Pearson pointed out to her blog-reader audience:

In newsroom lingo, [the Sakia Gunn murder] was treated as a "small murder"—deserving of scant coverage because it was not considered likely to be of interest to the advertiser-attractive consumers of most news outlets, even among LGBTQ and African American media.

For the hundreds of black lesbian and gay youth attending her funeral, however, the trauma of Sakia's death was anything but small. Mick Meenan of the *Gay City News* was stunned by the groundswell of grief and anger he witnessed as stricken youths passed by Sakia's open casket. Her corpse lay cradled in white—dressed in a neat, white jump suit, cushioned in soft, white pillows, cosseted in a steel casket enameled all-white. A rainbow patch was pinned to the interior fabric of the casket lid, and a large beribboned spray of blue-tinted carnations, white daisies, and fuji mums rested on the closed half of her coffin. So many gathered on the lawn outside the funeral home that the wait to file past her body grew excessively long, heightening frustrations and shortening tempers. Emotion overwhelmed many of the young mourners, some of them collapsing on the grass sobbing as they exited the funeral parlor building. Meenan reported that a young woman cried out in a piercing voice, "Why? Why? Why?" over and over in her anguish. The situation nearly got out of hand. No provision for grief counseling had been made by anyone, typical of the way that Newark related to its LGBTQ youth, as some long-time gay activists noted to the press. A few professionals, licensed counselors, HIV/AIDS workers and LGBTQ-friendly ministers who were in attendance to pay their own respects to Sakia, acted to comfort the waves of grieving young people, many of them teenaged lesbians. Leah McElrath, an out lesbian psychotherapist, told Meenan that she never intended to offer her services that day, but the need was so great, she stepped in to do what she could. "Most of these kids had shown up without any adult support," she said. "Many appeared to be overwhelmed with grief and their trauma stemmed from the realization that it could have been them who was killed." Adults besieged Mayor James to do something, not just stand there. He couldn't deny what he saw with his own eyes, so the mayor ordered in scores of officers from the Newark Police Department as well as workers from the Newark Department of Health. Mayor James's panicky calls were so strident that both the Chief of Police and his deputy hustled down to the teeming lawn where ambulances rolled in and paramedics were administering oxygen to prostrate teens. Surrounded and booed by angry voters, the mayor declared he would push for the establishment of a gay youth center in Sakia's name—a promise he never kept.

STAND IN THE DAY OF TROUBLE

Marginalized queers of color from the streets of Newark are the real heroes of this terrible story. They took up their own mission in Sakia's memory in the days following her murder. In the wake of her massive funeral, Aggressives and their allies struggled to bend outrage into empowerment, even though the specter of street violence loomed over the city for many days. Rev. Elder Kevin Taylor, pastor of New Brunswick's Unity Fellowship Church, was deeply involved in comforting anguished youth on the funeral home lawn on May 16. Professor Pearson recalls in her "News and Notes" blog that Taylor made two trenchant observations about the seething crowd of LGBTQ teenagers and their mood on that chaotic day. First, it was nearly miraculous that the spark of Sakia's brutal murder did not ignite the pent-up fury of these kids into a full-blown street rebellion. As Elder Taylor commented to his congregation the day after her funeral, "They were two tears away from a riot." Second, many of these kids came together that day out of a common need for security. Many of them had been harassed and beaten repeatedly in their schools and neighborhoods—even their own homes—for their actual or perceived gender non-conformity and sexual orientation. Protection had never come from the adults in their lives. They were truly afraid that what had happened to Sakia was going to happen to them as well. Professor Pearson also sensed that the surprisingly mixed multitude of youth—many Black and Latina lesbians, but also including good numbers of "thugged-out straight boys"—were united by much more than grief over Sakia's death. To a person, these young people feared an increase in murder and physical attacks against themselves because of what had happened to her. Some believed all they could do was fight and die, just like Sakia, since school, law enforcement, and church officials had proved totally unreliable, unwilling, or unable to help them.

Still others, however, organized themselves for security and protest. What they accomplished in the first year following 'Kia's murder kept her memory alive through a lingering period of political neglect. Young queers of color held the line until adult allies awakened to the horror and significance of a murder that led to the first anti-gay bias prosecution in New Jersey history. Sakia's closest friends and acquaintances formed the "Sakia Gunn Aggressive'z and Fem'z," a lesbian teen group, created to agitate for better police protection, heightened lesbian awareness in city schools, and to keep Sakia's memory alive. Members donned clothes similar to Sakia's for school, festooned with buttons bearing her picture and rainbow patches to identify themselves publically as LGBTQ. They pressed administrators at Sakia's West Side High School for a moment of silence in her memory, where an ugly unconfirmed rumor circulated that the principal, Fernand Williams, said the slain girl had gotten "about what she asked for." The school administration refused to grant even one second of silence for Sakia. Officials banned "Sakia clothes" and buttons throughout the 44,000-student school district, but the Aggressive'z and Fem'z found adult allies who helped them advance their demands for a safe place to gather, a gay community center, so that they wouldn't need to travel to New York City for solidarity and support.

Laquetta Nelson, a longtime human rights activist, was so distressed by Sakia's murder that she came out of retirement to launch the "Newark Pride Alliance, Inc.," an organization dedicated to securing the gay youth drop-in center Mayor Sharpe James had paid only lip service to. When asked in October 2003 by reporters for *The Advocate* why she decided to take up the cause of the Aggressive'z and Fem'z, Nelson said it was because of her jarring experience at the May 15 vigil for Sakia. "Those kids," she remembered, "I have never seen so many kids just falling apart. I mean, their grief and their pain was . . . it was just so deep. These were mostly young African-American lesbians. And I'm wondering, 'Where are their parents? The kids don't have any place to go.'" Nelson had a powerful natural affinity and admiration for Sakia. She found a kindred spirit in her and in the other young Aggressives and Fems who struggled to be true to themselves in Newark. "That little girl inside of me connected with Sakia," Nelson said, "and all the other lesbians I talked to felt the same thing. Because when we were 15 years old, guys hit on us all the time, and we just wouldn't say anything. We knew we would have been found dead somewhere. She was brave. Sakia's like our hero." Nelson's decades of work on LGBTQ issues in New Jersey made her the ideal organizer for promoting the idea of a gay community center where queer kids of all sexual identities could connect, take GED classes, and find lesbian and gay foster families to give security and acceptance in a hostile city.

The local chapter of Parents and Friends of Lesbians and Gays (PFLAG) supported Sakia's marginalized friends, too. After Shani Baraka (Sakia's favorite teacher and coach), and her partner were both killed in a domestic dispute in August 2003, the Gunns worked alongside the Baraka family to establish the Newark branch of PFLAG. Not only advocating for a community center serving queer youth of color, PFLAG members also raised enough money to establish a $2,500 scholarship in Sakia's name. On the first anniversary of her death in May 2004, Newark PFLAG awarded the first annual "Sakia Gunn College Scholarship for Gay, Lesbian, Bisexual and Transgender (GLBT) Community Involvement" to Alexa Punnamkuzhyil, a high school senior honor student from Arcata, California who had founded a Gay/Straight Alliance. PFLAG also played a role in the developing case against Sakia's killer, Richard McCullough. In February 2004, the local chapter released a letter sent to them from McCullough, who was then being held on $500,000 bail in the Essex County Jail. According to the *New York Times*, McCullough wrote PFLAG, saying that Sakia was responsible for her own death, which he called "an accident." "This little dude pounced on me and into the knife that I held in my hand," McCullough wrote. "I never wanted or intended to hurt him or anybody else. I never knew he was a she filled with such hate and aggression over a simple argument and nothing more." Stunned by the letter, McCullough's attorney disavowed that he had anything to do with its creation. The PFLAG letter complicated an already difficult defense for his big-mouthed client.

Newark Now became an ally, as well. Future Newark Mayor Cory A. Booker founded "Newark Now" in 2002, a grassroots non-profit organization seeking to connect low-to-moderate-income citizens with resources and services to improve their neighborhoods. By the first anniversary of Sakia's murder, violence against youth of color had become a political hot potato for longtime Mayor Sharpe James, and Booker simply adopted the cause for a drop-in center for LGBTQ and other kids of color.

The first annual observance of Sakia's murder included commemorative events in the Newark Public Schools and a vigil, largely brought about by the coalition of Aggressive'z and Fem'z, Newark Pride Alliance, PFLAG, and Newark Now. West Side High reversed its own decision not to allow recognition of Sakia's death, and the Superintendent of Schools belatedly approved a moment of silence at noon, followed by the reading of Sakia's name along with the names of twenty-five other Newark students who had died since 2002 of accidents or violence. Two hundred and fifty people gathered for the vigil at the corner of Market and Broad Streets to listen to songs, poetry, and speeches in Sakia's memory. Alice Leeds, speaking for the local PFLAG chapter, announced the recipient of the Sakia Gunn Scholarship to the crowd with the noisy grumble of city traffic serving as a backdrop. The *New York Times* covered the event, as well as a few Newark and LGBTQ papers. But those in it for the long haul knew keeping Sakia's memory alive would only become more difficult as the months and years elapsed.

"COME OUT THE WILDERNESS LEAN AND LONELY"

Amnesia and inertia, prime enforcers of the status quo, set in with a vengeance shortly after the first anniversary of Sakia's murder. Old, smoldering patterns of bigotry and backlash reasserted themselves as Sakia's memory submerged into a pool of community impotence that seemed bottomless. As early as June 2003, in their blog post for "The Gully," Kelly Cogswell and Ana Simo bitingly critiqued Newark's "Siamese Twins joined at the anus": white racist censorship and black homophobia. They argued in their post "Erasing Sakia: Who's to Blame?" that both white racists and black homophobes wanted black queer youth to vanish. Like gored oxen, many critics protested their argument, but Cogswell and Simo had merely voiced what other critics of conscience were noticing, as well.

Sakia Gunn sat uncomfortably at the center of this hate crime murder, a black, urban, lower class, lesbian girl who was often confused for a thugged-out black boy. In the American mind, each unwelcome layer of her life gradually diminished and obscured her remembrance. White editors most certainly downplayed Sakia's story since all the players, victims and victimizers alike, were black. Professor Pearson's comparison of media coverage of the Gunn murder with the slaying of LGBTQ icon Matthew Shepard in Laramie, Wyoming proved particularly telling. Pearson's careful *Lexis-Nexis* research month-by-month for the year following both murders showed that the stories in *all* news media on Sakia numbered 28, while stories appearing only in *major* newspapers about Shepard totaled 735. Had the stories on the young, white University of Wyoming student counted up in *all media* for this period, articles would surely number in the thousands. GLAAD (the Gay & Lesbian Alliance Against Defamation), concluded in its October 2003 report on hate crimes that the initial scant media coverage of Sakia's story received was never followed up. Dr. Gayle Baldwin, a passionately engaged researcher into Sakia's murder, pointed out, "Sakia died for reasons too stupid to imagine! All she got was twenty seconds on national media!" she said, the anger swelling beneath her words. "That was it! It was as if all of this community never existed!" Though black and LGBTQ news outlets must bear their share of the blame for diminishing Sakia's narrative, too, neither community had access enough to shine a national spotlight on her murder and its meaning. Corporate media, reflecting white community preferences and values among both straights and gays, buried Sakia Gunn's story as utterly as the undertakers had buried her body in Newark's Fairmount Cemetery. All these factors, combined with the endless legal maneuvers postponing McCullough's trial *ad nauseum.* Two long years squelched the little media interest in Sakia, allowing it to wither and die. Without the galvanizing power of a courtroom drama, the initial size and strength of the community response to her murder faded away with yesterday's headlines.

The homophobia of Newark's "black Democratic machine" and the virulently anti-gay Black Church set the pattern of apathy and attack that nearly snuffed out any movement for change. Mayor Sharpe James's pledges of a gay youth center amounted to nothing. While city school officials aimed homophobic innuendo at Sakia's memory, James sat by feigning deafness and assuming no responsibility. Without the leadership of the mayor, city government remained largely unmoved by the concerns of LGBTQ people, a conveniently ignorable segment of the population. To the historic Black churches of Newark, Sakia's fate simply served as an object lesson buttressing a divinely assumed condemnation of the "lesbian lifestyle," which they routinely read back into scripture before preaching it from their pulpits. For the most part, the religious communities of Newark, prominent national civil rights leaders, and the big, national advocacy organizations remained numbingly, homophobicly silent about 'Kia's slaughter in the streets. National leaders like Al Sharpton and Jesse Jackson expressed no interest in the story, either, as if there were something too radioactive about this blatant injustice to touch. Speaking to "The Gully" in June 2003, Laquetta Nelson said that silence in the face of injustice has dire consequences, particularly for the young:

The church people were quiet. All of them were quiet. There was nothing from the NAACP, nothing from any of those types of organizations. What kind of message do you think that sends to the young people of Newark? That their lives mean nothing to them.

The fragmented and divided Newark LGBTQ community, hampered activists like Nelson and a few clergy allies from moving ahead with the drop-in center effort. The causes of gay disunity were many, and they had crippling effects. Too many queer folk were closeted, unwilling to do anything public for fear of losing their jobs and status. They led divided lives, passing in the straight world, secretly gay behind closed doors. "Papa" Jeter, a black female-to-male transgender man familiar with the Gunns, remembered more was in play than rage back in the day. Fear was rampant, too. "When Kia was murdered," Jeter said, "people retreated back into their closets." Some had a hard time dealing with Sakia's AG identity. They were outraged that she had been so brutally murdered, but something about the Pepe Jeans and "fitted's" she wore made them balk at owning her as one "of theirs." By far, the largest obstacle to unifying the Newark LGBTQ community to resist amnesia and press ahead for change was the widely accepted notion that nothing black queer folks and poor women ever did seemed to count. Misogyny, racism and homophobia were deeply linked, each serving as a weapon of the other two. For as long as anyone could remember, gay folk of color were as invisible as ghosts in Newark. The Powers That Be doubted such a community even existed in New Jersey's largest city, since most LGBTQ people unobtrusively crossed the river to New York's Greenwich Village for gay nightlife and culture. Sakia's horrible death had rallied the young in the hundreds, and the street rage at the status quo had been real. But nearly two years after her murder, nothing much had changed for queer youth of color in the city. It was common knowledge that Sakia's slaughter was not an isolated incident, not by any means. But "money talks and bullshit walks"—and though poor black youth and women were murdered with distressing frequency, the increasing word on the street was "They never do anything when one of us gets killed—They never put it on TV—Hell, they never even talk about it!"

It seemed that Newark's "great big closet door" was about to slam shut on the children's crusade coalition of black queer youth and too few activist allies. But as Nelson tirelessly reminded whoever would listen, anger was on the side of remembrance and change, this time. Like the

Hebrew children ready to 'come out the wilderness,' Newark's black queer diaspora had been hardened in the lean and lonely time, and something was getting ready to explode.

RELENTLESS, THIS TIME?

After years of protests had fallen on deaf ears regarding the plight of Newark's LGBTQ community, the pent-up fury of the people demanded a hearing. Laquetta Nelson said her folk were in no mood for another derailed movement for change. In her October 2003 interview with *The Advocate*, Nelson made their determination abundantly clear: "We're getting ready to rise up—and I'm talking about the African American gays and lesbians," she said. "We're some angry people." The pressure for meaningful change refused to be choked off by pain, or by threats this time—no shriveling up like a raisin in the sun. The people's anger drove their pursuit for justice. And just about the same time Richard McCullough's trial started making news, Sakia LaTona Gunn was rediscovered.

Sakia's family and its supporters were relieved when McCullough's indictment for bias intimidation in the first degree was finally handed down by the grand jury. New Jersey's hate crimes statute was so rarely invoked that the indictment itself made local and state news. In mid November 2004, the *Newark Star-Ledger* reported that Sakia's murderer, Richard McCullough, was finally docketed to stand trial. For the first time in New Jersey judicial history, a man would be prosecuted for bias intimidation because of sexual orientation, second-degree murder, and aggravated assault. McCullough pled not guilty, and his trial was set for February 2005. The Essex County Prosecutors Office upset the Gunn family when it refused to seek the death penalty. Grandmother Thelma intuited that the behind the scenes plea-bargaining was not going in her family's favor. She told Mick Meehan of the *Gay City News*, "If he does get out, he won't last long on the street with the people looking to get him."

Sakia's rediscovery took place by a new cadre of highly motivated black and white advocates, most of whom had not been in Newark at the time of her murder. They took up her story in powerful and creative ways, and from a variety of perspectives: in arts and letters, in activism, and on film. Word of her life and death had not come to them from the usual mainstream media sources. Instead, these new advocates owed a debt to the early bloggers who kept lifting Sakia's story out of oblivion, and transmitting it to the wider world. The usual media had chosen not to carry Sakia's story beyond the starting gate. Dogged bloggers like Professor Pearson, however, showed that unconventional sources and methods could circumvent the old, racist media closet, and these new advocates for Sakia took all these important lessons to heart.

Among these new advocates was Charles Bennett Brack who started the "Sakia Gunn Film Project." A black gay filmmaker, "Chas" Brack, hailed from the Southside of Chicago. He became a human rights activist in the New York metro area, and heard about Sakia's murder on television. In 2008, he told Christopher Murray of the *Gay City News* that telling her story became a mission for him. Though the never met 'Kia in the flesh, directing the film transformed his life. He could not forget the image of Sakia he saw on the newscast. "The picture of Sakia said more to me than the newscaster," he said.

> It was clear to me that there was a gender and/or sexual orienta-
> tion slant to the story that was not being reported. The person that
> the media described was a 15-year-old girl, but the person I saw
> was a 15-year-old boy. I knew there was more to be revealed.

Sakia's story received much deserved exposure and critical analysis because of Brack's documentary project. Brack understood the project as a way to lift up the lives of black LGBTQ youth for the first time, to interrogate both white privilege and black homophobia. In his Director's Notes for the film project, Brack said:

> In my heart of hearts, I knew she was killed because of her sexu-
> ality. As Black or Gay people, when we walk out into the world,
> we walk out into a hostile environment—the world is not a safe
> place for us. This is especially true for Black GLBT . . . People will
> kill you because of who you are still . . . in America.

Brack drew strength from his own history as a gender non-con-forming youth, caught in the harsh web of homophobia and racism that plagues gay and lesbian teenagers of color:

> I remember being Sakia's age and the angst caused by my ambigu-
> ous gender. I remember feeling like I was cut off from amongst
> my people. My father had great disdain for me and my girlish
> ways and figure . . . No child should be subjected to the kind of
> fear and loathing I experienced, and no child should be mur-
> dered because of who she is.

Using uncommon care for Sakia's family and sensitivity to the fragile community of Black Aggressives in Newark, Brack worked for years to develop a film now acclaimed as an award-winner. *Dreams Deferred: The Sakia Gunn Film Project* was released in 2008, but its rippling effects in the Black LGBTQ population of Newark, and in Brack's own life, continue to be powerful. The film humanizes the plight of gender non-conforming youth of color for the larger LGBTQ and Black communities, appealing to them to appreciate the needs and dreams of children who are often treated as disposable. Conversely, it communicates to queer black youth that they are known and cared about widely. In Brack's own case, *Dreams Deferred* brought a whole new sense of wholeness and renewal to his life. In recovery from drug and alcohol addiction for seven-and-a-half years now, Brack credits the film project as his reason for getting "clean": "My life came to bloom again!" he said. One of the greatest moments in his life was when Sakia's mother LaTona claimed Brack as her "Brother." "Sakia took me to the place I am working now, Third World Newsreel," Brack claims with a thankful heart. He is Operations Manager for TWN, planning to launch a series of films about LGBTQ concerns.

Brack often says his motive for making the film was "love for his people," young African American queer folk who sit at the crossroads of so many oppressions at once. The very lack of access to media that made Sakia's story languish for so long while Matthew Shepard's flourished is both symptom and cause of an entire community's invisibility to the larger LGBTQ, white, and black worlds.

Brack's great accomplishment in *Dreams Deferred* is the way he tapped into the angry power Laquetta Nelson and James Credle, co-founders of the Newark Pride Alliance, talked about, taking that energy to a new constructive level. While they worked on the street to unite the Black LGBTQ community, and to bring pressure for meaningful social change to Newark's most discriminated against minority, Brack took Sakia's story and broke into the American consciousness. For fifty-eight minutes, Brack artfully interweaves encounters with Sakia's family, and her AG sisters with actual footage from the sentencing hearing for her killer. The grief and pathos of the vigils are interspersed with the swelling rage of protestors, drawing viewers into a confrontation with their own need to know more about a hip-hop girl who died in obscurity because of the brutal indifference of her hostile world. Above all, Brack said, bystanders to Sakia's outrageous murder must understand that they have lost "the ability to deny what is going on in our community. She was not the first to die like this, and she surely won't be the last," he declared. "Enough is enough!"

Brack's camera was the only one permitted in the Essex County courtroom when defendant Richard McCullough faced his trial, the lone video witness to the justice 'Kia and her sisters had so long been denied. True to the ominous feeling Grandmother Thelma had, the Essex County Prosecutor agreed to drop second-degree murder charges against McCullough in exchange for his guilty plea to aggravated manslaughter and anti-gay bias intimidation. Instead of 118 years in prison, the maximum sentence on all the original charges, Sakia's confessed murderer would be incarcerated twenty-five years or less because of the deal. On March 3, 2005, McCullough pled guilty in order to avoid a jury trial, but even then the burley 31-year-old nearly spoiled his deal with the court by trying to avoid blame for her death, according to the *Newark Star-Ledger*. McCullough claimed that Sakia had run upon the knife he held in his hand, impaling herself on it in a rumble that was due to misunderstanding and too much liquor. Superior Court Judge Paul Vichness sternly warned McCullough that he would call a trial unless he took complete responsibility for Sakia's murder. A chastised McCullough revised his testimony.

April 4, 2005 (ironically the anniversary of Martin Luther King Jr.'s 1968 assassination) was McCullough's sentencing day. Judge Vichness heard from Sakia's family and friends, and then from the McCullough family before pronouncing sentence. As Brack remembers it, the Gunns and Kia's best friend and cousin, Valencia Bailey, were extraordinarily forgiving. Thick with emotion, LaTona Gunn told the court that she had suffered countless nights with no sleep since McCullough took her beautiful child away from her. The Essex County courtroom stayed perfectly still when LaTona Gunn turned to McCullough and showed him two pictures: the first of Sakia in happier days, and the second of her body lying in the hospital dead on a gurney. "This is the way Sakia looked before you ran into her," LaTona said as McCullough stared at the floor, unable to meet her eyes, "And this is the way she looked the last time I saw her."

The McCullough family, on the other hand, shot looks at the Gunns throughout the hearing. Brack told *The Advocate* in September 2008,

"I think [the McCulloughs] simply don't get it. I think they weren't re-morseful; they were very recalcitrant, actually." Reading her prepared re-marks in a low montone, Benita McCullough said her son was a friendly person, non-violent, and very bright. Wistfully, she told the judge, "We all thought Rich was gonna be a genius."

After listening to the statements, Judge Vichness gave his sentencing rationale. The defendant had a relatively clean record. Aside from a mar-ijuana possession conviction, he had no priors. He had held down a job most of his adult life, too. But the judge did not believe that McCullough was therefore incapable of perpetrating violence against another person. The crime he committed was terrible. He should have been in control. He was the adult, not the girls he attacked. He bore full responsibility. "This is a young lady who would have accomplished a lot in her life," he explained as he sentenced McCullough to twenty years in prison.

Assistant Essex County Prosecutor Thomas McTigue told the *Star-Ledger* he was pleased with the sentence which conceivably could free McCullough on parole in seventeen years. "Seventeen years is a very long time," he said. His office had consulted with the Gunn family prior to accepting the deal, and they had signed off on it in order to get a conviction. "There is always frustration on sentencing day," he told re-porters. "What they truly wanted I couldn't give them. I couldn't give them Sakia back."

Was justice done for Sakia? Or did justice relent, in the last analysis, into something that looks like justice to the courts and the status quo, but remains frustratingly beyond the reach of those who lost the most when 'Kia fell, murdered in the mean streets of her city? In other words, did brave Sakia die in vain?

FOR THE LOVE OF THE PEOPLE

Justice for Sakia lies in the hands of those who are producing the knowl-edge about her life and death. Sakia's rediscovery by Chas Brack and his contemporaries puts her memory in good hands. As Michel Foucault, the mid-twentieth-century philosopher and parent of queer theory, might say, spreading Sakia's story empowers the people. Knowledge of her orientation and gender non-conformity shines a bold search lamp on old prejudices. As Brack told *The Advocate's* Louis Virtel after *Dreams Deferred* premiered in 2008, Sakia is like an angelic messenger calling people together. She enabled Brack to take up his vocation as storyteller for the love of the people:

> I always talk about being HIV-positive and being in recovery just because our communities, the black and gay communities, have such a high rate of substance abuse as well as HIV. It's like, we do have those things in common that we can use as a point of departure somewhat. The struggles are different, but there's something we can come together on. And that's that we're hated. That's the thing that upsets me about racism in the gay white community and homophobia in the straight black community. It's like, both groups should know better. It's that simple. They should know better. I don't want to be called a nigger or a faggot. They both hurt.

Sakia's story keeps demanding that whiteness be interrogated for the sake of a better life for everyone. Dr. Gayle Baldwin, author of a forthcoming book about Sakia, *Black Butterfly*, says, Sakia keeps her accountable for the privilege she has that others do not. In the circumstances surrounding her murder, Baldwin points out, "We can see how conditions can be set up for black-on-black crimes to occur." For five years, Baldwin, an Episcopal priest before becoming an academic, worked to build trust among the people of Newark so she could have the privilege of telling others about Sakia. She remembers a small photo of 'Kia held on her mother's keychain that perfectly captures Sakia's essence. She was in her basketball jersey, smiling, recalls Baldwin: "That person was strong and independent. She was going to be who she was—she was just herself. Everybody loved her for that." Then, pensively, Baldwin said, "She keeps me accountable. We are all accountable for the responsibility we have."

The ripple-effect of Sakia's story moved Garden State native Darnell Moore to take up the work of improving Newark schools. A scholar and activist at Rutgers University, Moore is Associate Director of the Newark Schools Collaborative. As a black gay man, he is keenly aware of the way economic disparity contributed to her murder. "We must remember," he says, "this was a girl, a teenager. Newark lost a *youth*, somebody who could have been an activist, a contributing member of the community." Her murder enabled people to face how the deaths of youths are commonly talked about in a disconnected way. "Sakia brings us to connect the dots between differing forms of oppression," Moore says, "and to take a stand against violence." Economics and lack of access helped kill her, he contends, since "some people do not have the money to ride in a cab, and have to walk to the bus at three in the morning." Her death was not a "tragedy" in his view. It was cold-blooded murder, and we need to call it what it was. "She didn't volunteer to be in this position," Moore says. "Her name has become a call to arms for change."

Newark has changed since Sakia the young tigress fought and died for her sisters. Though there is still no drop-in youth center in her name, Mayor Cory Booker has instituted an after-school program for LGBTQ youth of color that many have hailed as the first of its kind in the nation. It is hardly enough, but it is a start. Primarily because of her murder, the Newark Pride Alliance and its affiliate, Newark Essex Pride Coalition, came into being. So did PFLAG in Northern New Jersey. In June 2009, thanks to Sakia's memory, the Newark City Council created a commission to advise the mayor on LGBTQ issues. But the struggle for the hearts and minds of the "Brick City" is still fierce. Many of Newark's most vocal churches preach that homosexuality is a sin. When Mayor Booker raised the rainbow flag over City Hall for Pride Week the first time, he was stunned by the virulence of the backlash aimed at him and the entire LGBTQ community. The murder of young black gay youth has not abated in the Newark-New York City metro area, either. Now, added to Sakia's name, we must remember Rayshon, Shani, Rashawn, Dashon, Iofemi, Terrance, Carl, and Jaheem, as well. One hopes that over time the power of knowledge spawned by Sakia's story will finally breech the old walls that hold young LGBTQ souls captive. As James Credle, who took up the baton from Laquetta Nelson to lead the Newark Pride Alliance, said in an op-ed for "Black Gay Gossip" in May 2009:

> Much has been accomplished in the six years since that tragic Mother's Day in Newark; much more remains to be done. In particular, we must seek and find more ways to involve our youth in the development of systems and programs intended to serve them. We must address the breaking issues of the moment, even as we create structures to address them in the future.

When will justice for Sakia Gunn finally come? Not until all her gender non-conforming sisters and brothers may celebrate life on their own terms, and without fear. Until then, there can be no rest for her brave spirit. Or for us.

For Greater Understanding

Justice Deferred, Justice Denied: Sakia LaTona Gunn

BOOKS AND ARTICLES

Baldwin, Gayle R. "Rainbow Children Over Me: Parabolic Narratives for Sakia Gunn." *Cross Currents*, Summer 2004. No pages. Online: http://findarticles.com/p/articles /mi_m2096/is_2_54/ai_n7576567.

Boykin, Keith. *One More River to Cross: Black and Gay in America*. New York: Anchor /Doubleday, 1996.

Pearson, Kim. "Small Murders: Rethinking News Coverage of GLBT People." In *News and Sexuality: Media Portraits of Diversity*. Edited by Laura Casteñeda, and Shannon B. Campbell. Newbury Park, CA: Sage Publications, 2005.

Zook, Kristal Brent. *Black Women's Lives: Stories of Pain and Power*. New York: Nation Books, 2006.

FILMS AND VIDEOGRAPHY

Dreams Deferred: The Sakia Gunn Film Project. Third World Newsreel, 2008.
The Aggressives. Seventh Art Releasing, 2005.

ORGANIZATIONS AND WEBSITES

KeithBoykin.com, http://keithboykin.com/blog.

Newark Pride Alliance Youth Caucus, http://www.facebook.com/pages/Newark-NJ /Newark-Pride-Alliance-Youth-Caucus/307853645214.

Professor Kim's News Notes, http://professorkim.blogspot.com/2006/05/sakia-gunn -three-years-on-few-still.html.

The Sakia Gunn Film Project, http://www.sakiagunnfilmproject.com.

Unfinished Lives Project, http://unfinishedlivesblog.com.

Charles O. "Charlie" Howard
January 31, 1961—July 7, 1984

BANGOR, MAINE

9

Bridge of Sighs

Charles O. "Charlie" Howard

"This is the road we all have to take—over the Bridge of Sighs into eternity."

—Søren Kierkegaard, *Journals and Papers*

Before there was *Rent*, there was *La Cage aux Folles;* before there was Matthew Shepard, there was Charlie. The first Broadway musical paved the way for the other, pricking up the ears of America to receive and appreciate a more radicalized gender outlaw story a decade later. The callous anti-gay murder of Charlie Howard in 1980s New England was a regional atrocity, in contrast to the international media obsession with the Matthew Shepard killing in the late 1990s. Outside of Maine, Charlie's name and narrative remain largely unknown. Yet the impact of Charlie's story has caused more substantial change in the hearts and minds of Mainers, more measurable gains for LGBTQ equality throughout New England, than Matthew's story has brought about for the country as a whole. Without Charlie's agony in the cold, swirling waters of Bangor's Kenduskeag Stream, there might never have been a frame of reference for what happened to Matt, who was lashed to the rude timbers of a buck fence fourteen years later on a ridge overlooking Laramie.

The killing of Charlie Howard was the first fully recognized hate crime murder of a gay person. For that reason alone, his life and death should be remembered and wrestled with by a far wider audience than the story has ever received until now. Every characteristic so hideously familiar to us from the thousands of hate crime stories of American women and men killed because of their gender non-conformity was first driven into the body and soul of this gentle man from Bangor: community homophobia and heterosexism, bullying in neighborhoods and schools, name-calling, threats and physical assault, religious intolerance, character assassination, innuendo and the re-victimization of the victim, and, of course, the infamous "gay panic" defense. Passage of years has not made this story easier to bear. Neither has Charlie's memory become less turbulent, nor more accessible, no matter how much water has passed beneath the State Street Bridge since the summer of 1984.

"A PATHETIC LITTLE SECOND-RATE SUBSTITUTION FOR REALITY . . ."

Charles O. Howard was born to a family of stolid, rural Minnesota folk who had moved to Portsmouth, New Hampshire in search of better prospects. As Midwesterners who immigrated "Down East," the Howards were fringe people. They had no claim to a long New England heritage. They sounded and looked different to the native Yankee families, some of whom could trace their lineage back to the seventeenth century. Though Charlie was by birth in Portsmouth an authentic Seacoaster, he was never truly accepted that way. He didn't have the pedigree for it. As became evident in his adolescent years, Charlie was several shades more "different" than even his folks were perceived to be. He was beset by all the stereotypical characteristics Americans of the 1960s and 1970s attributed to a gay boy. He was small-boned, gracile instead of robust—"gangly" would be an accurate depiction of the slender boy with the long, blond bangs hooding his brow. His classmates called Charlie "sissy" and "fag," which under any circumstance is a detestable slur. To tell the truth, though, he could conform to type quite well. Charlie could be downright bitchy. He had a tendency to prattle on and on, and ignore what other people had to say. Even people who genuinely liked him admitted that he could be a royal pain in the ass. Plagued by severe asthma, Charlie couldn't have succeeded in sports if he had wanted to, and he was learning-disabled which screwed with his grades. By the time he got to high school, Charlie had constructed pretty sophisticated defense mechanisms just to endure the hazing he faced on a routine basis. Anyone who says that gays can "pass" at will in the unforgiving society of pubescent boys and girls on any American schoolyard hasn't lived in the skin of an effeminate gay boy. Charlie's couldn't hide his sexual orientation, plain as that. He was a sitting duck among swans.

Self-doubt and self-deprecation embossed themselves on his teen soul during what should have been his salad days in secondary school. On the outside, Charlie developed a tough hide to withstand the name-calling and the harassment of his peers, but he was never numb or oblivious to the pain. On the inside, Charlie struggled with his increasing attraction to other young men, and he succumbed (at least to some degree) to the internalized shame everyone told gay and lesbian people they should have for feeling that way. When the whole world seems to be telling you that you are a "deviant" and a "pervert," you tend to believe it. School for Charlie was a cruel glass closet. Everyone could see he was "that way." He was trapped inside like a specimen in a bottle—no way out, and nowhere to find sanctuary.

In order to grasp how the cards were stacked against gay kids like Charlie, we have to venture back into the American mindset toward homosexuality during his childhood and youth. Looking back, we see negative biases assumed to be true about gay men and lesbians that were stunningly foisted upon them in every aspect of life. *Time Magazine* in its January 21, 1966 issue, published a major article entitled, "The Homosexual in America." As a little boy, just shy of his fifth birthday, when the article hit newsstands, Charlie was growing up in a culture doing everything it could to keep its LGBTQ citizens silent and closeted. The essay commenced, "Society is torn between condemnation and compassion, fear and curiosity, between attempts to turn the problem into a joke and the knowledge that it is anything but funny, between the deviant's plea to be treated just like anyone else and the knowledge that he simply is not like everybody else." The tone of dehumanization runs roughshod throughout the text, oscillating between pity for tortured, maladjusted souls "fearful of the opposite sex," and full-throated chastisement of predatory men whose "constant tendency to prowl or 'cruise' in search of new [sex] partners" made them dangerous to children and the family. Every form of social authority was marshaled by *Time*, from the judgment of history to "the clear-cut condemnations of the Bible or of traditional moral philosophy" in order to support the thesis that "homosexuality is an offense against God and man."

In a crescendo of opprobrium, the *Time* essay sets forth the negative opinion of mid-twentieth-century America against lesbians and gay men in no uncertain terms:

[Homosexuality] is a pathetic little second-rate substitution for reality, a pitiable flight from life. As such it deserves fairness, compassion, understanding, and, when possible, treatment. But it deserves no encouragement, no glamorization, not rationalization, no fake status as minority martyrdom, not sophistry about simple difference in taste—and, above all, no pretense that it is anything but a pernicious sickness.

Against all these cultural, societal, and religious pressures, Charlie, to the contrary, came out as gay at a young age. Perhaps the futility of trying to pass as straight eased his decision to be true to himself and his sexual identity. Somehow, he mustered the courage to break it to his family that he liked boys. Charlie's relationship with his stepfather had never been good, but the revelation about his sexuality just made things worse. Instead of taking the easier road, denial or deceit, there was something stronger in Charlie's character. He chose integrity over safety—a decision few made, and many considered foolish. Thus, Charlie became a member of a small, clandestine group of gays and lesbians who lived the best they could in the region where Coastal New Hampshire touches Southern Maine, the Seacoast community.

A friend of Charlie's, identifying himself on the internet only as "Vacationland," reflected on what any young, gay person had to face in Portsmouth and environs. He commented on a blog in May of 2009:

I am glad that Charlie is not forgotten, and not just because his story is heartbreaking and his death a tragedy.

My home state—like many places—was unforgiving for gay people, especially *out* gay people, back in the day. Charlie paid the ultimate price for being true to himself, and the thought of it strikes a special kind of fear and sadness in my heart because it so easily might have been anyone—In fact, it could very easily have been my brother.

"Vacationland" continues:

See, my brother was good friends with Charlie Howard—had known him for years (we lived near Portsmouth and the Seacoast gay community was pretty small). My brother was a couple years older than Charlie; I was a couple years younger. Like Charlie, my brother came out when he was fairly young, at a time when there was precious little support for such a thing. Growing up I heard plenty of "war stories" involving abuse and gay bashing and homophobic acts, and I saw a lot of unnecessary cruelty directed at my kind, decent, never-hurt-a-fly brother and his friends, including Charlie. I was P-Flag before P-Flag was cool.

Graduation from Portsmouth High School was like being sprung from the state pen. Charlie's low grades ruled out college as an option for him. When everyone else donned their maroon and white for the graduation celebration dance, he didn't go. He didn't go to his own graduation ceremony, either. Some have speculated that he chose not to "walk" because he couldn't bear to have his parents, especially his mother, see how the other students treated him. Given what Charlie had to endure in school, he must have wrestled with his own sense of frustration, shame, and embarrassment, too.

Post-graduation, Charlie's poor relationship with his stepdad made it impossible for him to live at home anymore. The family booted him out, either to live in the streets or to depend upon the unreliable kindness of strangers. He drifted for a few years, doing odd jobs and living marginally, until his early twenties when he moved in with a man from the county seat town of Ellsworth, Maine. The relationship broke apart, and then in January 1984, Charlie decided to move up to the "big city," Bangor, Maine. Perhaps in Maine's third-largest town, he could find other gay people.

For a century, Bangor, whose population in 1984 was 31,000, has been the major commercial and cultural center for eastern and northern Maine. Settlement started where the Penobscot River and the Kenduskeag Stream flowed together. "City-consciousness" is vital to Bangorites. Though the whole metropolitan area covering two counties numbers fewer than 84,000 souls—tiny in comparison to mighty Boston or Portland, Maine's largest city—Bangor tried on much bigger britches, and liked them. Perhaps their outsized opinion came from the Victorian glory days when millions of trees were felled in Maine's North Woods, floated down the Penobscot, and milled in Bangor's busy port. Super-logger Paul Bunyan and his great Blue Ox, "Babe," were legendary residents of this "Queen City of the East," where lumber once was king. To prove it, a thirty-one-foot statue of Bunyan stands tall in a downtown park. "City of Bangor" is emblazoned everywhere to remind residents that they are no mere "town." The paradox of Bangor, though, is that it yearns to be a big city, and simultaneously clings to small-town culture. Save in name only, Bangor was still small town Maine as the 1980s dawned.

By the time Charlie got to the Queen City, the sands of its urban consciousness were shifting, and Bangor was becoming an increasingly divided place to live. Just a half-hour trip up Highway 2, the University of Maine at Orono had leavened Bangor with a degree of learning and urbanity that stretched long-time residents to acknowledge a world outside of its predominant small-town culture. Bangor Theological Seminary, the only accredited theological institution of higher learning in Northern New England, also supported a new intellectual and cultural world-view. Students and faculty from all over the United States and the world visited, shopped, bought homes, and settled down in Bangor thanks to UMaine and BTS.

Native Bangorites, however, still manipulated the machinery of government and set the small-town tone for the city. For all its New England propriety, Bangor was as deep-down blue-collar as Bunyan's ox. Its leading families had made their money the hard way back in the day, lumberjacking and supporting the timber industry. Though it was hard to see for the inexperienced eyes of outsiders, Bangor has a long and deep "redneck" streak, insular and provincial. Interlopers were referred to, politely, as "those people from away."

DOWN EAST PEACOCK

In January 1984, Charlie arrived in Bangor, a 22-year-old gay boy with no job, no prospects, no plan, and nowhere to stay. Fortunately, he met a gay couple who had restored a grand old Victorian house on Highland Avenue. Paul Noddin, an antiques dealer, and his partner, Scott Hamilton, offered Charlie a place to stay until he could get on his feet and find a job. A month passed, and Charlie was still unemployed. He grew increasingly frustrated and melancholy. Paul and Scott suggested to Charlie that he return to Portsmouth where he knew more people and might find more job prospects. His mother agreed to let Charlie move back for the time being, but Thomas Wolfe was right: "You really *can't* go home again." In less than a week, the situation in the Howard home deteriorated. Charlie tried moving in with another man, but things between them went sour, too. As a last resort, Charlie called Paul and Scott, pleading with them to give him another chance. In 2004 Scott told Renee Ordway of the *Bangor Daily News*, "He moved in with us because he wanted to leave a bad relationship, and to make a change in his life." They agreed, and bucked up by the good news, Charlie returned to Bangor, thrilled about the future.

Charlie exhibited a new self-confidence that paid off with new op-
portunities. Thanks to the help of one of Scott and Paul's neighbors, he
landed a job through Bangor's employment program. Newfound success
allowed Charlie to reveal the real sweetness of his character. At Easter
time, as a surprise, he decorated the house and cooked a banquet for
Scott and Paul as an expression of personal gratitude for their doing
so much for him. Within a few weeks, Charlie found an apartment in
a run-down building where he could afford the rent. It was a pretty
crummy place, but Charlie's enthusiasm for fixing it up seemed bound-
less. He festooned the walls with posters, brought in a modest jungle of
houseplants, and found himself a live-in companion: a tiny kitten.

Most significant, Charlie found a few good friends. The Unitarian
Church and its gay-friendly group, Interweave, became the incubator
for his budding sense of personal worth. Like so many gays and lesbians,
church for Charlie had been a place to avoid. But something was decidedly
different about these church folk. They were warm, community-oriented,
and the only spiritual home in Bangor for queer people. Charlie became a
regular. He loved the fellowship, the potluck dinners, and the new dimension of faith he discovered within himself. Just weeks before his murder,
he even started taking instruction for membership in the church.

As his spirits lifted, Charlie the ugly duckling of Portsmouth days
morphed into something of a "Yankee peacock," freer in his self-identity
than he had ever been. He unavoidably drew attention. Bangor wasn't
prepared for what the gay boy "from away" had to offer. Not only was
Charlie undeniably "that way," but he also refused to hide it. Unlike more
experienced Bangor queer folk who observed an unwritten code of gay
conduct that prohibited open disclosure, Charlie was, by consensus of
those who knew him, "flamboyant." That was the *nice* way to put it.

Douglas Watts, a sophomore Journalism major at UMaine, saw
Charlie around town and knew who he was. Watts, was a straight
man, and a self-described "Mass-hole" who migrated to Bangor from
Massachusetts and stayed there for years. He considers Charlie's story
a turning point in his life. Watts admits he didn't know any gay people
in his high school. "I didn't even know the concept of what that was,"
Watts said about his early days in Bangor. Yet Charlie Howard left an
indelible imprint on him, both as a man and a journalist. "Charlie's story
hit me so deeply," Watts said, "because I had a connection with this guy.
When [his murder] occurred, he was just walking down the street. He

could have been me." Watts would never see difference, humanity, or the power dynamics of a small town in the same way thanks to the in-your-face gay guy who lived his life as he chose, not as others proscribed it. To Watts, this gay man wasn't simply "flamboyant." In the vernacular of the day, Charlie was a "screaming queen," a cross-dressing flamer who matter-of-factly wore makeup and an earring in his left ear. Charlie was the sort of gay youth whom older gay people saw in public and thought to themselves, "Oh, no!" He could accessorize with the best of them: "man-bag" over the shoulder, bell-bottoms, and a blouse. He casually addressed Bangorites as "dearie," and when confronted, he was known to break out in a chorus of "I Am What I Am" from *La Cage*. Charlie once got himself thrown out of the West End Disco for dancing with a man. This Yankee peacock was about to "shake a tail feather," and that was dangerous in the Queen City.

Watts remembers the deep ire Charlie drew from Bangorites, and the reasons for it. When local high school kids harassed him with slurs, they were expressing the hidden outrage of their elders. Using epithets they were sending a message to Charlie, "How dare you not keep 'the way you are' hidden in our town!" "A lot of people didn't like that," Watts said. "He was not from Bangor. He didn't know a lot of people and had few friends. Most of all, he had no real support network, no big brothers to defend him or to teach him what the secret conduct rules were, to steer him clear of danger." Recalling the anti-gay attitudes rampant in Bangor in 1984, Watts continued:

> Bangor is such a small town. Charlie had only been in Bangor a
> few months at the time of his murder. If you are a young gay man
> in a town where everybody knows everybody else, you stick out
> like a sore thumb—Everybody knows that you are an outsider!
> They say, "That's the queer outsider!"

Dr. Mavin Ellison concurs with Doug Watts's estimate of Charlie. Ellison, a gay professor of Christian Ethics and an ordained Presbyterian clergyperson, had just arrived at Bangor Theological Seminary the year before Charlie was murdered. Ellison remembered him as an outsider with negligible support in the city. "Charlie Howard," he said, "was a young, effeminate person, an in-your-face guy. He was queeny, a cross-dresser with no standing in the community and no constituency." As Ellison saw it, Charlie was not only on the fringes of Bangor's straight majority. "He was on the margins of the LGBT community, too," he said.

Christine Palmer, who was news magazine editor for the *Bangor Daily News* in 1984, remembered Charlie as "bubbly and innocent," and also irritating to her sensibilities. In a 1998 book by Warren Blumenfeld and Diane Christine Raymond, *Looking at Gay and Lesbian Life*, Palmer recalled how she felt about him:

> [Charlie] didn't do things *my* way. And isn't that exactly why if we must find a reason that he died? Charlie didn't do things the way others thought he should. He didn't conform. It doesn't make much sense that Charlie, whether he wanted to carry a purse or even if he wanted to wear a dress, should be so hated!

Palmer saw something in Charlie others seemed to miss. As he grew more comfortable in his own gay skin, he went beyond personal acceptance. He developed a sense of pride with an edge to it. Palmer remembered that Charlie's personal anthem was a caustic gay protest song recorded by the Tom Robinson Band from Great Britain, called "Glad to be Gay." Robinson, a pioneer of the punk rock scene, wrote the song out-and-proud for London Gay Pride in 1976. In the United Kingdom and across the pond, gay people were routinely referred to in the late-1970s press as "self-confessed homosexuals," as if they were the same as rapists and ax-murderers. The lyrics of the song are direct and confrontational, chastising the police for raiding gay bars "for no reason at all," and accusing the authorities of prosecuting gay news outlets for obscenity rather than *Playboy Magazine*. Robinson's third verse condemned homophobia and every form of violence done to gay men and lesbians. "Sing, If You're Glad to Be Gay" became a rallying cry for people coming out of the closet in the English-speaking world. Charlie Howard knew the verses by heart, and sang them in the street if provoked, and afterward, throw a kiss.

The pastor of the Unitarian Church, Rev. Richard Forcier, worried about Charlie's safety. He and his parishioner had developed a friendship on Sundays and at Interweave meetings. Forcier, a student minister at Bangor Theological Seminary, knew the word on the street about Charlie was not good. When the time seemed right, Pastor Forcier diplomatically asked him why not tone down his appearance just a bit, and rein in his public persona to lessen the target he presented to antagonists. Charlie's answer was crystal-clear: "I can't participate in my own oppression," he said.

Palmer heard from her sources that Charlie told friends the week before he was murdered about a run-in he had with some hostile towns-folk. "The fag-beaters were after me today," he told them, "but they didn't get me." Just a few summer nights later, the bashers caught up with him, and this time, he didn't get away.

THE WISDOM OF CROCODILES

Just a few weeks before his murder, Charlie went to the market dressed as flamboyantly as usual. As he shopped, a woman in her middle age lashed out at him, shouting, "You pervert! You queer!" Everyone stood stock still, glaring at Charlie. Stunned and terrified, he lost his grip on the basket, spilling its contents in the floor, and made for the exit. At the last moment, trembling, he turned to the scold and her admirers, and blew them all a kiss. Friends remember that after that skirmish, something snapped in Charlie. He was fearful of unsolicited glances, and strangers tended to startle him. His friends noticed that he was more and more reluctant to venture outside his apartment alone after the tongue-lashing in the market. But the real shock came sometime later when he stepped outside his door looking for his kitten. He found its lifeless body lying in the doorway, strangled to death. Inconsolable, he reached out to his friends at Interweave for help.

Lest we conclude that Charlie was singled out for the spite of the community solely because of his flamboyance, Bangor police records for the 1980s show that violence against gay men took place routinely, but was seldom reported. Hate crimes laws did not exist in Maine at the time. There was no anti-discrimination statute to protect LGBTQ people in Bangor. According to Bangor Police Detective Bill Lawrence, who spoke to the *Bangor Daily News* for their coverage of the twentieth anniversary of Charlie's hate-murder, assaults were chillingly common along Valley Avenue and the Middle Street area where gay men congregated in 1984. In one rare reported instance, Detective Lawrence recalled that a young man was arrested for robbing the same gay man three weekends in a row on Valley Avenue. The victim never reported a thing. Like many other gay men in Bangor, he was too frightened of exposure to say a word to the police. Some of the victims were married, and they were scared of losing their families and their jobs if anyone knew the truth about their sexual identities. None of these men "flaunted" their sexual orientation—they hid it. But they were intimidated, beaten, and robbed nonetheless, just because of who they were. The 1966 *Time* article portrayed the dominant heterosexist attitude of the age perfectly: to the vast majority of Bangorites, even the sympathetic ones, all gays were *de facto* "deviants," "perverts," and "perniciously" *sick*. That was Bangor's frame of reference for gay people, a dangerous bias held along with the vast majority of Americans. The woman in the market had expressed community disdain for queers exactly right. Hidden from sight or not, gays were perceived to be at best a headache, and at worst a menace. In the wake of Charlie's murder, these politely shrouded homophobic beliefs became shockingly clear in the way the story was framed by the press, and the umbrage the town took at any suggestion that hate was behind the deadly acts of their children against a "twisted little person who ran risks by the way he led his life out in the open." To be sure, there were many, perhaps even the majority of Bangorites, who deplored the violence against Charlie and others like him. Nonetheless they remained totally silent, passively assenting to the routine gay bashing that was Bangor's dirty little secret. Perhaps hardest of all to take was the insincere pity people expressed for the demise of "poor Charlie."

There is an old wives' tale claiming that crocodiles weep when they consume their prey, in mock grief for their victims. Sir Francis Bacon wrote in 1625, "It is the wisdom of *crocodiles* that shed *tears* when they would devour," (*Of Wisdom for a Man's Self*, emphasis in the original). Such sentiment is amusing when the crocodile in Walt Disney's *Peter Pan* gorges on an evildoer like Cap'n Hook. But citizens do not have the excuse of reptilian instinct when they devour the young, nor are their quarry mere cartoons. Charlie was flesh and blood, a boy, barely a man, and what was done to him on the State Street Bridge could not be rationalized away, or taken back. It was not a "tragedy;" it was murder. Teenage boys from some of Bangor's leading families turned out to be the sharpened teeth of the crocodile, prowling in the night until they found hapless Charlie Howard; and Bangor's elders squeezed out crocodile tears when confronted with the news of what their children had done. Such is the reptilian logic of bigotry.

The weather was pleasant on the Saturday night in July when Charlie was murdered. The daytime rain had ceased, and a nice breeze was blowing. Temperatures lingered in the mid-60s. The moon was waxing 70 percent full, like a lantern hanging in the night sky. Interweave had sponsored a potluck dinner at the church, and Charlie came. Shortly after 10 p.m., when the meeting broke up, Charlie talked his gay friend, Roy Ogden, into walking with him to check his post office box. Charlie was reluctant to walk alone at night, even though it was barely dark yet, thanks to daylight saving time. Plenty of people strolled outside, enjoying the weather. Charlie and Roy headed down State Street and began crossing the bridge across Kenduskeag Stream. This area is the very core of the business district, fewer than one hundred yards from the confluence of the Kenduskeag and the Penobscot River. A camera-man standing on the State Street Bridge could pan full-circle and take in the whole of downtown. Pedestrians used the eighty-foot bridge all the time. Doug Watts estimates that in the couple of years he lived in Bangor he walked back and forth across that bridge hundreds of times. Four-storied buildings lined the Kenduskeag on both sides, brandishing their sheer concrete walls from the streets above down to the channel below. Because of a six-foot tidal fluctuation coming up the Kenduskeag from the Penobscot, the Corps of Engineers had turned the watercourse in the 1960s into an immense concrete chute with no ledges or banks, to prevent flooding. The drop from the bridge to the water surface below was a good eighteen feet, and the depth of the swift water was around twelve feet most of the time. Anyone falling into the Kenduskeag from the State Street Bridge would have a long swim before reaching any place to clamber out of the water.

Midway across the bridge, Charlie and Roy sensed a car slowing down behind them. It looked ominous, like one belonging to some high school toughs who had harassed Charlie only a few days before. It was. Shawn Mabry, the driver, recalled that Daniel Ness was beside him in the passenger seat, while Jim Baines sat in the back with two girls. Mabry, sixteen; Ness, seventeen; and Baines, just fifteen, had been binge-drinking that evening, and now were headed with the girls to a party. All of them were drunk. They had stopped at a 7-11 store and tried to buy more beer, but unsuccessfully, with some fake ID belonging to one of the girls. On their way to try and hoodwink another vendor, Mabry caught sight of "the fags" and followed them onto the bridge.

Roy testified that, earlier that night, he had been verbally harassed by Baines, and had made a complaint to the police about him. Officers turned a deaf ear, he said. No one was going to take the word of a "self-avowed, practicing homosexual," anyway. Reviewing the complaint after Charlie's murder, the Bangor Police Department found Ogden's claim of negligence, "wholly without merit." Had the police even questioned young Baines about the incident that night, the whole course of Bangor's history might have been very different.

As Charlie and Roy became conscious of the threat behind them, the three young men got out of the car. Baines shouted out, "Hey, fags!" Mabry, Ness and Baines broke into a run, as the two gay men scrambled to escape. Roy got clear, running for the far steps on the opposite side of the bridge, looking back as Charlie, terrified, tripped and fell so hard that his asthma kicked in, making an awful wheezing sound. In an instant, the three attackers were on him.

"CHUCK-A-HOMO"

Ten years after the fact, Shawn Mabry was still haunted by what they did to Charlie. In the first interview he gave in a decade, Mabry told Renee Ordway of the *Bangor Daily News*, "I remember he was on the ground. We punched and kicked him. I was barefoot." Gasping from acute asthma, Charlie was completely defenseless. The high school boys were nearly as old as he, but much stronger, and much bigger. Doug Watts who had seen him often around town described Charlie as "rail-thin, a bone-rack." Against three brawny young men, fired up by beer and anti-gay bias, Charlie had no chance in the world. Roy, by now too far away to rescue Charlie, cried out for the assailants to leave him alone. Charlie begged them to stop—*please, stop!* Struggling for air, he shouted "fire!" and "help!" as best he could, using his arms and legs to protect his face and torso. Then one of his attackers stunned him with a kick to the head. Jim Baines yelled, "Over the bridge!" Mabry recalled that Ness got Charlie by the legs, Baines got him by the arms, and he himself took him by the mid-section. Charlie managed to scream loudly enough that Roy, the girls in the car, and others in the area distinctly heard him, "I don't know how to swim!"

"We just picked him up and threw him over," Mabry said.

That instant transfixed State Street Bridge in time. It would never be just another span over the Kenduskeag again. Embedded in local mythology, in a mockery of First Nations nomenclature, it would thereafter be known as *"Chuck-a-Homo Bridge."* For twenty-five years to come, the bridge would be a battleground, fought over by people who demanded that Charlie's murder be remembered with dignity, and others who wanted him to be held in derision. Soon after the "Bangor

Three" drowned Charlie, pitching him over the rail eighteen feet into the inky water, memorial marchers found the words stenciled at the spot, "Faggots Jump Here."

Charlie hit the water with a sickening splash, gurgling and crying out hysterically for help, fighting a losing battle against suffocation. Because the stream ran swiftly along smooth concrete walls, there was nowhere for him to stand and nothing for him to cling to. Roy, horrified, lost sight of him, and ran frantically along the stream to see him come up for air. Charlie didn't. Death comes hard in twelve feet of water.

Up on the bridge, the girls yelled for their gay-basher friends to come back to the car. Mabry, Ness, and Baines were *adrenalized*. They were *pumped*. Mabry said that bashing a gay person always made him feel "powerful." They heard Roy shouting Charlie's name, running wildly along the Kenduskeag. One of them shouted that Roy better not report this to anyone, if he knew what was good for him. Roy heard them laughing as they got back into their car to drive away. The celebration already started: they really bashed that "queer" good, didn't they.

Mabry said to Renee Ordway in July 1994:

> We never considered that he might not get out of there. We never gave it any consideration that he might drown. We drove away, laughing. To us, this was just another day. Another incident that would go unreported and life would go on.

According to a court affidavit, Mabry, Ness and Baines finally got to the party, and bragged to friends that they "had jumped a fag and kicked the shit out of him, then threw him in the stream." The other partiers cheered them as heroes for what they had done, then they got back to the main business of Saturday night: drinking and dancing till dawn.

Roy raced to the nearest fire alarm and pulled it. Within a very few minutes, squads of fire fighters and police were shining powerful searchlights into the stream, and rescue teams were combing the water for Charlie. At 12:10 a.m., they found Charlie's waterlogged corpse at a depth of about three feet, not a hundred yards from the bridge. A large eel had wrapped itself around his neck. The autopsy confirmed that Charlie had died of drowning, most likely hastened by a severe attack of asthma. He was twenty-three.

As Sunday morning dawned, the news of Charlie's murder spread quickly. Roy had recognized the boys, and the police started a dragnet.

Daniel Ness turned himself in when he heard the news that the gay man they had assaulted was dead. Shawn Mabry and Jim Baines tried to make a getaway by jumping a freight train, but the train was sidetracked before going very far. The two fugitives decided to spend the night hiding in the woods, and grab another train in the morning. As the police searched near the tracks, they caught Mabry and Baines. On July 9, the trio was charged with the murder of Charles O. Howard, booked, and jailed for a day.

Judge David Cox decided to release them without bond into the custody of their parents, and the news exploded into *the* story of the summer. "A man was killed, thrown off Kenduskeag Bridge, right in the heart of downtown Bangor!" This was how the story was initially framed. The combination of murder, a rarity in Bangor, and the audacious location of the crime, in the town center, made the news take off like a rocket locally. Doug Watts, 19 at the time, keenly observed how everything about this atrocity played out in the hours following the recovery of Charlie's drowned body. Within a day, the alleged perps were in police custody. "Basically," Watts said, "the reason these kids got bagged so quickly was there was no way they could deny what they had done. There was too much evidence to pin it to them." The trio had no alibis. Too many people, besides Roy Ogden, were in the area when the attack started, and they had heard everything. Even if Bangorites wanted to discount the word of a "known homosexual" like Ogden, they couldn't get away with it. Watts remembered, "There was no denial about it. They were nailed. [The boys] didn't even try to say somebody else did it." Watts continued, "Since 'Who did it?' was already settled, 'Who started it?' became the question almost immediately . . . Then it got ugly."

HOW TO TORTURE A DEAD MAN

On Monday, July 9, as the trio was being charged with murder, fright and mourning swept over the people who knew Charlie. Pastor Forcier and other progressive leaders organized a memorial march for that evening, starting at the Unitarian Church and moving through Bangor to the State Street Bridge. Two hundred people turned out. Richard Forcier's teacher, Dr. Marvin Ellison, came out in part to support Forcier. Another part of Ellison marched to protest Charlie's murder, and to express his personal grief and outrage as a gay man. "It was a scary time," he recalled. "Charlie's death was a community trauma." As the marchers moved down the street holding hands and singing softly, angry bystanders hurled anti-gay epithets at them. Ellison said, "We were scared—young men in trucks with shotguns drove by and shouted things at us." When they got to the site where Charlie had been thrown into the stream, they saw the repulsive sign inviting gays to jump off the bridge, "Fags Jump Here." Mourners prayed, sang, and dropped flowers into the water below, a tradition honoring Charlie that continues to this day.

Among the awful things Ellison experienced in the early days of the crisis was the blatant lack of shame of the citizenry of Bangor. People were worried about what the news meant for their beautiful town, but there was no official expression of sorrow or introspection as to why this murder took place in the civic heart of their community—a murder carried out by local young men from respected Bangor families. To the contrary, people treated the Bangor Three as celebrities, lauding them for "teaching a queer a thing or two." Ellison remembered a court-ordered psychiatric evaluation of the three young men. The evaluation diagnosed the three as "conforming personalities." That is, these boys were not initiators of lethal prejudice against gay people, but instead were foot soldiers who carried out what community mores dictated. The three acted upon what was commonly believed, that gay people were somehow subhuman—"disposable property," as Ellison put it. Pitifully few townsfolk comprehended this terrible weakness in their community's character or felt shame because of it. Ellison said, "Until there is a public sense of shame, nothing changes."

The second scandal Ellison experienced was the deafening silence of Bangor's pulpits. All the standard Protestant denominations had nothing to say about Charlie's murder. Neither did the leadership of the Roman Catholic community. Of all religious organizations in the city, only the Unitarians and the Jews expressed any lamentation or righteous anger about a vulnerable person who had been put to death in their midst. Unitarian and Jewish leadership alone was not enough to dispel the religious community's silence surrounding Charlie. According to Ellison, this sense of oppressive silence draped over the whole sorry affair like a pall all year long. Ellison's fellow Presbyterian minister and friend, Dr. William Sloane Coffin, accepted the invitation to speak at the first anniversary of Charlie's murder in July 1985. Preaching a week later to his flock at Riverside Church in New York City, Coffin made observations similar to Ellison's:

> What was sick was the absence of the straight community . . .
> To take part, you didn't have to think homosexuality was right,
> only that murder was wrong. But precious few came for the same
> reason Abraham and God couldn't find ten righteous people in
> Sodom: fear that the majority would view their righteousness as
> deviant activity.

Charlie was buried on July 12, in quiet obscurity after a simple memorial service in Kittery, Maine, near his family's home.

On July 17, the three perpetrators pled innocent to the murder charges against them. The defense strategy was (1) to go flat out for juvenile status for the defendants, subjecting them to Maine's juvenile penal code instead of the full force of prosecution for murder as adults; (2) to argue for a reduction in charge, from murder to manslaughter, on the grounds that "the lads" never intended to kill anybody—the "tragic incident" just got out of hand; and (3) to victimize the victim by employing the prevalent community bias against him as a "self-avowed and practicing homosexual;" to put Charlie on trial instead of "the boys," appealing to the deep-seated prejudice against gay people in the community by emphasizing Jim Baines's claim that Charlie had come onto him sexually, saying suggestive things to him some weeks before the "incident that just got out of hand" on the bridge.

Though LGBTQ people and their allies organized protests and bombarded the court with demands that the Bangor Three face the full brunt of the law as adults for the murder they had committed, the defense always had the advantage in a town like Bangor. When dozens of Charlie's supporters packed into the courtroom on July 18, wearing lavender ribbons on their lapels, the reports in the press portrayed them as an angry mob. A woman carrying a sign saying, "Justice for Charlie," was told she had to leave. Frustration boiled over at the lenient treatment Mabry, Baines, and Ness received, especially the judge's ruling that allowed them to go home, bail-free, to sleep in their own beds at night. The paper quoted Bangor Police Department Sergeant Thomas Placella, the detective in charge of the case, to quell the unrest. "I'm not trying to lessen the severity of the crime," he said, "but it's not like these were ax murderers. These people came from respectable families who own property in the city of Bangor." By implication, Charlie, who had few to defend his character, was an immigrant "from away" who had no family to speak of, and rented a slummy little apartment. The three killers were perceived as no threat to public safety, but the undertone of menace attributed to Charlie's "queer lifestyle" caused strong irrational feelings in many of the townsfolk, especially among some of the men. Such was the case with Mabry, who admitted how he felt about gays during the time of the murder. He said to the *Bangor Daily News* in July 1994 that gays simply made him angry. When pressed to explain, he said, "It was something different, totally odd. I didn't like it. Some of the things they said and did angered me"—lethal anger, as it turned out.

The truth was that Bangor's "respectable boys" were very dangerous indeed, and a whole youth culture of physical violence against gay men and lesbians flourished like noxious weeds in the shadows of Bangor virtually every night. Mabry revealed to *Bangor Daily News* reporter Renee Ordway that he had participated in the bashing of gays on a routine basis for at least eight months before the attack on Charlie—facts that never surfaced during the trials in 1984. Mabry, a high school dropout who still managed to hang out regularly with his former school chums, got invited to a bashing and liked the power rush it gave him. Violent attacks on gay men, Mabry admitted, were "a nightly activity." The bashers in Bangor were young men like Mabry: bored, testosterone-soaked, and violence-prone. Like a pack of wolves or a pride of lions, they coordinated their attacks on the unsuspecting gay men who congregated in the steep, hilly Middle Street area of town. They had it down to a science: Mabry often served as "bait," tempting a potential gay target to believe Mabry himself was gay. Once inside the victim's car, the bait-boy (Mabry or someone else) snatched the car keys out of the ignition, and threw them out the window to prevent the victim from getting away. A waiting ambush squad, brandishing ball bats and pool cues, would burst from the bushes to smash the victim's windshield, mirrors, and lights. Then they fell upon their prey, yelling anti-gay epithets like war whoops, bludgeoning him with their weapons, fists, and feet until he either ran away wounded and bloody, or succumbed to unconsciousness. The boys preferred their quarry to run. They liked the chase, Mabry remembered. And the beautiful thing to Mabry about this nightly ritual of violence was that these "poor queer slobs" never reported anything to anybody. They were too fearful and ashamed to say a word.

Looking back on what they did to Charlie, Doug Watts surmised:

> In hindsight, we should not have been surprised by Charlie Howard being murdered in Bangor for being gay, because this hate was there all the time. We all knew it was there. We just deliberately chose not to see it. It's easy when you're not gay.

Gays and lesbians got the message of Charlie's murder loud and clear. Though the definition of anti-LGBTQ murder as a hate crime hadn't yet entered the lexicon of American prejudice, Maine's gay and gender non-conforming youth understood that one of their own had fallen to hatred—and the next victim might be . . . *me*. Mel Vassey, now a doctor of veterinary medicine in Southern Maine, reflected on the chilling effect Charlie's murder had on him as a gay teenager:

> I was fifteen years old at the time and spending the Summer with my grandparents in Hancock County. I vividly remember watching the news report of Howard's murder on Channel 2. I learned a frightening lesson that day: Faggots get killed. It would take me another seven years to learn to stop running from the fear that message caused and to reclaim my identity and soul. Charlie Howard's murderers did more than rob him of his life. They helped rob me of my adolescence.

According to Doug Watts, the fledgling "gay panic defense" aimed at Charlie was a mechanism of avoidance, the function of a community unable to face what their youth had done and the malicious reasons behind it. These young men had not thrown women, or blacks, or other minorities off bridges—why throw *this* young man to his death? The contortions began almost immediately in the local and national press. The youths had absolutely no way to avoid culpability for throwing a gay man off the bridge, and still the twisted logic of denial dictated that the victim somehow brought all this on himself—that the "real victims" of this whole incident were the three young defendants, even though they harassed, assaulted, and pitched Charlie Howard headlong off the State Street Bridge. For Charlie to be a viable scapegoat for his own death, Charlie (1) had to seem threatening to the average person; and (2) had to have given a "good" or "understandable" reason for the gang's aggression against him.

Insinuation and innuendo did the trick. It was almost impossible to find any accurate description of Charlie Howard as a real person in the Bangor press. Watts tried repeatedly to learn something about Charlie the human being from news stories with little success. In District Court, the legal battle to discredit Charlie's status as a victim moved swiftly. The media moved along a parallel track, engaged in what Watts called the "weird morphing" of Charlie Howard. This weird morphing would not allow the media to call Charlie a "peer" of his killers, though in his early twenties he was virtually their age, and far more physically frail than any of them. Such admissions would (God forbid) undoubtedly lead the public mind to assume that the Bangor Three were murders. So, the "bone-rack" thin, non-menacing 23-year-old gay man was subtly morphed into "Homo Menace-Man," innocent Charlie's sinister *doppelgänger*, who threatened to undermine morals, and corrupt the youth. The local media therefore provided only his name, his age, and his vaguely menacing status as a "homosexual," who originally came to Bangor "from away" in New Hampshire. When the culture is, by default, heterosexist and homophobic, the homosexual moniker alone is enough to burden a victim with a presumed guilt, making it virtually impossible to expunge bias from the public mind. As a cipher instead of a human being, the artificial Charlie was voided of character content, conveniently rendered into an empty bucket, and made available to be filled by prejudicial ignorance about gay men. Watts believed that the media construct of Charlie—never presented in so many words, mind you—resembled nothing less than a middle-aged, sinister "Charles Nelson Reilly-character," hot to cruise for youth to molest (Reilly, a television and film actor-comedian, often portrayed a campy, gay man).

The scapegoat logic could turn to another distracting question: "How did the 'homo' start it?" The *casus belli*, the precipitating event, for the attack was conveniently provided by an unsubstantiated claim from the youngest of Charlie's killers, Jim Baines. Baines alleged to police that Charlie had made sexualized comments to him weeks before the assault. The media grabbed the accusation, and ran it frequently to sensationalize the story. Here was a "plausible reason" their hometown youth could not leave Charlie alone and still be "real men." Picking up the narrative as framed by local sources, even the venerable *New York Times* made the same erroneous assumptions in September 1984 when the "three juveniles" were reprieved from standing trial for murder as adults by Judge Cox. By then, all three defendants were singing the same tune—they were just trying to "frighten him for what they said was a sexual advance he had once made to one of them." They were defending their masculinity against the blandishments of a corrupter of youth, a "Homo Menace-Man." And the public by and large bought it. Charlie was dead, unable to speak for himself from the grave, or to defend his own character. The real Charlie Howard didn't appear in print for years. Only a few news stories carried any mention of him, and the articles described him unsympathetically virtually for a decade, until the media had been chastised into portraying LGBTQ people in less biased ways than in the mid-1980s. The classic pattern of the "gay panic defense," which haunts courtrooms and newsrooms even today, was inscribed first on the corpse of frail Charlie Howard.

LEARNING THE HARD WAY

The story of Charlie's murder bubbled and boiled all summer, until his killers came to trial in the fall of 1984. On September 14, Judge Cox ruled that Shawn I. Mabry, Daniel Ness, and James Francis Baines would be tried as juveniles, and the judge set the stage for them to plead guilty on October 1 to manslaughter instead of murder. Four days later, the Bangor Three appeared at their sentencing hearing. District Judge Cox gave them each the maximum sentence under the Maine Juvenile Code, remanding them to the Maine Youth Center in South Portland to serve "an indeterminate stay not to exceed their twenty-first birthdays." Ness, the eldest of the three, served the least amount of time. Mabry served twenty-two months. Baines was released last, two years after his incarceration.

Mainers, it seems, learn the hard way. Of all the killers, Baines has taken his guilt the most seriously, lecturing to school groups on the evils of prejudice. With the assistance of journalist Ed Armstrong, he published his *mea culpa, Penitence: A True Story,* in 1994. Mabry and Ness have been more wary of the public eye. In his 1994 interview in the *Sun Journal* for the *Bangor Daily News,* Mabry gave a rare glimpse of a killer's remorse. "How could you not feel guilty? Of course, I do," he said. "Charlie Howard was so young. He was helpless that night, and three reckless kids come along and just for the hell of it toss him over the bridge. Because of our actions, Charlie Howard lost his life." Ness has never spoken out publicly. Now, more than twenty-five years after the murder, the Bangor Three are in their middle age and have dropped out of sight. Mabry has continued to be in trouble with the law through the years. Rumor has it that Baines is married with children, living somewhere in the Midwest. Roy Ogden, Charlie's companion on his last night, is nowhere to be found.

"Gone, But Not Forgotten," could have been coined just for Charlie. His memory has been kept alive in Maine longer than his whole earthly lifetime. For a quarter century, advocates and opponents of LGBTQ

equality have fought over his legacy. The Christian Civic League, a regional arm of the Christian Coalition, memorably characterized Charlie
and all the gay people of Maine as "a lie from the Pit of Hell." Equality
Maine, first known as the Maine Lesbian/Gay Political Alliance, was
founded in 1984 in response to Charlie's murder, to address "the impact
of violence and discrimination in LGBTQ Mainers' lives." Like *yin* and
yang, the two opposing forces have grappled with each other, struggling
to change the ethos of the Pine Tree State. In May 2009, Governor John
Baldacci, a young Bangor City Councilman at the time of Charlie's murder, signed Maine's gay marriage act into law. Many heralded the legislation as a victory for Charlie, whose memory was invoked throughout the
state as the patron saint of marriage equality. Maine balked at same-sex
marriage equality, however, and in a hard fought statewide referendum
the following November, marriage equality was repealed, 53 percent to
47. Bangor's most famous citizen, Stephen King, immortalized Charlie's
murder by drowning in his 1986 horror novel, *It*. King, who lived right
down the street from the State Street Bridge in 1984, was deeply affected
by Charlie's death. For his 1987 book, *Turtle Swan*, National Book Award
winning poet, Mark Doty, wrote "Charlie Howard's Descent," a powerful indictment of homophobia. The Yankee Queer author, John Preston,
wrote movingly about Charlie in his book, *Winter's Light*, published
posthumously in 1995. "I was enraged," Preston wrote.

> It wasn't just that a brutal act had occurred. I was also furious that
> my own right to be in this place, Maine, was challenged. I took
> the murder personally. I knew they would have killed *me* if I had
> been walking down that street that night . . . I moved through
> the streets of Portland in the subsequent weeks daring someone
> to hassle me. I wasn't going to let anyone take me out so casually.
> There was going to be a fight . . . I spoke with fury to any audience
> who would listen.

Compared to Harvey Milk, and often these days to Matthew
Shepard, Charlie has gone through an *apotheosis* of sorts. He has taken
his place among the honor roll of the LGBTQ dead, remembered each
year at the State Street Bridge across the Kenduskeag in Bangor. Charlie's
mother, Patience Berounsky of Portsmouth, New Hampshire, will never
set foot in Bangor again. But each year her words are conveyed to those
who have not forgotten her son, as a white rose, wreathed in baby's
breath and tied with a lavender and white ribbon is dropped into the

stream: "Be careful of the crazies out there and those with closed minds."
A blog contributor named Scott wrote for the twenty-fifth anniversary
of Charlie's murder, "Charlie, by his death, made our lives as gay people
better. He couldn't know what his death would mean for the LGBTQ
rights movement, but I hope he had even a small sense of what a hero
he was just by living his life authentically." It took twenty-five years of
wrangling, but a modest granite memorial, complete with a stone bench,
is now installed in the park beside the bridge where Charlie was thrown
to his death, far more local recognition than any other gay hate crime
victim currently enjoys. Carved on a tablet are the words, "May we, the
citizens of Bangor, continue to change the world around us until hatred
becomes peacemaking and ignorance becomes understanding."

Because of Charlie, Bangor has changed—and so has Maine. It takes
time for Down-Easterners to learn something new, but once they do,
they can be tenacious about it. Today Maine has a hate crimes law on the
books, and many cities and towns have anti-discrimination ordinances.
The Attorney General's Office in Augusta has established Civil Rights
Teams in two hundred Maine high schools to combat unreasoning
prejudice against minority groups, including gays, lesbians, and transgender people. But Bangor does not have one in the very same school
that bred Charlie's three killers. Bangorites have a good deal more to do
in Charlie's memory before heterosexism and homophobia become no
more than bad dreams in the northern night.

In an interview with the *Bangor Daily News* in 2004, Dan Williams
confessed that he still fears a bit for his own safety in the Queen City.
Williams, who founded the Charles O. Howard Foundation, and spear-
headed the effort to pass an anti-discrimination ordinance in the city,
said, "Bangor has become a good place to live. However, there is still
prejudice here. I think I'm safe 99 percent of the time, but do I still look
for an escape route when I'm about to walk through a group of people on
the sidewalk? Of course!"

Joseph V. Keelan, a native of nearby Lewiston, has a similarly guarded attitude toward the degree of change in Maine. For a June 2010 retro-
spective in the *Sun Journal* on Charlie's murder, he mused, "Twenty-five
years later, things have changed in Maine and if nothing else, it's a safer
place to live for Maine's gay, lesbian, bisexual and transgendered citizens.
But I wonder how much some times." Keelan continued:

Earlier this year, when I was still living in Lewiston, my partner and I were walking our dogs down the street when a young man shouted from his window a long line of disgusting slurs at us. And for what reason?

Just because we're gay. That small incident upset me a great deal. I wondered why after twenty-five years Charlie Howard still comes to my mind. I believe we should always remember Charlie Howard and not only because of what happened to him. But because of what could happen again."

For Greater Understanding

Bridge of Sighs: Charles O. "Charlie" Howard

BOOKS

Armstrong, Edward J. *Penitence: A True Story*. Bangor, ME: Lucy Madden Associates, 1994.

Coffin, William Sloane. "Thirsting for Righteousness (July 14, 1985)." In *Collected Sermons of William Sloane Coffin: Volume 2 – The Riverside Years: Years 1983—1987*. Louisville, KY: Westminster John Knox Press, 2008.

Doty, Mark. *Turtle Swan*. Boston, MA: David R. Godine, Publishers, 1987.

Preston, John. *Winter's Light: Confessions of a Yankee Queer*. Hanover, NH: University Press of New England, 1995.

FILMS AND VIDEOGRAPHY

Charlie Howard: A Memorial. Scruffy Productions, 2004.

ORGANIZATIONS AND WEBSITES

Equality Maine, http://www.equalitymaine.org.

Unfinished Lives Project, http://unfinishedlivesblog.com.

Satendar Singh
July 21, 1980—July 5, 2007

LAKE NATOMA STATE PARK, FOLSOM, CALIFORNIA

10

Dancing with Shiva

Satendar Singh

"Because Thou lovest the Burning-ground,
I have made a Burning-ground of my heart -
That Thou, Dark One, haunter of the Burning-ground,
Mayest dance Thy eternal dance."

—FROM A BENGALI HYMN TO SHIVA

THE SHORES OF LAKE Natoma State Park became a tragic *Burning-ground* for the young gay Sikh nicknamed, "The Lucky One." Satendar Singh was gay-bashed to death on the first day of July 2007 in a distinctively American collision of immigrant ethnicities and belief systems. On the Indian subcontinent, where Satendar's ancestors originated, the corpses of the dead are cremated beside bodies of water. Where the pyres are built and burnt, Hindus believe Shiva the Destroyer dances in the midst of the *Burning-ground*. Though he was not a Hindu, as his Russian émigré killers mistakenly assumed, Satendar's forebears knew the stories of Lord Nataraja, the Dancing Shiva, and held the faith of their neighbors in sacred honor. Lake Natoma, a popular recreation area for runners, cyclists, and holidaymakers just fifteen miles northeast of Sacramento, California, is half a world away from the banks of the Holy River Ganges, aflame with the last rites of the faithful dead. But on the verge of that most American of all holidays, the Fourth of July, Satendar the gentle, gay East Indian who joyously danced with his friends all afternoon under the hot California sun, encountered the Destroyer in a fatal choreography of clashing cultures, religions, races, and homophobic rage.

Satendar Simmon Nicolas Johal Singh was born on the Pacific island paradise of Fiji. There, his married elder brother Shalender Singh, and Satendar's parents, Jaswat and Akesa Singh, belonged to a dwindling Sikh community who were emigrating from the islands to almost anywhere else. At the height of their population, the Sikhs in Fiji boasted around ten thousand souls. They had removed from the Punjab, the ancestral home of the Sikh religion, in the mid-nineteenth century to work in the sugar cane fields of their British overlords. Fiji once had been a fertile ground for their religious culture. The Sikhs brought along their proud heritage, understanding themselves as the Lions of their Holy Book, *Guru Granth Sahib*, regarded by Sikhs as the eternal and final guru of the youngest of the world's great religions. They built five temples, called "Gurdwaras," in Fiji, where they welcomed all people, Sikh or not, to find shelter, food, and worship. As the most feared soldiers of the British Empire, Sikhs had won respect for their orderly lives, co-operative civic mindedness, and ferocious loyalty. Their turbans were crowns of piety and purity of life. But life on Fiji had turned hard after the sugar cane fields played out. Indebtedness, domestic strife, and restlessness set in over time. Young Sikhs emigrated by the thousands during the 1970s, '80s, and '90s for the greener pastures of Canada and the United States. By the time Satendar arrived in California, there were only three thousand or so of his people remaining back home, mostly on Viti Levu, the larger island of the Fiji archipelago.

As the 2000 millennium approached, tales of the American Dream filled Satendar with hope. Relatives and friends sent back stories of the charms of the American West Coast, a land of opportunity where it seemed anything was possible for a young man who was willing to work hard. So as he entered the annual lottery for a visa and a green card to the United States, Satendar said his prayers for a miracle. He won, and along with the documents unlocking his future in the New World, he also won the moniker he would own for the rest of his life, "The Fortunate One."

Members of Satendar's family had already established themselves in California's Sacramento area, so it was convenient for Satendar to live with them while he settled into his new country. He lived for a time with his uncle and aunt, Camie and Suvin Bhuie, and his grandmother, Chand Johal. He landed a good job with an AT&T Call Center, and thrived there. His family back in Fiji took pride in his accomplishments. In barely seven years in the United States, Satendar had advanced in the company, and had got a series of good raises in pay. Just before the Fourth of July holiday weekend in 2007, his bosses informed him that he had earned yet another substantial promotion. So, together with three young East Indian married couples he knew and liked, Satendar planned a great day at Lake Natoma, picnicking, grilling, and celebrating how good it was to be in America. The partiers took blankets, a video camera, a "boom box" with familiar music they all liked, plenty of good food and drink, and they headed out happily for a Sunday on the lake.

DESIS, QUEERS, AND SLAVIC FUNDAMENTALISTS

The *desi* population in Sacramento was booming in 2007. *"Desi"* refers to anyone of subcontinental heritage, usually from India, Pakistan, Bangladesh, or Sri Lanka, but also from other immigrant communities such as Fiji. The Sanskrit root of the term means, in South Asian slang, "one from the home country," in effect a brown-skinned homeboy. The most recent census had counted nearly 17,000 people of South and East Asian descent living in Sacramento, a number that was multiplying rapidly in the greater metro area. IT and telecom jobs beckoned them to move to the River City. With a reputation since 2002 as one of America's "most integrated" large cities, California's capital attracted many of South Asia's best and brightest. It was also a metropolitan environment where a young gay *desi* could learn how to express his sexuality in *relative* safety.

Satendar was indeed gay, but out only to a select few of his friends and family. In the glare of publicity after his murder, loved ones initially claimed that he was not homosexual. After the early shock had worn off a bit, however, family members admitted to journalists that they had known about Satendar's sexual orientation for a long while, and that it had never interfered with the love he and they shared for each other. Whether he had a same-sex love interest in July 2007 remains unknown. A general heterosexist agreement seems to exist in the *desi* community not to speak openly of such things as same-sex attraction. South Asians are a discreet people.

When Alexandr Shevchenko stood trial for Satendar's murder, Romil Sharma, an eyewitness who had been with Satendar at the lake, said that though he had not met "the Lucky One" before that day, Singh reminded Sharma of his native Fiji. "He was open, he was funny," Sharma said. Under oath, the prosecutor asked Sharma if he thought Satendar was gay. He replied that he had never asked him about it, but "probably, I would say, 'Yes.'"

Satendar's death ignited a hot debate that raged for weeks on the blogosphere, concerning appropriate responses to violence among members of the *desi* community. Some bloggers accused their community of "wimpishness" in the face of aggression. Out of frustration, a certain ethnic and cultural reticence became the target for their ire. Others attributed the deafening silence of the desi community toward this brutal hate crime to less excusable motivations. Writing on the "Sepia Mutiny" site on August 10, little more than a month after Satendar suffered the fatal punch in the face, "Krish****" (as he was known on the internet) straightforwardly contended that *desi* notions of shame were behind the community's mum response. "Mental illness, homosexuality, domestic violence, are examples of issues we'd rather ignore because of 'shame,'" he wrote. "There's something to South Asian psychology that tells us to keep these problems at a distance, because even talking about them is inviting these 'misfortunes' to pop up in your family." Then Krish**** cut to the chase: "Let's face it . . . the vast majority of [*desis*] (even the progressive ones on here) have this feeling in the back of their mind that because of his sexual orientation, 'he had it coming.'"

No doubt, Satendar would have carried painful awareness all his life of the *desi* community's aversion to his sexual orientation. Being gay on Fiji was an extremely tricky thing to pull off. As a boy, he would have grown up understanding that homosexuality was illegal in his home country. Though seldom enforced in recent years, Fiji has one of the toughest anti-gay laws in the South Pacific, as an Australian tourist found out in 2005 when he and a Fijian man were arrested, tried, and sentenced to two years in prison for consensual sex. If the full penalty of the law had been imposed, the two men could have faced fourteen years at hard labor for homosexual activity. The Australian, Thomas McCosker, and his sexual partner served four months of that sentence before having their conviction overturned by a Fiji High Court judge in response to an international outcry. $60,000 poorer and badly shaken, McCosker immediately returned to his homeland, where Australian gays subsequently issued a travel advisory warning, directing LGBTQ tourists away from Fiji. Satendar would have known about this infamous case since it made headlines throughout the South Pacific. As any sensitive, closeted gay man would have done, he took it to heart. In addition to Fijian conservatism on homosexuality and a stern *desi* attitude toward any form of queer expression, Satendar's native Sikh religious heritage also held a deeply ingrained negativity toward openly gay people.

Though he was in a triple bind of sorts about his gayness, there was another side to the story. The one mitigating element in Satendar's sexual self-awareness was the presence of a large, vibrant LGBTQ culture in the Sacramento metro area.

Sacramento County is home to one of the largest per capita LGBTQ populations in the United States. In California, only San Francisco itself exceeds the River City. An estimated 45,000 gays, lesbians, bisexuals, and transgenders live there, enjoying the freedoms the "Left Coast" has to offer. Satendar would have known about and probably discreetly participated in the festivals, social events, organizations, and groups that this burgeoning queer community created for themselves in the golden city by the banks of the Sacramento and American Rivers. LGBTQ heritage stretched back at least a generation there, and while he would have been characteristically quiet about it, Satendar had enough liberated gay life going on around him that he could have grown into a deeper awareness of himself, despite any of the inhibitions he may have faced on a daily basis.

Satendar, known as "Simon" at work, would have felt freer to be an openly gay man on the job in Sacramento than he would have in his own native cultural setting. AT&T, where he worked for seven years, is one of the most LGBTQ-affirmative companies in corporate America. Even as early as 1975, the telecom giant had a sexual orientation non-discrimination policy in effect, and LEAGUE, the AT&T LGBTQ employee organization, is the first and largest queer corporate business resource group in the nation, having been founded in Denver in 1987. Every year since 2004, AT&T's inclusive policies have received a 100 percent rating from the Human Rights Campaign's Corporate Equality Index. Through his job at the call center, Satendar would have known about these policies thoroughly thanks to his local Sacramento LEAGUE chapter.

Sacramento was an attractive place for San Francisco LGBTQ people to spend a vacation weekend. In April 2007, Andrew Collins, writer for the *About.com Guide to Gay and Lesbian Travel*, encouraged queer San Franciscans to make the three-hour trip down to the capital city: "If you're looking for a relatively affordable Northern California destination that has a highly visible and quite fun gay community, consider planning a trip to Sacramento, an underrated city with lots to see and do." What Collins did not address in his post, "Exploring Gay Sacramento," however, was the increasing friction gays were having with a burgeoning Slavic Christian fundamentalist community that considered itself to have a divine mandate to oppose any expression of LGBTQ life world-wide.

Local leaders in the gay community had feared for months that violence could break out against them from the Slavs, and for good reason.

WATCHMEN ON THE WALLS

Wtihin Sacramento's Slavic community, aggressive, militant Christian fundamentalism took control away from moderate leadership in the months before Satendar's murder. Florin Cuiriuc, former director of the Slavic Community Center of Sacramento, at one time led anti-gay protests among his fellow Slavs, but stopped for fear of what these demonstrations might become. He told the *Sacramento Bee*, "I saw that people were hungry for violence, for blood. I don't want people from my community killing each other or other people because they are getting aggressive." In the spring of 2006, at a "Queer Youth Advocacy Day" for young gay rights activists to lobby state government on LGBTQ issues, some two hundred youth were confronted in the streets by an estimated 350 Slavic anti-gay demonstrators. Wendy Hill, a lesbian and gay rights activist in Sacramento since the 1990s witnessed the scene. She told the Southern Poverty Law Center (SPLC), "They were blocking sidewalks, physically intimidating [us] . . . We realized how complacent [the LGBTQ community] had become. We weren't used to that type of behavior." Commenting on the composition of the anti-gay protesters, she pointed directly at the Slavic fundamentalists, "I'd say about 90 percent to 95 percent were from Slavic churches." Hill and her partner of eight years became frightened for their two little children, a three-year-old and a one-year-old, after the angry confrontation. Once, they had considered Sacramento a good place to rear a family. Not now. "It scares me," Hill continued, "to think that something's going to happen to my daughter because of who her parents are."

Since 2005, according to the Montgomery-based SPLC, "a growing and ferociously anti-gay movement in the Sacramento Valley . . . centered among Russian- and Ukrainian-speaking immigrants" has been asserting itself at nearly every public LGBTQ event. Of the 100,000 immigrants from the Ukraine, Uzbekistan, and Russia, approximately 30,000 are self-styled evangelicals, mostly Russian-speaking "Russian Baptists" and Pentecostals who, since the 1980s, had immigrated to the United States from the former Soviet Union to find relief from religious persecution. These Slavic fundamentalist Christians are organized in some seventy churches in Sacramento and environs, and one of these churches boasts over 3,200 members and bills itself the largest Slavic evangelical church outside Europe. These congregations have rallied thousands of their parishioners to picket LGBTQ events. In a *Sacramento Bee* article from the summer of 2006, the threat LGBTQ people felt in the year leading up to Satendar's murder came through loud and clear: "Gays say the Slavic protesters have hit them with signs, spit on them and displayed a menacing lack of civility. Gay leaders have met with local police and press to say they're worried about violence, and now they're forming a 'Q Crew'—a new political activism group—to tell the public their fears." Placards wielded by anti-LGBTQ Slavs often purposefully muddle homosexuality, pedophilia, and bestiality, and assert that the AIDS epidemic is a plague sent upon gays by God. The *Seattle Times* reports that one of the demonstrators' favorite tactics is to "tap" LGBTQ people forcefully on their heads and proclaim that they are now "saved."

Many Russian immigrants first learned about the Sacramento area from two media sources espousing an apocalyptic view of history: a shortwave radio program called, "A Word to Russia," and the local Russian-language paper, *Our Days,* printed in Sacramento and smuggled into the old Soviet Union for circulation among underground churches. Like the Puritan pilgrims who settled Plymouth, Massachusetts in the seventeenth century, Russian Baptists and Pentecostals believe that God has chosen America to be a sanctuary for present-day pilgrims seeking religious freedom. When they came to this country, however, the Slavs found that the power of secular culture and social diversity challenged their mores and lured their children into a melting pot that threatened to erode the same beliefs they had immigrated to the United States to preserve. These religious fundamentalists look at American churches as soft on issues such as homosexuality, abortion, and "family values." In order for true Christian values to survive, they believe, the Slavic churches must battle for the soul of their adopted country to cleanse the way for the Second Coming of Jesus Christ. A twenty-four-hour Russian-language cable television station, a number of newspapers, and two radio stations keep broadcasting their conservative Christian screed, hallmarked by a stalwart, anti-LGBTQ party line. Vitaly Prokopchuk, a Sacramento County Sheriff's Deputy interviewed by the *Los Angeles Times* in 2006, tried to put the aggressive political program of his countrymen in context. The combination of culture shock and homegrown Russian prejudice has created a hornets' nest of opposition to liberalizing American attitudes toward homosexuality. "Back home," he said, "homosexuality was looked at as kind of a disgrace and a lifestyle for immoral people and prisoners."

For every anti-gay protester shouting "Repent or be damned, you Sodomites!" however, there have been pro-LGBTQ push-backs, advocating the deportation of Russians and their Ukrainian cohorts. Nathan Feldman, for example, a gay activist in Sacramento, formed his LGBTQ group, Stand Up for Sacramento, as an act of community self-defense after being surrounded by an angry mob of Russian-speaking demonstrators in June 2006. "I ended up getting spit on and yelled at," he told the *Los Angeles Times*. In a Craigslist web forum cited by the SPLC entitled "DEPORT RUSSIANS NOW!" in boldface capital letters, the forum leader wrote, "They came here [as] religious refugees and turn their newfound freedom on our citizenry. If they are going to [use] evangelical religious rhetoric, then I say give some Old [Testament] eye for eye."

Many LGBTQ activists in Sacramento point to the United States branch of a Latvian-based extremist organization as the ultimate impetus for Satendar's murder, the "Watchmen On the Walls." Both of the Russians who carried out the fatal attack on Satendar were affiliated with the Watchmen through their local church. Drawing their name from the Hebrew Bible book of Nehemiah, whose armed lookouts sat upon the broken walls of Jerusalem as the ruins of the city were repaired, modern-day Watchmen see an allegorical connection between their extremist brand of religion and the ancient restoration of the City of David. Bending the Bible to their own ideological needs and prejudices, Slavic leaders preach that "Jerusalem," the current world-wide membership of "true" Christianity, has been sacked and pillaged by an ungodly cabal of homosexuals, their "homosexualist" boosters, and even Muslim fundamentalists. As Watchman Alexey Ledyaev says in his 2002 book, *New World Order,* "The first devastating wave of homosexuality makes a way for the second and more dangerous wave of islamization [sic]." American Watchmen accuse secretive "homosexual activists" with undermining the "natural family," and therefore Western civilization by spawning the pornography industry, the pro-abortion movement, and "the destruction of marriage by divorce," according to Liz Meyer, reporting for *Seattle Gay News*. Like a sexually transmitted disease, say the Watchmen, LGBTQ people and their "homosexual agenda" are threatening the life and health of the "true Christian faith" (read, *their* brand of exclusive Christian fundamentalism). In the summer of 2006, according to the SPLC, a Russian-language newspaper with an English title, *The Speaker*, whipped up attendance at an anti-LGBTQ rally by sewing fear:

"Make a choice," the paper demanded, "It's your decision. Homosexuality is knocking on your doors and asking, 'Can I make your son gay and your daughter lesbian?'" The only thing that will save Christianity from annihilation is drastic action, according to Pacific Coast Watchmen leader and Russian-language radio host, Vlad Kusakin, a.k.a. Wade Kusak. In January 2007, he told the *Seattle Times* that the disease of homosexuality had prompted God to make "a divine injection" of massive numbers of anti-LGBTQ Slavic Christians into gay-friendly cities on the West Coast. "In those places where the disease is progressing," Kusakin said, "God made a divine penicillin."

The only way to combat this "blue plague," as Watchmen co-founder Scott Lively calls the LGBTQ community, is aggressive, head-to-head confrontation—just a whisker shy of full-throated incitement to violence. In his widely distributed screed, "Masculine Christianity," Lively presses for testosterone-saturated confrontation wherever possible:

> We church leaders need to stop being such, for lack of a better word, sissies when it comes to social and political issues. For every motherly, feminine ministry of the church such as Crisis Pregnancy Center or ex-gay support group, we need a battle-hardened, take-it-to-the-enemy masculine ministry like Operation Rescue [which opposes abortion].

The SPLC reports that Lively is fully willing to use violence in the name of his hate agenda. A civil court judge ordered him to pay $20,000 in damages to lesbian photojournalist Cathrine Stauffer for throwing her down by the hair of the head and dragging her through the corridors of a Portland, Oregon church in 1991.

Lively cemented his strongest rhetorical connection to Satendar's Russian émigré attackers by the cunning way he tapped into the mingled feelings of anti-Nazi loathing and nationalist pride borne by the Russian people since the "Great Patriotic War" against Adolph Hitler. Millions of Russians died at the hands of the Nazis, so when Lively published his single claim to fame in Eastern Europe, *The Pink Swastika: Homosexuality in the Nazi Party,* many veterans and their families were predisposed to believe its claims. A blatant piece of historical revisionism, *The Pink Swastika* has been debunked time and again by conservative and liberal scholars alike. Nonetheless, its publication in 1995 made Lively a minor celebrity in right-wing Russian circles. Briefly, the book perverts history by making homosexuals, one of the "Final Solution's"

most infamous targets for annihilation, into the architects and willing executioners of Jews and Slavs alike. Not only the Nazi Party, but also Hitler
himself was homosexual, Lively claims. His twisted but diabolically effective logic takes the visceral fear and hatred reserved for the Third Reich,
and transfers it to a new kind of *pink menace* threatening Christian faith
and the Motherland: LGBTQ people. This erroneous, highly dangerous
mythology permeated the "New Generation" church movement instituted
by right-wing Latvian pastor, Alexey Ledyaev, whose Riga megachurch
has spun off two hundred satellite congregations in Argentina, Israel, the
United States, and throughout Eastern Europe. Ledyaev was so taken
with *The Pink Swastika* that he opened speaking engagements for Lively
throughout the former Soviet Union. A straight line connects these events
in Eastern Europe to the gathering storm in the Sacramento Valley. Besides
the efforts of two congregations of Ledyaev's New Generation Church
movement in Sacramento, the Russian-language newspaper, *The Speaker*,
pushed sales of Lively's book through its editorial pages for weeks and
weeks. With the growth of Watchman Lively's prestige in the Slavic fundamentalist community in Sacramento, and hefty sales of his mind-warping,
virulently anti-LGBTQ book, an almost hormonal loathing of anything
or anyone perceived to be gay or lesbian spliced itself into the DNA of
the evangelical Russian community in Satendar's hometown. Though he
could not have known it, the likeable gay *desi*, dancing with his friends
on the shores of Lake Natoma, had been randomly targeted for attack all
the way from Mother Russia by Slavic fundamentalists who saw his very
existence as a threat to their marriages, their families, their religion, and
their entire worldview.

ONWARD, CHRISTIAN SOLDIERS

At 26 years old, Satendar Singh had everything to live for. An Indo-
Fijian of medium height and build, his family and friends remember
him as quick to share a smile, with a loud, nearly musical laugh that
communicated joy. His grandmother, aunt, and uncle said that they
appreciated his humble, loving nature and his sincere affection for everyone, especially for his elder brother, his sister-in-law and nephew,
and his large extended family. They also highlighted Satendar's gift for
making everyone around him feel special, as if he had a specific place in
his heart reserved for each of them. A friend said, "He had a smile and a
laugh that always lit up the room whenever he came in." Another friend

pondered on the irony of how Satendar died in such a shocking outburst of bigoted violence. "Satendar lived each day to the fullest," she said, "as if it was going to be his last. We just never thought that it would be his last day so soon."

Though a Sikh by ancestry, like many younger members of his generation's *diaspora*, Satendar wore neither a turban nor a beard, except for the small goatee he sported on the day of the attack. He was attentive to the way he looked, especially about his clothes. Though he might not have owned the most expensive wardrobe in town, he had learned how to wear what he had to the maximum effect. His preferred style was casual, urban, and simple. On the day he died, Satendar wore blue jeans, a chocolate-brown crew shirt, and a brown ball cap. Ever mindful of his waist, he consciously watched what he ate, with the exception of his one food weakness: chicken tenders. Friends say that his favorite restaurant was Kentucky Fried Chicken, but Satendar's looks on July 1, 2007 implied he had successfully resisted temptation.

The small group of *desis* who picnicked at Lake Natoma State Park that Sunday had lots to celebrate. The Sharmas, the Naidus, and a third couple (who are still fearful and wish to remain anonymous), invited Satendar to bring his special brand of *joie de vivre* to make a red-letter day of it. The unnamed couple came to celebrate their engagement. Another couple was preparing very soon to welcome their first child into the world. Satendar had been promoted at the call center, and everyone in the group congratulated him for that achievement. The young *desi* community was prospering in its adopted homeland. The seven friends chose a nice shaded spot, spread blankets, set up their barbeque grill, and began to twist open bottles of ice-cold beer. Somebody brought along a stack of East Indian CDs, and soon the lakeshore vibrated with the beat of *desi* hip hop artists like Punjabi M.C. and Rishi Risky Raj, and the point-counterpoint of women's and men's laughter. Like a contagion, the rhythm claimed them, one-by-one, beckoning the whole party to rise up and dance.

Desis say that Punjabi Sikhs are just better at dancing than other South Asians. For centuries, they have been gyrating to up-tempo music in a style called *"bhangra,"* that involves swiveling hips and rotating wrists that one tongue-in-cheek admirer has called a combination of twisting in a light bulb and molesting a dog. Of course, it wasn't like that at all, but the exaggerated movements, the swaying torso, and the twirling hands of a good *bhangra* dancer always capture attention, and Satendar was one of the best. As the day wore on and as the beer flowed freely, the intermittent dancing moved from a show to audience participation. An eighteen-minute video shot by one of the women in Satendar's party captures the giddy joy of the day. Like a dancing honey bee, Satendar buzzed from one person to the next, taking this one and now that one by the hand, got them up, and led them in a crazy *bhangra*. To the delight of the woman heavy with child, Satendar reached for her hand, saying in that melodious sing-song of his, "Get up here and dance, pregnant lady!" As the remixes of Punjabi, *desi*, and Indian hip hop throbbed, he spun another of the women around and around, ending with a flourish of his wrists, a broad smile reaching from ear-to-ear. Satendar's attentions did not exempt the men, either. It is not uncommon for *desi* men to dance together at weddings and other grand occasions, so they forgot any North American reserve they might have acquired, and clapped to the beat along with Satendar who was giving some deep shoulder action, bobbing and weaving with the men to the delight of the women. With playful abandon, one of the men took up a little switch fallen from one of the trees, and mock-whipped Satendar's derriere to torrents of laughter. Before long, a goofy conga line formed under the lakeside trees. Video captured the last moments of carefree dancing for Satendar's group: woman, man, woman, man, man, man.

Seven minutes into the eighteen-minute-long video, another group of Sunday picnickers appear. Fresh from church services, a gathering of Russian fundamentalist Christians chose the area adjacent to the Indo-Fijians for their fresh-air day of fun, too. This was a larger group than the *desis,* with several families present. Among them was Andrey Vusik, 29, an auto export trader, his wife Tatyana, and their three little children who lived in a Slavic enclave in West Sacramento. Unused to both East Indian hip hop, and to men dancing together as the *desis* were doing nearby, Vusik immediately took offense at what he saw. To him the music sounded like noise, something like "honky dinky dinky dinky dinky honky dinky dinky . . ." He and his muscular young friend, a 21-year-old construction worker named Alexandr Shevchenko, had also come to the lake after church with his date, Vusik's sister-in-law Dasha. Both Andrey and Alexandr grew less and less tolerant of what they watched going on among the *desis,* and more and more belligerent about it as the day wore on. The strong Russian brews began to take effect.

The Russians saw immediately that Satendar was the only single man in his group, provocatively dateless. They steamed and breathed disgust among themselves about the way he hugged men as well as women, and danced with both genders in an altogether too friendly manner. Huddling their women and children in a tight circle, the Russian men, led by Andrey and Alexandr, began to hurl slurs at the Fijian group, along with demands that they stop and go home, or go back to India. When the members of Satendar's group refused to leave, and actually barked back that the Russians should leave and not them—especially since the *desis* got to the lake first—the verbal brickbats got meaner. The Russian men shouted that the "brownies" were "taxi drivers," "7-11 Workers," "Hindus," and "Sodomites." The *desis*, though uncomfortable, refused to back down, and threw back some verbal bombs of their own, like "go back to Russia!"

About 5 p.m., bystander Wolfgang Chargin called 911 and reported to the California State Police that two groups at Lake Natoma State Park were at each other's throats. Chargin, a resident of Folsom, said he had watched the exchanges escalate between the two groups, and he told the police that he feared there might be a fight. He decided to pack up his family and go because of the impending violence, he told the authorities. Chargin mentioned that the Russians seemed particularly incensed at the actions of one of the East Indians, the one in the brown ball cap. Chagrin went so far as to say that, though the Russians confronted the East Indians repeatedly, he had not seen any of them become aggressive in return. At one point, he said, Satendar's group went down to the water for a swim, and some of the Russian men walked over into the *desis'* area to spit on their blankets. Before leaving the park, Chargin stopped by the gate kiosk and let a park worker know that the shouting match between the two groups was changing into a shoving match.

The California State Police passed Chargin's warning along to the Lake Natoma Park Rangers, a process that lagged response time almost three hours. Just about the time the park rangers were getting the news of the impending problem, around 8 p.m., Satendar's group tried to leave the lakeshore and go home. Had the rangers gone to the correct area of the park at that moment, they probably could have averted an impending disaster. Instead, unclear about where to go, they couldn't find where the fight was brewing.

Men from the Russian group blocked the Indo-Fijians in the parking lot. One of Satendar's friends (speaking anonymously because of fear of Russian reprisals) said the violence started when two men from their group returned from the restroom and were accosted verbally by a couple of the Russian men. The Russians were in a rage, saying that they had seen Satendar and another man kiss each other. They demanded that Satendar apologize to them and their families for being obscene. Singh and his friends denied kissing anybody, and refused to apologize for something they didn't do. The Russians growled homophobic and racist slurs and one of them threatened, "If there weren't any park rangers here you'd see what I would do. We're waiting for you."

At that fateful moment, with violence heavy in the air, Lord Nataraja, the Dancing Shiva, stepped onto the asphalt of the parking lot, and commenced his deadly *Burning-ground* dance. Unknown to Vusik, a fundamentalist Christian who would deny that he even existed, Lord Shiva made his entrance, hidden within the big Russian's anger. Unknown to Satendar, the target of Vusik's rage, Sri Nataraja had chosen him to be his dance partner on the *Burning-ground*.

According to Sharma and Naidu, Satendar finally responded to the goading insults, and Vusik and Shevchenko turned on him. They shouted that they belonged to a Russian evangelical church, and that he should start going to a "good church" like theirs. Several witnesses, both Russians and *desis* alike, testified that at that point the Russian men sent their wives and children away, and called on their cell phones for more men to come and back them up. The *desi* who was pregnant tried to leave, but the Russians bodily-blocked her and other members of their party. She said in a terrified voice that she didn't want to fight them, and one of the other *desi* men, identified in court as the "big Fijian," tried to defuse the situation. Vusik and Shevchenko rebuffed him out of hand. The Russian fundamentalists were now in full Christian soldier mode, fueled by misguided piety, Watchmen-paranoid hatred, and too much beer. One of them said to her, "We don't want to fight you, either, we just want your faggot friend."

At that moment, the "big Russian" threw a cup of beer in the face of one of the *desis*, and then "sucker-punched" Satendar full in the face with such force that Satendar fell back, hard and fast. Later Vusik claimed to his wife that he had only thrown a "soft punch" at the "faggot," who was so drunk that he lost his footing and fell. Another person, commenting on the blow said that it was not soft at all, but rather "the punch of the century." Satendar was hit with such power that it rattled his brain, and he fell with a crack, hitting the back of his skull on the edge of the concrete sidewalk, fatally wounding his brain stem. Either it was the un-luckiest sucker-punch the Golden State had ever seen, or Vusik, who by then was drenched with self-righteousness, machismo, and adrenaline, had loosed a killing blow. Satendar suffered a gaping head wound from the concrete edge of the walk, and bled profusely. As the *desi* women turned to aid Satendar, some of the men lunged toward the Russians. Shevchenko tossed a beer bottle at Romil Sharma, backing him off long enough for Schevchenko and Vusik to clamber into their cars, and flee the scene. Paramedics were already loading Satendar into an ambulance when the park rangers finally arrived at the right place—much too late.

After remaining unconscious for a short while, Satendar seemed to rouse a bit, regaining consciousness temporarily. But he was doomed the moment he sustained the blow. The brain stem, which controls most of the autonomic systems that sustain human life, has only the tiniest tolerance for trauma. Its boney sleeve cannot accommodate even slight swelling, and the hit Satendar suffered caused massive engorgement of the brain stem's tissues. As the brain stem swelled with injury, the life supports built into his body began to shut down one-by-one. He was rushed by paramedics to nearby Mercy San Juan Hospital, where a trauma team fought to save his life. Satendar fell back into unconscious oblivion. Then the telltale signs of a wounded brain stem took hold. His wrists that had once turned in time to the music, now grotesquely con-torted with a deadly rigor; his feet once so sure on the dancing ground, spasmed and twisted downward and inward; and his face bent into a frightening rictus as Lord Nataraja, the Destroyer, approached the cli-max of his lethal *pas de deux.*

Vusik raced home from the lake, and told Tatyana that something terrible had happened back at the picnic ground. Initially, he described what he had done as a soft, little punch that caught the "faggot" off bal-ance so that he hit his head. Though he didn't remain long enough to see how badly his victim was hurt, he had guilty presence of mind enough to claim to his wife that it had been "an accident."

Satendar's farewell drama unfolded with agonizing slowness at Mercy San Juan Hospital. His family and friends hurried to be near him as doctors fought the losing battle to save his life. At one point, over a hundred people stood vigil at the hospital, hoping against hope that "the Lucky One," "the Fortunate One," would awaken from his coma. His uncle and aunt kept in constant touch with Satendar's parents back home in Fiji. The waiting was terrible to endure for Jaswant and Akesa, who could not afford the 5,000 mile flight to be at their younger son's bedside. When doctors finally explained Satendar's prognosis, the finality of the news hit his Uncle Camie and his Aunt Suvin like a kick in the stomach. Satendar's brain stem injury was too severe. He would never recover. His brain wave activity was already minimal, implying that, in a best case scenario, Satendar would exist in a persistent, comatose, vegetative state—the very antithesis of their vivacious, loving nephew. Satendar's parents knew they could not manage his care or make life-and-death decisions from half way around the world. They left that burden to their brother-in-law and sister, Camie and Suvin Bhuie. After Satendar existed four unbelievably long days in ICU hooked up to life-support machines, the Bhuies and Grandmother Johal went to Satendar's bedside to hold his hand and say good-bye for the last time. Afterward, the doctors respected the decision of the family: they detached him from the devices that supported his life, and ever so slowly, Satendar Singh's life ebbed away.

Among the scores of friends and concerned Sacramentans who camped out at the hospital, were many LGBTQ activists, and they responded to the news of Satendar's death with grief and anger. Marghe Covino, a longtime lesbian advocate in the Sacramento Valley, had been warning the authorities for months that American Christian fundamentalists were using Slavic church groups as proxies in their campaign to deny equal rights to LGBTQ people. After comforting Satendar's family, Covino, Nathan Feldman, and Michael Gorman spread the word as swiftly as they could: the struggle with Slavic fundamentalism had finally turned deadly. Satendar Singh must not be forgotten. The Sacramento LGBTQ community felt it had a responsibility to Satendar and to his family, to see that the attackers would be brought to justice. A memorial service was hastily planned for the coming Saturday at Lake Natoma. Uncle Camie urged the public to attend out of respect for Satendar, and as an expression of opposition to anti-LGBTQ violence. The lakeside memorial service would be the first among many rallies and vigils for the gentle Fijian with the sparkling laugh.

The Sacramento County Sheriff's Department issued arrest warrants for Vusik on August 6 and Shevchenko on August 7. Hearing the news of Satendar's death, "the Big Russian," Andrey Vusik, fled the country as quickly as he could, hiding out in Russia, his exact location unknown.

He was charged with involuntary manslaughter, and with committing a hate crime for the intimidating homophobic slurs he hurled so liberally at his victim before punching him into oblivion. The FBI was called in to co-operate with the local sheriff's office to locate and extradite Vusik from Russia. Though the *Sacramento Bee* reported that Vusik's family was co-operating with law enforcement in an effort to bring him back for trial, his wife, Tatyana, spoke to whatever news source would listen, arguing that the real victim was not the dead man, but instead her husband and family. "We are a Christian family," she repeated again and again, contending that any suggestion her husband was guilty was a lie. She blamed Satendar and his friends for drunkenness, lewd behavior, lustful dancing, brandishing a broken beer bottle, and escalating the situation throughout the day at the park. The Russians saw the single man kiss another man, she said, satisfied that anyone who heard such a thing would be swayed to defend her husband. Her husband was "a good man," she said. Andrey acted only in self-defense, trying to protect his three children from the debauched behavior of the man who had no female partner at the lake. No witnesses have ever been identified by the police to substantiate the allegations Vusik's wife made against Satendar and his group of friends.

Immediately, Vusik's attorney cut Tatyana off from the press before she did any more damage to his case. Nothing, however, is more revealing than the two major justifications she gave for the "street fight" that turned into what she believed was a homosexual persecution of her family. First, the Vusiks were *Christian,* meaning that their whole sectarian existence opposed the assumed sinfulness of this gay man; and, second, her husband had to act *to protect the children.* Once the Russians had determined that one of the "Hindus" was gay, their defensive aggression switched on immediately, revealing their bedrock belief that gay men are invariably predatory and a threat to little children—the oldest homophobic red herring in the creel of hate groups like the Watchmen On the Walls.

Scott Lively, co-founder of the Watchmen, spun the story of Satendar's murder like a hungry spider. In an August 2007, at a conference held in Novosibirsk, the capital of Siberia, he interpreted the previous month's events in California as evidence of the insidious way gays and lesbians undermine the Christian family, and threaten the overthrow of all moral law. In this transcript of Lively's sermon to the Siberians (provided by Jim Burroway of *Box Turtle Bulletin*), Lively comes danger-ously close to full incitement to violence:

> "Now, I've been working with the Russian community in Sacramento. And I want to tell you this is an example of how bad things are in the United States. Because we've come to a place in the United States where the homosexuals have achieved a very high power. And they've begun to punish . . . They've begun to cause the political powers to punish anyone who says that homo-sexuality is wrong.

"There was a situation in Sacramento a few weeks ago in a pub-lic park. There was a group of homosexuals and they were very drunk and one of the homosexual men was taking off his pants. And there were children in the park. And a Russian man went over to these ho-mosexuals and he was rebuking them and there started a fight. And the Russian man punched the homosexual." [The audience starts to shout and applaud.] "No, no, no, don't . . . The man was very drunk . . . the homosexual was very drunk. He was very drunk and he fell down and he hit his head and he died." [Some in the audience start to applaud and laugh.] "No . . . no . . ."

> "Now the Russian man has been accused of murder and the FBI is seeking him. And all of the powers in Sacramento have been accusing all of the Russian community of being murderers. And the goal is to silence everyone who speaks against homosexual-ity. And this is a very dangerous situation because we don't want homosexuals to be killed. We want them to be saved. Amen?"

THE ONLY DANCE THERE IS

Satendar's family and friends followed the advice of the District Attorney to keep statements to the press to a minimum. Satendar's friends who partied with him at the lake were particularly circumspect, perhaps fearing Russian retribution. Friends established a fund to pay for the local memorial service held in Sacrameto on July 13. After the autopsy, Satendar's remains were transported back to Fiji where, an obituary said, "the last rites of the funeral shall be performed." "The Satendar Justice Coalition" formed in the wake of the killing, and raised $10,000 in re-ward money for leads to the men who attacked Singh. In addition to "MySpace" and "Facebook" web pages, www.satendar.com was launched to keep the public informed about latest developments in the case. While some *desi*-specific news outlets carried the story for a time, outside the Sacramento area very few national news media paid much attention to the case. The young Indo-Fijian, who won the Diversity Lottery in Fiji seven years before his murder, would depart American consciousness just as he had entered it: unknown and unheralded. Comparisons of how the mainstream news services, and even the LGBTQ press, treated Satendar's hate crime case alongside the coverage given to homicides of American-born gay white men, proved that white privilege and a raft of other biases are as evident in the press as in American society at large.

Shevchenko, charged with inciting a fight, assault, and interfering with a victim's rights (which is a felony hate crime in California), went on trial in California Superior Court in May 2008. Throughout the trial, clashing cultural values, and perceptions of what constitutes appropriate behavior, dominated the proceedings. The prosecutor portrayed Satendar and his group as fun-loving young people, doing what virtually all high-spirited young adults like to do at the lake: play, dance, eat, drink, and celebrate their lives. The defense attempted to spin the behavior of Satendar's group as provocative and lewd. The eighteen-minute video shot by one of Satendar's friends was shown repeatedly, each side drawing conclusions from it, seeking to influence the jury favorably for their clients. Dozens of witnesses took the stand, but, as in so many hate crimes trials, the person lost to the view of the court was the victim himself.

After three days of deliberation, the jury brought back a verdict of guilty on the misdemeanor charges of inciting a fight and assault, but admitted they were hopelessly deadlocked on the felony hate crime charge. Seven of the jurors believed that Shevchenko had committed a hate crime against Satendar, and five dissented. Judge Gary Mullen declared a mistrial on the hate crime charge, and proceeded to sentence Shevchenko to 150 days in jail, a stiffer sentence than most had expected after the jury failed to reach a verdict on the hate crime charge. Shevchenko's attorney, Michael Long, appealed to the judge to give his client some weeks to set his life in order before serving his sentence, but Judge Mullen refused, ordering the young Russian to be cuffed and led away.

Few people went away from this debacle satisfied. The Slavic fundamentalist community still seethes with spite against gay Sacramento, contending that they are being unfairly scapegoated for an accidental death in what actually amounted to a brawl, and not a gay bashing. The LGBTQ community remains nervously on guard against the Slavs. Ed Bennett, a gay Democratic activist, characterizes the attitudes of his people, "The gut feeling of the [gay] community is that preaching among the local Russian evangelical community was breeding hate and that something would happen. And Satender was the something that happened." Both groups now have recruited new, albeit unwitting, martyrs to their causes. *Desis* continue to argue about their motives for staying largely silent about the sexual orientation of one of their own. "Justice" had become an elusive byword in the streets of the River City, and a contentiously fluid one, at that. None of Satendar's family believes justice has been done for the loss they sustained in that single, brutal flash of bigotry at Lake Natoma. Young Shevchenko managed to dodge the hate crime conviction, but still took the heat for his older partner in crime, and was forced to "cool his heels" in prison. Vusik, ostensibly still in Russia on auto export business, remains a fugitive more than two years after donning his Christian armor to punish the queer infidel. His wife Tatyana admits that she talks with him by phone at least twice a week, but refuses to divulge his whereabouts. Apparently, the FBI does not consider him a big enough fish to fry, and Vusik still avoids arrest and extradition. His mother, Ludmila Vusik, speaking through a Russian translator, has identified one of the cruel ironies at the heart of this story. "I really love my son," she said. Then, speaking of Satendar's family as well as her own, she sobbed, "This tragedy touches upon both of us. We both lost our sons." The difference is, of course, that the Singhs will never see their sweet boy alive again.

Satendar, once called "Lucky," stumbled unknowingly into a fault line between great, opposing social forces in American life, and as they collided, they crushed him to dust. *Desis* and Russians alike, seeking opportunity for a better life, not only settled here from far away, but also brought with them their cultural treasures and their easily exploited vices. Shamelessly, home grown hate-inducing groups like the "Aryan Nation," "Defend the Family," and "Abiding Truth Ministries" were poised to take advantage of immigrant phobias and weaknesses as soon as these new pilgrims cleared customs. American history is replete with stories of ethnic and religious conflict involving immigrant communities—Irish Catholics versus Protestant nativists in Boston, Southeast Asians versus redneck whites on the Gulf Coast, Mexican illegals versus Minutemen throughout the Sunbelt, to name but a few. But there is an additional element to this particularly angular drama about natives and their uneasy immigrant neighbors. Like a hidden thread woven throughout the fabric of all these histories, no matter the demographic or the ethnicity, LGBTQ people like Satendar have always been the least told part of the story. But just like grains of grit in an oyster, queer folk are enduringly, irritatingly present throughout the entire saga of this nation of immigrants.

Satendar was not a two-dimensional, "issue" person. Instead, he was a man who loved other men, and he danced gingerly through the minefield of homophobia and heterosexism in his adopted country. His story, as well as that of his antagonists, is an object lesson on the ills of xenophobic hatred that are as American as the Fourth of July. It is also a reprimand to a society too apt to tolerate intolerance. Simply put, it is easier to hate than to do the hard work of reconciliation. Satendar was a Sikh, a *desi*, a Fijian, an immigrant who invested his life and death here, and he was a queer. None of these protected him when the Destroyer demanded that he dance with him on the *Burning-ground*. As a visitor to a *desi* blog site wrote some days after he died, "He doesn't look very lucky to me."

But who would say that belief in reincarnation by the Sikhs and their Hindu counterparts has not opened, or could never open, a door to a different resolution to a story so *Red, White, and Sad?* Huston Smith, the foremost interpreter of the world's great religions to the West, writes that for all the violent conflict between Hindus and Muslims in the Punjab, where the Sikh religion was born, no more conciliatory faith exists on the planet than the one Satendar inherited. From the beginning, though persecuted as unbelievers by both sides, Sikhs have obeyed a deep spiritual intuition that hopes even enemies may one day be reconciled in the bliss of theological compromise. Sikhs believe in the ultimacy of a supreme and formless God of love, who is beyond all human conception. Rejecting avatars, Sikh faith affirms that Allah, and the great Hindu trinity Brahma, Vishnu, and Shiva, are, in the great summation of all things, One.

For Sikhs, in the unity of God, Lord Shiva does not remain distinct from enlightened mortals. He is the one Hindu deity honored in their national anthem by name, *Deh Shiva bar mohe,* for all who do righteousness are Shiva, and Shiva is in them all. The Dancing Shiva, in this blaze of insight, is neither only the frenetic demon of the burning ground nor the enigmatic, arch-yogi of creation and evolution. He is Sri Nataraja, the Dance Master of the only dance there is: life through death, the reconciliation of all dualities, and an open future in the ceaseless whirling of time. Could this be why South Asians agree that Sikhs are such good dancers? Perhaps the Sikh gurus are right, and Satendar has danced his way into the heart of the cosmos. Though Sikhism has yet to repeal its negativity toward homosexuality, surely in such a generous theology there is room for a smiling, laughing man who yearned to dance with the men he loved.

When Satendar's mortal remains were shipped home to Fiji, the family observed the last rites of their faith. Called *Antam Sanskaar,* the Celebration of the Completion of Life, a Sikh funeral teaches the faithful not to lament the passing of an individual, but rather to focus on the opportunity of the soul to reunite with the Creator. At a chosen burning ground, the purifying flames wrapped Satendar's broken body in light and the heat of a new creation. After the cremation, his ashes would have been buried in the earth, or, even more probably, spread on the waves of his beloved South Pacific. Though we have no details of the service as it was performed in the summer of 2007, one traditional hymn, *Merging with the Divine Light* or *Jot Milee Sang Jot,* particularly recommends itself to those who knew him, and offers a fitting benediction to his life with hope for a better world for everyone. In part, the singers chant their tender good-bye:

Simar simar daataar manorath poor-i-aa.
> *Meditating, in contemplation of the great Giver, the heart's desires are fulfilled.*

Ichh punnee man aas ga-e visoor-i-aa.
> *The craving and hopes of the mind are realized, and sorrows are forgotten.*

Paa-i-aa naam nidhaan jis no bhaal-daa.
> *The treasure of the name is obtained after a long search.*

Jot milee sang jot reh-i-aa ghaal-daa.
> *My light merges with the Supreme light, and my labors are over.*

For Greater Understanding

Dancing With Shiva: Satendar Singh

BOOKS AND ARTICLES

Bouma, Gary D., et al. *Religious Diversity in Southeast Asia and the Pacific: National Case Studies.* New York: Springer Publishing Company, 2009.

Kompes, Gregory A. *50 Fabulous Gay-friendly Places to Live.* Pompton Plains, NJ: Career Press, 2005.

Mann, Gurider Singh. *Sikhism.* New York: Prentice Hall, 2004.

Sanchez, Casey. "The Latvian Connection: West Coast Anti-Gay Movement on the March." In *SPLC Intelligence Report 127,* Fall 2007. No pages. Online: http://www .splcenter.org/get-informed/intelligence-report/browse-all-issues/2007/fall/the -latvian-connection.

Shankar, Shalini. *Desi Land: Teen Culture, Class, and Success in Silicon Valley.* Durham, NC: Duke University Press, 2008.

ORGANIZATIONS AND WEBSITES

Box Turtle Bulletin, http://www.boxturtlebulletin.com/category/activists-anti-gay/watch men-on-the-walls.

OutSacramento.com, http://www.outsacramento.com.

Unfinished Lives Project, http://unfinishedlivesblog.com.

Allen R. Schindler Jr.
Petty Officer Third Class, United States Navy
December 13, 1969—October 28, 1992

CHICAGO HEIGHTS, ILLINOIS, AND SASEBO,
NAGASAKI PREFECTURE, JAPAN

11

Hell to Pay on the Belleau Wood

Allen R. Schindler Jr.

"There's nothing to do in Sasebo unless you are a homo killer."

—Shipmate's offhand comment
on the murder of Allen Schindler

RADIOMAN ALLEN R. SCHINDLER Jr. was murdered in cold blood 9,500 miles from home in a Japanese public toilet because he was gay. He was 22. Schindler had come out as a gay man to his superiors aboard the USS Belleau Wood, and his captain had straightaway commenced the administrative process to discharge him from the Navy. In a phone call to his mother barely twenty-four hours before the murder, he told her to expect him home by Christmas. Instead, she was to have his body home for burial in time for Thanksgiving, battered beyond recognition after one of the most savage personal attacks recorded in naval history.

Petty Officer Schindler died at the hands of two shipmates, both Airman Apprentices and both 20 years of age. Terry M. Helvey took the rap for murdering Schindler with uncommonly brutal zest, and is serving a life sentence in Disciplinary Barracks at Fort Leavenworth, Kansas. By statute, Helvey is granted a clemency hearing every year. Charles A. Vins, who turned state's evidence on Helvey, received a real sweetheart of a deal from the Navy in return. He served a total of only seventy-eight days in the brig for the murder. At last report, Vins lives quietly as a free man in Lyons, Illinois within thirty miles of Allen Schindler's mother, Dorothy Hajdys. He is still permitted to wear his medals and military ribbons if he likes.

In contrast to its core values of "Honor, Courage, and Commitment," the United States Navy created one of the most notorious military scandals during the Clinton presidential era, mismanaging the Schindler story with a combination of arrogant, institutional heterosexism, bureaucratic bungling, and crass strategies—all intended to deceive a working class mother, the press, and the American public. With poignant irony, Allen Schindler's remains were escorted home for burial with full military honors—dress blues, flag-draped casket, and official condolences—all perfunctorily arranged for a "homosexual pervert" the Navy scorned to wear the uniform in the first place. According to his mother, no one informed her who had killed her son until the officer in charge of the burial detail let slip that the suspects in custody from the Belleau Wood. All the Navy had told her was that her boy had been killed in a Sasebo park near the naval base. She recognized the name of Allen's ship immediately, and murmured in stunned disbelief, "*United States Sailors* killed my son?" "Yes, ma'am. They were shipmates of his."

Only a journalist from the independent military newspaper, *Pacific Stars and Stripes*, let Dorothy know definitively that Allen openly identified himself as gay, and that her son's murder was almost certainly a gay bashing. Reporter Rick Rogers revealed to her that Allen had met with his superiors, confessed to them that he was a gay man, and started discharge proceedings so he could leave the ship he loathed and a crew he feared. Rogers said that three gay entertainers who had known and befriended Allen in Sasebo wrote *Pacific Stars and Stripes* to alert the world that their friend was murdered because of rampant homophobia in the Navy. The gay dancers, one of whom would later become like a son to Dorothy, wrote, "Why should the death of an admitted homosexual be swept under the carpet by the U.S. Navy? Why does the U.S. military get away with this discrimination? This letter is being written in hopes that Al did not die in vain."

Allen's murder became the eye of a typhoon of controversy surrounding gays in the military. He and his killers became the main fetishistic characters in what might have been a classic *kabuki* drama, entangling presidential candidate Bill Clinton, the military high command, the U.S. Senate, and thousands of gay and lesbian patriots serving in silence in the U.S. military throughout the world. Schindler, Helvey, and Vins had all enlisted in the Navy to escape the hardships of rotten childhoods and broken homes, to find adventure, and to get their G.I. benefits in a desperate gambit for a better life on the other side of the service. No amount of rice powder makeup and face paint could differentiate victim from killer successfully. Schindler had grown up, maligned by a harsh stepfather, in hardscrabble Chicago Heights, Illinois. Dorothy's second husband, who managed a Burger King restaurant, lavished money and attention on his own son while ignoring 12-year-old Allen. Schindler's killers, Helvey and Vins grew up similarly in blue-collar Michigan towns. Vins grew up in Sturgis, a southern Michigan town where the biggest event all year was the celebration of a dam opening in 1911. He left his hometown as soon as he could to enlist in the Navy. Helvey, from Eloise, Michigan, probably had the hardest childhood of the three. In a bizarre attempt to save water, his stepfather punished Terry and his brother Wade if they used the toilet at home. If they used the one at school instead, he raged at the boys, there wouldn't be such a high water bill to pay. One day bursting at the seams, the boys crapped in a roll of linoleum in their sister's closet, unable to hold it any longer. When their stepfather found it, he forced Terry and Wade to eat their excrement with a fork while he watched them.

The trio's dreams for the future were even similar. Helvey wanted to parlay his height and athletic prowess into a basketball scholarship that never materialized. Vins longed to be an elite Navy SEAL, even undergoing an operation to improve his poor eyesight so the SEALS would accept him, but he never made the grade. Schindler, a mediocre student at best, worked at a pet store and wanted to become a veterinarian some day, caring for the snakes and lizards he adored. Like Seymour Krelborn in *Little Shop of Horrors*, all three longed to escape the clutches of skid row, and the Navy was their ticket up and out.

While military life gave these young men much needed structure and discipline, it also immersed them in a warrior cult of homo-hatred starting in boot camp and permeating the service from bottom to top. "Faggots," "pussies," and "nancy-boys" were the foils for everything wrong with raw recruits. Washouts and failures were despised as "queers," and drill sergeants, from day one, hammered anybody they considered substandard with homophobic epithets. A sailor in Sasebo, interviewed in February 1993 for a British newspaper, *The Independent*, said that impressionable 18-year-old recruits in the Navy are conditioned to despise gays. "When I went to boot camp," the anonymous sailor said, "the officer stood up on the first day and asked, 'Is anyone here a faggot?

Because I would rather kill a faggot than work with one.'" As Nathaniel Franks shows in his definitive 2009 history of the gay ban in the military, *Unfriendly Fire*, the criminalization of homosexual behavior in the armed services since 1950 has created an insular, paranoid culture, a "closed society" exempt from civilian law and mores. Gays and lesbians, who enlisted to serve their country, were not simply deemed "unfit for military service," but considered a "homosexual menace." During the final days of the Carter presidency in 1981, the Deputy Secretary of Defense succeeded in promulgating a service-wide policy on homosexual exclusion, declaring without any substantiating evidence that:

> Homosexuality is incompatible with military service . . . The presence of such members adversely affects the ability of the armed forces to maintain discipline, good order and morale; to foster mutual trust and confidence among servicemembers; to ensure the integrity of the system of rank and command; to facilitate assignment and worldwide deployment of servicemembers who frequently must live and work under close conditions affording minimal privacy; to recruit and retain members of the armed forces; to maintain the public acceptability of military service; and to prevent breaches of security [by the threat of blackmail] (Franks 2009, 10).

The Navy in particular allowed the fear of gay service to override any objections of conscience, rationality, or good sense. Franks quotes Rear Admiral John Hutson as saying in 2008:

> "We were all a bunch of white guys who were born in the 1940s. And the decisions [about how to deal with gay service in the Navy's JAG office] were based on nothing. It wasn't empirical, it wasn't studied, it was completely visceral, intuitive. It was all ridiculous, it was by the seat of our pants . . . The leadership of the military was essentially telling the young people that we really don't trust you to deal with this, we think you're all pretty bigoted, and you're not very open minded and we're going to end up with blood in the streets and the units are all going to fall apart" (Franks 2009, 122).

Rear Admiral Hutson said the idea of gays sent down through the ranks "to boots on the ground was a very, very negative message." Based on what Hutson told him, and his own careful research into the matter, Franks surmised that the Navy brass "did not tell people under their command that they were capable, mature, and well-disciplined; instead, *they welcomed their homophobia and used it as an excuse for inaction"* [emphasis mine] (Franks 2009, 122-123).

The Navy Allen Schindler joined out of high school in 1988, soon to be followed by Terry Helvey and Charles Vins, taught bigots to despise gays and lesbians, and frightened gays and lesbians into closets aboard their submarines and surface ships. Three Midwestern kids surrendered their futures to a military organization that on one hand cultivated fear and loathing of gays and lesbians, and on the other allowed the homophobia of the troops to lead the Navy into tacit approval of violence against them. One wound up battered beyond recognition on the floor of a granite-steel-and-glass park toilet, and the other two unquestionably did the horrible deed, but it was the U.S. Navy that victimized all three of them that October night in 1992.

A SHIP, A SHARK, AND A TIGER

Allen Schindler kept a diary. It was a cheap little volume, faded green, filled with scribbles, drawings of snakes and lizards, and the musings of a C-average student who dreamed he could enroll in veterinary school one day. On page one he exulted, "I am finally going to a special place, the mighty, mighty Midway!" Allen's family was "true blue Navy." He had never known his grandfather, a World War II sailor whose uniformed photo was on display in Allen's childhood home. His stepfather, Frank Hajdys, had escaped fiery death and drowning on the Battleship Arizona, sunk by the Japanese at Pearl Harbor. Allen enlisted when he turned eighteen, and in November 1988 he graduated from boot camp. The day he shipped out for his first assignment in San Diego, his mom believed she was the proudest mother in America. He looked so handsome in his uniform, blond-headed and blue-eyed, 6'1" tall, well muscled and approaching 180 lbs. Since he stood a head taller than she, Dorothy had to reach up on her tiptoes to hug him and peck him on the cheek. Chip Brown tells in "The Accidental Martyr," an article written on Schindler's murder for *Esquire* in 1993, that Allen left his mother with a veritable menagerie to care for: a dog, a rabbit, a duck, four turtles, parrots, a big fish tank, and a couple of hundred garter snakes. Allen was crazy about animals, especially reptiles, and everybody knew it. The best job he ever held was at a local pet shop, while he attended Bloom High School. Dorothy said he wanted to work at Sea World or in a zoo after his discharge from the Navy. Just before Mother's Day, the year after

Allen sailed away, she signed the delivery slip for the scaliest gift she ever received—a rare, little Chinese crocodile lizard.

During his year and two months stationed in San Diego, Allen carefully opened himself to the possibility that he might be gay. The late 1980s were difficult times to identify as a gay sailor, even in relatively liberal San Diego with its large gay and lesbian population. The U.S. Naval Base in San Diego was huge—921 acres, offering barracks accommodations for 380 officers and 18,000 enlisted men. Given the usually accepted percentages of gays in the general population, there were easily over a thousand gay sailors on base at any time. In the then-recent past, naval command had eased its attitude toward homoerotic expression on base. In an uncharacteristic expression of "campiness," the Navy conceived a recruiting campaign in 1979 based on the hit, "In the Navy," by the popular disco group, The Village People. The hyper-masculine fantasy group was flown to the San Diego Naval Base to film the music video, and was provided a warship, the USS Reasoner (FF-1063), several warplanes as scenery props, and the ship's entire crew. A precondition said that the crew would not be allowed to dance in the video. After a storm of criticism from conservative politicians upset about the use of taxpayer money to film a controversial ad campaign aboard a missile frigate, the Navy scrubbed the Village People idea. By the early 1980s, the Navy's official policy on the gay ban took effect, and attitudes toward gays returned to a grim version of naval homophobia—described by some as the American variation on "rum, sodomy, and the lash." Radioman Schindler learned quickly how gays in the military found ways to discover each other, even in a climate of repression. In his diary, he hinted about his affairs with the type of men he was most drawn to—gay men, like himself—on base and off. He called them his "blond things." According to Chip Brown, Allen started smoking clove cigarettes and wearing an earring in his right earlobe that resembled a salamander. He reveled in concealing his pet three-foot monitor lizard, "Junior," under his clothes, and then exposing it to his "blond things" on gay barhopping sprees.

Some guys considered him attractive and nice to be with. They liked his wide-eyed, Midwestern sexual innocence and his insatiable curiosity. Others found him goofy and insufferable. Allen not only obsessed over his reptiles, but he also became a *Star Trek* fanatic of the first rank. A little Klingon-ese here and there might have been alright, but Allen, who had memorized the whole Klingon lexicon, habitually took it to the guttural extreme. One gay sailor, James "Jim" Jennings, however, never minded Allen's odd sense of humor and Trekkie-madness. The two sailors met in San Diego's gay clubs and became lovers in 1990. All through the years, Jim has treasured Allen's memory. Honorably discharged from the Navy, Jim now works as a nurse in San Diego. "Al was sweet," he says, storing a whole trove of memories behind his words. Sailors are far more mobile than soldiers, a fact that is both blessing and curse. Relationships are rarely long-term. The sailor's life could be described as one long good-bye. He is always leaving some girl or boy in port for another deployment.

When Allen went home to Chicago Heights on leave in June 1990, he took the plunge and came out of the closet to his mother, his sister Kathy, and the rest of the family. At first, Dorothy wasn't having any of it. Allen had been raised in the church, and he should know better. She had seen to his religious upbringing in between the two full-time jobs she held down just to keep food on the table and clothes on the backs of her children. She was sure Allen had a screw loose somewhere—that this "gay thing" was some sort of phase he would just have to get over. Dorothy had no frame of reference for understanding what being a gay man meant. Until her son's death, she had never met a gay person face-to-face that she knew of. She believed the gays in San Diego must have brainwashed her boy. Dorothy was a fundamentalist Christian. Religious intolerance of homosexuality came as a standard feature of the faith communities she relied on to make it through her awful marriages and hard knock life. When Allen came out to her, Dorothy was working as a bookkeeper for the Salvation Army. She refused to hear Allen, and just denied the whole thing. Meanwhile, big sister Kathy worried about AIDS. Allen did his best to reassure her that he was careful sexually, and that gay men were not what she feared they were. When he looked into their faces for reassurance, Allen did not see rejection. All he discerned there instead was confusion. His coming out mission had been a snafu. Mom was in denial, and sister Kathy fretted about his health. Allen left home for San Diego to return to Jim, brooding over how much disappointment and damage he had caused the family.

In January 1991, Allen left Jim to join the crew of the USS Midway (CV-41), commencing what Jim described as "the happiest time Allen ever had in the Navy." The eleven months he spent aboard the aircraft carrier Midway fulfilled his wishes about what the Navy should be. "Some dreams do come true," he wrote in his diary. "The Mighty, Mighty Midway" was a floating city, nearly a fifth of a mile long from bow to stern. At full complement, 4,104 officers and men lived and worked in one of the most formidable warships of the Vietnam and First Gulf War eras. Until August 1991, she was the forward-deployed carrier at Yokosuka Naval Base in Japan. Her last voyage was from Yokosuka to Pearl Harbor; to then Bremerton, Washington; and then finally to San Diego to be decommissioned. Allen re-enlisted so he would be aboard for Midway's final cruise, and under a special Navy program, he arranged for his 16-year-old half brother Billy to join him from Washington State to San Diego. His diary was not the only evidence of how fulfilled he was on the Midway. In addition to the shark and tiger tattoos he had gotten on his left forearm, Allen went under the needle for the insignia of the Mighty Midway, a mark he carried on his right forearm to his grave.

The atmosphere for gay sailors on the Midway was best described as "tolerant." The old salts used to say, "It ain't queer till you're tied to the pier." Straights and gays mingled with little evidence of discomfort or friction. It was a "happy ship," in the proud parlance of the enlisted men. Seaman Stuart Kalbrofsky, a sailor from the USS Germantown, said Allen described the Midway in even more glowing terms, as a "people's ship." As long as he was not too indiscreet, then, Allen felt he could live out his sea duty in relative security as a gay man. All that changed the day he got his orders to join the Belleau Wood.

THE HOUNDS OF HELL

In December 1991, Seaman Schindler transferred from the USS Midway (which was being mothballed for eventual mooring in San Diego as a museum ship), to the USS Belleau Wood (LHA-3), an amphibious assault ship in the Tarawa class. The two ships were as different as night and day, physically and psychically. The "Wood," as she was called, was named in honor of the U.S. Marines' decisive victory during the Battle of Belleau Wood in 1918. She was considerably smaller than an aircraft carrier. Although usually crewed by 930 women and men, when a Marine battalion was billeted aboard, the ship's complement could top 3,000. The Wood was designed to carry assault helicopters, jump jets, and landing craft. There was nothing elegant about her lines. Neither was there anything flattering about her reputation at sea or in port. If nomenclature indicates character, then nicknamers nailed the Wood right between the eyes. Taking a cue from Kaiser Wilhelm's troops, who called the ferocious marines they fought in the Bois de Belleau *"Teufelshunden,"* or "dogs from Hell," the warriors on the Wood were dubbed "Devil Dogs."

The hellhounds picked up Allen's scent soon after the Wood steamed out of San Diego for her forward deployment at Sasebo Naval Base in Japan. Swiftly, Allen's happiness with life in the Navy turned to bitter disappointment, all because of anti-gay harassment on the Belleau Wood. Ricky Gonzales, a gay former Navy officer who liked and befriended Allen, attributed part of the problem to Allen's strange sense of humor and wonky obsessions. Gonzales told the *Chicago Sun-Times* in February 1993, "He wouldn't talk about the usual things. I think that's why he didn't get along with anyone on his new ship." On a more broad-minded ship, idiosyncrasies like Allen's were given a pass. But the Wood's homo-averse culture was decidedly less humane than the Midway's had been. If a sailor didn't blend in, then he would be ostracized.

Dorothy knew that Allen was unhappy on the Belleau Wood. She said he called the ship the "Helleau Wood," and had altered the stitching on his embroidered cap to reflect his feelings, transforming the "B" to an "H." He kept a lot of his troubles to himself when he communicated with Gonzales and his mother. Though they both knew how he felt about his new ship, they said Allen never talked to them about harassment by the crew. Confiding in Jim Jennings, his former lover, however, Allen was far more candid about his experiences of anti-gay discrimination. "He didn't like the people on that ship," Jim said. "Right off the bat the harassment started." Allen told Jim that he had been called "faggot" and "queer" to his face, on numerous occasions, and someone had glued the door of his sea locker shut. There had been times when he was walking down the corridor and somebody would yell out, "Do you know there are faggots on this ship?" or "We gotta do something about these faggots on the ship!" as he passed by. After docking at Sasebo, Allen confided in gay friends that he felt lucky to be unharmed on the ship. Others had not been so lucky. He told Valan Cain, a Southern California gay singer and dancer, about the story of a young gay sailor who had been soaked in lighter fluid and set on fire because of his sexual orientation. He had survived, badly burned. The sailor refused to report the attack, however, because he didn't want to reveal he was gay, Allen told Cain. As Cain said to the *Los Angeles Times* in early 1993, "He hated the ship . . . He called it a floating prison."

Allen told his friends that he had repeatedly complained to his superiors between March and April of 1992 about anti-gay harassment, but to no avail. The Navy has never acknowledged any such of Schindler's reports. But his surviving gay friends from the ship know he was telling the truth. Richard Eastman, Allen's shipmate and a fellow member of a guarded group of gay sailors, calling themselves "The Fabulous Five," told *Esquire* in 1993, "I saw the harassment personally. People bumped into him and shoved him out of the way. They made comments," Eastman said, like "'Queers coming down the passageway!'" According to another member of the Fabulous Five, Gunner's Mate Keith Sims, sailors carrying hot soup pretended more than once to stumble so they could dump it on Allen.

During the summer of 1992, Allen was a regular in the Navy Alcohol Rehabilitation Center, San Diego. Whether Schindler actually had an alcohol problem is in dispute. Many sailors drank too much, and it would have been unremarkable had he been an alcoholic. He continued to go to Alcoholics Anonymous meetings in Sasebo, however, and even attended one on the day of his murder, according to friends in Sailor Town. But an anonymous active-duty sailor who claimed to know him well from the San Diego rehab center said Allen flatly denied being an alcoholic. He told the sailor that his superiors aboard the Belleau Wood had ordered him to go to the center in order to "cool" him off, after his repeated complaints about harassment by the crew.

As the Belleau Wood steamed from Hawaii to Japan, on the last leg of her forward deployment, the harassment finally got intolerable for Allen. While on radio duty one September night, in what he described in his diary as an attempt to let his "true colors" out, Allen transmitted the prank message, "2-Q-T-2-B-S-T-R-8" ("[I'm] too cute to be straight"). The entire Pacific Fleet heard Allen's defiant admission, if they were listening. Retribution was swift. He was charged with broadcasting an "unauthorized statement" while on duty.

Allen requested an audience with his Commanding Officer, Captain Douglas J. Bradt, and the ship's Legal Officer, Captain Bernard Meyer. According to Navy records, Allen got his requested audience on September 24. At that meeting, he formally came out as a gay man, effectively ending his four-year career as a sailor. Writing about his admission in his diary, Allen vented, "If you can't be yourself, then who are you?" Bradt and Meyer informed him the administrative discharge proceeding would take a couple of weeks, and during that time he was to report any harassing behavior against him. Allen told Fabulous Five member Rich Eastman about reporting the many incidents of anti-gay harassment against him to the two officers, though nothing in the ship's records acknowledges Schindler ever reported a thing.

On September 25, Allen was called before the captain's mast, a non-judicial proceeding, to deal with his unauthorized radio message. Since Captain Bradt had the discretion to hold a closed or open proceeding, Allen requested that the mast be closed to the crew. Bradt denied his request, and over two hundred sailors crowded into the area to gawk and snicker at the subject of all those queer rumors on the Wood. In a jaunty act of non-verbal defiance, Allen wore one of his favorite earrings. Still, it is hard to imagine that the pressure of public exposure would not have hurt him deeply. He made no open admission of his homosexuality at the hearing. Yet *Esquire's* Chip Brown discovered that something in the proceedings prompted Allen to cover the microphone in front of him with his hand, and say to the captain in a hushed voice, "You know what I am." Taken in the context of his admission of homosexuality to Captain Bradt only the day before, this was not simply an offhanded or self-mocking little comment. Bradt *did* know "what" his radioman was, definitively, and still exposed him to public humiliation before the mast without due consideration for his sailor's welfare. For his peccadillo, Allen was punished by a reduction in rank from RM1 to RM3, and sentenced to a thirty-day restriction aboard ship.

Why would officers in the U.S. Navy drop a shroud of silence around Allen Schindler's complaints that he was mercilessly harassed on numerous occasions for being a homosexual? Why would the Navy feign ignorance or inaction when they reasonably knew violent acts of retribution against him were likely to come from members of their own crew, or why would they claim inability to prevent some homophobic atrocity from happening to him after the fact? What were they protecting? Steven Zeeland's 1995 study of how sailors and marines experience sex with each other, *Sailors and Sexual Identity: Crossing the Line Between "Straight" and "Gay" in the U.S. Navy,* gives us at least a partial answer. There are things the military does not want the civilian world calling "homosexual." Zeeland writes:

Boundaries between what is homo- and heterosexual, and what is sexual and nonsexual are subject to disagreement. It is convenient to define a homosexual as the U.S. Navy does, as "a person, regardless of sex, who engages in, desires to engage in, or intends to engage in homosexual acts. These are defined as "bodily contact, actively undertaken or passively permitted, between members of the same sex for the purpose of satisfying sexual desires." ... But homosexuality comes in many flavors, some known to the Joint Chiefs of Staff to be a natural part of military life.

A desire to be in close quarters with other military men in a tightly knit brotherhood might be homosexual. Navy initiation rituals involving cross-dressing, spanking, simulated oral and anal sex, simulated ejaculation, nipple piercing, and anal penetration with objects or fingers might be homosexual. An officer's love for his men might be homosexual. The intimate buddy relationships men form in barracks, aboard ship, and most especially in combat—often described as being a love greater than between man and woman—might be homosexual—whether or not penetration or ejaculation ever occur.

The U.S. military does not want these things called homosexual. To maintain the illusion that these aspects of military life are heterosexually pure it is necessary to maintain the illusion that there is no homosexuality in the military. This is the function of "Don't Ask, Don't Tell": for boys to play with boys—and not get called queers and not get called girls (Zeeland 1995, 6-7).

From the day Allen Schindler came out to his superior officers on September 24, he was no longer "theoretically" gay to anyone privy to that information. His murder was no mere happenstance. The presence of an actual, self-avowing, practicing gay man on a ship at sea uncomfortably called into question many other "straight" sailors and marines who behaved in gay and bisexual ways. According to Zeeland, this eventuality was too terrible for senior officers to contemplate. The open, public presence of a person such as Schindler threatened to dispel the illusion of heterosexual purity so dear to the Navy. Reactions to his self-revelation exposed the lengths to which the military was willing to use passive and active institutional violence against gay and lesbian servicemembers. Opening the captain's mast to the crew intensified Allen's vulnerability to an already hostile segment of the ship's company. If Captain Bradt in fact turned a deaf ear to Allen's complaints of maltreatment, he passively condoned the cruelty to which his sailors were subjecting his radioman. Once public discharge proceedings had begun for Schindler, Captain

Bradt's duty of rank was to protect a vulnerable member of his crew for (perhaps lethal) violence and harm. Instead, the evidence suggests Bradt may have dishonorably abdicated his duty. With tacit Pentagon approval, Captain Bradt may have written Schindler off as a threat to the sexual equilibrium of his ship, and then feigned impotence to do anything about the "consequences" of Schindler's candor.

Confidentiality broke down. Word spread quickly aboard the "Helleau Wood" that Allen had come out, dispelling any further conjecture about Schindler's orientation. The "queer" was jumping ship. To the cruel, he was now fair game. When the Wood docked at Sasebo Naval Base on September 30, Allen still had three weeks of confinement to the ship. The mood aboard ship turned darkly sullen. Even friends avoided him. Jim, his ex-lover, heard how increasingly difficult it was becoming for Allen to avoid confrontation. On October 2, Allen wrote in his diary, "More people are finding out about me. It scares me a little. You never know who will want to harm me or cease my existence."

DYING CHERRY BLOSSOM

Sasebo was a small seaside city by Japanese standards in 1992. Two hundred and fifty thousand people nestled among the hills on the island of Kyushu, a thirty-mile train ride from Nagasaki. When the three thousand sailors and marines from the Belleau Wood came ashore on September 30, both the base and the city felt the strain. The Wood had a rough, brawling reputation both in the fleet, and among the locals. Entries in Allen's diary, confirmed by interviews with local residents, said that Japanese fishermen in small boats sailed out to the Belleau Wood and formed a cordon to discourage her from docking.

Most sailors thought Sasebo was a decent port, though it tended to be expensive. The native Japanese were not particularly friendly to servicemembers, and were rather perfunctory about doing business with them. Average Japanese citizens spoke no English. Long gone were the heydays of American naval presence during the Cold War, when drinks and women were cheap, and the United States was admired for holding the Soviet Union at bay. Now the role of the Wood and her sister ships was "maintaining stability in Asia," which meant defending sea lanes, watching the Red Chinese, and reassuring the rest of Asia that Japan was not becoming militarily expansionist again—a mission no one thought glamorous in the wake of Vietnam.

There wasn't very much to see or do in town. Sailors could go to "the mile long mall," properly called the *Ginza*. For after dark activities, there were two parts of town a new sailor needed to know about: "Saki Town" (ruefully called, "Sucky Town"), which was decidedly sailor-unfriendly, and Japanese-only unless you had a Japanese escort; and "Sailor Town," a maze of narrow streets and alleys dotted with Karaoke bars selling beers at $5 a pop—cash only. Filipinas almost exclusively owned these bars, and they catered to the military trade. Any new face in Sailor Town was identified right away and given the standard interrogation: "How long you here for? Are you single? What ship you on? You an officer?" Old squids said that the vast majority of the bargirls were from the Philippines and stayed in Sasebo on temporary work permits. Many were divorced from Japanese men, looking for an American military man to hook up with and raise their standard of living. Most nights the bars of Sailor Town were crowded, and the bargirls were pushing a legendary local drink called "Habu Sake"—rice wine spiked with a snake carcass. The snake venom reputedly kicked up the potency of the alcohol.

Lovers of culture had little to admire in Sasebo, except perhaps in springtime when the cherry trees bloomed in Nimitz Park. The Cherry Blossom Festival, with its happy celebrations, contrasted with the poetic melancholy attached to the fleeting beauty and short lives of the tiny flowers. Buddhist and Shinto teaching says the vigor of life is ephemeral, and often involves suffering. An anonymous Japanese poet of long ago wrote:

> Let us ride, our horses abreast,
> To the old home whither we go,
> To contemplate the cherry blossoms,
> Falling perchance like the flakes of snow.

Vital, lovely, and cut short—this was the way of the *Samurai*, who lived for today, taking no thought of tomorrow. It was a blessing not to know one's end, but to be ready to face it with courage when it came.

On Friday evening, October 23, Schindler got off restriction. The only times he had been permitted to leave the "Helleau Wood" were with an escort to AA meetings on base. He couldn't wait to get ashore under his own steam. The ship was scheduled to weigh anchor for the Philippines in only five days. He felt he had a lot to do in order to get home for the holidays. He was a dying cherry blossom, unaware how short a time he had left.

Allen felt compelled to address two existential matters during the last days of his life. First, Allen desired to leave the ship he loathed in better shape for gays than when he found it; and second, Allen needed to connect with others who could understand him. On October 20 he wrote in his diary, "It would be a great idea for people of our type to stay together, especially when times are rough. I don't want anybody else to go through the torture I did." He wrote that he had taken a leadership role in organizing a gay support group aboard the Wood. Naturally, the Fabulous Five was its core. Allen offered to draft rudimentary procedures for organization and membership. Twenty-five members of the crew came to the first secret meeting, and what they established together was a combination of self-defense association and political action group. Allen had researched support groups on the mainland, both for himself and his gay shipmates. He had written down the name and telephone number of James Woodward. Woodward was a long-time activist who provided military counseling for the "Lesbian & Gay Men's Community Center" of San Diego which had challenged the Navy's anti-gay policies in the 1970s and 1980s. Perhaps Allen and his friends were considering mounting a challenge of their own. Woodward wrote in 2003 to his LGBTQ alumni newsletter at Williams College, the *BiGLATA News*, "Allen Schindler had my phone number among his effects when he died. Unfortunately, he waited too long to call."

Straight sailors who had befriended Allen knew he needed a connection with other gay men. There were no gay bars in Sailor Town, or anywhere else in Sasebo. But the entertainment industry brought lesbians and gays to the area from Europe and America. A Dutch theme park, *Huis ten Bosch*, had opened earlier that year on Omura Bay, just a thirty-minute ride from downtown. Gay singers and dancers employed at the park would travel to Sailor Town for their nights out. Allen's straight friends knew one of them, Valan Cain, a dancer from Irvine, California, and they offered to introduce him to Allen. On Saturday night, Cain and Allen met at Captain's Bar. Through Cain, Allen also met two other gay entertainers from Southern California, Eric Underwood and Rod Burton. Cain told the *Los Angeles Times* in February 1993 that Allen latched onto the three of them for dear life. "We talked three or four hours a night," Cain said. "He was so hungry to be around people who would understand him." Allen especially liked Eric. He was a blond haired model, actor, singer and dancer. "He was just enamored of Eric,"

Cain told the *Times*. Underwood was up-front about a monogamous relationship he was already in, but generously gave his time to the lonely all-American sailor with the "beautiful blue eyes."

Allen poured out his heart to his three new friends, talking about his interests, coming out to his mother, and the difficulties he had aboard the Belleau Wood. Underwood found Allen to be genuine, sweet, and inquisitive. Allen was fascinated with the life of an openly gay entertainer so unlike anything he had ever known. Like a kid with a crush, Allen showed Underwood his sketches of reptiles, photos of a Long Beach Pride Parade he attended, his mom's picture, and before-and-after snapshots of himself showing how he had lost twenty-five pounds. "Allen was an easy going, gentle good guy," Eric told the *Times*. "He was not ashamed of who he was." The stories Allen told his three new friends about life aboard the Belleau Wood concerned them a great deal. "Valan and I asked him about what had happened on the ship," Underwood told Chip Brown for his *Esquire* article, "and he said as far as harassment goes, he felt lucky not to have seen more."

Allen also reached out to Seaman Stuart Joseph Kalbrofsky, a 29-year-old sailor serving on the USS Germantown. The two sailors met on Sunday afternoon in a toy store in the Ginza, looking at the same Godzilla dolls. In a statement to the Naval Investigative Service (NIS), Kalbrofsky said that he and Allen spent the afternoon walking and talking. Though he stopped short of revealing he was gay, Allen shared that he had been put on restriction and demoted for "some sort of message on the radio." Kalbrofsky said that he claimed to hate the Belleau Wood, and when Kalbrofsky suggested the ship couldn't be as bad as that, Allen said, "Well, people have threatened me, but I'll be going home soon." He told Kalbrofsky about his administrative discharge, and when asked directly if he were gay, Allen said, "Well, maybe." "I subsequently told him that if he was gay, I didn't care," Kalbrofsky said, adding that he had friends and a brother who were gay. "He told me that I was one of the few people who would talk to him and then claimed no one would talk to him 'because of all the things that happened.'" Ominously, Allen told his new friend he did not want to deploy to the Philippines with the Belleau Wood because there were "gangs" on the ship.

On Monday October 26, Allen came to see Kalbrofsky again. This time he was much more forthcoming about his orientation, stopping just short of divulging he was gay. He showed Kalbrofsky snapshots of his lizards, his gay pride parade pictures, and a photo card of a male model (Eric Underwood), "a white male wearing bikini-style swimwear and had his physical measurements on the back." The model had autographed the picture for Allen, who bragged that the guy was "all over him." Allen said that he had gone to gay bars in San Diego before. Then Allen said he would be leaving with the Belleau Wood on Wednesday. Kalbrofsky genuinely liked Allen, and regretted having to work late on Tuesday night and miss Allen before he shipped out. "We ended up exchanging addresses, said our good byes and RSMN Schindler left my BEQ (Bachelor Enlisted Quarters) room at 22:30, 26 October 1992," Kalbrofsky concluded for the NIS. "This was the last time I saw him."

NAVY DAY

Dorothy expected Allen's phone call. He called her every week when his ship was in port. The call on Tuesday, October 27 was a good one, she recalled, lasting about eight or nine minutes. He was chatty. They talked about his upcoming discharge, and how much he looked forward to being home and off that ship. Everything seemed routine to her. Within twenty-four hours, two Navy officers in dress blues, one of them a chaplain, knocked at her door. When she saw them, the blood cascaded to her feet. Navy mothers know what it means when officers in dress blues pay a visit. Stunned, she listened as they informed her that her son had been attacked and killed in a Sasebo park.

After putting in his call to his mother, Allen saw Valan Cain on his way to an AA meeting. He told Cain that he would come by later to say his farewells to Cain, Eric, and Rod. The Belleau Wood was set to leave Sasebo on Wednesday morning. The two friends parted, and Allen walked alone into the autumn night.

Terry Helvey and Charles Vins were buddies. The two Airman Apprentices had been assigned to the Belleau Wood earlier in the year, and lifted weights together in the ship's gym. Since the Wood was departing for the Philippines in the morning, Helvey and Vins had some serious unwinding to do ashore. To start the evening, they and two other buddies went to the base theater to see *Single White Female*, a thriller starring Bridget Fonda and Jennifer Jason Leigh. Then, like most sailors with limited funds, the quartet tanked up on beer on base, since drinks were too expensive in Sailor Town. Preparing for a long night, they bought extra beer, as well as whiskey, vodka, orange juice, and peppermint schnapps, and headed for the bleachers in Nimitz Park to continue drinking. At 11 p.m., shore patrol officers rousted the four tipplers because the park was closing for the night. Crossing over the Sasebo River, the four buddies split up in Sailor Town. Helvey and Vins were headed for a bar, but caught sight of a sailor they knew from the Wood—the one everybody said was a queer. It was Allen Schindler, strolling along the street. Helvey, who had often avowed his utter disgust for gays to his shipmates, forgot all about going to another bar. Instead, he turned to Vins and said, "Let's go fuck with him."

Sailor Town with its warren of narrow lanes and alleys stretches along the east bank of the Sasebo River. Allen took a meandering route past the brightly lit bars and fast food shops, almost as if he were taking one last look at the sights before shipping out in the morning. Helvey and Vins kept him in sight, hanging back just out of his range of vision. About 11:30 p.m., Allen took Albuquerque Bridge (a footbridge dedicated to the "eternal friendship" between sister cities Sasebo and Albuquerque, New Mexico) across the river, and headed back to base. Unaware he was being stalked, Allen entered Sasebo Park. Rather than make for the back entrance to Nimitz Park, he turned left to take the shortcut to the main gate to the base. He ambled past a series of playgrounds and benches, through some bushes and camphor trees where the stalkers lost him momentarily. But Helvey glimpsed Allen entering a doorless public toilet situated beside an indoor swimming pool, and he broke into a trot. Covering the distance quickly, Helvey disappeared into the toilet. Entering the urinal area a moment later, Vins saw Allen facing one of the porcelain and steel urinals, with Helvey beside him at the next one pretending to take a piss. Helvey had his right arm cocked over his head with his hand bunched into a fist. No words were exchanged, no sound except the buzz of the fluorescent lights. Allen glanced to his side ever so slightly, just to register that someone was standing beside him—and, like a thunderbolt, Helvey's blow fell.

The next lethal minutes robbed Allen Schindler of everything. Helvey's fist caught Allen on the bridge of his nose, smashed the bone, and snapped cartilage. Allen crashed to the tile floor as if he had been pole-axed. At least two more of Helvey's blows hammered Allen, sending a fine mist of blood and saliva spraying into the air. Helvey sprang behind the gay sailor, deftly clamping him in a headlock. Fighting for his life, Allen reached up to grab his assailant, and bit down on Helvey's arm.

"Chuck!" Helvey screamed in pain and rage, "son of a bitch bit me!" Helvey released his victim, recoiling from the pain of the bite. Vins threw a kick that caught Allen in the forehead. Hurt by the kick, Allen turned loose and crouched on his haunches, struggling to catch his breath. Vins launched at least three more kicks into Allen's side, hard enough to break ribs. With a whoosh of air and blood rushing from his mouth, Allen turned turtle, falling onto his back. He was helpless, unable to defend himself.

Bellowing Vin's name in an invitation to join in on the kill, Helvey swung his foot into the side of Allen's head, kicking him again and again and again. "It looked like he was kicking a soccer ball," Vins later testified. "I kept hearing thuds every time he kicked him. I would have to say Helvey kicked Schindler to the right side of his head at least five to ten times." The scene looked horrible to Vins, like an *abattoir*. "Blood was all over the place. His face was covered with blood," he said. "Helvey then started down and began to kick and stomp on Schindler's chest and torso—It lasted for at least thirty seconds—I could not tell you how many times he kicked and stomped on his chest." In one last act of terrifying rage, Helvey stamped his foot onto Allen's throat as he lay on the floor, and shifted his entire 240 lbs. onto the dying gay man, as one might crush a spider.

The hellish rhythm of the stamping and grunting drew Allen's fellow Fab Five member, Keith Sims, to the park toilet as he was passing by, just to see what was going on. From about thirty-five yards away, all he could make out was the frenzied shadow play upon the backlit restroom window. Sims described that the "big shadow" was doing "choreography" to the *New York Times* in a September 1993 interview: "It seemed like he was dancing." Sims said he recognized Terry Helvey and Charles Vins as they ran from the bathroom into the night.

Sims, and a second curious passer-by who witnessed the last seconds of the assault, found a bloody wreck inside the toilet, more dead than alive. His face was a ruin. His nose was gone and his skull was crushed. His jaw was unhinged, floating free. Two shore patrolmen responded to their alarm. Assisted by Sims and the other sailor, the two patrolmen carried Allen's shattered body to Albuquerque Bridge where they waited forty-five agonizing minutes for an ambulance. Though Sims and Allen were friends, he didn't even recognize his fellow Fab Fiver. In an interview for the *Los Angeles Times* in February 1993, Sims said, "He was beaten so badly I didn't know it was Allen until the hospital called the ship at 2 a.m. or 2:30 a.m. to notify us that he had died ten minutes earlier." No one could have saved him. "Allen was gasping for air and having epileptic fits," Sims recalled. "When the ambulance arrived, they put a breather bottle on his face to get air into his lungs. They squeezed the bottle and blood started flowing out of his mouth," he told the *Times*.

Meanwhile, Helvey and Vins raced down to the Sasebo River to wash the blood off as best they could. Then they decided to cook up an alibi, so they went back to Sailor Town and tried to be conspicuous before going back to the ship.

The coincidence of the date, October 27–28, caused a pain nearly too sharp to bear—on the old national calendar, it was Navy Day.

It took weeks for the horror of what Helvey and Vins did to Allen that night to be comprehendible. His corpse was shipped to Okinawa for the autopsy, and then transported to California to be prepared for shipment home to his mother. The pathologist testified that Schindler's beating was the most severe he had seen in his entire career. Allen's injuries were consistent with those usually sustained in low speed air crashes or high-speed automobile wrecks. The pathologist said he had seen horse tramplings that were not so extensive. The bones of Allen's face and skull were shattered. The globes of his beautiful blue eyes were burst and ruptured. Force of impact imprinted the tread marks from a shoe on his forehead and chest. His Adam's apple was obliterated. All but two of his ribs were broken. Every organ system of his body was destroyed, his aorta was torn, and the liver was "smushed" like a tomato in its skin—so perforated, the pathologist testified, that he could pick Allen's liver up and see through the holes in it. Allen's groin was blue-black with bruises, his bladder was popped like a balloon, and his penis was lacerated.

On November 4, the Navy delivered the coffin bearing Allen's remains to Steger Memorial Funeral Home in Chicago Heights, escorted by a petty officer from the Wood. Naval officials advised that the casket remain closed. Dorothy wanted to see her son's body, and requested the lid be lifted. What she and her family saw was unrecognizable as Allen. All the military embalmer's skill had been able to produce no more than a flattened face with eyes so far apart they crowded the corpse's ears. Revolted by what he saw, Allen's uncle shouted for the morticians to shut the lid immediately. This ruin of a body was not Allen's—*could not* be Allen's. On the day of the visitation, after most guests had left the funeral home, Dorothy's daughter Kathy asked to have the casket opened one last time to see if she could find Allen's tattoos. As they rolled up the sleeves of his uniform, there on his pallid left arm were the inky remains of a tiger and a shark, and on his right was the insignia of his beloved "Mighty, Mighty Midway." Allen was finally home.

ANYBODY'S CHILD

Terry Helvey was arrested and charged with the murder of Allen R. Schindler Jr. the day after the body was found battered and broken on the men's room floor. His accomplice, Charles Vins, initially confessed to his part in the beating, but turned states-evidence against Helvey for the sweetheart deal of the century. In return for his testimony, he pled guilty to lesser crimes, including resisting arrest and failing to report a crime. In November 1992, Vins was court-martialed, convicted, and sentenced to only four months. He served a total of seventy-eight days, and received a general discharge from the Navy. Helvey pled guilty to murder in a U.S. military court on May 3, 1993, claiming that his acts were unpremeditated—a move calculated to save his life. On May 28, a jury of eight Marine and Navy officers took less than three hours to sentence Helvey to life in prison, though, by statute, he must receive a clemency hearing every year. Though he admitted he had done horrible things, Helvey always contended he was not a bad person . . . just a sailor in a bad situation. He denied under oath that he had killed Allen because he was a gay man, a claim refuted by Navy Investigator Kennon F. Privette, who told the jury that Helvey had slain his victim because "he hated homosexuals. He was disgusted by them." Privette quoted Helvey as saying under interrogation the day after the murder, "I don't regret it. I'd do it again. The bastard deserved it." The whole regrettable incident, Helvey said, would never have occurred if the Navy had just prevented all gays and lesbians from entering the service—in effect, then, according to Helvey, *the Navy made him do it.*

On one patently absurd level, the insouciant bigotry of Terry Helvey indicts military intolerance toward gays and lesbians: any branch of the military service unwilling to take responsibility for its own institutional prejudice deserves a degree of the blame when the unchecked hatred of its soldiers and sailors draws blood. The only two things Allen Schindler ever did to his killers and the United States Navy were to love his country, and serve it honorably in the armed forces.

After the sentencing phase of Helvey's trial, Dorothy Hajdys and her son's killer were ushered into a small conference room. Helvey tried to give her a copy of an apology letter he had written. She wouldn't take it from him. Instead, she demanded to know what Allen had ever done to him. He said, "Nothing." "Then why did you kill him?" Dorothy rumbled. Helvey couldn't look at her. "I don't know," he said. Dorothy had been warned to remain in control throughout the trial—while all she wanted to do was stomp this man's head in. But now, in this cramped little room with her nemesis, she lost control, and began shouting, "What did my son ever do to you?" All Helvey could do was bow his head and say, "I'm sorry," over and over again. In a January 25, 1994 article for *The Advocate*, Dorothy said,

> "I explained to [Helvey] how he had ruined my life. I told him that I have an 8-year-old granddaughter and she cries about how Allen is dead. 'What did Uncle Allen ever do to anybody?' she asks. How do you explain to an 8-year-old what you can't explain to yourself? She's afraid now when her mom and dad go some-where that someone will do to them what he did to Allen. She used to take Uncle Allen's picture to bed with her, and we've just gotten it so that she'll let his picture be on her nightstand. I told him to think about that as he sat in jail."

The U.S. Navy, once a surrogate parent for wayward young men, failed its Midwestern sons, Allen, Charles, and Terry, by trapping them each in a homophobic web of the Navy's own weaving. One was betrayed, dying on the white tile of a Japanese toilet, surrounded by an ocean of red. Another was slapped on the wrist, escaping the full penalty for the murder of a shipmate—but not escaping his own guilt. The last was incarcerated for life—ironically in a detention facility with men as gay as the fellow sailor he dashed to pieces against a urinal. Where is the "honor, courage and commitment" of the Navy to be found in any of this?

In the intervening years since Helvey's trial, some things have changed a great deal. Dorothy, now divorced and remarried, found out gay people were pretty wonderful, and not caricatures like Klinger on the hit television series, *M*A*S*H* at all. Eric Underwood has become like a surrogate son to her. In a way, Allen's story might be justly called, "The Transformation of Dorothy Hajdys." Having defeated her own deep-seated homophobia, Dorothy has become one of the most effective and sought after advocates for the LGBTQ community's right to serve openly in the military. She speaks out in her own, plain, powerful way about her son and the injustice that killed him. Her courage was portrayed in the acclaimed 1997 made-for-television film, *Any Mother's Son*, with veteran actor Bonnie Bedelia playing Dorothy. Every year at Terry Helvey's clemency hearing, the Servicemembers Legal Defense Network (SLDN), the nation's leading advocacy organization working for the full repeal of the "Don't Ask, Don't Tell" policy, works with Dorothy to keep her son's killer behind bars—a vow Dorothy made on Allen's grave.

There can be no doubt that the furor surrounding Allen's horrible murder, and the subsequent cover-up attempt by the Navy, ignited the debate over gays in the military in an unprecedented way. President Bill Clinton's administration was stamped forever as the one enshrining anti-gay prejudice in the United States military—largely because of the horror associated with the hate crime killing of this lone gay sailor. Allen's story put an individual face on that debate, and both sides have repeatedly used his murder to legitimize their positions.

The USS Belleau Wood is no longer with us. She was decommissioned in 2005 and used for target practice off Hawaii a year later. She had a proud life as a Navy warship, and now lies at the bottom of the Pacific as an artificial reef. The "Helleau Wood" proved particularly hard to sink, and so has the anti-gay prejudice that became part of her legacy of national service. In its third annual report on Don't Ask, Don't Tell, issued for the period between February 28, 1996 and February 26, 1997, the SLDN recounted that Petty Officer Schindler's murder seemed to have changed very little aboard the Wood. A 21-year-old sailor aboard the ship faced a discharge for alleged gay conduct in 1996. The Chief Master at Arms advised him not to fight the charges, and go quietly, if he knew what was good for him. Referring to Allen's murder, the Chief reportedly said, "The same thing will happen to you. You will be killed." The young sailor took the advice and accepted his discharge.

Allen's name comes up frequently at the offices of SLDN, from gay and lesbian members of the armed forces who fear a similar fate to his. But in the wake of the passage of the repeal of Don't Ask, Don't Tell during the "lame duck session" of the 111th Congress in December 2010, it cannot be denied that a significant portion of the energy to achieve this watershed victory for full equality in the military came from Allen's story—the story of a mother's son who could have been anybody's child—who loved his country, loved other men, and died as no one ever should again.

For Greater Understanding

Hell To Pay On the Belleau Wood: Allen R. Schindler Jr.

BOOKS AND ARTICLES

Brown, Chip. "The Accidental Martyr." *Esquire Magazine*, December 1993. No pages. Online: http://www.chipbrown.net/articles/martyr.htm.

Frank, Nathaniel. *Unfriendly Fire: How the Gay Ban Undermines the Military and Weakens America*. New York: Thomas Dunne Books, 2009.

Zeeland, Steven. *Sailors and Sexual Identity: Crossing the Line Between "Straight" and "Gay" in the U.S. Navy*. New York: Harrington Park Press, 1995.

FILMS AND VIDEOGRAPHY

Any Mother's Son. ABC Pictures, 1997.

ORGANIZATIONS AND WEBSITES

Servicemembers Legal Defense Network (SLDN), http://www.sldn.org.
Servicemembers United, http://servicemembersunited.org.
Unfinished Lives Project, http://unfinishedlivesblog.com.

Adolphus B. "Dolphus" Simmons
1990—January 21, 2008

NORTH CHARLESTON, SOUTH CAROLINA

Lawrence Fobes "Larry" King
January 13, 1993—February 14, 2008

Oxnard, California

Simmie Lewis Williams Jr.
November 25, 1990—February 22, 2008

FORT LAUDERDALE, FLORIDA

12

Baby Boys, You Stay On My Mind

Adolphus Simmons, Lawrence Fobes "Larry" King, and
Simmie Lewis "Beyoncé" Williams Jr.

"What greater pain could mortals have than this:
To see their children dead before their eyes?"

—EURIPIDES, *THE SUPPLIANT WOMEN*

SINCE 2008, AN OMINOUS new dimension of the slow-rolling decimation of LGBTQ people has appeared in America's schoolyards and
neighborhoods. Youths are being targeted for violence at an alarming
rate, as much for their non-traditional presentation of gender as for
their sexual orientation. This phenomenon is taking place from coast-
to-coast, especially among queer youth of color. Three youths—two of
them boys and one of them barely an adult—were savagely murdered
in the first two months of 2008 because they presented femininely and
refused to conform to common gender stereotypes: Adolphus Simmons,
18, of North Charleston, South Carolina, who died on January 21; Larry
King, 15, of Oxnard, California, who was fatally attacked on February
12, though he remained brain dead in a medically induced coma for
two more days; and Simmie Lewis Williams Jr., 17, of Fort Lauderdale,
Florida, who died on February 22. These are their stories, and the familiar back-story of a deadly culture unable or (perhaps more accurately)
unwilling to tolerate difference among its young.

　None of these three youths knew each other, nor had they heard
of each other. Each one was as extraordinary as a snowflake—one of a
kind in beauty, potential, and fragility. Yet in life as well as in death, these

three shared a great deal in common. All were members of racial/ethnic minorities. Simmons and Williams were African American. King was bi-racial. All came from economically disadvantaged circumstances, and inherited limited-opportunity horizons from their parents and their communities. Not only were they young, but so were their willing executioners—all of whom used handguns to slay their victims. Simmons's killer was 15 years old. King's murderer was barely 14. Williams was shot down in the street by two unidentified assailants, probably young men as well, who still remain at large. We must not ignore the role of race, poverty, and class if we ever want to understand what cut the lives of these three "Baby Boys" so brutally short.

And there is another maleficent ingredient to the toxic brew that took the lives of these three: gender hatred. Riki Wilchins, formerly Executive Director of GenderPAC (the Gender Public Advocacy Coalition), which she directed until it closed its doors in 2009, says the deaths of Simmons, King, and Williams were hardly unique. When the "Baby Boys" died in 2008, fifty-nine other gender non-conforming people had preceded them in lethal hate crime attacks since 1995. The majority of these murders victimized racial/ethnic minority youth. Most of these victims were born biologically male but presented femininely. One-third were teenagers at the time of their murders. In every case, their attackers were male, two-thirds of whom were within five years of age of the youths they killed. The American press carried sustained coverage of only 20 percent of these gender variant homicide stories. In over half of these murders, their killers were still free in 2009, as opposed to merely 31 percent of other homicidal killers in this country. *This is hard news to bear*: better than even odds exist for someone who murders a femininely presenting youth of color in the United States to get away with it. *Scot free.* As a teenage African American transperson said to me in New Haven, Connecticut, "Mister, they [the police] don't catch people who do things like this to folk like us."

Like other LGBTQ murders, gender non-conformist murders are exceptionally brutal, as Wilchins explains in an interview with *The Advocate* on March 8, 2008. "Gender hatred," she said, "is one reason these killings have been so spectacularly vicious. Half the young victims GenderPAC has documented since 1995 were attacked with some combination of shooting, bludgeoning, and stabbing. Many were assaulted further even after the victim was clearly dead." Wilchins then drove home her point with the full conviction of a big sister defending her family:

> "Our assailants are enraged by how we look, act, and dress—our gender. We camp it up; we wear high-heeled boots or even mascara. Like frail, blond Matthew Shepard, we fail to be paragons of masculinity, or like 15-year-old Sakia Gunn, we go out at night dressed as boys. How can we combat this kind of hatred as a community until we fully understand and acknowledge its roots?"

None of us has a full grasp of the extent of this problem in American society—not the FBI, nor the National Coalition of Anti-Violence Programs, nor even organizations like TrueChild and GLSEN (Gay, Lesbian and Straight Education Network), dedicated to combating gender stereotyping, gender dualisms, and school bullying. But we do know the problem is immense and growing. In her 2007 book, *Dude, You're a Fag: Masculinity and Sexuality in High School,* C.J. Pascoe says a sea change is taking place regarding sexual identity and gender among school-age youth—one that is deadly to those who do not conform to gender expectations. Adolescent boys who hurl epithets at each other in school may not mean literally that a "fag" is always a homosexual person, but the moniker always carries the weight and threat of un-masculinity with it. Four decades of success by the human rights movement for LGBTQ equality has enabled gay men, bisexual people, and lesbians to come out of their closets by the hundreds of thousands, if not millions. But the promise of gender freedom and expression has not come true for them after coming out. This is especially true for the young. When boys of color come to school, emboldened, or just freed-up enough to "camp-it-up," they meet the backlash of masculine insecurity in the corridors of our middle and high schools. "Fag identity" as Pascoe says, may indeed be fluid enough to permit contemporary boys to move in-and-out of "fag-dom" as they contest each other's masculinity. But femininely presenting boys, no matter how well adjusted to their own gender identities, are ill equipped to survive such contests when fists and bullets take the place of posturing and name-calling. Just ask the "Baby Boys."

DESTINY'S CHILDREN

Simmons, King, and Williams were also linked by a set of fashion characteristics the press frequently noted, but invariably, perhaps deliberately, misunderstood. In the early reports of each murder, journalists found the fact that the victims all wore women's clothing too sensational to resist. Cross-dressing gave the stories a "hook," a bizarre twist that made these youths exotic, sensual, and scented with a whiff of indecency that sold copy. From the favorite color of Larry King's eye-shadow (blue), to Adolphus Simmons's elaborate coiffures, and to Simmie Williams's knotted tee shirts and exposed midriff, the media labored to make their audiences approach these accounts of brutal murder through the lens of abnormality. It did not matter that each of these youths deliberately chose feminine identities to express their budding sense of self. Reporters chronically used male pronouns in reference to them, and seemed hell-bent on insisting that all three of them be known as "boys in dresses." So incurious were reporters that when writing about King's feminine alter ego "Leticia," and Simmons's and Williams's self-identifications as "Beyoncé" or "Chris," these reporters never bothered to ask the basic journalistic question why something so dissonant with majority culture seemed so important to each of these victims. None seemed interested in why the danger to these trans youths in communities of color, especially African American communities, made the construction of separate, yet parallel, male and female identities an absolute necessity. Whether the journalists intended or not, their portrayal of the unexplained freak-ish aspect of how these youths dressed and accessorized foregrounded media-fabricated flamboyance that carried with it innuendoes of the victims' personal failures, mental instability, and at least partial blame for the fate that befell them. Remember *Newsweek* reporter Ramin Setoodeh's image of Larry King's imbalance and abnormality: a diminu-tive, effeminate urchin, mincing along in cheap stiletto heels, "teetering" and "chasing the boys around the school in them." The effect is to turn innocent, gender-variant teenage boys into predatory sex offenders— and such yellow journalism is inexcusable.

Oddly enough, given the history of antagonism between the trans community and organized religion, a Christian minister—and not the journalists—got the image right for these murdered youths. In his eulogy for Larry King, Rev. Dan Birchfield, pastor of Westminster Presbyterian Church of Hueneme, California, called the 15-year-old *a masterpiece*. Each was a masterpiece of metamorphosis, in the process of becoming more beautiful in the most difficult of circumstances. School is hell on earth for femininely presenting teenage boys. Adolphus Simmons faced name-calling and discrimination in high school, and managed to get through it by becoming a jokester, clowning around to make people laugh. Williams's mother, Denise King, on the other hand, gave Simmie permission to drop out of the daily hazing he suffered in the Fort Lauderdale schools. She told reporters from the *Sun-Sentinel* that students regularly called her son "Gay!" and "Faggot!" Even in their neighborhood, men mistook Simmie for a girl, shouting after him, "Hey, lil momma!" Simmie ran away as fast as he could, fearing what would happen to him when the men found out that he was biologically male. GED classes and the promise of training in the Job Corps were safer for him than another year of high school. And last, Larry King went back into the furnace of ridicule at E.O. Green Junior High in Oxnard after winter break, and boldly made his transformation public by his manner of dress and use of cosmetics. But, in truth, he had faced verbal battering for gender non-conformity as far back as the third grade. By junior high, Larry was a past master in the struggle to assume a fuller feminine identity.

The word these three young gender outlaws invariably used to describe their socio-sexual identities was "gay." That is what Dolphus had said to his mother, Felicia Moultrie. At the age of ten, Larry had matter-of-factly responded to his friend's question, "Are you gay?" "Yeah," he answered. "So what?" In 2006, Simmie had told his mom not to expect grandchildren from him because he was "gay." "Gay" was the term early twenty-first-century culture offered them to describe who and what they were, but the neatly bordered lines demarcating one sexual orientation from another hand blurred into gender fluidity by the time these boys adopted the language. To some degree, each of these "Baby Boys" was in transition throughout his school years, becoming more fully identified as female in a variety of ways. Were they "gay"? Yes. Were they "transgender" as well? Yes, again.

Wolfgang Eli, in an online comment for *Reason Magazine* on February 19, 2008, shortly after Larry King's murder, explained the degree of difficulty trans youth face as they physically mature:

> For transsexual teens, puberty itself is a living hell. Imagine what it's like to watch in horror as your body develops in a way that is completely at odds with your inner identity. The emerging secondary sex characteristics are grotesque and alien to the trans teen who spent his childhood praying for a miracle to transform his body into alignment with his mind. Now a teen, nature's cruel betrayal is complete. Trans teens often lose all self-esteem; survival becomes a constant struggle. Now imagine being ridiculed and teased relentlessly by other kids on top of that.

Fashion and style were not simply diversions for these three boys. Dress, cosmetics, coif, and affect were sacramental in the broadest sense: outward signs of inward transformation. They were doing what all young people do—pressing the envelope of experience, transcending who and what they were to explore who and what they were becoming. Glamour, fantasy, and experimentation were the emergent means by which they could "try on" the personas that made sense of their developing femininity. In poor, black communities, and in Latina/o-predominant communities, this trans emergence presented particular characteristics and problems.

Dolphus, Larry, and Simmie did not find their role models in sports, politics, or the military; instead they turned to the world of Arts and Entertainment. Beyoncé Knowles of the R&B group, "Destiny's Child," became their avatar of hope. Knowles, born in 1981, was a superstar when the Baby Boys entered puberty. She epitomized African American pop success: singer-songwriter, record producer, actress, dancer, choreographer, model, fashion trendsetter, and video director. Knowles also embodied black feminine elegance. Her vocal hits dominated American radio, and her 2003 Grammy Award winning album, *Dangerously in Love*, propelled "Crazy in Love" and "Baby Boy" to number one hits. An aspiring singer, with a fine voice that got him noticed, Larry King memorized and sang her tracks. Dolphus Simmons borrowed her name and lip-synched her lyrics for friends and on stage. Simmie Williams adored her so much that he adopted "Beyoncé" as his *alter ego* for the "gay family" that gathered in and around Sistrunk Boulevard in Fort Lauderdale.

Having a strong avatar like Beyoncé Knowles who embodied success and hope, a "gay family," and a loving mother back home kept Williams sane, willing to wake up every day and face what might seem insufferable circumstances to many. This is the crucial element most journalists miss when reporting the stories of trans teen hate crimes victims. These reporters misread and therefore misreport what fashion and style represent for gender variant youth of color: the need to identify with beauty and racial/ethnic success in a world stacked against poor trans teens.

DOLPHUS SIMMONS STAYS ON MY MIND

He was the perfect houseguest, cooking dinner for his hosts, cleaning up, and then carrying out the trash afterwards. Adolphus B. Simmons, affectionately called "Dolphus" by his family and friends, was staying temporarily at the home of Debra Mack, a neighbor of Dolphus's who lived in the Bradford Apartments on Bream Road in North Charleston, South Carolina. Dolphus loved to cook, and he loved to style hair for women. He was good at both—very good, in fact. But the way Dolphus endeared himself to neighbors up and down the apartment complex was by his infectious good humor. No matter what he did, whether creating one-of-a-kind elaborate hair weaves for his clients, or putting that special touch to the Lowcountry cooking he had learned from his mother and grandmothers, ever-cheerful Dolphus made people feel better just by being around him. Many have remembered his wonderful sense of humor, and his inexhaustible flood of quick-witted jokes. One of his sister's teachers, Marisa Jacobs, remembered, "Adolphus always put a smile on my face and made me laugh no matter what kind of day I was having." Like Lowcountry folk say, *Lord, he could cut the fool, that child!*

Monday evening, January 21, 2008 was chilly, downright cold for North Charleston—just right for crab, boiled and baked, caught fresh from the estuaries nearby. Dolphus got Debra just to sit back and relax while he bustled around the kitchen fixing supper (there is no such thing as "dinner" in South Carolina, except for the evening meals of transplanted Yankees!). Since he felt so much at home with Debra and her friends, Dolphus slipped on one of his favorite everyday dresses which he took care to cover with an apron as he prepared the meal. Nobody thought twice about it. That was how Dolphus felt most comfortable, and, to tell the truth, he made dresses look *good*. At eighteen, he was tall and slender, and he could "work it" as well as any biologically born girl in the complex. Femininity truly was second nature to Dolphus, and if anyone got uptight about it, he would just laugh it off, tell one of a hundred jokes he knew, and move along with the life God meant for him to live. The consensus of his many friends was that Dolphus didn't have an enemy in the world . . . but they were wrong about that. Horribly wrong.

Back in 2007, Dolphus had moved to the Bradford Apartments to make a new life for himself. He came from a big family, and he was the eldest. His folks, Russell and Felicia Moultrie, had seven other children: LaKenya, Richard, Katrina, Russell Jr., Marissa, Jordan, and Michaela. Dolphus was the gender-variant child of the family, a fact any mother would recognize even early in his life. There was a special bond between Felicia Moultrie and her femininely presenting son. She was the apple of his eye, and he was hers. When she looked at Dolphus, all she saw was a loving human being. Nothing else mattered. Reflecting on her child's life to a reporter from Charleston's *Post and Courier*, Mrs. Moultrie said, "He chose the life the way he wanted it. We all accepted him for who he was."

It had been another story for Dolphus in school, however. School children can be exceptionally cruel to anyone different. At some point, this sweet, effeminate boy understood that he had to defend himself. So, he played the jokester to deflect the stinging, anti-queer slurs aimed at him by his classmates. The theory: if you can get them laughing, even at your own expense, they usually aren't beating you up at the same time. Everybody loves a clown, don't they? But, like Smokey Robinson and the Miracles sang about Pagliaccio back in the day, there is nothing much sadder than a clown's tears. Scar tissue lay beneath the smiles. The jokes became a hallmark of his, a life skill, and he learned how to "fake it 'till you make it." When he bade Stall High School good-bye, Dolphus determined to live freely—to march to the beat of his own drummer.

Life went well for Dolphus at the Bradford Apartments. People accepted his gender variance, for the most part, and the coifs he wore were so colorful and unique that women asked him to do their hair. He experimented with varieties of weave and color techniques, and made a modest living at it. Before Christmas, he quit his job at Captain D's fast-food restaurant to concentrate on hairstyling. On January 7, 2008, though, at about 5 p.m., somebody kicked in the door to his apartment. Thankfully, no one was home. To the untrained eye, it appeared to be a petty robbery. The place was ransacked. Compact discs and earrings were missing. Dolphus never believed that robbery was the only motivation for the break-in, and neither did his mother. From the beginning, she suspected that a group of people was trying to get at him. The break-in disturbed Dolphus enough that he refused to sleep in the apartment again. Instead, he accepted Debra Mack's offer of hospitality. Precautions notwithstanding, barely two weeks later, Dolphus was dead.

Homophobia and transphobia are virulent in some of Charleston's black neighborhoods. In an online commentary about a *Post and Courier* story on Dolphus's murder from January 23, 2008, two "chatters" highlighted the depth of the anti-transgender and anti-gay bias in the Charleston metro area. "Brant" wrote:

> If you've looked closely at anything concerning a gay individual who has been bashed, shot, killed, etc., . . . it's never thought of as a hate crime. Think Matthew Shepard. My opinion is that we're

afraid, as a nation, to admit we HAVE such a thing. Ironically, if he hadn't been Gay, it'd be thought of strictly on a racial basis. . . . The LGBT community, whether it's in Charleston or someplace else, gets little respect and this is just another example.

"Eyfigueroa" responded:

It may have been [an anti-gay hate crime]. Homophobia is rampant in the black community, more so now with the influx of the "gangsta" lifestyle. I find it very plausible that someone in or near the community that may have known of the victim [killed him] out of hate or desire to seem "hard."

Two weeks after Dolphus had abandoned his apartment for the friendly security of Debra Mack's home, he had forgotten the shock over his home invasion—as well as the uneasiness about who could have done such a thing, and why. A couple of hours before supper, he had called his mother to invite her to come over for crab. Mrs. Moultrie recalled the conversation vividly. "He was cuttin' a fool, and laughing and joking," she said to the *Post and Courier* two days after his murder. She was out shopping, and told Dolphus she would call him back later. To this day, she regrets never returning his call.

The supper party ended around 8 p.m. Only scraps remained from the feast. Dolphus's immediate concern was to get supper's fishy smelling residue out of his host's apartment. He didn't bother taking off the dress; the dumpster was just a quick trip across the parking lot. So he collected the trash, stepped out into the frigid night air, and shut the door behind him.

Gunfire exploded just as Dolphus stepped off the porch onto the apartment steps. We will never know whether he saw his assailants in the muzzle flash. They were waiting for him, screened by the foliage flanking the stoop. Dolphus crumpled on the steps, shot in the gut and in the right leg above his ankle. Police investigators found multiple shell casings left carelessly at the crime scene.

Mary Ivory, a neighbor from a couple of doors down, heard the shots, but didn't think much about it. Gunshots were part of the usual atmospherics in this section of South Carolina's third-largest city. The clamor on the stoop, though, made her open the door to a scene she will never forget. Dolphus lay like a broken doll on the bloody steps, chaos swirling around him. Tiffany Wells, his best friend, remembered how cold it was, and how desperate she felt because the Emergency Medical Service responders seemed to take forever to get there. According to *ABC News 4*, by the time Officer Daniel Pritchard arrived, Dolphus was catching his breath in ragged gasps, and his pulse was fading. Like a Renaissance tableau, a black transgender Pietà, Dolphus slumped unconscious in the arms of his weeping brother, who happened to be at the complex that night. EMS rushed him to Medical University Hospital, where he died at 9:08 p.m.

By Wednesday, a 15-year-old was arrested and charged with the murder. On Saturday, two more teens were arrested and charged with accessory after the fact of murder, a second 15-year-old, and a 19-year-old named Jackeuz Witherspoon. All the defendants were local boys. Under questioning, Witherspoon, also suspect in the January 7 break-in at Dolphus's apartment, hindered the investigation by lying to interrogators. Ninth Circuit Solicitor Scarlett Wilson wrapped the identities of the juveniles in a cloak of confidentiality, assuming that their cases would be tried in Family Court because of their youth. Solicitor Wilson eventually routed the 15-year-olds to Community Juvenile Arbitration, and no more presently is known of their cases.

So many questions about the murder of Adolphus B. Simmons remain unanswered. His mother still wants to know why these killers took the life of her first-born. "Right now," she told *Post and Courier* reporter Noah Haglund on January 25, "I need to know why. What triggered them to take my son away from me?" Debra Mack wants answers, too. In an interview with Nadine Parks of the *Post and Courier* the next day, Mack said she couldn't get the picture of Dolphus dying on the stoop in front of her apartment out of her mind. "I'm moving," she said. "I haven't slept since this thing happened. This is really eating me alive. He was no threat to anybody. He was a nice person. He was just like my child."

Initially, North Charleston police refused to label the murder a hate crime. Police spokesperson Spencer Pryor said there was no evidence to suggest it was. As the investigation proceeded, though, detectives admitted that the real reason they did not do so was because South Carolina has no anti-LGBTQ hate crime statute on the books. The Palmetto State is one of five in the nation that has so far refrained from passing hate crimes protections for their transgender and gay residents. Under criticism from everyday citizens as well as activists, North Charleston officials have backtracked, now saying that they could not rule out the possibility that Dolphus was killed because of his perceived sexual orientation, gender identity, and gender expression. But even if they determined that gender-variant Dolphus, who presented femininely in a clearly transphobic, homophobic Lowcountry culture, and who died in women's clothing, South Carolina would simply sniff and move on. Elke Kennedy of Greenville learned that same lesson when Stephen Moller, an 18-year-old white boy, killed her 20-year-old gay son, Sean William Kennedy, outside a popular local club on May 16, 2007. Because South Carolina has no anti-LGBTQ hate crime statute, Moller served less than a year for homicide. Kennedy's killer was granted early release, a three-year suspended sentence with thirty days community service, and a few mandatory anger management classes. Sean's mother decried the injustice in a press release:

> There was no justice today for my son, Sean. The sentence [his killer] received was a joke and a slap on the wrist. Once again it proves that in the state of South Carolina there is no justice for the victim, especially the victim of a senseless, violent, bias-motivated crime . . . No mother should have to bury her child. No mother should have to lose her child to violence and hate. No mother should have to fight to see justice for her child.

Charleston State House Representative Seth Whipper unsuccessfully introduced legislation to remedy this gross injustice. In the *Charleston City Paper* on March 19, 2008, Whipper admitted that the hypocrisy of state law boggles the mind. "For example," he said, "if you put two cats in a ring to fight, that person would receive a felony charge for animal fighting and face up to five years in prison or a $5,000 fine. But if it's two birds, there would be an additional misdemeanor charge with another year in jail or $1,000 fine." In the case of a transgender or gay person, of any race or ethnicity, however, a human life is worth less before the eyes of South Carolina law than brawling cats or fighting roosters.

Dolphus made his last journey on Saturday, January 26, the same day two more teenage suspects in his murder were being arrested. His family escorted his body to the Lovely Hill Baptist Church on Bear Swamp Road, Johns Island, where he lay in state for an hour before the Rev. Robert Dees Sr. officiated at his funeral. His remains were interred in the Red Top Community Cemetery. We might wonder if anyone that day remembered how special Adolphus used to look on a Saturday night, dressed to the nines like the Lady he really was. Or just how important to him it was to feel so feminine and alive? Like his forebears, Dolphus came home to Johns Island, laid to rest by a grieving family. He was beautiful in life, outrageously abused in death, and, as his friend Tiffany Wells lamented, "He was *so* young." But not forgotten.

Baby Boy, we cannot forget you.

LARRY KING LIVES IN MY MEMORY

The memory of 15-year-old Lawrence Fobes "Larry" King is like the corpse of a fallen antique warrior on a Trojan field—opposing forces fight back and forth to claim it. His murder in a California middle school computer lab has inflamed public opinion more than any other LGBTQ hate crime since Matthew Shepard was killed in Wyoming in 1998. Larry was shot execution-style—two bullets from a .22-calibre pistol, fired at close range in the back of his skull—by a 14-year-old-classmate. He died barely three weeks after Dolphus Simmons was gunned down on the steps of his apartment complex on the East Coast. But while news of the murder of Dolphus never grabbed the attention of the national media, and took months to leak out bit-by-bit to the regional LGBTQ press, Larry's slaying seized the West Coast news media by the collar and shook it hard. Larry's execution-style killing spawned a national maelstrom of fury at parental abdication, school bullying, gender variance discrimination, juvenile crime, the gun lobby, and LGBTQ politics. Everybody wanted a piece of Larry either to support or to oppose an agenda. But the eye of the storm was a Baby Boy we must not forget—a diminutive, proudly emergent queer naïf who asserted his forming gender identity with breathtaking abandon.

Larry was small for his age, but impossible to ignore, at E.O. Green Junior High School in Oxnard, California, where he was an eighth grader. His smooth, beige face was preternaturally young looking, and displayed hints of character that were by turns cherubic and mischievous depending on his mood. At 5'4" tall, he weighed 101 lbs. He was mixed race, half African American, and was just beginning to explore his black heritage. But it was his gender non-conformity that triggered the buzz among students at E.O. Green. Every day when the van from Casa Pacifica Center pulled up in the schoolyard, gawking students craned to see what Larry the queer kid was wearing this morning. News of his makeup, or nail polish, or footwear, or whatever garment he had put on over his regulation school clothes (white shirt and dark pants for boys) spread like California wildfires amid giggling knots of teens throughout the campus halls and locker rooms. "He was like Britney Spears," a teacher said to Setoodeh. "Everyone wanted to know what's the next thing he's going to do."

His school was wedged into a densely populated residential area five minutes from downtown Oxnard; Larry, however, lived at Casa Pacifica, a residential center for abused, neglected, and severely emotionally traumatized children, twenty-five minutes away in rural Camarillo. In November 2007, the court placed him there after trouble with his adoptive parents, Greg and Dawn King, with whom he had lived since he was two years old. His biological father never played a major part in his life. His birth mother was a drug addict, and neglected to feed him regularly. After the story of his murder broke into the "big time," investigative reporters sought out every source they could to profile Larry. The results rendered two types of "Larrys" in press accounts. One "Larry" is disturbed and chronically difficult to live with, a Tasmanian devil of a kid. The other "Larry" is a boy whose rocky, early life took its toll on his family, but all-in-all he showed promise as a bright, effeminate soul. He struggled to come to terms with a growing gender identity that complicated his life in the public schools. The Kings have remained mum about the reasons he was removed from their care except to a few reporters they deem to be sympathetic. His parents characterized Larry to the minister who preached his funeral as a fun-loving person who was fascinated by insects, loved to fish for crawdads with licorice, was nerdy enough to enjoy playing chess, and had learned to crochet so that he could help his mom make woolens for American soldiers overseas in Iraq. He was even rehearsing his exceptional singing voice to perform the National Anthem at his brother's ball game.

By the time he got to junior high, Larry was a five-year veteran of sexual harassment. As early as the third grade, kids needled him about being gay and shunned him during recess period. In the sixth grade, according to a July 2008 account of his childhood in *Newsweek*, malicious pranksters threw a smoke bomb into the King's house, almost killing Larry's dog. He told his dad that he was bisexual when he turned 14, but Greg King assumed it was just a phase. At E.O. Green where he had enrolled since the seventh grade, Larry was ridiculed and harassed with a sickening regularity. Students called him "fag" and "queer." They would jostle him the halls, trying to knock him down. They threw wet, wadded-up paper towels at him in the boys' toilet. Still, Larry had discovered friends and defenders in the student body, especially a group of girls who accepted him for who he was. Miriam Lopez, a 13-year-old friend, told the online news blog, EDGE, in March 2008, "He didn't like people insulting him. Larry was brave enough to bring high heels and makeup to school and he wasn't afraid of anything."

Casa Pacifica was a welcome sanctuary for Larry. Though the center has a policy of confidentiality about personal characteristics, counselors say almost everyone knew Larry was gay. He was obvious. Supervision was close at Casa, but Larry seemed never to mind the presence of psychologists and caseworkers. He welcomed their attention and support. The Casa mascot, a big, gentle Newfoundland dog named Archibald RazzMaTazz ("Archie," for short), became a special favorite of Larry's. Others often saw Larry with Archie talking quietly as if the Newfoundland understood and empathized with Larry's every word. By Christmas 2007, he had become a personality of sorts on the sprawling twenty-five-acre campus.

Larry was legally entitled to attend gay-straight alliance meetings since he identified as gay and queer at Casa Pacifica. Weekly, a staff member would drive him to Ventura County Rainbow Alliance youth gatherings. Neal Broverman of *The Advocate* discovered for the April 8, 2008 issue that Larry blossomed when he interacted with other self-identified LGBTQ youth. Jay Smith, Executive Director of the Rainbow Alliance told Broverman that Larry was doing well both at Casa and at the Alliance. The policy of Casa was that any person in their care would have to be in the actual presence of a staff member from the center whenever attending events off campus. So Casa had worked out an exception to the Alliance's "youth-only" rule for rap sessions to permit an adult supervisor from Casa to attend the meetings and keep their residents in sight at all times. Smith said that Larry was comfortable with this arrangement, even appreciative of it. The attentive presence of the Casa Pacifica staff gave Larry a sense of belonging and security, Smith observed. "I think [Larry] felt somebody was at least listening to him," he said to Broverman, "and he was starting to connect with an adult figure supportive of him which I am not certain he was receiving at home, and it sounds like he wasn't really receiving at school either."

Larry's personality had always been confident, even when he was a small child. Now that he had regular adult attention at Casa Pacifica, and had made friends with other LGBTQ kids at the Rainbow Alliance,

Larry began to express his budding feminine persona with a growing pride. During the winter break from junior high, he integrated more and more of his queer identity, and apparently determined that no antagonist would cow him into shame and silence any more. When school started up again in January 2008, Larry was prepared to let students and faculty at E.O. Green deal with who he was. Classmates saw the difference immediately. In an often quoted comment made to reporters from the *Los Angeles Times*, eighth-grader Michael Sweeney said, "[Larry] would come to school in high-heeled boots, makeup, jewelry, and painted nails—the whole thing. That was freaking the guys out."

One of those "freaked-out guys," 14-year-old Brandon McInerney, couldn't cope with Larry's metamorphosis. So, when Larry pushed back against the heckling and harassment coming from the super-"het" crowd Brandon belonged to, Brandon got irritated. When Larry camped it up, using public flamboyance as a defense against the epithets and pranks, Brandon got increasingly angry. And when Larry went as far as to express a crush on him, asking him to be his Valentine, Brandon didn't seek school official intervention. Instead, Brandon took matters into his own hands, and he reacted with soul-crushing violence.

On Monday, February 11, the day before his lethal attack, Larry got into a heated argument with Brandon's clique in the school cafeteria. One of the boys snarled that Larry "better watch [his] ass." Brandon seethed after the incident, and ranted to a girl who knew both Larry and himself, "You better say goodbye to him because you won't see him again." The girl thought Brandon was just blowing off steam, and she mentioned the threat to no one until Larry was already dead.

Ironically, Brandon had come from a difficult family situation similar to Larry's in several respects. Brandon's father, a real estate salesman, was regularly in trouble with the law. His mother, a drug addict, allegedly got physically violent with Brandon. As a result, she lost custody of him. Brandon's parents got mutual restraining orders against each other. For a time, the boy lived with his father, but that arrangement had lasted only briefly. Brandon had lived with his Grandfather McInerney since he was twelve. Junior high had been a boost for Brandon. He was growing up into a good-looking, well-muscled young man, tall for his age. Girls liked him. Since he was athletic, and was a member of a group called the "Young Marines," other boys looked up to him and thought he was cool—something of a "stud duck" on campus. One of the cool things his circle of friends liked to do was to bully and pick on the queer kid, the "little fag" from Casa Pacifica. When the "little fag" turned the tables on him, however, Brandon was caught unprepared.

The news media constructed contrasting accounts of Brandon McInerney just as it had for Larry King, once the story caught fire. A legion of journalists combed through every source available to construct a profile of this 14-year-old killer. As with Larry King, their conflicting agendas *vis-à-vis* Brandon came to light from the images they constructed of him in the press. The first "Brandon" they constructed was an early adolescent boy developmentally unable to understand his emotions when beset by an aggressive queer. This juvenile "Brandon" was the target of a flamboyant, sexually harassing gay boy who threatened Brandon's masculinity and pushed him into violence. This "juvenile" image served the purposes of his defense team who desperately wanted the presiding judge to remand his case for trial in juvenile court. On the other had, the second construction of "Brandon" was a troubled soul who grew up neglected by his parents, someone who secretly idolized Adolph Hitler and who was influenced by a neo-Nazi white supremacist mentor. Though he was barely 14, he nonetheless acted as an adult with premeditated malice, lying in wait to snuff out the life of a boy he loathed—an innocent boy who was just trying to live his life. While the prosecution may not have fabricated this portrayal, it undoubtedly worked to sway public opinion enough toward trying Brandon as an adult.

Indeed, these two boys were both abused by a media establishment determined to give a voracious public the news it was hungry to have: digestible pictures of a victim and his alleged killer to feed the insatiable American fascination with teen-on-teen violence. In this sense, at least, both Brandon and Larry were victims of a system that skewed public images of them in ways beyond their influence, and beyond the control of those who loved them. But there is a stark difference between the boys that no media wizard can resolve. While Brandon remains alive and able to defend himself against negative portrayals of his identity, Larry King cannot. He lost his voice in death.

Valentine's Day, coming up on Thursday, February 14, was special to Larry. He was excited about the approaching school dance, and was full of suggestions about how to make it fun for everyone. Elizabeth Castillo, Co-president of the Associate Student Body at E.O. Green, told the *Ventura County Star*, "He'd come up to me and offer different ideas for the dance. He thought about getting a photo booth." She knew that he was being harassed because the school administration had transferred Larry to her gym class. Everybody seemed to know it. In an effort to lessen the verbal attacks, Larry started wearing regular school clothes and sneakers. When the van from Casa Pacifica pulled up on Tuesday morning, February 12, his classmates noticed that Larry seemed more subdued than usual. His clothes were boringly normal.

Brandon came to school that day, habitually early. He was carried a black backpack. Plenty of people knew about the previous day's altercation between Larry and Brandon and his clique in the cafeteria. Some wondered if Brandon would confront Larry again before class, either at the school entrance or before first period classes. He did not.

School officials must have known that tensions were running high between Larry and his tormentors. They also surely knew about the incident in the school cafeteria. The Superintendent of Hueneme School District, Jerry Dannenberg, told various reporters that he and other authorities had tried to settle things between the boys, but Dannenberg made it sound as though their hands were tied by the law and by the informal power of community opinion. Larry had the right to wear anything that was decent, and that posed no safety hazard, Dannenberg said. Though Larry couldn't wear steel-toed shoes, for example, he could wear stiletto heels if he wanted. Like Oxnard generally, school was not a welcoming place for obviously different children, especially those perceived to be LGBTQ. Community resistance had been high enough to disown queer kids publically, determining that no Gay-Straight Alliance could exist at E.O. Green, though there were scores of GSAs in junior high and high schools throughout Southern California. Teachers and school administrators knew more than enough to act. Principal Joel Lovestedt had the power to call an emergency assembly to address the rising tensions, and chose not to do so. The day after the shooting, Lovestedt said to Rob Hayes of *KABC-TV News—Los Angeles*, "Could we have prevented this or was this one of those unfortunate things where all of the preparations in the world can't [protect] you from a crazy person?" If such an assembly had been called, would there have been any news story on Wednesday at all? Who can say?

Both Larry and Brandon were in Joy Boldrin's first-period English class. After beginning class, Ms. Boldrin took her students to the computer lab, where they could work on their latest assignment, a paper on the Second World War. Brandon chose a seat directly behind Larry, in the middle of the classroom. Approximately a half-hour into the class period, Brandon reached into his black backpack, and removed a small black handgun he had smuggled into school. He stood up and walked behind Larry. Brandon raised the pistol, pointing it directly at the back of Larry's head. He pulled the trigger once, then twice. The blast was deafening in the confines of the classroom. Ms. Boldrin screamed at Brandon, "What the hell are you doing?" The 14-year-old dropped the weapon on the floor, and walked briskly out of the room. Police apprehended him only seven minutes later, a few blocks away from the school.

Chaos lurched and streaked throughout the school as word of the shooting spread from class to class. The school went into lockdown. Students were using text messages and cell phone calls to spread the news almost immediately to the outside world. Twenty-four traumatized and hysterical classmates witnessed the cold-blooded execution of one of their own by another. The horror of Columbine and Jonesboro, Arkansas had come to E.O. Green Junior High School.

Larry was rushed to St. John's Hospital. While doctors fought to save Larry's life, the judicial system charged Brandon as an adult for premeditated hate crime murder, and then jailed him in a juvenile detention facility with a bail amount set at $770,000. By Wednesday, Larry was declared brain-dead. Greg and Dawn King, in consultation with Larry's physicians, decided to keep his body on life-support until Thursday—Valentine's Day—when his organs could be harvested. All his major organs, and the retinas from his eyes, were donated to those who needed them. With almost unbearable irony, Larry's strong heart finally found a way to be shared with another—today it beats in the chest of a young girl.

The years have passed since Larry was gunned down in his computer lab. Literally tens of thousands have marched in his memory in Oxnard and around the nation. Unlike most LGBTQ hate crimes stories, especially those of young, gender variant victims of color, Larry's saga has shown stronger legs than that of any other hate crimes victim in more than a decade. Hundreds of articles and weblog posts debate the morality of his life and death. Meanwhile, Brandon McInerney grows older, languishing in jail as he awaits trial. On his behalf, his attorneys entered a plea of not guilty to the charge of murder. His defense team argued successfully for the venue of his trial to be shifted from Ventura

County to Santa Barbara County, where McInerney may stand a better chance of a fairer trial. But his attorneys were not successful in persuading the court to try Brandon as a juvenile. After three days of hearings in July 2009, Ventura County Superior Court Judge Ken Riley ruled that it was appropriate for him to be tried as an adult for first-degree murder as a hate crime, particularly in view of McInerney's declaration of intent to kill Larry, the cool calculation with which he "laid in wait" several minutes into the class to shoot his victim, and the "the cold-blooded precision of an executioner" with which he carried out the crime. A State Appeals Court upheld Judge Riley's ruling in January 2010, clearing the way for the trial. According to Maeve Fox, the senior deputy district attorney prosecuting McInerney, if convicted as charged, Brandon could face a maximum sentence of fifty-three years in prison.

Larry wanted to be known as "Leticia." That is the way he signed a paper due for class the day before he was killed for refusing to conform to the gender expectations imposed on him by others. He blew kisses at boys in school. He stretched the limits of the dress code by wearing regulation colors in Leticia's own inimitable style. A spiritual grandchild of Helen Reddy, Larry's persona Leticia sometimes spoke in a roar to assert the right to live in gender freedom. Most of the time, however, Leticia remained quietly within Larry, feeling secure enough at Casa Pacifica to curl up beside Archie, the shaggy black Newfoundland dog, and dream of a time when boys who present as girls, no longer afraid, could grow up to be strong and invincible in a transformed world. That world has not yet come. Larry's memory lingers on a contested field, where America's non-white young and poor die at an alarming rate. Today in this country, femininely presenting trans youths like Larry die at the rate of two a month. But tomorrow belongs to those who have rejected a world where children like Larry and Brandon suffer for our sins. Tomorrow belongs to those who are committed to the long, hard work of bringing all our insecure brothers to understand they need not fear or hate anyone beautiful.

Baby Boy, we will not forget you.

SIMMIE WILLIAMS STAYS IN MY DREAMS

Simmie Lewis Williams Jr. loved three things most of all: family, cooking, and a fantasy connection with Beyoncé Knowles. On February 22, 2008, "Beyoncé" (as Simmie was known on the street) was shot and killed in

Fort Lauderdale, Florida, beside a chain link fence bordering an urban wasteland known as the "Transvestite Stroll." She died within a week of Larry King's murder, and only a month after Dolphus Simmons's. Like them, Simmie/Beyoncé's[1*] story shows how easy it is to kill a transgender person of color in twenty-first-century America, . . . *and what an incalculable loss to the world it is when someone does.*

The facts of the case are both fragmentary and hideous. It was Friday, February 22, 2008, a balmy night of the full moon. At approximately 12:45 a.m., on the blighted corner of the 1000 block of Sistrunk Boulevard and Northwest Tenth Avenue, a well-known area where transgender folk were known to congregate, two men dressed in black clothing approached young Beyoncé Williams. According to the police report, a loud argument broke out along the chain link fence that extended across the front of a vacant lot to the corner. One of the men fired two shots at close range. Beyoncé fell to the sidewalk, mortally wounded. A can of partially discharged pepper spray was found in her hand. She had not gone down without a fight. The assailants ran into the moon shadows, and disappeared. They have never been identified, though they are thought to be from the Sistrunk neighborhood. Beyoncé was taken to Broward General Medical Center where she was pronounced dead an hour later.

Broward County Crime Stoppers received only two tips from the community, but neither amounted to anything. Seasoned investigators remarked that so few leads in a homicide case are unusual. The Transvestite Stroll knows how to keep its secrets. Densely populated and desperately poor, the neighborhood is far enough away from the ritzy homes, Venetian-like canals, and yacht clubs along the Atlantic Ocean that transgender people of color can gather under the radar of the Fort Lauderdale city fathers. Some even ply their trade as sex workers along the Stroll, though no one should assume that the only trans people who come to Sistrunk are in the sex-for-hire trade. People with privilege may like to make thumping generalizations about poor people of color, but *they* don't know. The Sistrunk folk just "know what they know," with the

---

1. `I use this dual designation for Williams both to respect Denise King's way of identifying her 17-year-old son, and to honor the self-identification of this remarkable person in the gender and persona Williams chose on the street. Simmie/Beyoncé was in transition at the time of her murder. At home, Simmie lived as a son. On Sistrunk Boulevard, Beyoncé blossomed into the female she was becoming.

wisdom common to hard-living people—and they pretty much keep it to themselves.

Beyoncé was in her full "Baby Boy" persona that night. She was wearing a stylish pair of women's pants and a white tee shirt knotted in the front to expose her ebony midriff. According to friends at the Gay American Heroes Foundation, she had also chosen to wear "a fierce pair of pumps." That girl was ready to "rock dat world," dressed out as her pop idol, "BeyBey" Knowles. Like songs, dreams are not just recreation for a young, gender variant black kid from the 'hood. They are absolute necessities.

In March 2008, Brittany Anderson, Simmie/Beyoncé's best friend from Hollywood Hills High School, recalled for the *Sun-Sentinel* that she would perform Beyoncé's greatest hits for Brittany "loud and off-key." Thought to be shy by people who knew her slightly, "Beyoncé Williams" (aka "Chris" and "Lil Rick"), as she was known in the Sistrunk neighborhood, was social, happy, and full of dance moves. Simmie/Beyoncé stretched her meager dollars to put together *chichi* outfits, wore her hair in long braids, glossed her lips, and plucked her eyebrows to accentuate her attractive facial features. Everyone knew she was a boy who presented femininely. But around Sistrunk Boulevard, she was part of a subculture that relied on separate identities to allow its members freedom and to protect them from people who might otherwise cause problems among their families and friends.

Beyoncé's separate identity from Simmie on the street was a form of both self-expression and self-defense in the black community. Danny Sol, like Simmie/Beyoncé, was a femininely presenting black male. Sol, who was twenty-six, told the *Sun Sentinel* on March 28, 2008 that Simmie/Beyoncé had been her "gay daughter." Sol explained that it was customary for gender non-conforming black males to go by different names of their own choosing to defend themselves from neighborhood ridicule, religious disapproval, or even from their own families, who might disown them (or worse) if they found out the truth. "You learn from an early age not to trust anybody," Sol said, "so you make up an identity so they don't know who you really are." Life is led on two separate but parallel tracks. Ideally, family life at home remains undisturbed. But life along Sistrunk revolves around family, too, a "gay family." Sol explained, "Especially with us African-Americans, there is really no 'gay community' and [having a gay family] lets you have a circle of friends."

Older gay and transgender friends like Sol helped Simmie/Beyoncé deal with a whole raft of problems: with the shame so many black trans teens face, with struggles "in the life," and with questions like whether she was going to hell (as all the right-wing preachers say) for being gender non-conforming.

No one knows you better than someone who lives like you do. Simmie/Beyoncé loved her mom, Denise King, so much it hurt—and she would do anything for her mom. But her "gay family" along the Stroll understood how to live the dream against the odds. Simmie/Beyoncé was black, poor, and transgender. Grant Lynn Ford, Dean of Fort Laud's Sunshine Cathedral, a church that ministers to the LGBTQ community, called her "a minority within a minority within a minority." Tammy Wynette, an artist from a completely different cultural context but a similar female experience, sang, " . . . Sometimes it's hard to be a woman." Young Simmie/Beyoncé needed the sisterhood of older trans women who knew how to live the hard life of the Beautiful. That, above all else, is why she went down to the Stroll every chance she got—not to sell her body, as the police, the press, and the moralistic preachers assumed—but instead to be with big sisters with whom she could laugh, cut up, sing, dance, *and dream.*

At home, "Simmie" (as Denise King would always know her child) kept house, baby-sat for his[2]* toddler nephew, Jamar, and took care of the woman who took care of him. Mrs. King worked in a nursing home, and paced all day long on hard floors. When she got off the metro bus at her apartment complex, off U.S. Highway 441 west of Fort Lauderdale, Simmie was usually at home waiting for her with a meal he had cooked himself. On Wednesday evening, February 21, Simmie prepared a hot meal she loved: steak, creamed potatoes, gravy, and mixed vegetables. "Simmie loved to cook," Mrs. King told *The Miami Herald's* Audra Burch. "He would watch the *Food Network*, then experiment." After cleaning up from dinner, Simmie took Mrs. King's shoes off and soothingly massaged the life back into her feet. Mrs. King adored her son, not only for what he did for her, but because of who Simmie was. "He was a quiet person, kept to himself," she shared with Scott Hall of Gay American Heroes Foundation. "He had a lot of friends. He wasn't a troubled child. He was a happy person."

2. In deference to the identity Simmie/Beyoncé maintained at home, I use pronouns here in the way Mrs. King used them in reference to her son.

Wednesday the twenty-first had been an eventful day for Simmie. He had signed up for the Job Corps, a federal vocational training program for youth. He was so animated while he told his mom all about it. Simmie had big plans. First, he was going to use the Job Corps to get his GED, and then he planned to go to culinary school. He was determined to work his way up and up until he owned a fancy restaurant, and could afford to move his mother out of the projects. "He was so happy because he was going to finally be able to work toward becoming a cook," Mrs. King remembered. The cable television service was broken in the apartment, and the repairman had neglected to show (again), so Simmie was unable to watch one of his favorite TV shows that night, *Make Me a Supermodel*. So, he asked his mom for money to catch the cross-town bus "to go meet friends." Mrs. King handed over $2 for bus fare, and Simmie/Beyoncé left home with a change of clothes and a pair of pumps in the black Adidas bag she always carried. She was steppin' out to the Stroll on Sistrunk to share the big news with her "gay family" and friends about enrolling in the Job Corps.

So many things collide at the scene of Beyoncé Williams's murder: gender expectations and stereotypes; white and black versions of transgender life; skin privilege and poverty; dreams and brute reality. Even pronouns collide, in the struggle to find the proper language to give this remarkable trans teen her dignity and worth. Simultaneously, the struggle to find the right language collides and clashes with the memories of a mother who loved her child selflessly, but in the end could not surrender the masculinity of the man her child would never become. For the funeral, Mrs. King chose to clothe Simme/Beyoncé in a classy beige suit and a pair of white gloves—the first and only suit her child ever wore. She told Scott Hall, "Simmie's friends asked me if I was going to dress him as a woman for the funeral. I said no. I gave birth to a boy, and my baby would be buried as a boy." Then, with passion born of a mother's pain, she said, "I don't know what he did or didn't do across town. What I know is that he was gay and didn't deserve to be gunned down because of who he was."

Until her untimely death on New Year's Eve 2010, Mrs. King never gave up trying to find her child's murderers. Though the police announced that they never had enough evidence to classify the murder as a hate crime, Mrs. King, like all the Sistrunk folk, "knew what she knew." Simmie/Beyoncé was a casualty of hatred: of women, of difference, and of the gentle and the beautiful. As long as Mrs. King lived, she, her family, and her friends in the LGBTQ community pounded the pavement all over Fort Lauderdale, hanging up hundreds of handbills and asking people for help to bring her baby's killers to justice. After laying Simmie/Beyoncé to rest with the help of friends and activists who raised the money for the funeral, she became a staunch advocate for human rights and gay equality, especially for youth. Denise King died never having seen justice done for her child. Her death at forty years of age delivered another blow to a family already decimated by hatred of gender and sexual orientation. Her friend, Waymon Hudson, said that we caught a glimpse of who this remarkable transperson was through the love of a mother. It is up to us now. We must not forget the beautiful one whose murder interrupted her metamorphosis, and killed her before she fully left her old cocoon behind.

Baby Boy, we must not forget you.

LOW MOAN

This "Baby Boys" chapter began in anger, picked up sorrow along the way, and moved to the place where no one is satisfied. There are no words for how we feel about the outrageousness of two months of murder, when three trans teens had their lives senselessly snatched away from them by hatred. Dolphus, Larry, and Simmie/Beyoncé could have been anybody's children, but because of the way they proudly presented themselves to a xenophobic, transphobic society—the society *we* created for them—they were singled out for destruction by the wolfish ignorance and prejudice of our time. Who can possibly find satisfaction from such an outcome?

In the African American spiritual tradition, a gospel singer doesn't need lyrics to express the depths of anguish she feels. When a song descends into the pit where the memories of "being 'buked and scorned" and "being treated like anything but a child of God" come thick and fast in a Black church service, a singer sometimes utters a combination of hums and sighs too deep for words—deeper even than screams or tears, and this is called the "low moan." Beyond concepts, such a moan captures the agony and resolve of a people who have been "'round the rough side of the mountain." That is what we are left with here, in the wake of the murder of children. We wish the same church would no longer betray its spiritual heritage and mission by shunning its trans and gay children, and, by finding the courage to repent, moan itself into embracing them as their dear sons and daughters.

Whose children are they now? The musical conceit of this concluding chapter has attempted to say, they are Beyoncé's, the "Baby Boys" and "Baby Girls" we think about all the time, the innocent inhabitants of our dreams. Like Beyoncé says, we hold them in our memory, for they will not let us go. The better angels of our nature know that these arresting, gender variant youths are *our* children now. The unwanted now become the unforgettable, and their memories clamor for us to do something we are singularly uncomfortable about. They call upon us to change—to change our minds about gender, race, sexual orientation and economic class; to change our hearts from cold indifference to the blue heat of justice for all those who are different.

Anger is a good thing when it does no sin, but instead fires up our bellies for the long, demanding work of personal and societal transformation. Without a certain amount of unquenchable anger, no change ever comes. We know that. We also know that love is stronger than death, as clichéd as that may sound. Love abides, even when anger fades—and love, if it is real, has to set things right. Dolphus, Larry, Simmie/Beyoncé, and the multitudes of young strangers among us they represent deserve better than our good intentions. They deserve to be remembered. That is what love does. And, in the end, those whom we love are all that is worth remembering.

Baby Boys and Baby Girls, you are so damn fine! You stay on my mind.

For Greater Understanding

Baby Boys, Stay On My Mind: Adolphus Simmons, Lawrence Fobes "Larry" King, and Simmie Lewis "Beyoncé" Williams Jr.

BOOKS AND ARTICLES

Johnson, E. Patrick, and Mae G. Henderson. *Black Queer Studies: A Critical Anthology.* Durham, NC: 2005.

Pascoe, C. J. *Dude, You're a Fag: Masculinity and Sexuality in High School.* Berkeley, CA: University of California Press, 2007.

Setoodeh, Ramin. "Young, Gay and Murdered." *Newsweek*, July 19, 2008. No pages. Online: http://www.newsweek.com/2008/07/18/young-gay-and-murdered.html.

Wilchins, Riki. *Queer Theory, Gender Theory: An Instant Primer.* New York: Alyson Books, 2004.

FILMS AND VIDEOGRAPHY

Teach Your Children Well: A Film About Homophobia and School Violence. Left Coast Flix (in development).

ORGANIZATIONS AND WEBSITES

Beyoncé Knowles: "Baby Boy" Lyrics, http://www.lyrics007.com/Beyonce%20Lyrics/Baby%20Boy%20Lyrics.html.

Gay, Lesbian, and Straight Education Network (GLSEN), http://www.glsen.org.

Gender Public Advocacy Coalition (GenderPac), http://www.gpac.org.

Milkboys: The Boys Blog, http://www.milkboys.org.

Sean's Last Wish, http://www.seanslastwish.org.

Teach Your Children Well: A Documentary Film Project, http://www.facebook.com/group.php?gid=58159774696.

Unfinished Lives Project, http://unfinishedlivesblog.com.

13

Afterword

The Prerogatives of Love and Justice

"THERE IS NO CLOSURE." When Pat Mulder, the mother of Ryan Skipper, spoke these words to me in her Auburndale, Florida home during one of our interviews about the murder of her son, I heard the voice of every person harmed in the aftermath of a hate crime homicide. I accept her word as a given. It carries the authority of a mother's grief. How can there be any closure when lives like Ryan's, or Sakia's, or F.C.'s have been so brutally, irrationally torn from their loved ones (and from us) and left so . . . unfinished?

The writer of the book of Ecclesiastes says, "For everything there is a season, and a time for every matter under heaven" (3:1 NRSV). There must be room for grief and anger in response to the monstrosity of these hate crimes. We need time to mourn, to undergo the stages of grief and loss as we struggle to find a way to live with stories like these. Anger has its place, too. As I have argued throughout this volume, anti-LGBTQ hate crimes murders are not "tragedies." They are *outrages* against human civilization. As gay scholar Marvin Ellison says, "Anti-gay violence is an intentionally employed weapon of mass terror, and religion is often its accomplice." To deny the outrage we feel against these killings, enacted as they are not only against individual victims, but also intended to terrorize the whole LGBTQ community, is to allow the killers and their ideological sponsors to "own" these stories and the future that flows from them. None of us can allow that to happen. The same ragged emotions we are left with in the ruins of these difficult stories are the beginning point to conceive responses of love and justice to them. As Ecclesiastes says, it is time.

There can be no closure in the work of remembrance. To remember the dead is not to dwell in morbidity. Rather, it is an act of identity, decency, and justice, if we choose to make it so. The dead, of course, offer us no guarantees. Nothing in these accounts of hateful death automatically manufactures anything better in us. Confronting the raw realities of a harsh, apathetic society, one that honestly *does* value the lives of others more than it values yours or mine may just leave us embittered, or—worse than that—numb. My work on this project has caused me to live as closely to the stories of these hate crimes victims as anyone, outside of their own immediate families. Handling the broken pieces of their memories for four years, I slowly began to understand that these victims had much to teach me, if I would only learn from them. So I chose against despair, and enrolled in the school of remembrance, with the dead as my teachers. The obdurate fact of their lives and the manner of their deaths was the first and most seminal gift these victims ever gave to me: they presented me the occasion *to decide*, to choose to commemorate queer lives. Everything else has flowed from that initial gift of choice. They offer the same choice to each one of us, as well.

To remember the victims of anti-LGBTQ hate crimes is to take responsibility for who we are to them. We are their successors, their witnesses, and their larger family. In memory, they become our ancestors, and when we stand close to the stories of their lives and deaths, we *commune* with our ancestors—not in order to linger in some melancholy past, but in order to understand the struggles of the living. The stories of our ancestors, fallen at the hands of hatred and irrational fear, are portals to a deeper, richer, and more just community of LGBTQ people and our allies. *We* are the community who takes responsibility for the memory of our dead ancestors—not the killers and their religio-political masters.

There must also be no foreclosure of the work of lament. Lamentation and remembrance have always been political acts of love and justice, as well as acts of communal therapy. When feminist scholar Phyllis Trible wrote her classic, *Texts of Terror* (Fortress Press, 1984), in which she tells the sad stories of four representative women from the Hebrew Scriptures who were victims of male violence, she invited her readers to lament their outrageous fortune with her. She told the stories in such a way that modern readers could communally grieve over Hagar, the abused slave; Tamar, the raped princess; the unnamed concubine, dismembered and discarded; and Jephthah's virgin daughter, sacrificed to male arrogance.

Trible did so, she writes, "in order to recover a neglected history, to re-member a past that the present embodies, and to pray that these terrors shall not come to pass again" (Trible 1984, 3). Behind each of these tales of victimized biblical women stand stories of countless women in our own time brutalized by misogyny and gender-hatred in an irrational at-tempt to buttress the wobbly walls of male domination. The lamentation Trible ignited with her stories galvanized women and their male allies for the long, hard work of strengthening female self-esteem and political power.

Womanist scholar Emilie Townes, in her study of African American health issues, *Breaking the Fine Rain of Death* (Continuum, 1998), writes that communal lament, when a people grieve publicly for the members of their community who have suffered terror, has the power to require the group to admit the full reality of their shared pain and to experi-ence it together. No group in American life today needs the ability to ac-knowledge and share the suffering wrought by domestic terrorism more than LGBTQ people and our straight allies. Townes speaks directly to the condition of queer Americans in the wake of hate crimes horror:

> The formfulness of communal lament has a deep moral charac-ter that helps the discipline of social ethics do its work in our contemporary contexts . . . Communal lament, as a corporate experience of calling for healing, makes suffering bearable and manageable *in* community . . . It is only then we can begin to heal (Townes 1998, 24).

In other words, lamentation not only commences the healing process of a group. It also forms communities of moral purpose out of the very oppression that sought to destroy the group in the first place. The LGBTQ community must take up its hard-earned prerogative to lead the nation in lamentation over our dead and to invite all persons of good conscience to remember them with us, because through com-muning with our ancestors who have died at the hands of hatred and falsehood, we have begun our healing and seek to become people of love and integrity.

But the LGBTQ community must do more than that, if our fallen ancestors are to be honored aright. The stories told in this book, and the thousands of others they represent, are a call and challenge to queer folk to become *a people* with a distinct communal character, a justice-char-acter that does not coerce others to be like us. There have been plenty of communities in the history of the planet for whom "justice" meant conformity to the expectations of the group. Old regimes of coercive power fell, only to find newer regimes in their place, all-too-ready to enforce a new "justice," a new oppressive uniformity, on those who were deemed to be "different." All the familiar temptations and prejudices that plague the heterosexual world are also alive and well in queer community. The stories of our murdered ancestors bear the wounds and scars of racism, abuse of privilege, gender-hatred, greed and poverty, xenophobia and ignorance, as well as the heterosexism and homophobia that killed them. But if we are a community discovered in sexual difference and gender non-conformity, one that, like our beloved queer ancestors, emerged in every condition and social demographic on earth, then we must resist the fundamentalist impulse to coerce others into familiar and comfortable images of ourselves. All that coercion and uniformity ever gave the queer community was a graveyard filled with our dead. The justice we seek must be different. We are called to identify and root out the causes of fear, loathing, and sexual oppression wherever they are found, not only in others, but within our own communities, as well. Our forebear, Audre Lorde, lesbian poet and writer of color, describes how the search for justice among queer folk must start. In *Sister Outsider* (Crossing Press, 1984), she writes:

> Without community there is no liberation, only the most vulnerable and temporary armistice between an individual and her oppression. But community must not mean the shedding of our differences, nor the pathetic pretense that these differences do not exist . . . *I urge each one of us to reach down into that deep place of knowledge inside herself and touch the terror and loathing of any difference that lives there. See whose face it wears. Then the personal as the political can begin to illuminate all our choices* (Lorde 1984, 112-113; emphasis in the original).

There is, therefore, no closure to the work of justice, either. For the just and right thing to do, in response to the harm done by anti-LGBTQ hate crimes, is not "an eye for an eye." Instead, it is the hard work of evolution and education: the evolution of disparate collectives of sexual outlaws into a community of justice-in-difference that demands respect, and honors our fallen ancestors by educating ourselves and others that the strange is something to understand and celebrate, rather than to loathe.

In the interim, however long it may be until justice comes, we cannot rest. The LGBTQ community must organize for responsible political action to eradicate hate crimes, the passage of enforceable laws that protect communities of difference of every kind, and the development of a better society where those resembling our beloved dead need never fear to live openly as they truly are. We must summon from within ourselves and arouse within others the spiritual resources and moral courage to confront religious intolerance and bigotry, so often the accomplices to hate violence in our world. Like Pat Mulder said, there is no closure for any of us who have been touched by the stories of these unfinished lives—only a hope that captivates us—a stubborn hope for a nation that finally lives up to the best of its ideals, and that steels us for the labor it will take to get all us there . . . *together.*

CPSIA information can be obtained at www.ICGtesting.com
Printed in the USA
LVOW102005270613

340559LV00022B/1159/P